O9-CFU-195

616.85
Of33

c.1

Ofshe, Richard
  Making monsters

COLLEGE OF THE SEQUOIAS
LIBRARY

GAYLORD M

MAKING MONSTERS

False Memories, Psychotherapy, and Sexual Hysteria

Richard Ofshe
and Ethan Watters

CHARLES SCRIBNER'S SONS

NEW YORK   LONDON   TORONTO   SYDNEY   TOKYO   SINGAPORE

COLLEGE OF THE SEQUOIAS
— LIBRARY

CHARLES SCRIBNER'S SONS
Rockefeller Center
1230 Avenue of the Americas
New York, New York 10020

Copyright © 1994 by Richard Ofshe and Ethan Watters

All rights reserved, including the right to reproduce this book or portions thereof in any form whatsoever.

SCRIBNERS and colophon are registered trademarks of Macmillan, Inc.

DESIGNED BY ERICH HOBBING

Manufactured in the United States of America

1   3   5   7   9   10   8   6   4   2

Library of Congress Cataloging-in-Publication Data

Ofshe, Richard.
Making monsters: false memories, psychotherapy, and sexual
hysteria/Richard Ofshe and Ethan Watters.
p.   cm.
Includes bibliographical references and index.
1. False memory syndrome.   I. Watters, Ethan.   II. Title.
RC455.2.F35037   1994   94-15642   CIP
616.85′82239′0651—dc20

ISBN 0-684-19698-0

For our parents,
with whom we share cherished memories

Contents

Preface

We have written this book as a bitter debate has raged over the practices of recovered memory therapy and the treatment of multiple personality disorder. Accordingly, this work is part applied social science and part dispatches from the front lines of a growing controversy. Our goal is to prove beyond doubt that devastating mistakes are being made within certain therapy settings. By relying on the published works of recovered memory clinicians for the bulk of our evidence, we intend to show that these mistakes are not being made by aberrant clinicians but by a substantial group of therapists who have created a movement replete with scholarly and how-to books, conferences for clinicians, journals, newsletters, and a raft of prominent experts. This work is intended as an exposé of a pseudoscientific enterprise that is damaging the lives of people in need.

While we have tried, for the most part, to evaluate the recovered memory movement dispassionately, we make no attempt to hide—or apologize for—the anger that exists between the lines of this book. Over the last several years, as we have conducted research and written together and separately about recovered memory therapy, we have witnessed the damage this therapeutic enthusiasm has caused to patients and their families. The anguish and sadness we have seen has motivated our work.

We would like to thank Dr. Frank Watters for his tireless research work over the course of this project. Our editor at Scribners, Hamilton Cain, deserves recognition for his guidance, commitment, and vision, as does Bonnie Nadell of Frederick Hill and Associates for her support throughout. We would also like to thank Michelle Coddle, Scott Johnson, Laura Martin, Jenia Walter, Fred Sawyer, and Andrew Attaway for their contributions. Po Bronson and Hillary Fox were kind and thoughtful readers of special note. We gratefully acknowledge *Society* magazine for publishing our article, "Making Monsters" (March-April 1993).

Ethan Watters gratefully acknowledges several past and present editors at *Mother Jones* magazine—Doug Foster, Jeffrey Klein, Peggy Orenstein, and David Weir—for their unflinching support of his early work on this

controversial topic. In addition, he would like to recognize the encour-
agement of others over the years, including Charis Conn, Jim Conklin,
Jeff Davis, Sarah Donohoe, Lawrence Gallagher, Jody Hood, Jim Humes,
David Robertson, Paul Tough, Sean Wagstaff, and Mark Warren.

Richard Ofshe would like to recognize Martin Orne, Margaret Singer,
Elizabeth Loftus, and Ulric Neisser, whose work has influenced his own
research and has had a major impact on the debate over recovered memory therapy. He also would like to express his appreciation to the Thurston
County Prosecutor's Office for retaining him to analyze the allegations
against Paul Ingram and thereby giving him the opportunity to study the
effects of recovered memory techniques in a unique fashion. He would
also like to thank Larry Wright for bringing international attention to the
plight of Paul Ingram. In particular he would like to acknowledge the
patience, understanding, and support of Bonnie Blair Ofshe.

MAKING MONSTERS

Introduction

For nearly a decade a segment of the psychotherapy community has offered recovered memory therapy to women and a few men suffering from disorders ranging from depression and headaches to schizophrenia and arthritis. These recovered memory specialists maintain that patients often carry buried memories of having been sexually abused as children or infants and that those abuses, while hidden, are the root to their current troubles. Further, these therapists believe that helping their clients unearth these repressed memories can cure the disorder the patient presents. This treatment is not specific to one branch of psychotherapy. Recovered memory specialists come from the ranks of psychiatrists, psychologists, social workers, new-age gurus, marriage and family counselors, and those who, without a degree, simply proclaim themselves "therapists." Because therapists from many schools of therapy share fundamentally similar beliefs in the power of the unconscious and in their ability to retrieve long-banished knowledge, recovered memory therapy can be found in psychoanalysis, hypnotherapy, gestalt, new-age counseling, and many other of the two hundred talk therapies that populate our social landscape.

Unlike treatments intended to aid patients suffering from the shock of rape or grappling with lifelong memories of childhood sexual abuse, the axiom of recovered memory therapy is that the patient will have no knowledge of the sexual trauma before treatment. Patients can begin the therapy with no memories of abuse and finish with the belief that they suffered endless horrible molestations or rapes—often by their parents. Recovered memory therapists expect that patients will not only be amnesiac for the trauma in their past but that they will also disbelieve the therapist's initial suggestion that they suffered sexual assaults as children.

In general, patients who come to believe they have recovered memories of child abuse fall into three categories. The most common example of a recovered memory involves the individual coming to believe that she* was sexually abused, usually by a parent or another adult family member. In the end she may conclude that the abuse happened once or that she was molested routinely for decades. She may believe that she drove the knowledge into her unconscious within seconds of the abuse or that she held it consciously for years before banishing it from memory. In her mind's eye she may see the images of abuse vividly or the knowledge may remain only a vague feeling.

The second general category consists of those who believe that they were abused at the hands of an organized satanic cult. These stories account for perhaps one in five of all those who believe they have re-covered memories of abuse. These cults, according to recovered memory patients and their therapists, operate underneath the surface of American and Western European society and have done so for hundreds of years. Some clinicians and patients maintain that these cults represent a secret cabal that controls the world economy. The ceremonies recounted rou-tinely involved ritualized rape, abortions, and the murder and canni-balization of adults, children, and infants.

The third category consists of those who believe that they harbor mul-tiple personalities. Those with this diagnosis of multiple personality dis-order learn to accept that they embody dozens or hundreds of separate personalities, each with its own memory and set of experiences. Because of its use in recovered memory therapy, MPD has grown in a single decade from an exceptionally rare diagnosis to an epidemic.

These three categories are not mutually exclusive. While virtually all start in the first category, some patients continue to uncover increasingly brutal images of abuse until the scenes eventually lead them to conclude they were ritually abused by satanists. Others start in the first category and then begin to manifest symptoms of multiple personality disorder. It is also very common for recovered memory patients to end up repre-senting all three categories.

In a little over a decade the inroads this therapy has made into American culture have been impressive, or chilling, depending on our perspective. Recovered memory patients and self-proclaimed experts on the subject have become staples of television talk shows. Popular books explaining the ideas of memory repression and the curative power of uncovering those memories have sold millions of copies and have been incorporated into college curricula and accredited training seminars for practicing

---

*Because the large majority of recovered memory patients are women, we will use female pronouns throughout this book.

psychotherapists. Insurance companies over the last dozen years have paid out hundreds of millions of dollars for memory therapy, while about half the states have enacted changes in their statutes of limitation to allow recently recovered memories of abuse to become the basis for civil lawsuits and in some cases criminal prosecution. Practitioners of the therapy hold annual national and regional conferences where new discoveries in the field are discussed. To find a psychotherapist who specializes in recovering memories of abuse, one need only tap into a network of hot lines and publications devoted specifically to the topic or to the more general field of adult recovery. Some therapists have gone so far as to advertise in airline magazines, newspapers, and telephone books their ability to un-cover repressed memories. "Remembering Is the First Step to Healing," proclaims the headline of one prominent advertisement in the South-western Bell Yellow Pages. The advertisement, which is not uncommon for the movement, lists twenty-five problems believed to be associated with sexual abuse, and promises that "through our powerful combination of massage, bodywork, hypnosis, psychodrama & sodium brevital inter-viewing, we can remember and heal." Recently, enterprising recovered memory therapists have begun giving professional seminars and selling their books and literature in Europe.

Because of the rapid proliferation of recovered memory therapy, it's now becoming popularly accepted that the unconscious mind has the power to hide horrible histories for decades and that psychotherapists possess the tools to uncover those truths. As a society, we are moving toward accepting recovered memory therapy as a legitimate treatment that benefits patients.

Put simply, there are two possible explanations for what has happened over the last decade in the realm of recovered memory therapy. The first possibility is that recovered memory therapists in our time have made, as they claim, a fundamental breakthrough in the understanding of the human mind and memory. If true, the theories surrounding repressed memory therapy, multiple personality disorder, and the discovery of satanic-cult abuse are a leap out of what will surely become known as the mental-health dark ages. In light of these new discoveries researchers will have to discard or fundamentally reinterpret most of the accepted research surrounding memory retrieval, the effects of hypnosis, and the impact of trauma on the human psyche and perhaps the soul.

The idea that will so transform our understanding of ourselves is the discovery of the mind's remarkable powers of repression. In the new conception of the repression mechanism, the unconscious mind can not only steal away the memories of decades of horrible torture—often hiding the memory as the abuse takes place—but also has the power to store that information in such crystalline form that the abuse can be vividly relived during therapy as an adult. Through this new understanding of this repression mechanism, therapists can now identify patients who are suffering the aftereffects of abuse and, by helping them uncover and relive the memories buried in their subconscious, cure them of those symptoms. These accomplishments are more remarkable considering that, as they have recovered the secret past of their patients, they have also discovered the shockingly high frequency of multiple personality disorder—a pathology once believed as rare as Siamese twins. In exploring the subconscious minds of their patients, therapists have not only discovered hidden memories but hidden *personalities* that rise up and appear to take control of the patients' bodies.

The implications of recovered memory therapy have not been lost on the experts of the movements. Their discoveries, they agree, will go far beyond the confines of the mental-health industry. "Denial, repression, and dissociation operate on a social as well as individual level," writes Harvard psychiatrist Dr. Judith Herman in her book *Trauma and Recovery*.[1] Herman, a leading figure in the recovered memory movement, boldly applies the mechanism of memory repression to society as a whole. She implies that not only will individuals embrace the new truths of memory, but we will be the first society to root out horrible crimes that we have *collectively* forgotten or forced from consciousness. In the same way patients supposedly overcame their disorders by discovering repressed memories, society will be "cured" by the uncovering of a previously unacknowledged epidemic of incest and sexual abuse. Chief among the atrocities that we will collectively bring into consciousness, according to the movement's literature, is a vast network of satanic cults that have "ritually abused" and murdered children for hundreds of years with impunity. A 1991 survey found not only that 12 percent of clinical members of the American Psychological Association had treated a patient with memories of ritual abuse by these evil cults, but that virtually all of these treating clinicians believed the accounts to be true.[2] Because of our societal "dissociation," all of our mechanisms for exposing and controlling aberrant behavior (including investigation by law enforcement, academic inquiry, and exposure by the media) have failed not only to stop these groups but to turn up any evidence that they exist. After centuries of our forcing the knowledge of these groups into our societal subconscious, a crusading band of recovered memory therapists intend to lead society out of the darkness of denial and repression and into the light.

The alternative explanation of the sudden nationwide spread of this therapy is no less dramatic. We will argue that the practice of uncovering repressed memories, along with the attendant theories of multiple personality disorder and satanic-cult abuse, are fads as widespread and as damaging as any the mental-health field has produced this century. We will show that recovered memory therapists are not, as they portray themselves, brave healers but professionals who have built a pseudoscience out of an unfounded consensus about how the mind reacts to sexual trauma. In the process they have slipped the ties that bind their professions to scientific method and sound research. Free from any burden of proof, these therapists have created an Alice-in-Wonderland world in which opinion, metaphor, and ideological preference substitute for objective evidence. While claiming to uncover the truth of their clients' past, these therapists have pursued a treatment regime that persuades clients to accept hynotically generated images, gut feelings, dreams, and imaginings as valid memories. Without an understanding of the damage they have caused, these therapists have employed methods that blur the already perilously thin line that separates memory from imagination and have unwittingly coerced their patients to mold their beliefs and behaviors to the expectations of the therapy.

While to the uninitiated, the two scenarios outlined above may sound overly dramatic, for those schooled in the debate they may be considered understatements. The options for those taking sides in this debate are quite unambiguous: the mind either has the ability to repress vast numbers of events, as described by recovered memory therapists, or it does not. The satanic cults, which have been reported by a substantial percentage of recovered memory patients and their therapists, either exist or have been created in therapy. Multiple personality disorder is either a widespread pathology or, like demonic possession, a role that has been forced on vulnerable people in a misguided attempt to cure them. The therapy setting and the special techniques used either access life histories previously unknown to the patient, or these procedures create pseudomemories. Because of the clear nature of these positions, this professional debate is not likely to be settled amicably or on some mutually agreed upon middle ground. While it may take another decade for the debate to run its course, there is now no backing away from the fact that this debate must be resolved.

We believe that there is now sufficient evidence—within the therapists' own accounts of their techniques—to show that a significant cadre of poorly trained, overzealous, or ideologically driven psychotherapists have pursued a series of pseudoscientific notions that have ultimately damaged the patients who have come to them for help. If our conclusion is correct, the epidemic of repressed memories "discovered" daily in therapy settings prove not that our society is exploding with the most vicious sort of child molesters and satanists, but rather that psychotherapists—if they are possessed with a predisposition to uncover memories of abuse—can unintentionally spark and then build false beliefs in a patient's mind.

For the most part, the techniques of influence employed in recovered memory therapy are not intended simply to force the patient to agree with the therapist's conclusions. Although we will illustrate some notable exceptions, recovered memory therapists are not the equivalent of interrogators threatening and berating the patient in an attempt to force a confession. Rather, the techniques are persuasive ones, which result in the patient internalizing the idea that she was abused. If used improperly, hypnosis, to choose a prominent example, can effectively induce a patient to vividly imagine the abuse that the therapist presumes to have happened. Other techniques such as dream analysis or the constant revisiting and rewriting of vague early childhood memories offer innumerable opportunities for the therapist to assemble hunches, metaphorical clues, and feelings into a body of evidence that points to a history of abuse.

Through the therapy process, patients come to believe, essentially, that they have memories of two separate childhoods—one maintained in normal memory, and another, recorded in their subconscious minds, during which they were repeatedly and horribly abused. Patients face a dilemma that logic and their therapists demand they resolve. The size of the gap between their pretherapy memories of their childhoods and the beliefs that come out of therapy varies from client to client. For some patients the newly uncovered "memories" of childhood abuse may augment pretherapy memories of an upbringing that was, in fact, dismal and abusive. For many others, the beliefs created in therapy may darkly contrast pretherapy memories of a warm and cherished childhood.

Faced with choosing between their memories before and after the influence of therapy, therapists often encourage patients to redefine their life histories based on the new pseudomemories and, by doing so, redefine their most basic understanding of their families and themselves. For patients who enter therapy with happy memories of childhood, believing the reality of their newly recovered memories comes hard. They must first admit that their normal memories were essentially fantasies—a trick their minds employed to shield them from an awful truth. Memories once presumed real, valid, and normal are reinterpreted, seen as nothing but a false front, a movie set of a happy home. Any positive memories must be redefined as imagined or as events their parents cynically sub-jected them to in order to direct attention away from the true horror of their childhood. In this way, the therapy not only builds new memories but discredits the pretherapy recollections. Often the memories discovered during therapy turn what the patient once thought was a relatively normal upbringing into a vision of hell.

Perhaps most disturbingly, recovered memory therapists often train their patients to "reexperience" the emotional pain of rape, sexual abuse, and other horrors that they "discover" in therapy. Believing it therapeutic, therapists encourage abreactions—where the patient, often in hypnotic trance, "relives" the imagined abuses and in doing so supposedly punc-tures and drains the psychological abscess that has formed around the repressed memory. Patients are persuaded to literally feel the pain of rape and torture and the humiliation of unspeakable degradation. The power of the therapists' suggestions is so great that some patients can develop observable physiological reactions, often in the form of welts or rashes. Therapists sometimes induce these abreactions weekly over years of ther-apy. In describing the intense torment they subject their patients to, therapists often portray themselves as if they were heroic doctors who could save their patients' lives only by performing amputations without anesthesia. If their treatments are invalid and unnecessary, as we have concluded, then these reports of the pain induced by therapy are in reality a documentation of the brutalization and psychological torture of the people who have come to them for help. Although we don't suggest that these recovered memory therapists take sexual pleasure from these abuse "re-creations," some recovered memory therapists perhaps deserve rec-ognition as a new class of sexual predator. If, for no defensible reason, some therapists are causing the same emotional and psychological trauma as an actual rape or sexual assault, then they, like those who physically victimize people, deserve moral condemnation.

Patients usually come to view their parents as far worse than pedophiles. To explain away the contradiction between preexisting memories and memories found in therapy, the patient often casts one parent as a master manipulator who—working in concert with the rest of the family, teach-ers, neighbors, and other authority figures from the child's life—controlled a complex conspiracy to keep society and the patient herself unaware that anything was wrong. As the recovered memories of abuse increase in severity and duration, each subsequent contradiction between the patient's normal memories and the evil uncovered in therapy can be explained by a further twist of this conspiracy. In the narrative created, the abusing parents not only sought sexual gratification from their children but took pleasure from inflicting psychological and physical pain and gross humiliation. Through the process of therapy, patients often come to believe that their childhoods were abusive wastelands and their parents were the worst sort of monsters.

Many parents have described the horror of watching as their children become cold, then estranged, as they go through this therapy. Patients are often encouraged to accuse and denounce their parents, often in confrontations overseen by the therapist. In these confrontations parents are told that they must acknowledge their hideous guilt in order to speed their child's healing process. Many parents have been sued by children who have read recovered memory literature that attests that filing lawsuits can speed their recovery. Parents have told of witnessing their children turn into another type of monster—one filled with the righteous hatred born of recovered memory therapy.

On another level, this book is not about the current fad in the psycho-therapy community but what that fad represents. While the results of the mistakes made in recovered memory therapy are so egregious that they can no longer be ignored, the mistakes themselves are not new but have been made, to varying degrees, by many talk therapies both past and present. They include the presumption that psychotherapy increases clients' accurate knowledge of their pasts, the belief that therapists can trace the etiology of a given behavior to its true source, and their stubborn insistence that patients, at the beginning of treatment, have only a minimal understanding of their true selves and their true pasts. Recovered memory therapy has emerged out of a tradition of treatment that is filled with fatal flaws—but flaws left unexposed because results, up to now, have been largely benign.

The fact that recovered memory therapists could so damage their patients and yet, until recently, largely escape criticism illustrates how incapable the mental-health profession is of evaluating and curbing fad treatments that grow within its ranks. While mental-health professionals look with horror at the seemingly barbaric mistakes of their predecessors, each generation appears unable to stop the birth of new damaging practices. Of the lessons learned from the wide use of prefrontal lobotomy only two generations ago, University of Michigan professor Elliot Valenstein writes in *Great and Desperate Cures* that fad treatments continue to be the "very bone and marrow" of the profession. "Premature reports of spectacular cures with minimal risks are still accepted uncritically," he points out, and "the popular media promote innovative therapies even

more enthusiastically; . . . conflicts persist within and between specialties; and ambitious physicians still strive for 'fame and name.' "[3]

In addition, recovered memory therapy illustrates how easily the "science" of psychotherapy changes to confirm our society's current phobias
and beliefs. Even the experts of the recovered memory therapy movement
acknowledge that the field has been driven by political and social forces.
For those who promote the therapy, these social forces, namely, the
women's movement, the self-help movement, and an increased concern
for child protection, are seen as having been only positive influences.
And indeed there has been positive change to the extent that these movements have succeeded in making society more concerned with the un-
derreporting of abuse and the damage that abuse can cause. But there is
now much evidence to show that the line between political advocacy and
science has become blurred.

"The systematic study of psychological trauma depends on the support
of a political movement," maintains Herman in *Trauma and Recovery*.
"Advances in the field [of trauma] occur only when they are supported
by a political movement."[4] Herman is correct that changes in science
often come in tandem with changes in social thought. What she ignores
is that movements in scientific theory brought about in this way aren't
necessarily advances. Despite the popular assumption to the contrary,
science is not on a linear course to the truth: social movements and
popular ideas can just as easily mislead science as bring it toward truth.

Harvard professor Stephen Jay Gould, in *The Mismeasure of Man*,
illustrates this malleability of science. In his examination of once respected scientific work supporting the idea that intelligence could be
judged by brain size (along with other supposedly objective measures),
Gould found that the research surrounding this hypothesis was profoundly
influenced by the assumptions and predisposition of the scientists. If the
scientist holds an assumption at the outset of the research, Gould theo-
rizes, and there are enough pieces of data to manipulate or selectively
choose among, the conclusions found will often simply mirror the scientist's assumptions, and, by extension, reflect the conclusions of whatever political, ideological, or social movement the scientist subscribes to.
"Much of [science's] change through time does not record a closer approach to absolute truth, but the alteration of cultural contexts that influences it so strongly."[5]

That is not to say that science is powerless, a twig in a river of social
beliefs. As Gould points out, scientists rightly should assume that reality
does exist and that it can be documented through careful work. Unfor-

tunately some areas of study don't lend themselves well to the collection of hard data or provable hypothesis and end up, therefore, more at the will of the social currents than others. "The history of many scientific subjects is virtually freed from . . . constraints of fact," he writes, ". . . some topics are invested with enormous social importance but blessed with very little reliable information. When the ratio of data to social impact is so low, a history of scientific attitudes may be little more than an oblique record of social change."[6]

Our review of the recovered memory literature leads us to the conclusion that the science surrounding recovered memory therapy suffers from precisely these problems with one caveat: the mistakes made in this therapy are not due to the lack of reliable information but are largely the result of reliable information being ignored. Although much research has been conducted regarding human memory, the coercive nature of the therapy setting, and the effect of techniques like hypnosis, this knowledge has been ignored by recovered memory therapists.

As for Gould's other criteria, it is clear that the issues of child abuse, sexual assault, and the victimization of women and children have in our time been "invested with enormous social importance." The 1980s were a reckoning time for many of the darker issues relating to human sexuality, including date rape, spousal battery, and sexual harassment. In particular, sexual crimes against children became a national concern. As the issue of child abuse grew into a political rallying cause, dispassionate analysis and debate was set aside, while unadulterated advocacy on behalf of the children and adult survivors was applauded. Researchers Janice Haaken and Astrid Schlaps noted that sexual abuse became a focus of the women's movement during the 1980s because "it represented the convergence of clinical knowledge and feminist consciousness. Feminist analyses of abuse within the family and feminist challenges to authoritarian practices became a palpable presence in the discourse on sexual abuse."[7] Andrea Dworkin went so far as to argue that fathers often rape their daughters as a way of socializing them to their female status. "In the United States, incest is increasingly the sadism of choice," she wrote. "Perhaps incestuous rape is becoming a central paradigm for intercourse in our time." In a paper entitled "The Dynamics of Feminist Therapy," Kathy Swink and Antoinette Leveille write: "Incest is the extreme expression of a patriarchal society. It trains the young victims from the start that their place/purpose/function in society is for the needs of others, especially men."[8] On the cover of *Secret Survivors*, a book promoting recovered memory therapy, Gloria Steinem gushed that the work "explores the constellation of symptoms that result from a crime too cruel for the mind and memory to face. This book, like the truth it helps uncover, can set millions free." In her book *The Revolution from Within*, Steinem uncritically touts the methods and conclusions of recovered memory therapy, stating that by learning to access the "timeless" unconscious you can "retrieve repressed trauma—a process that is vital to freeing yourself from old patterns."[9]

Recovering memories of abuse has proved a powerful metaphor for the larger goal of exposing the unfairness of patriarchal family structures and of a male-dominated society. Society, some said, was finally facing the long-hidden mistreatment of women just as individual women were discovering that they had been sexually abused. As recovered memory therapy became a metaphor for feminism, defense of the therapy became synonymous with defense of the women's movement. "The sexual-abuse-victim story crystallized many of society's anxieties, in these insecure times, about the vulnerability of children, the changing roles of women, and the norms of sexuality. It draws like a magnet those who feel vulnerable and victimized," writes Carol Tavris in *The Mismeasure of Woman*. ". . . it is a lightning rod for the inchoate feelings of victimization they have as a result of their status in society at large. It provides a clearer focus than such vague enemies as 'the system,' sexism, deadening work, welfare, or boredom. For them, 'sexual abuse' is a metaphor for all that is wrong with women's lives."[10]

Remarkably, some even proposed that the rise of the women's movement was directly related to women's ability to unlock their hidden memories. Some psychotherapists implied that the women's movement had actually altered the psyche of women, allowing them not just to tell their stories of abuse but to *remember* them as well. "To hold reality in consciousness requires a social context that affirms and protects the victim and that joins victim and witness in common alliance . . . ," writes Herman in *Trauma and Recovery*. "For a larger society, the social context is created by political movements that give voice to the disempowered." The women's movement has not only encouraged the disclosure of abuse, according to Herman, but been responsible for the very ability to recall the memories—the ability to "hold reality in consciousness."[11]

Such a close link between a type of treatment and a popular political movement does not come without costs. While academics and scientists have often been called upon to ratify the conclusions and beliefs of a given social, religious, or political movement, the resulting science has often been distorted by the predilection to find data that confirm the assumptions of the movement. The conclusions drawn by such science are often bitterly defended, not because of their scientific merit but because they further the cause at hand. If, as Herman attests, political and social forces have pushed recovered memory therapy into prominence, she should also recognize that up until now those same social forces have shielded the therapy from clear analysis, serious scientific criticism, and demands that its claims about human memory be documented. For much of the past decade, to wonder aloud whether the frequency of childhood sexual abuse could actually be as high as one in every two women (as was theorized) was to be labeled "in denial." Those who express concern for the rights of the accused were charged with "protecting the perpe-trator." One misstep, and even well-intentioned researchers or journalists could find themselves accused of secretly trying to prolong centuries of ignorance of child abuse.

Those who have written critically about recovered memory therapy understand the difficulty of discussing the merits of its techniques without being attacked as a misogynist. As Tavris wrote, childhood sexual abuse became difficult to address because it lay at "the misty intersection of political analysis and psychological trauma." Many in the media, politics, and the mental-health professions reacted to this climate by expressing unqualified belief in the accuracy of all accounts of abuse—regardless of whether these accounts came from children, adults in therapy, or "experts" who claimed to monitor the problem nationwide.

For many years, recovered memory psychotherapists were not subject to criticism because at the basis of any criticism lay a simple truth that was, for a time, unspeakable: it is indeed possible for adults and children to be coerced into making false claims of being abused or sexually as-saulted. To say as much in polite company was for a time (and in certain circles still is) morally stigmatizing. To make such a statement as a person of liberal leanings was to betray yourself as unenlightened. But this truth being said, we must turn to the task of determining how false memories of abuse come about. If we cannot separate truth from fantasy, we will not be able to discern or effectively address the true nature and conse-quences of child abuse in our time.

To address sexual abuse and other problems in society, we must have a clear vision of those problems. Although metaphors speak to the truth, they are not the truth themselves. If we come to believe that every other woman is suffering the debilitating effects of sexual trauma, and that millions carry festering hidden memories of abuse, we will surely direct our resources and energy to address this problem. If this turns out not to be true, we have ignored the "vague enemies"—the truth behind the metaphor—at our peril.

*   *   *

Until recently there was no opposition to the theories and practice of recovered memory therapists. Only in the last few years have those accused of child abuse based on memories recovered in therapy begun to join their voices in questioning the techniques and direction of the therapy. In 1992 the False Memory Syndrome Foundation was formed in Philadelphia to promote education and public awareness of the damage recovered memory therapy continues to cause. More recently, a similar organization has begun in the United Kingdom. Patients who believe they were badly served by their therapists have also joined the chorus. Most importantly, searing criticism of the therapy can now also be heard from many mental-health professionals in the mainstream of the industry, as well as from research scientists and scholars who specialize in memory, hypnosis, and the study of influence.

As the criticism grows, those inside the recovered memory movement are becoming increasingly unwilling to discuss, much less admit, any possible problems wrought by their methods. They ignore all previous research into memory and trauma because, they say, memories of repressed childhood sexual trauma are different—a special case without parallel. They shield themselves from any criticism that they are damaging patients, attesting that any criticism comes only from those intent on protecting the perpetrator. Those who question this therapy are labeled misogynists and turned away.

Many sincerely intent on uncovering victimization of women and men have overlooked exactly what they intended to root out. Because recovered memory therapy offered advocacy for those who came to believe that they were victimized, these therapists were welcomed as allies. And because the metaphor of memory recovery was so appealing, the ideas were lionized as a dramatic leap forward. In the midst of all the congratulations, no one considered the possibility that these therapy patients might indeed be victims not of their parents—but of their psychotherapists.

We intend to show that the evidence is now overwhelming that something has gone tragically wrong in certain therapy settings. If those who are concerned with the victimization of women ignore this evidence, they run the risk of sacrificing the well-being and happiness of thousands of women and their families for the sake of the politically expedient assumption that recovered memory therapy cannot create false memories of abuse. To look away from the brutalization of patients in therapy is now nothing less than an act of willful blindness and betrayal.

CHAPTER ONE

The Myths of Memory

The victims have come out of the closet and clinics are overwhelmed with sexually molested adults wanting treatment. The progress in ten years is truly gratifying.
> —Charlotte Krause Prozan
> *The Technique of Feminist Psychoanalytic Psychotherapy*

Patients of recovered memory therapy—whether they eventually reject the abuse beliefs created in treatment or not—agree that the treatment provokes a torturous reassessment of selfhood. Sometimes pursued for years, recovered memory therapy often leads patients not only to believe that they suffered abuse of which they previously had no knowledge, but also to accept the abuse as symbolic of their entire childhood—and often their pretherapy adult life. In the first paragraph of *The Courage to Heal: A Guide for Women Survivors of Child Sexual Abuse*, Ellen Bass and Laura Davis list the alleged long-term effects of child abuse. "It permeates everything: your sense of self, your intimate relationships, your sexuality, your parenting, your work life, even your sanity. Everywhere you look you see its effects." While this may be true for some who have experienced molestation as children, Bass and Davis might also be describing the experience of uncovering previously unknown memories of abuse during therapy.

In recovered memory therapy, beliefs are maintained in many ways, chief among them being the weekly therapy session the patient attends. Recasting the identity in the "survivor" mold often requires that the patient pursue the belief far beyond the therapy hour. Patients may attend weekly group-therapy sessions or body-massage treatments aimed at releasing memories from muscle tissue. The patients might also participate in various conferences and retreats offered by these therapists. In off-hours, the patients often devote time to reading newsletters, pamphlets, and the seemingly endless stream of self-help books that promote the idea of memory recovery. In addition, many therapy patients have described spending dozens of hours each week on the phone with other survivors from their groups, discussing the progress of their new memories.

Taken as a whole, the influence of the therapy can go far beyond the acceptance of the belief that one suffered sexual abuse and then repressed the memory for many years. Patients often re-create themselves in the mold of the survivor, their beliefs forming the basis of a new identity and world view.

There is perhaps no other way to understand the broad nature of this process than to explore the lives of the individual women and men this therapy has touched. For this reason, we have scattered the stories of individual patients throughout the book. We begin with Christine Philips's story, not because her story allows a great deal of insight into the process of therapy or to attempt to prove that her memories were undoubtedly false, but because it illustrates the ways in which the abuse-survivor identity can take over the lives of patients and their families. * What makes Christine's story particularly tragic is that Christine first came to believe she was uncovering memories of sexual assaults by her father only a month before she was diagnosed with myelofibrosis, a terminal disease that slowly transforms bone marrow into scar tissue. It is evidence of the force of this belief system that it was her new memories and not her terminal illness that remained the focus of her therapy, dominating the last years of her life.

Christine, who was twenty-six the year that she began therapy, had known all her life that she had not come from a perfect family.[1] Her father was an alcoholic who often angrily lashed out at her mother, Helen, when he was drunk. By the time Christine was eight years old her father's heavy drinking had affected his ability to be rational when he was sober, and he could rarely remember what he had said or done after his third drink. When Christine was eleven her mother gathered the courage to divorce her husband, Jack, and take her daughters away from his destructive behavior. Helen had a difficult time making a home for her two daughters on her salary as a draftsman. After her mother was laid off during the recession of the 1970s, the family went on welfare for a time before Helen could start her own business selling food supplements and household products out of her home. Still, there had been good times. Talking on the phone with her mother, who lived a few states away, Christine sometimes reminisces about the trips she and her mother and sister had taken together while her father had been away for his two-week

---

*All the names in this case study have been changed, along with some identifying details.

army reserve training. Christine had been a straight-A student during grade school and, although her grades slipped some during high school, she had been popular among other students and had a steady boyfriend whom her mother thought very highly of.

While Christine could clearly recall her father's angry drinking binges, it wasn't until a year into therapy that she and her therapist began to suspect that sexual abuse might be at the root of her problems. Christine was a picky eater, and had recently been drinking too much herself. In addition, she seemed to have had only sketchy memories of some parts of her childhood. All of these symptoms, her therapist knew from the recovered memory literature, were common among adults who had repressed memories of childhood molestation. The fact that her father had been an alcoholic made identifying the likely perpetrator an easy task. As a supplement to her therapy Christine joined a group for "survivors" of childhood sexual abuse. She also bought several books on the subject, including *The Courage to Heal*, which she found particularly helpful. In the book she learned that alcoholism in families and other "dysfunctional patterns often accompany sexual abuse" and that victims often abuse alcohol as a way to deny their memories of molestation.

Through therapy and her support groups she learned how to "relive" her newly recovered memories. The sessions in which she reexperienced these scenes were intensely painful. Her body often reacted as if she were actually being assaulted. Describing one session with her therapist, she wrote, "Today I had a physical flashback—which means I physically reexperienced my father's hands on my breasts and I choked and gagged because it felt like his penis was in my mouth again."

In her first letter to her mother after Christine learned that she was dying, she wrote nothing of her disease but only of her new beliefs. "I have some things I need to say to you that I have been afraid to say on the phone because they are painful things. It is clear to me that large blocks of time have been completely wiped from my mind. This came as quite a surprise to me. . . . I have begun having memories of things that happened a long time ago, things that I didn't even know I had forgotten. These memories hit me with the force of a freight train, and there is absolutely no doubt in my mind of their accuracy. . . . I remember being alone in the house with my father at night in front of the TV. I remember a lot of what he did to me during those nights, but not all. I clearly remember him molesting me repeatedly. I believe today that he raped me. . . . I do not know whether the incest went on for months or years, but I do know that the emotional damage has lasted close to twenty years so far, and it will take a few more for me to heal."

Reading the letter, Helen broke down and decided that she would buy a gun, track down her ex-husband, and kill him. Raping one's own daughter was as abhorrent a crime as she could imagine. The impulse to murder her ex-husband lasted only a few days, however. Killing him, she realized, would do nothing to change what had happened or to help her daughter. She decided the best course would be to support her daughter any way she could. Rereading the letter, she realized that a measure of her daughter's anger was directed at her. Christine had determined that the sexual abuse had occurred at about the same time her mother had founded a teen group at the local Unitarian church. Because Christine was ten years old at the time, her mother took only her older sister, Janice, to the weekly meetings. Christine wrote, "I believe today [the creation of the teen group] was an effort on your part to protect Janice from my father."

Because Christine specifically told her mother in the letter that she did not want to discuss this issue over the phone, Helen mailed a series of letters apologizing for the abuse Christine had suffered. She wrote that she had no idea the abuse was taking place and that if she had known she certainly would have immediately taken Christine and Janice out of the home. A week later Helen first learned from Janice that Christine had been diagnosed with myelofibrosis and might have as little as three months to live. After going to the library and reading all she could find on the disease, she decided to call her daughter. The call was received coldly and lasted only a few minutes.

In the weeks following her diagnosis, Christine's abuse beliefs had increased in number and severity. The more memories came, the more she and her counselor determined that her mother must have approved— either tacitly or directly—of the abuse. In one recovered memory she saw her father dangling her off the porch by her wrists. Her mother was standing in the doorway, watching but refusing to intervene. Because of the symptoms she and her therapist identified in retrospect—including picky eating habits, bed-wetting, and straight-A report cards in grammar school—Christine and her therapist determined that her mother must have been aware that something was wrong.

With the support of the therapist and therapy group, she finally overcame her "denial" and accepted her mother as an abuser. Rereading *The Courage to Heal*, she learned that it was always inappropriate for abusers to try to control the relationship with the abused. Only the survivor should be allowed to choose "if, when, and how much she wants to interact." Abusers should never "minimize or criticize" a survivor's anger.[2] After discussing her mother's phone call—which they agreed was intrusive and manipulative on its face—Christine and her counselor decided that Christine's mother's encouragement that she strive for happiness and peace every day she had left was in fact the very sort of minimizing that *The Courage to Heal* had warned of. Christine wrote her mother a long, angry letter.

"This abuse requires years of recovery," she wrote. "I feel that when you say, 'live in today,' that you have completely discounted my experience—my reality. I feel so angry that I need to severely limit our communication. I do not want you to call me on the telephone, I will accept a letter from you—if and only if you can say: 'Christine, I minimized your feelings and I am sorry,' or, 'Christine, your childhood was hell and I didn't help you,' or, 'Christine, I realize that you are entitled to be angry about it for the rest of your life if you want to.' I believe it would help me to hear you admit: 'Yes, Christine, I saw you being abused and I didn't help you.' If you cannot say these things to me, please do not contact me by mail, either."

Helen couldn't decide what to do. She had never seen Christine dangled from the porch, nor suspected sexual abuse. Helen would never have left one daughter vulnerable. If she conceded to her daughter's demands, she felt as though she would be lying, but she desperately wanted to keep open communication with her daughter. For the first time she wondered about the competence of Christine's therapy. Could it be healthy for a woman who was dying to be focused so intently in therapy on memories of being abused? Helen read a book on the terminally ill that helped her understand the process of dying; she sent it to Janice in hopes that she would pass it on to Christine. As the three-month deadline approached, Helen located Christine's doctor, who told her that the disease was moving more slowly than they had expected. Christine might live for a few years, Helen learned to her relief. A week later, a letter arrived from a law firm in Denver. "Our firm represents your biological daughter, Christine Philips," the letter began. "It has come to our attention that you have acted fraudulently and illegally and in direct invasion of her federal and state protected right of privacy in your recent contacts with certain medical personnel. This letter is to inform you that if any future actions are taken by you in violation of her rights, we will immediately institute all appropriate actions."

During this time, Christine continued to focus on her childhood in therapy. She tried to contact her father to confront him, but learned that he was languishing in a residential hospital, his mind severely damaged by the effects of alcoholism and several recent strokes. In a few incoherent notes, he denied that he had ever done anything wrong. The anger

Christine was learning to express in therapy became more and more directed at her mother. She and her therapist began to focus less on the specific memories of sexual abuse that her mother tacitly allowed than on more subtle forms of abuse that she came to believe permeated her childhood. The flashbacks of the sexual abuse by her father became a symbol of her upbringing. Her abuse, she determined, spanned her entire childhood.

With her therapist's help, Christine redefined many of the things she always remembered about her childhood. For example, her sister Janice had played the flute and the guitar but her mother had not encouraged Christine to learn a musical instrument. Her mother's joking admonition, "Be happy, that's an order," seemed in retrospect more malevolent— perhaps an attempt to control Christine's emotions. Drinking beer in high school indicated an early abuse of alcohol. That her mother had not noticed her drinking, she decided, was a type of negligence. As Christine's sickness worsened and her vision of her childhood grew bleaker, she found acceptance within the community of other adult survivors. She began giving speeches around the Denver community, telling church groups, women's studies classes, and community-center gatherings what it was like being a survivor of sexual abuse with a terminal illness. Finally she came to believe that the abuse—which she learned had so permeated her life—was the true cause of disease. When her spleen swelled and had to be removed, many of the women from her survivors' therapy group visited her in the hospital.

After the letter from the lawyer, Helen kept informed of her daughter's condition through Janice, instructing her older daughter to pass on her love and best wishes for health. One Sunday morning a few months later, Helen got a call from Christine's therapist, who told her that Christine might consider allowing a visit if several conditions were met. Before a meeting would be possible, the therapist said, Helen would have to read *The Courage to Heal*. Then she would have to go into therapy. Helen expressed her excitement over the possibility of a meeting and also stressed that she had no idea that Christine's father had sexually abused her. The therapist proceeded to berate her for over an hour about how she brought up Christine. The signs were everywhere that there was something wrong with her daughter, the therapist told Helen, and only a negligent mother could have missed them. Further, the phone calls to the doctors and the book on dying she had sent Christine through Janice were brazen attempts to manipulate Christine. If she was going to see her daughter, her actions would have to be monitored very closely. By the end of the phone call, Helen was in tears.

That day Helen bought *The Courage to Heal*—a thick, large-format book of nearly five hundred pages—and quickly read it cover to cover. She paid particular attention to the section entitled "Families of Origin," and the chapter that followed, which gave advice for the partners and loved ones of victims. She read, "If you are abused within your family or if your family is generally unsupportive, critical, or withholding, continued relations can be very difficult. Sometimes survivors receive genuine support and understanding from members of their families, but this is unusual. Most survivors look back from their own changed perspective at families who are still caught in the patterns that existed when they were children. And as they step out of the family system, they are confronted with the possibility that there will no longer be a place for them."[3] Helen redoubled her resolve to make sure that Christine knew that there would always be a place for her in their family. A few pages later she read that loved ones should always "Believe the survivor. Even if she sometimes doubts herself, even if her memories are vague, even if what she tells you sounds too extreme, believe her." Helen also learned that she should "validate" her daughter's feelings of anger and pain, "These are healthy responses. She needs to feel them, express them, and be heard."

Helen found a local therapist, and after the first few sessions she asked her to call her daughter's therapist to see when a meeting could be arranged. When Helen came back for her fifth session, the demeanor of her counselor seemed sour. The counselor had talked to Christine's therapist, but had learned there were many issues that Helen must first address before she could see her daughter. The therapist then suggested that Helen herself might have repressed memories of abuse she had suffered as a child: "But the first thing we have to find out is why you chose to marry an abuser."

After leaving the session, Helen became angry at the accusation and decided not to return. She wrote a letter to Christine's counselor, lying that she had stopped therapy because it was too expensive but assuring her that she would find other types of counseling and that she still wanted very much to see her daughter. She received a letter back from Christine's therapist chastising her for stopping therapy: "I believe I was clear that you needed to be emotionally able [in order] to actively listen to Christine express her anger."

Months later, anxious to see her dying daughter, Helen finally wrote a letter in which she decided to accede as best she could to her daughter's newfound beliefs about the horrors of her upbringing. She decided that defending her parenting was not as important as providing support to

Christine. "How I wish I could see you so I could apologize to you—greatly apologize to you for so many things I did wrong that hurt my Christine whom I truly love. The fact that I did these things unintentionally is beside the point—they hurt you, Christine, and I'm so sorry. . . . Not a day goes by that I don't think of you often, and long for you to be happy and healthy and wonder how you are doing. Would it be too much for you to let me come see you very briefly? How I wish I could hear your voice!" Through Christine's counselor, Helen's wish was granted. The meeting would have to take place in the presence of Christine's therapist. Helen agreed immediately.

On the day of the scheduled meeting in Denver, Helen arrived at the therapist's house a half hour early, and waited in her car. The house was large and beautiful, and she had to push a button to be let in a gate at the front of the driveway. A woman counselor, not her daughter's therapist, came out and led Helen into a wood-paneled study.

Helen managed to keep from crying when she saw Christine's emaciated state: her eyes were hollow and her body was limp. She slumped, and an intravenous tube fed morphine into her shoulder. When Helen moved to embrace her daughter, the counselors who had led Helen to the room took her by the arm and invited her to sit down on the couch across the study from Christine. Christine's therapist sat by Christine, holding her hand. Helen told her daughter how good it was to see her and how she had cherished her in her thoughts and heart every day. Christine didn't respond.

Christine and her therapist knew that the meeting had not been planned as a social get-together, but rather, in the parlance of the movement, as a "confrontation," and the pair had spent many of the preceding therapy sessions preparing for this day. Christine had compiled a long list of the abuses that included the sexual assaults she believed her mother had allowed. After whispering something into Christine's ear, the therapist told Helen that Christine had a statement she had prepared for the meeting. Christine picked up the sheets of lined paper from her lap and began to read:

"Mother, I am experiencing problems trusting myself and others and expressing and letting go of my emotions as opposed to stuffing them in. I have a hard time knowing who I am." Her voice was weak and she had to take two shallow breaths between each sentence. She went on:

— When I heard you say, "Both my girls are smart and talented," I
   heard you saying, "I was insignificant as an individual and that
   alone I didn't possess any qualities worth noting."

— Whenever you said, "When my kids hurt I hurt," or "Don't cry, I'll cry too," I heard that my feeling hurt you and that I was bad.

— When I resisted doing something just as you told me to and you said, "Why must you aggravate me so?" I heard that my need to be independent hurt you.

— When I missed my curfew and you said, "Why do you hate me so much?" I heard you saying that everything I did was intended to hurt you.

— When you said, "I don't mind buying clothes for you as long as you're going to wear them," I heard you saying that spending money on me was a waste of money.

— I got the message from you that I am worthless . . . when you said you loved all your children equally but let Janice enter a beauty pageant but I couldn't have short-term modeling school.

Helen had a hard time focusing on what her daughter was saying. She knew that she didn't think her daughter was insignificant or worthless, and she had certainly never intended to send her these messages. How could there be such a huge discrepancy between her memories of Christine's upbringing and what her daughter had come to believe? Hearing the complaint that she had favored her older daughter, Helen interrupted to explain this one simple misunderstanding. She hadn't allowed Christine to take modeling classes because they were too expensive and the opportunity had come up when she was barely able to provide for her daughters. The children's beauty pageant that Janice had entered some time before had been different—it had been *free*, and the clothes for the contestants had been donated by a local department store. Christine's counselor cut her short. "You need to just listen now," the therapist said sternly. "You need to just listen to Christine's anger." Helen was given a pen and pad of paper so she could write down her responses. Helen tried for a few minutes to write down her thoughts but was so flustered by her daughter's bitterness she quickly gave up trying. Christine continued reading:

— Forcing me to sit at the table until I ate precisely what you wanted me to, I consider abuse and your lack of remedial action to determine why I had no appetite was neglect.

— I got the message that I wasn't worth your time and attention when you said I should have singing lessons, but I wasn't worth it because you didn't do anything about it.

— When you said, "Lying is the one thing I won't tolerate—I don't do it to you," I heard you saying that you were a better person than I am.

— Whenever I heard, "You're always trying to bring people down," I heard that you wish I wasn't alive in our family and that you would be happier if I was dead.

— Whenever you said, "I try so hard to please you but you're never happy," I heard that I didn't have adequate gratitude for you.

— Whenever you said, "Why do you always need to be right?" I heard that I never was right and did not deserve self-esteem.

— Whenever you said, "I know you can do better than that," I heard that what I was doing was no good. . . .

The full list took Christine almost an hour to read and concluded: "Today I choose to recognize these things for what they really are: blatant child abuse that has no bearing on who I am or who I was then. I use my anger about them as a source of strength . . . I reject these messages about me as the falsehoods they have always been. The hatred and shame I thought were mine all these years I now return to you, their rightful owner. I believe the scar tissue in my bone marrow is simply a manifestation of my belief that I was rotten to the core and my wish to please you by ceasing to exist."

There was a long silence. One of the therapists told Helen that she could now respond to Christine's accusations. Helen wondered what she could say to her daughter; where she could begin to set the record straight. Perhaps if she could tell Christine how happy she had seemed as a child. She tried to recall the best evidence to demonstrate to Christine that she had always loved her. Helen looked at her daughter who was folding the paper in her lap as though it took great strength. Helen knew this visit would be the last time she would ever see Christine. Helen realized that the truth no longer mattered and that there would not be enough time to set the record straight. "I'm sorry, Christine," was all she could think to say, so she repeated it over and over. "I'm sorry, baby. I'm so sorry for everything . . ." At the end of the meeting Christine's therapist handed Helen a copy of the list of accusations.

Christine died a few months later, leaving instructions that no one in her family be notified of her death until a week after her memorial service.

Helen cannot understand what happened to her daughter in therapy; she still puzzles over the letters and the list her daughter wrote. Considering all the ways Christine reinterpreted her childhood, Helen is beginning to wonder whether the sexual-abuse accusations against her ex-husband might be as false as the accusation that she had allowed the abuse to take place. Most of all, Helen is sad that she was unable to support and comfort her daughter during her illness.

The truth of what transpired in Christine's childhood can never be known with absolute certainty. Like most recovered memory therapy cases, the patient's beliefs sharply contrast with the claims of the parents. In many cases the story built in therapy so alters the client's view of the past that the resulting beliefs share practically no common ground with parental memories. What is clear in many of these cases, such as Christine's, is that patients often enter therapy without any notion that they were abused by their parents or that their childhood was abusive from beginning to end. Since the process of therapy leads persons such as Christine to these beliefs, the only way to understand what has happened to these women is to investigate the ideas, techniques, and practices of the therapy.

*   *   *

To justify the beliefs created in therapy, the experts of the recovered memory movement have offered up a series of new theories purporting to explain the mind's ability to repress trauma. While the theories surrounding the movement are often vague and contradictory, those who practice and promote the therapy share one general belief: a young mind has the ability to repress years or decades of repeated sexual abuse so that the child or adolescent victim loses all conscious knowledge of the abuse. While the idea of repression has been toyed with in psychoanalytic circles for a hundred years, this conception of repression proves wholly new— a more powerful mechanism than ever imagined by Freud. While psychotherapy has long put forward the idea that we can consciously avoid thoughts of unpleasant experiences and thereby minimize the impact of those memories—in most references, this is how Freud initially used the term[4]—the robust repression mechanism supposedly allows the subconscious to willfully steal away from our conscious mind virtually any traumatic memory. With this mechanism, our mind not only avoids unpleasant ideas and memories, it blocks them completely from consciousness. Not only are the memories of trauma hidden, but they lie frozen in pristine form, awaiting a time when the person is emotionally prepared to remember. The final magic of this new robust repression mechanism is the belief among recovered memory therapists that these traumatic events can be "relived" during therapy. So real are these repressed memories said to be that therapists claim clients reexperience the event as if it were happening at the moment.

Those who offer the idea of robust repression can be split into two categories. First are the many experts who sell their ideas directly to the public through books, tapes, and seminars. The second are those who claim status as scientists or academics and direct their research and writing to a community of experts. Insofar as the ideas, theories, and justifications behind recovered memory therapy are concerned, the distinction between academic and nonacademic is moot. Except for differences in tone and types of jargon, the theories offered by the two groups are largely the same.

"Most women begin recovery with little or no certainty that they are survivors of sexual abuse," writes Mary Beth McClure in her popular book on the subject. "This is because most incest survivors experience either partial or full amnesia about the actual event. . . . When the body and mind become overwhelmed with stimuli, they simply shut down and stop processing information until the system is no longer overloaded. This is perfectly natural."[5]

"Forgetting is one of the most common and effective ways children deal with sexual abuse," agree Ellen Bass and Laura Davis in their bestseller, *The Courage to Heal*. "The human mind has tremendous powers of repression. Many children are able to forget about the abuse even as it is happening to them."[6] According to Mike Lew, author of *Victims No Longer*, repression may include not just the memories of abuse, but all childhood memories in between the molestation: ". . . enormous pieces of childhood may be pushed into hiding. . . . When an adult client tells me that he can't remember whole chunks of his childhood, I assume the likelihood of some sort of abuse."[7]

These experts also agree that these memories often stay hidden until clients reach adulthood and enter therapy. As Laura Davis explains in her book *Allies in Healing*, "Children actually forget the abuse happened; they store it away in part of themselves that isn't available to their conscious minds. . . . Then, ten or twenty years later, these repressed childhood memories surface, often creating havoc in their lives . . . the process of recovering traumatic memories years after the original trauma is a well-documented psychological phenomenon."[8]

According to these books, the subconscious releases these longrepressed memories into consciousness when it is somehow signaled that the adult mind is ready to remember. "Repressed memories are pieces of your past that have become a mystery," writes Renee Fredrickson in *Repressed Memories*. "They stalk your unconscious and hamper your life with their aftermath. . . . When you were abused you were too young and too fragile to retain the memory. . . . So your wonderful, powerful mind hid some or all of the abuse until you were strong enough to face it. Your repressed memories were held in storage not only for your readiness but also for society's readiness to deal with them. There has been an evolution of consciousness in our culture, resulting in a renewed awareness and ability to humanely respond to abuse."[9]

Explanation and definitions surrounding the idea of repression taken from supposedly academic books and journal articles are nearly identical: "Repression is an effective way of handling data about the self: what is not remembered is put into cold storage, to be retrieved if necessary," writes therapist Karla Clark in the *Clinical Social Work Journal*, adding, ". . . Such matters, when retrieved, may astonish us by their existence or by their nature."[10] Psychiatrist Eugene Bliss in his book on multiple personality, published by Oxford University Press, writes that "Early [traumatic experiences] are carefully guarded. . . . Events thus relegated to the unconscious remain unaltered unless they are hypnotically recovered and reinserted into the stream of consciousness."[11] Therapist Elaine Westerlund, in the professional journal *Women & Therapy*, contributes that "sometimes the memories have been so successfully repressed that a woman may be in therapy for years before she is able to recall the experiences."[12]

The overall theory of this repression mechanism can be summed up in the first line of Judith Herman's *Trauma and Recovery*. She states unequivocally: "The ordinary response to atrocities is to banish them from consciousness." These self-proclaimed experts, like Herman, report that massive repression is commonplace. They claim that the mental-health profession and society at large are only now starting to understand the extent of this remarkable, innate ability. Psychologist John Briere, one of the movement's most influential experts, admits that this sort of total repression capable of causing the "complete loss of child sexual abuse memories" is a phenomenon "only recently appreciated" thanks to the work of "abuse-oriented therapists."[13]

Beyond the shared belief in a powerful repression mechanism, the movement's literature is rife with a seemingly endless number of ideas and explanations for how this repression mechanism works and how memories can be recovered. Trying to examine the many theories that explain this concept of robust repression is like trying to get a grip on fog. While these experts would clearly like to believe they are all referring to the same phenomenon, once one gets past the idea that the mind has the ability to hide vast knowledge of trauma in the unconscious, the theories about why repression happens vary widely from expert to expert.

For example, although they never openly contradict one another, the authors disagree whether children repress memories after each incident of abuse or as a whole set of experiences some point later in time. In some accounts of memory repression, children go from abuse to abuse without any previous knowledge of the last incident. In other accounts they survive long periods of abuse remembering their experiences, and then, at some later time, push the knowledge into their unconscious. This leads to some obvious questions: if children forget trauma instantly, wouldn't this phenomenon have been documented again and again over human history as well as in contemporaneous cases of childhood trauma? Or, if children store up memories of abuse and then repress them en masse, what triggers the repression if it is not the abuse itself?

There are also contradicting theories about the reasons why a child would repress experiences of sexual abuse. One theory often offered is that abuse is so physically traumatic that the mind fails to encode the memory, in the same way a car accident victim might not encode a memory of the moment of impact. However, if physical trauma is the triggering mechanism, how does the child repress the memories surrounding the attack that would indicate something traumatic had occurred? Why are so few patients recovering repressed memories of beatings and other physical punishments commonly inflicted on children? Why are many patients discovering memories of more subtle molestation that was not physically painful? And how do infants or very young children know the difference between nonpainful touching by a doctor that is appropriate and nonpainful touching by a pedophile that is inappropriate and therefore know which experience to repress? Are there properties specific to all types of sexual abuse, which makes it likely, above all other possible experiences, to be repressed into the subconscious for later retrieval?

One might reasonably ask Ellen Bass, co-author of *The Courage to Heal*, to answer these questions. She is, without a doubt, one of the most prominent figures in the recovered memory movement, appearing often on television talk shows to promote, and more recently to defend, the theories offered in her book. *The Courage to Heal*, which has sold an astonishing three quarters of a million copies, is often referred to as the bible of the adult survivor movement. While she is not a psychotherapist, and claims no academic background in the field, because of the prominence of her book she has led seminars for thousands of psychotherapists and other mental-health professionals. The book is filled with confident and unqualified statements about how adult women can uncover hidden memories of abuse they suffered as children. Among other things, Bass and Davis write that to their knowledge the suspicion that someone was abused has *always* led to the confirmation of those suspicions. They also admonish therapists to stay firm in their belief that their clients were abused, even if the clients come to believe that they were not.

In person, Bass is as friendly and engaging a person as one is likely to meet. When we interviewed her at her modest house in Santa Cruz, California, Bass showed no pretense of being a celebrity. When we asked her to explain what makes a child repress the memory of being abused, she began by explaining that the discomfort of remembering something so painful is the motivation for the mind to push a memory into the subconscious. "I think that is just kind of a commonsense reason," she said. "If something terrible happens to you, then if you think about it you feel terrible. That's the bottom line. It's a survival mechanism. Children don't have that many ways to cope."

She was then asked why a young child, who wouldn't yet understand society's delineation between sexual and nonsexual touching, would re-press the memory of nonpainful molestation.

"If it's not painful, I think the child knows it's bad because of the emotional state of the abuser," she explained. "If the abuser is afraid someone is going to walk into the room, the child can pick that up. The abuser may be in his or her own altered state of consciousness. Kind of glassy-eyed—kind of an icky state of mind. Infants don't know anything about sexual propriety, but they can read you perfectly."

What if a parent was washing an infant while he or she was tense, distracted, or upset? Would the infant repress that experience?

"Well, if the child is not old enough to know what is wrong, then at that point she might be just fine. But as the child gets a little older, the cultural view is going to be obvious. When the child realizes what was done to it, then it will repress the memory. It's sort of like delayed damage in that way. Although I'm not really sure. I don't know about this because I'm not really trained. But maybe a child remembers for a time and then represses. Maybe the repression is not instantaneous. Maybe if you ask a five-year-old child who was abused at three what happened to them, maybe they could tell you. But maybe at eight they couldn't. Why would that happen? Maybe they would get a sense from society that repression was necessary. I don't know."

We then asked why so few adult survivors repress physical beatings, devoid of sexual intent. That is, why does the mind's memory-repression mechanism seem to primarily work with sexual-abuse memories?

"I guess [physical abuse] doesn't have the same sense of shame," she explained. "It's acknowledged and is less confusing. With sexual abuse it's very hard for a child to interpret what is going on. Maybe we repress memories because there isn't a conceptual framework for abuse. It's hard to remember things that don't have a concept. Anything that isn't acknowledged around you takes on a kind of unreality."

Bass seemed unaware, or unconcerned, that in one short conversation the theory she offered to explain the mind's ability to repress memories drifted dramatically. In less than a half hour, the cause of memory repression changed from an involuntary self-defense mechanism against trauma to a more complex reaction to feelings of sexual shame or to the child's confusion and lack of a "conceptual framework" surrounding sexual experiences. Bass argues all sides. Perhaps children repress experiences because they are traumatic; perhaps because they don't understand what is being done to them; and perhaps because they learn from society later in their life to view the experience as shameful.

When it was pointed out to Bass that she seemed to offer not one but several explanations of repression, she protested that her theories about why children repress memories were based on common sense. "Maybe I don't even think a lot about why people repress," she then said. "I can't necessarily give you the arguments that would be convincing. I can't give you the research proof, but I don't really operate like that in the world. I'm a really commonsense, practical person." The idea of sexual abuse is so horrible, she offers, that it just made sense that a child's consciousness couldn't hold such an experience. Asked if there was any scientific research to back up any one of her theories, she said: "Look, if we waited for scientific knowledge to catch up, we could just forget the whole thing. My ideas are not based on any scientific theories. As you can hear, I don't really have too many theories."

Like many who promote recovered memory therapy, instead of sticking with one theory about repression, Bass chooses to cover all the bases. Physical trauma cannot be the sole reason for tripping the repression mechanism because it would have been noted more often in nonsexual trauma. Shame cannot be the sole cause because young children do not always understand the social taboos that make certain acts shameful and others not. The unexpectedness of a molestation cannot be the cause either, for patients are often said to repress abuse that has gone on for years and would have become quite predictable. Anyone intent on critiquing the theories of memory repression must get used to a moving target.

In truth, the theories behind repression move and change as necessary to defend the observable results of the therapy. Within the orthodoxy of the movement, it is paramount that no memory of abuse be questioned.

(Indeed, it is often suggested that to question a memory of abuse is tantamount to becoming an abuser.) Because questioning a particular theory of repression would inevitably mean questioning memories of at least some patients, such analysis is nonexistent. It is necessary that the theories of repression be able to change as needed, for if certain types of repressed memories are questioned, attention would immediately be focused on how those beliefs might have been formed in therapy. And to address this question properly, the entire therapy would be called into question.

In reading the popular books and scholarly works promoting the idea of repression, it becomes clear that what the child feels is not at issue. The experiences of the children are important only insofar as they can be used to justify and reinforce an adult horror of childhood abuse. Because we have agreed as a society that molesting one's child is the most abhorrent of crimes, it is assumed that, out of all possible negative experiences, sexual abuse would have the most dramatic impact on the psyche of the child-victim. If incest is the most disturbing crime we can imagine, then surely, these therapists implicitly argue, it is the most damaging crime to be a victim of. All sexual abuse, recovered memory proponents imply again and again, exists separately from other experience. Sexual abuse is assumed to be unique from, and more psychologically damaging than, physical abuse, or the effects of poverty, or the death of a parent, or even surviving experiences like the Holocaust. The remarkable, and newly claimed, ability of the mind to hide all memories of sexual abuse is, therefore, a reasonable and understandable response to such a horrible event. As Bass insists: it only makes sense. These therapists have elevated our shared abhorrence of child sexual abuse from a strongly held culture value and norm to an innate, biological reality.

Further, because as adults we make little moral distinction beween violent and nonviolent sexual abuse of children—we are rightly horrified by all types of child sexual abuse—recovered memory therapists assume that in a child's mind any type of sexual encounter will be as traumatic as any other type. "The fact that someone else has suffered from abuse more severe than your own does not lessen your suffering. Comparisons of pain are simply not useful," write Bass and Davis in *The Courage to Heal*. "Violation is determined by your experience as a child—your body, your feelings, your spirit. . . . Nor is frequency of abuse what's at issue. Betrayal takes only a minute. A father can slip his fingers into his daughter's underpants in thirty seconds. After that the world is not the same."[14]

But does this make sense? Does our adult disgust at the scene Bass and

Davis describe mean that the mind of the child or infant would have—
as a product of human evolution—the ability to remove from consciousness the awareness of this specific type of deplorable act? An inappropriate
touch or even a sexual stare can, according to this logic, be as damaging
as a violent rape and therefore just as likely to be repressed. To say
anything different is to risk being seen as shrugging off certain types of
abuse when society understandably demands uniform condemnation.
Here lies the true rationale for the ever-shifting theories behind the idea
of the robust repression mechanism: all types of sexual abuse are grouped
together (and can therefore be said to trigger memory repression) for no
more sophisticated a reason than that we have—as adults—labeled all
sexual encounters with children as abhorrent. This assumption that the
internal workings of the mind mirror the moral and ethical demands of
society is just one way that specific cultural ideas about sex, children,
the devil, and, ultimately, good and evil, have crept into the supposedly
objective facts and theories put forward by the recovered memory
movement.

Often, one of the first defenses of the concept of repression is that the
idea has been around for a hundred years and has found wide acceptance
in the therapy community. While this may be true (and is, of course,
proof of nothing), it should be pointed out that while the word has been
used in the talk-therapy field for a century, what the word *meant* has
been far from constant. Even today, if you were to ask two different
therapists what repression is and how it works, you are likely to get two
substantially different answers.

Some therapists have defined the term so broadly as to include any of
the ways in which a memory might fail to be encoded as well as the
numerous means by which it might fade or be forgotten. "Repression
has . . . often been called the 'queen of the defenses,' the most general
form of avoidance of conscious representation of frightening memories,
wishes, or fantasies or of the unwanted emotions," writes Professor Jerome
Singer in the book he edited on the subject. He notes that repression can
incorporate "specific defense mechanisms of isolation, denial, rationalization, projection, reaction formation, intellectualization, or sublima-
tion." In this general form, Singer admits, "repression proves to be more
of a metapsychological principle rather than a testable hypothesis about
human behavior."[15]

Another researcher puts it even more strongly: "In seeking evidence
for repression, one could take the position of Humpty-Dumpty, who
pointed out, 'When I use a word, it means just what I choose it to

mean—neither more or less,' and then simply define as 'repression' the various processes that have been demonstrated to result in differential recall," writes David Holmes of the University of Kansas. "That saves the term, but most of the important connotative features of the concept would have to be stripped away."[16]

While all agree that the term refers to the idea that the mind has the ability to keep troubling wishes, thoughts, and memories out of consciousness, the "connotative features" Holmes refers to have to do with the belief that this defense happens involuntarily and that the memory that is repressed in such a way remains fundamentally intact. Holmes defines the "repression" offered in recovered memory circles as having three elements: "(1) repression is the selective forgetting of materials that cause the individual pain, (2) repression is not under voluntary control, and (3) repressed material is not lost but instead stored in the unconscious and can be returned to consciousness if the anxiety that is associated with the memory is removed."[17]

These factors distinguish repression from the normal and accepted idea of "motivated forgetting," that is, our ability to consciously distract ourselves from memories we find troubling. The distinctions are critical: motivated forgetting does not happen unconsciously or immediately, nor does the memory go to some solid-state holding ground where it remains in pristine form. In addition, until the avoided memory is lost through the normal process of forgetting, it remains accessible.

It is unfortunate that therapists often fail to distinguish the idea of "repression" from "suppression," defined in *The Diagnostic and Statistical Manual of Mental Disorders* as "a mechanism in which the person intentionally avoids thinking about disturbing problems, desires, feelings, or experiences."[18] This blending of the ideas of repression and supression goes back over the history of psychoanalysis. Professor Matthew Hugh Erdelyi in his essay on the history of the idea of repression notes that conscious motivated forgetting was what Freud labeled as "repression" for much of his career. He points out that Freud, throughout his career, referred to repression as a conscious "pushing away" or "fending off" an idea. Indeed, most of Freud's definitions of repression do not invoke a powerful unconscious mechanism or suppose that the avoided memory exists in some pristine form awaiting a specialist to apply the appropriate techniques to uncover the recollection. Indeed the mechanism, as Erdelyi notes, need not be thought of as solely a defensive one, employed only to avoid the pain of a particular idea or memory. "Psychologists and psychoanalysts have tended to confuse the psychological mechanism with the purpose for which it is deployed. Repression—intentional not-thinking of some matter—can be used for defense, in which case it is a mechanism of defense, but it can also be used for a variety of other purposes, in which case it remains the same mechanism but not a mechanism of defense."[19]

Of course, memories that are intentionally avoided may exist in some form for years or even decades before they are fully forgotten. (For them to be intentionally avoided requires some awareness that there be something to avoid.) Take the example of a fifty-year-old woman whose mother died suddenly when the woman was a child. The woman may have created a number of unique ways of distracting herself from thinking about the details of those events. If the woman began, in therapy or elsewhere, to search her memory for details surrounding her mother's death, she might be disturbed to find not much there; for, by avoiding thinking about the details for so long, much of the memory will have simply been forgotten. However, if she concentrates for a period of time, she might be able to acquire more details that she initially hadn't been able to recall. These details might be confabulated (perhaps incorporating details of other funerals she had seen or heard of) or have elements of wish and fantasy (perhaps remembering details that she later wished had happened), or be real bits of long-avoided memory. Regardless, the remembered event would grow at least marginally with an amount of concentrated effort. If details of the funeral, which had been avoided for many years, were dredged up in therapy, the therapist and patient may label that memory as having been "repressed" and then "recovered."

But this use of the term "repression" belies its use in the recovered memory circles. In the recovered memory field, "repression" is often described as an automatic mechanism in which the unconscious hides all knowledge of an event or set of events from the conscious mind. The memories are not avoided—*they are inaccessible.* What becomes hidden includes all details of the trauma, both disturbing and mundane, as well as the overall knowledge that the trauma took place at all. The forgetting of all the material around the experience clearly separates this idea of repression from what is called "traumatic amnesia," when parts of a highly stressful event are simply not encoded into memory. With the concept of repression offered by some therapists today, an apparently loving and caring father can rape his daughter and, thanks to repression, remain a loving and caring father in the daughter's eyes. She would supposedly be able to repress not only the memory of the event, but the feelings of betrayal and fear as well as any knowledge that there might be a danger in the future.

The difference between revisiting an avoided memory and recovering a supposedly repressed one is crucial because it is through the latter idea that therapists convince clients not only that it is normal to have no awareness of childhood trauma, but that new abuse "memories" will likely utterly contradict their pretherapy memories of childhood. Applied to the funeral analogy, the repressed memory theory would imply that the woman would have not only been able to avoid thinking of details surrounding her mother's death, but that she would have had no access to those memories even if she had tried to recall them by visiting the gravesite or talking with those who also attended the service. Further, she would have become completely unaware of the events leading up to and away from the funeral—perhaps even forcing from conscious awareness that her mother had died. In recovered memory therapy, patients do not describe simply revisiting long-avoided memories, but rather they tell of the process of uncovering whole sets of experiences of which they had been totally unaware.

This idea of repression stands in clear contrast to the woman who has managed to avoid only certain unpleasant memories surrounding her mother's death. Obviously this woman would know of her mother's death and of the fact that a funeral had taken place. No doubt she would have integrated the knowledge of her mother's death into the overall story she told herself about her relationship with her mother. Further, any memories she retained of the funeral would have been accessible through a number of ways—only one of which would be the focusing on them in the therapy setting. Like all memories, these recollections would have deteriorated over time and become a mixture of reality and imagination, but they would likely contain the crucial elements. No doubt many of the details of the experience, perhaps even large chunks of it, would have been lost due to the mechanism of forgetting.

Examining sixty years of laboratory research directed at finding evidence for the current idea of repression, Holmes concluded that ". . . at the present time, there is no laboratory evidence supporting [this] concept of repression." Those who support the idea of repression, Holmes notes, tend to agree with his conclusion that the experimental evidence is not on their side. Instead of allowing this fact to throw doubt on the mechanism, they offer the argument that the laboratory research is not applicable to what happens in the clinical setting. (Although they have no problem embracing such experimental evidence if it initially shows evidence for repression.) "After dismissing the laboratory research, the clinicians retreat to their consulting rooms for evidence for repression, but what evidence have they produced there? The 'evidence' they offer consists only of impressionistic case studies, and, in view of the data concerning the reliability and validity of clinical judgments, those observations cannot be counted as anything more than unconfirmed clinical speculations—certainly not as 'evidence' for repression."[20]

Considering the powerful and automatic nature of the newly proposed robust repression mechanism, the obvious question becomes: Why are we the first generation to notice that people can repress often-repeated trauma so completely as to have no knowledge that they experienced a life filled with horror and brutality? Does it make sense that although adults and children have experienced trauma throughout the history of the human race, we are the first generation to document the fact that victims can walk away from endless brutalizing experiences with no knowledge that something bad has happened to them? To make the case that we are the first generation to embrace and understand this powerful ability of the mind, recovered memory therapists perform all sorts of logical backflips and somersaults, changing theories as needed to cover the clinical results of those using the word. Often, recovered memory theorists simply vilify all the generations that have come before us as evil or stupid. As a prominent psychiatrist in the field noted, we have un-covered these new truths because we are finally becoming "a caring society,"[21] implying that all societies and generations that came before us were something less.

                    *   *   *

The belief that memory can stay frozen in the subconscious has found quick acceptance, for it matches the conception of memory most ther-apists and laymen already hold. In an informal survey conducted early last decade, two groups, one of mental-health professionals and one from the general population, were asked which of the following statements best described their belief in how memory worked.[22]

> Everything we learn is permanently stored in the mind, although some-times particular details are not accessible. With hypnosis or other special techniques these inaccessible details could eventually be recovered.
>
>   or
>
> Some details that we learn may be permanently lost from memory. Such details would never be able to be recovered by hypnosis or any other special technique because these details are simply no longer there.

Eighty-four percent of those with training in the mental-health field responded that the first statement best reflected their belief, as did 69 percent of the general public surveyed. These results clearly show the popularity of the idea that the brain can store almost every bit of information it takes in—or, at the very least, every truly important moment in one's life. Therapists who believe in the permanence of memory often compare the brain to a computer or a video camera. Using these metaphors, past events can be "replayed" or "called up." With the video-recorder analogy, those trying to recall events are sometimes told that they can "zoom in" on details of the replayed event. Any inability to come up with the details of an experience is explained away as either a failure of the recall techniques or the result of a mechanism in the brain that willfully denies access to that information.

The belief that almost all memory is stored permanently in the brain is pervasive in the recovered memory movement, and it comes with a corollary idea: that all failures at recall are abnormal. Since beginning the search for her hidden memories, one survivor writes in a book on the subject, "I have learned that . . . everything that ever happens to us is recorded in our brain."[23] Another therapy patient quoted in *The Courage to Heal* says of her recovered memories, "It's like it's all recorded in your skin, in your body. We have in our bodies exact, 100-percent recall of what's happened to us. All we have to do is connect with it." Gloria Steinem, a strong proponent of recovered memory therapy, writes that the unconscious holds not only all the events and emotions of our personal past, but the "wisdom of our species." "Precisely because past emotions and events are stored timelessly," she writes, "we can enter that realm of the unconscious and reprocess them. . . . If we ever had a second chance at the past, it is the unconscious that gives it to us. We can go home again—because a part of us never left."[24]

Most recovered memory therapists insist that a patient's important memories can always be found if the therapist and client search long and hard enough. While memory searches can take years, the resulting beliefs are nearly always assumed to be memories. The idea that all experiences are stored somewhere in our brain, that traumatic experiences can be held in crystalline form in the unconscious, and that therapists possess tools and procedures that can bring us in closer touch with our past are the central myths recovered memory therapy relies on.

Patients starting recovered memory therapy probably do not know the research surrounding the permanence of information in the mind, but most assuredly carry a set of beliefs about memory—a belief informed by their own experiences and the knowledge gained from the culture at large. In the survey just mentioned, those who believed that memory was permanently stored most often went on to explain that their belief was based on the personal experience of spontaneously remembering trivial events from long ago. Others who selected the first proposition mentioned their faith in the effectiveness of hypnosis, sodium brevital, and the psychoanalytic process in being able to access memories that were seemingly forgotten. These popular conceptions have made the marketing of recovered memory therapy much easier than it might have been otherwise.

Everyone has had the experience of being unable to remember a piece of information or an experience, only to have the detail later pop into consciousness. Sometimes we have a sense that we possess the memory we are looking for (protesting, often, that the information is on the tip of our tongue), but more often we can't determine whether we might have only temporarily lost access to the information or forgotten it entirely. Given these two options, we often prefer to believe that we have only temporarily misplaced the information and that if we truly needed it, or if we worked hard enough, we could locate it. To further bolster the comforting idea that our whole past exists somewhere in our memory is the common experience of spontaneously remembering long-ago events or moments. Sometimes these memories are sparked by associations such as smells or noises. The vividness of the images and feelings conjured up in these inconsequential memories can take one's breath away. If these memories exist in such a potent form, then why, we think, couldn't all the other similarly inconsequential details exist somewhere in our mind, awaiting the correct chord to bring them to the surface? Even among those who believe that some information is forgotten, there are those who believe that important experiences, including those of great joy and great pain, must be permanently stored, if not always accessible. It is disquieting to think that we might be able to forget the moments that most shaped us.

While it's comforting to believe that all our experiences (or, at the very least, the important ones) are stored somewhere in our minds, this model of memory runs directly counter to almost all scientific studies and experiments on the topic. Reviewing the scientific research, a much less perfect, more malleable, and ultimately more troubling picture of memory is formed. Not only does memory appear to deteriorate and often disappear utterly, but it also shows the disturbing tendency to change and drift—even without any outside influence—becoming an amalgam of imagined and real events. Further, with the addition of subtle and not-so-subtle techniques of influence, laboratory experiments have shown that memory can be easily changed and even created.

Professor Ulric Neisser and Nicole Harsch, of Emory University, in a study on the permanence of the memory of the *Challenger* space shuttle explosion, dramatically illustrated how memory can change over time.[25] When the *Challenger* exploded on the morning of January 28, 1986, Neisser immediately recognized the opportunity to study the properties of what are called "flashbulb" memories—that is, the belief that certain events in life are so significant that they leave indelible memories. While the assassination of John F. Kennedy is probably the best-known example, Neisser realized that the shock of hearing of the *Challenger* explosion would likely become such a "flashbulb," giving a new generation a similar sense that they would always remember the moment they heard the tragic news. The day following the disaster, Neisser gave a short questionnaire to students in his introductory psychology class, asking them to record how they heard of the explosion, including where they were, who told them, who they were with, what they were doing, and what time they had heard about it. He put the students' completed questionnaires away in his desk drawer for nearly three years, until the freshmen became seniors. Enlisting the aid of graduate student Nicole Harsch, he regrouped the students and asked them to fill out the same questionnaire with one addition. After answering each question, students were asked to rate their confidence in the memory on a scale of 1 to 5, 1 meaning "just guessing" and 5 indicating absolute certainty that the remembered account was true. The questionnaires were then compared to the original surveys and rated on a 7-point accuracy scale—2 points awarded for each of the three principal questions (location, way of learning, and activity at the time) and 1 possible point for accurately remembering peripheral details such as other people who were present or the time of day.

Remarkably, only 3 of 44 students who completed the second questionnaire ranked sevens, while 11 were ranked flat zeros—that is, for a full quarter of the sample not one piece of their memory proved true. One such senior, identified as RT, reported the event three years after the fact this way: "When I first heard about the explosion I was sitting in my freshman dorm room with my roommate and we were watching TV. It came on a news flash and we were both totally shocked. I was really upset and I went upstairs to talk to a friend of mine and then I called my parents." Her memory, reported the day after the event, however, showed no resemblance: "I was in my religion class and some people walked in and started talking about [it]. I didn't know any details except that it had exploded and the schoolteacher's students had all been watching which I thought was so sad." While RT's recall was particularly bad (out of the 7 points possible for accuracy, the students averaged a score of 2.95), it was by no means unusual. Another student, for example, remembered three years later that she had heard the results while at home with his parents when he had in fact been at college. The high level of inaccuracy in the memories three years later provided just the first surprise in store for the researchers.

The second surprise came when the researchers examined the results of the students' confidence in their memories. It turned out that those students who reported supreme confidence in their memories were just as likely to be wrong as those who were less confident. RT's confidence level, along with two other students who scored flat zeros in accuracy, rated at the top of the 5-point scale. "I must confess this result surprised even me," Neisser says of the study. "I had expected to find small errors, but not highly confident memories which were totally wrong." The results were so intriguing that the researchers decided to add to the study by interviewing each of the subjects personally the following spring. At the end of the interview, Harsch gave the students both copies of their surveys to read. At this point the researchers got the third surprise of the experiment. Confronted with proof of their original experience, the researchers believed many of the students would change their stories and recall at least some of the details of their original experience, saying in effect, "Oh, yes—*now* I remember how it was." To their surprise, none of the students did this. Many of them who were highly confident in their memories appeared visibly shaken by this evidence that their memories were inaccurate. While none disputed the validity of the evidence they were given, their "memories" proved unaffected. One protested after reading the survey he had filled out three years before, "I still remember everything happening the way I told you. I can't help it."

When and exactly why these memories changed is an interesting but difficult question. Neisser notes that some of the subjects' memories changed from hearing about the disaster through another person to hearing about it on television, perhaps remembering dramatic video footage of the explosion more clearly than the verbal descriptions. This theory, however, can't explain many of the memory shifts. One subject, who reported the day following the accident that she had heard the news in the cafeteria, recalled three years later: "I was in my dorm room when some girl came running down the hall screaming, 'The space shuttle just blew up.' " She went on to say that at first she wanted to run after the screaming girl but instead turned on the television. Where did this screaming apparition come from?

"In my opinion there never was any screaming girl running through the hall," says Neisser. "I think that [the subject] imagined her. Exactly what she imagined, and when, is hard to know. Perhaps she originally felt like screaming herself. Later, the screaming fantasy became the most vivid part of her memory. And finally she began to believe it."

Because it's unlikely that anyone took the time and effort to influence the memories of these students, or that the students had any ulterior motive for lying or desiring the memory to change, Neisser's study can best be seen as an illustration of how a single novel event can change over time with no particular outside influence. It also shows that once people have invested a measure of certainty in their memories—in this case by filling out the second questionnaire—they are likely to stick by their beliefs even with absolute proof that their recollection is incorrect. It's clear from his results that not only are memories forgotten, but that portions or all of some events can change in our memories without our losing confidence as to their accuracy. As Neisser concludes, the study shows that it is possible "to have vivid recollections of things that never occurred. Once you have such recollections, they are very hard to change. Our study shows that this can happen even in the ordinary course of events, without any particular outside suggestion."

This study alone does not of course prove that beliefs formed in therapy are false memories, only that memories—even ones we have great confidence in—are not necessarily what they seem. To counter this and all other disconfirming experimental research, recovered memory therapists often make the case that experiences of great trauma are a special case because they are so deeply etched in the mind. It makes certain intuitive sense that a memory of something really important or shocking would be stored indelibly somewhere in our mind; however, this too is contradicted by the available research.

A study of 133 school-aged children's memories of a sniper attack on their elementary school showed that within a short period (the interviews were conducted from six to sixteen weeks after the event), many of their memories substantially changed, proving a mixture of memory, fantasy, and wish.[26] Interestingly, the children who were safely away from the area of the playground where the fourteen children were shot tended in their retelling to overemphasize the danger they experienced by incorrectly reporting that they were closer to the danger or by misremembering that the sniper was closer to them. One girl initially said she was at the school gate nearest the sniper when the shooting bgan, while in truth she was a half a block away. Similarly, a boy remembered seeing someone lying on the ground while he was on his way to school when in actuality he was away on vacation on the day of the shooting. Those children in the direct line of fire, however, showed a tendency to move themselves away from the danger in their memory. In addition, many of the children seemed to want to make sense of the randomness of the attack by incorrectly remembering that the children who were injured had been clustered together near the one child who was killed.

From this study, it seems that memories of trauma are just as susceptible as other memories to distortion through the inclusion of wish and fantasy. In the case of this study, at least, these distortions can result in the subject remembering the event as either more or less traumatic. While the ability of the children in danger to downplay the trauma of the experience does speak to the possibility that the mind has a tendency in retrospect to lessen the intensity of a traumatic experience, this should not be seen as evidence for a stronger repression mechanism. While the study of the schoolchildren shows that the mind can incorporate wish into a traumatic memory, it did not show that any of the children could wish the memory away, or that the true memory of the experience lay undisturbed in their unconscious.

A researcher who studied the group of children who had witnessed the murder of a parent also found that while the memories are often distorted, not one child repressed the memory of the experience.[27] Not only had they not forgotten the experience, but the researchers noted that they all had recurrent thoughts of the episode that often came back at unwanted and unexpected moments. Their intrusive memories occurred even though they reported they did not like to speak of the events and seldom had to talk about the experience to anyone. They also showed the ability to integrate their memory of the murder with a larger understanding of their relationship with their parents.

This is not to say that memory of trauma cannot be forgotten. Memory of trauma has properties that might in some cases make it more likely to be remembered, and in other cases increase the likelihood that the event is forgotten. It has often been noted that the memories we continue to remember are ones we tend to retell or revisit in our minds. If, as in the case of the children who witnessed the murder of a parent, the memory of the trauma becomes intrusive, flashing images and other recollections into consciousness even when not called for, the effect ought to be to instill the memory. The exact opposite might also be true. Because our minds have the imperfect ability to consciously control what we dwell on, if a person can successfully avoid thinking about certain traumatic moments, it seems possible that he or she could increase the likelihood that the memory, through disuse, might be forgotten. However, as we have noted, forgetting a memory of trauma differs from the idea of repression because (a) it does not happen automatically, instantaneously (or even quickly), and (b) there is no assumption that the forgotten memory exists somewhere in the brain, waiting to be relived.

The other questionable property of robust repression is the idea that the memory can be recovered *intact*—filled not only with all the visual and sensory detail of the original event but with all the emotional and cognitive material as well. The woman believed to have repressed the memory of her mother's funeral, then, would be told by a recovered memory therapist that together they would not only be able to remember the event but also able to access exactly what she felt, thought, and said at the time. Some repressed memory therapists would, often under hypnosis, even help the woman "relive" the event.

The pain involved in "reliving" previously unknown rapes during what are called "abreactions" is not only tolerated in recovered memory therapy, it is encouraged. The idea of an abreaction is built from the belief that a patient must "relive" the repressed scene of abuse as if it is happening in the present. Once the details of the scene have been fleshed out from beginning to end through techniques such as guided visualization, dream interpretation, or artwork, the patient is often expected to relive the scene with all the appropriate emotion, fear, and psychological pain that would be appropriate to the actual event.

"Movement in therapy will be much greater if the woman is able to sob like a child, to shake with terror and to scream with rage," writes Elaine Westerlund in the journal *Women & Therapy*. "They may reexperience the events quite vividly. Physical responses such as vomiting, incontinence or fainting will sometimes occur."[28]

"Unless one works with these patients or has experience with excellent hypnotic subjects, it is difficult to grasp how *real* deep hypnotic experiences can be," writes Eugene Bliss, a prominent psychiatrist who works with clients to find their hidden pasts. "When a patient enters the world of hypnosis and encounters an early traumatic episode, whether it is induced by hypnosis or it occurs spontaneously, the event can be relived with the intensity of the original event. The patient is literally there reexperiencing all."[29]

Exploring the world of recovered memory therapy, one finds many accounts both from patients and therapists to substantiate these descriptions of the pain of reliving memories. Often before "reliving" scenes of torture and rape, patients are strapped down to beds with leather restraints and given trance-inducing drugs. "Survivors who experience abreactions feel as if they are right there, and the abuse is happening all over again," writes Margaret Smith in her book on recovered memories of ritual abuse. Another patient quoted later in this book describes what an abreaction can be like. "We [referring to herself and her alter personalities] can see the people involved clearly; we can feel them, smell them, taste them, and hear them. . . . Our body moves as though someone is hurting it. If we are involved in a rape, the body is pushed as though someone is on top of us having intercourse. The breath is knocked out of us. The whole body stiffens in defense. Sometimes there is spontaneous bleeding. There is intense fear."[30]

The gap between accepted research on memory and the theories offered by recovered memory therapists is perhaps widest in regard to the belief that abreactions are beneficial and an effective way to treat patients. A growing number of mental-health professionals who balk at the repression mechanism offered by these therapists have begun to identify these abreactions for what they are: the unnecessary torture of vulnerable people.

Writing in general of the new theories surrounding recovered memory therapy, David Holmes concludes "that our current regulations concerning 'truth in packaging' and 'protective product warnings' should be extended to the concept of repression. The use of the concept might be preceded by some such statement as, 'Warning. The concept of repression has not been validated with experimental research and its use may be hazardous to the accurate interpretation of clinical behavior.' "[31] We would add to this warning that these new myths of memory may also be hazardous to the patient's mental health.

CHAPTER TWO

Effort After Meaning

In a first-person article in the October 1992 issue of *Self* magazine, A. G. Britton describes living a relatively happy and successful life until she hit a series of unexpected crises during an eight-month period when she was thirty-three. "I was fired. But losing my job was just the capper. During those eight short months, I had watched, helpless, as my two-and-a-half-year-old son got hit by a car; he was unhurt but I couldn't stop worrying about him. I had miscarried in my third month of pregnancy, begun hemorrhaging and required emergency surgery. And I had arrived home one day to find the four-story building next door engulfed in flames. An underground electrical transformer had exploded, and in doing so had created a kind of mass hysteria among the mothers on the block."[1]

Britton then tells of the onset of depression and of going into therapy, where she determined that the actual cause of her depression was not the firing, the accident, the miscarriage, or the fire. Under the guidance of her therapist she determined that the cause of her present unhappiness was the previously unknown fact that "my father had sexually violated and otherwise tortured me from the age of six months to the age of eighteen months."

This article can be read in a number of ways. Reading this narrative, some critics of repressed memory have pointed to the obvious incongruity between the crises that brought on the author's depression, and the memories uncovered in therapy. The events that sparked the crises in her life, they point out, have a questionable correspondence to the conclusion that all her problems can be traced to a single source: sexual abuse by her father. The miscarriage, her dismissal, and certainly the fire, some have noted, were not likely results of being abused in early childhood. While this non sequitur is certainly troubling, the story can also be read in another, broader way. It illustrates what those who study the practice of psychology often call "effort after meaning." We desire to create a comprehensive cause-and-effect story out of our lives, and at those times when we seem unable to do this for ourselves, we are most vulnerable to the simple explanations offered by others.

The human mind seeks patterns. We tell ourselves stories about why one event might have been the cause of a second event and might therefore be a predictor of a third. In many areas, say religion or economics, we often offer such post hoc reasoning without requiring that the validity of those connections be demonstrated. Astrology, for another example, is an elaborate apparatus for creating the appearance of meaningful connections where none exist. All of us are experts at making such cause-and-effect conclusions within our own lives. "We tell ourselves stories in order to live," writes Joan Didion in her *White Album* collection. "We interpret what we see, select the most workable of multiple choices. We live entirely . . . by the imposition of a narrative line upon disparate images, by the 'ideas' with which we have learned to freeze the shifting phantasmagoria which is our actual experience."

For differing duration there inevitably comes a time when we lose our ability to create the connective tissue that helps us make sense of our lives. Events from day to day or even year to year become discordant or a hurried blur. At these times we can even begin to question the truth of the old stories we told ourselves in our younger years, for the person whom these stories describe appears different from the person we see in the mirror. For people in the depths of such a crisis, there exists an entire profession waiting to assist.

Within the general profession of psychotherapy, there is no agreed-upon training or procedure for treating such a client. The term "psychotherapist" describes a broad range of professionals and lay people, including psychologists, psychiatrists, social workers, educational counselors, drug-abuse counselors, family counselors, and psychoanalysts. While much of psychotherapy masquerades as a quasi-medical specialty and is funded by private insurance and government health-care programs, the training and methods vary enormously. In most states the profession is so poorly regulated that one needs no training at all to assume the title of therapist or psychotherapist. Regardless of these differences in training, in the most general terms, all psychotherapists attempt to offer help to those demoralized by their lives. As Jerome Frank suggests in *Persuasion and Healing*, this demoralization may stem from a feeling of powerlessness to affect oneself and one's environment. "Psychotherapies may combat the patient's demoralization," he writes, "not only by alleviating his specific symptoms of subjective distress and disordered behavior but also, and more importantly, by employing measures to restore his self-confidence and to help him to find more effective ways of mastering his problems."[2]

The psychotherapy Frank writes of has little to do with the treatment of major mental illness such as life-threatening depression, mania that leads to delusion, schizophrenia, or debilitating anxiety, but rather the more common forms of unhappiness and confusion. Serious mental illnesses have become viewed increasingly as medical problems, and psychotherapists have been increasingly shut out of their treatment. Currently, in American society, psychotherapy deals primarily with simple human unhappiness—the failure of life to be what we want it to be and the gap between our idealized image of ourselves and the realities of who we are.

Often the way psychotherapists offer to restore our self-confidence is by helping us to create new narratives intended to tell us why we are the way we are. Linking "present to past experience reflects the very structure of man's mental apparatus," wrote prominent psychiatrist Ernst Kris in a 1955 essay on recovering childhood memories. "It is part and parcel of many types of introspection and, in higher civilization, part of the tradition of contemplative and speculative thinking. The study of the interaction between past and present stood at the beginning of psychoanalytic work and has remained alive throughout its development."[3]

By understanding the "true" nature of the forces that have formed us, therapists often promise, we will learn to better control and affect our behavior. In the best-case scenario, a therapist can help the client to this new understanding, while at the same time providing a fuller appreciation of the complexity of his or her life and behavior.

In its most simplistic form, however, therapy offers pat answers. Some therapists, for instance, make their living explaining to patients that their current problems stem from not having fully come to terms with the trauma of childbirth. Other therapists are more savvy but just as simplistic in continually hunting the patient's past for events they can identify as the direct cause of the current distress. The method of tracing current behavior to some past cause, which we will refer to as the etiological model of therapy, has taken root not only in the mental-health community but in our culture as well. The scene in which the therapist, through thoughtful questioning of the client's past, reaches epiphanies of understanding has become standard fare for movies, books, and television. Books and movies such as *Ordinary People, Spellbound,* and *The Prince of Tides* exalt this idea and endow the finding of such a connection with remarkable curative powers. The story of the therapist and patient endeavoring to courageously face the mind's unknown terrain is told so often it's nearly a cliché.

French psychoanalyst Serge Viderman wrote in an essay in *The Psychological Quarterly* that patients' symptoms are a kind of "subverted memory, inserting themselves into a mnemonic net torn as a result of defensive operation, for the purpose of restoring the continuity of broken links. The spoken interpretation aims at retying, reweaving the net, by substituting the repressed memory for the symptom."[4] In this romantic and metaphorical description of what treatment is capable of, symptoms are merely the outward manifestation of past events, and are expected to disappear when the events are brought into awareness. Some therapists who follow this model offer patients a string of seductive ideas: First, that there exist specific, identifiable events for every problem or disorder. Second, that those reasons remain in the patient's memory or in the unconscious (or both, as with the idea of repressed memory). Third, that it is possible to make a causal connection between the symptom and cause by talking to the patient. And, finally, that digging up and understanding this connection can cure the disorder.

In all the dozens of incarnations of etiological therapies, therapists claim the same ability to identify the events or forces that have derailed a patient's life. The therapists often hold that the theory they are marketing is a newly discovered truth that can identify and set right the factors that sent the patient's promising life off the tracks. Once the treatment is applied, the patient will be restored to a healthy condition and be spared the problems and self-defeating behaviors that were never really his or her fault in the first place.

The proposition that we are unconsciously controlled by specific events in our histories is a seductive one for prospective patients because it lifts responsibility for seemingly self-inflicted problems off the patient, while at the same time promising to solve problems that may in fact have no satisfactory solution. For those plagued by anything from serious mental disorders that cannot presently be effectively treated to those haunted by the simple feeling that their lives are not as fulfilling as those of the people around them, the message that they are controlled by subterranean forces carries a type of absolution: the patient is forgiven the sins she appears to have committed against herself. At the moment the patient receives this forgiveness, she is offered the promise that through therapy she can learn to understand the deep currents that move her, and, through that understanding, take a greater measure of control of her life and the events that befall her.

"The challenge today is to take responsibility for your life by asking the hard questions without the blame and guilt and bad feelings of yesterday," writes J. Patrick Gannon in *Soul Survivors*, one of the books of the recovered memory movement. The hard questions are not about what choices the patient made and what she might do to change her current circumstances but rather what was done *to* her. "It may still be difficult to look at yourself and your current life," Gannon warns, "without hitting yourself over the head with shame and condemnation."[5]

"It is very important that self-destructive behaviors be linked with child-hood self-disgust and that a victimized life-style be linked with childhood powerlessness," write two clinicians in the journal *Social Casework*. "As a woman begins to see herself objectively as having been a helpless, victimized child, she sees that she was not responsible and she begins to like and respect herself."[6]

Accounts of patients accepting this absolution can be found throughout the literature of the movement. "Until that day [when she began to uncover her repressed memories], I never knew where my rage came from," writes Connie Brewer in *Escaping the Shadows, Seeking the Light*. "It was not until I began dealing with what had been done to me that I could begin dealing with the emotional, verbal, and physical abuse I had inflicted on my own children. . . . Although I had promised myself I would never slap my children in the face as my mother had done to me, I found myself doing so, totally unable to stop myself. But now that my repressed memories are emerging, I know the origins of my rage."[7]

"Before I knew my father had molested me," writes another survivor in the book *Dancing with Daddy*, "the feelings cycled endlessly and attached themselves to the world outside of my skin: If only my children weren't so demanding, I could think, I wouldn't feel so crazy."[8]

A woman who identified herself as Rosemary told a New York State legislative panel that was considering the extension of the statute of lim-itations on abuse cases that discovering her repressed memories explained many troubles in her life. "In my early twenties, I dated a very nice man. When things became serious and he started talking marriage, I broke off the relationship. I thought of any excuse to get him out of my life. At the time I didn't recall my sexual abuse, which I now believe is directly related to my rejection of him. Because of the abuse, I have been denied a husband and children."[9]

Over most of the history of talk therapy, discerning the truth of those connections drawn between events dating back decades and behavior problems in the present has largely been moot. Indeed, from an end-justifies-the-means standpoint, it often didn't seem to matter much what type of explanation was offered for a client's distress or whether that story was complex or simplistic. Just believing in the reason proffered by the therapist seemed to have at least a small curative effect. If a patient became to some measure healthier while in therapy because, for example, she

believed she had come to terms with the pain of being born or the belief
that she once witnessed her parents having sex, it didn't much matter if
that experience was truly at the root of her problems. With the advent
of recovered memory therapy the question of the historical accuracy of
the narratives must finally be addressed. "[The etiological model of ther-
apy] is predicated on the assumption that the psychotherapeutic process
offers the only valid basis for laying bare the nexus of psychological forces
that are etiologically responsible for the patient's illness," writes Samuel
Guze, Professor of Psychiatry at Washington University, in *Why Psychiatry Is a Branch of Medicine*. "The etiological model . . . is inherently
dramatic and appealing. By dealing with etiology, it seems to offer the
best possibility that the patient can be cured and that future relapses can
be prevented. Its success, however, depends directly on the validity of
the etiological hypotheses. To the extent that these are in error, the
ultimate justification for the psychotherapy is seriously undermined."[10]

Guze rejects the etiological therapy, as do many other professionals,
because he questions whether meaningful causal relationships between
sets of events and behavior are possible, given the complex forces that
drive behavior. Guze finds "little scientific basis for the assumption that
psychotherapy serves as a vehicle to uncover the etiology of psychiatric
disorders."[11]

The sheer number of different "schools" of etiologically based therapy
gives weight to Guze's argument. Because different groups of therapists
focus on different types of etiological theories, the cause patients come
to believe is at the root of their current demoralization is arbitrarily
determined by the therapy they select. As Guze suggests, it is likely that
"a therapist's interpretations may actually reflect his or her own assumptions and expectations, thus constituting 'suggestion' . . . this is reflected
in the old and cynical adage that every therapist finds in patients just
what his or her orientation leads the therapist to expect."[12]

If the causal connections created between events in the patients' past
and their current behavior are somewhat arbitrary, why then do they
seem to hold so much meaning for the patients? The answer comes by
examining the ways in which the therapist and patient conspire to manufacture a believable narrative. In the vast amount of evidence a client
presents to a therapist—including memories, dreams, behaviors, feelings,
and thoughts—there exists grist for any number of answers to the question
of why the client is currently troubled. The therapist and patient are
forced to pick and choose from this wealth of information to create a
sense of meaning. While there is no doubt that some therapies (and
some therapists) will come closer to the true historical antecedents—the

causes—of the client's behavior than others, in practice these causes are impossible to identify with certainty. In addition, because they must package that narrative in a manageable form, all etiologically based therapies must to a great degree simplify the story. However, while the narrative created can be partly true, it can also be wholly a creation of the therapy. As we will see, this arises when the therapist leads the client to create the evidence (as in the case of repressed memories) as well as the resulting narrative.

In his book *Narrative Truth and Historical Truth: Meaning and Interpretation in Psychoanalysis*, Donald Spence offers a profound critique of the theories and connections made in the therapy setting. He argues that those who practice psychotherapy often fail to make a distinction between the historical truth of the patient's life and the narrative created in therapy—mistakenly believing that they are one and the same. "The model of the patient as unbiased reporter and the analyst as unbiased listener suggests a kind of naive realism that is hard to imagine, harder to practice, and runs counter to everything we have learned about the way we come to understand the world." The model continues because it "heightens the special virtues" of the therapy setting in the mind of both patient and therapist. Each is tempted to believe that in the hallowed setting of the therapist's office "the patient does indeed have privileged access to the past, and the analyst, by virtue of his special training, is in fact a rather special reporter of a kind who makes almost no mistakes."[13]

This paradigm is problematic for a number of reasons. Before the patient's history is focused into meaningful theories by the therapist, the information from the patient travels through several lenses, each of which has the ability to magnify, diffuse, or distort the actual events of a person's life. As Spence notes, this process begins when the patient attempts to translate thoughts, feelings, and memories into words and sentences during the therapy hour. While this seems an innocuous step, there is little doubt that patients' access to their own life histories, while vast, has already been affected by their pretherapy assumptions about cause and effect relationships between events in their lives and their current behavior. Further, the patients' understanding of what sort of language and topics are appropriate to a given therapeutic setting—and a given therapist—will further influence the patients' offerings.

The second lens is how the therapist hears those words. Spence challenges the idea that a therapist can listen with evenly hovering attention without filtering what he or she hears through his or her own set of assumptions. It is human nature, after all, to give more attention to detail

COLLEGE OF THE SEQUOIAS
LIBRARY

that contributes to a sense of coherence (perhaps to a theory about the client's problems that the therapist is considering) than to details that do not fit. "Each interpretation is guided, unwittingly, by our favorite paradigm," Spence writes. "We are, in effect, constructing an interpretation that supports our private theory or collection of paradigms. . . . Interpretations are persuasive, not because of their evidential value but because of their rhetorical appeal. Conviction emerges because the fit is good, not because we have necessarily made contact with the past."[14]

Interestingly, Spence does not damn psychotherapy for its ability to create a believable but fundamentally untrue narrative. Ordinarily, the fictional elements that develop in the therapy narrative do not necessarily mean the narrative developed in therapy has no value. Spence argues that, on the contrary, the narrative created in therapy can provide the patient with an important sense of understanding about his or her life— *even if that narrative truth has a questionable relation to his or her true history*. In this sense, we can see therapy as an exaggeration of our natural inclination to create a meaningful story about the events in our lives. This story can not only give meaning to our past but, by providing a sense of understanding as to what type of person we are, also influences our future actions and decisions.

Spence draws a parallel between the analyst and an artist or fiction writer who creates works that seem to carry fundamental truths but do not necessarily represent real-life images or sets of events. Using the grist the patient provides during the hour, the therapist, in effect, tells a believable story that answers the patient's question: "Why am I like I am?" In the story's believability, depth, and complexity, the patient finds meaning and a measure of truth. In this view, Spence notes, therapy becomes an "aesthetic experience."[15] The historical truth of the story told becomes as moot as the historical truth of a novel. The story's *sense* of truth becomes paramount. "Narrative truth is what we have in mind when we say that such and such is a good story," writes Spence, "that a given explanation carries conviction, that one solution to a mystery must be true. Once a given construction has acquired narrative truth, it becomes just as real as any other kind of truth; this new reality becomes a significant part of the psychoanalytic cure."[16]

As Spence notes, even Freud came to partially concede that a narrative can have curative powers even if it doesn't lead to the memory of a specific event. "The path that starts from the analyst's construction ought to end in the patient's recollection; but it does not always lead that far," Freud wrote. "Quite often we do not succeed in bringing the patient to recollect what has been repressed. Instead of that, if the analysis is carried out correctly, we produce in him an assured conviction of the truth of the construction which achieves the same therapeutic result as a recaptured memory."

Viderman, who quite clearly believes in the curative powers of exposing repressed material, agrees with Spence that the psychotherapist must not be constrained to the particulars of the patient's true history. The interpretation should not be "obliged to respect the manifest content" of the material the patient provides. He goes on, "This is one of the advantages of the coherence we regain when we no longer feel so strictly bound to retrace, stroke by stroke, a history nowhere to be found."[17]

The most disturbing part of this narrative creation is the extent to which it can be influenced by the therapist's preconceived notions about what the likely causes are to the patient's problems. Because an unlimited number of stories can be made from any given patient's history, most therapists offer a limited number of narrative structures (or interpretations) onto which the patient, with the help of the therapist, can apply evidence. If the therapist didn't have these preexisting interpretations to offer, as Viderman points out, "the observable facts and realities [of the patient's life] can be looked at indefinitely and remain mute indefinitely."[18]

As an example of how these interpretations can be applied almost regardless of the evidence presented, he points to Freud's interpretation of a dream of his Wolf Man patient. From a dream of seeing half a dozen wolves sitting on the branches of a walnut tree, Freud deduced that the patient was suffering "infantile neurosis" from having witnessed his parents engaged in sexual intercourse. In order to make the intuitive leaps and logical backflips necessary to render the dream of the wolves into a "memory" of witnessing a "primal scene," Freud obviously must have predetermined his conclusion. That is, he must have brought the idea of the primal scene (and the further presumption that witnessing such an event could cause neurosis) to the therapy setting and saw the dream as an opportunity to graft his theory onto the experience of his patient.

As Viderman puts it, "Nobody could 'discover' the primal scene from the manifest content of the [Wolf Man's] dream . . . unless the end of the operation had been established—and anticipated—from its beginning. . . . Without the model that organized the meaning of the scene a priori, it is out of the question that it could have emerged from the ambiguous and contradictory material; *hence* [the memory] *could not be discovered but only imagined*" (emphasis in the original).[19]

Viderman implies that the reality of the client's past is too hard to grasp and too inconsistent and random to hope that it will reveal the type of fundamental truth necessary to provide the sort of memory that would carry an explanatory punch. Because our true lives are filled with partiality and caprice, the therapist cannot limit himself or herself to that reality, but rather hunts our memories and fantasy lives, looking for an opportunity to use one of a set of fundamentally compelling interpretations the therapist holds at the ready. What the quiver of interpretations might include varies greatly depending on the type of therapy, the predisposition of the therapist, and the mood of the times.

The idea that the narrative truth created in therapy can be rewarding and yet ahistorical seems at first a distressing one. What good, after all, is the creation of a life narrative that is largely unconcerned with the literal truth of the connections drawn? The answer to this question is that it is the wrong question to ask. The importance of the created narrative truth is not in its ability to re-create a person's history—for in this it fails—but to affect a patient's outlook, sense of continuity, and future behavior.

"The truth [of the narrative] lies more in the present and future than the past," explains Spence. "We are primarily interested in the effect it produces rather than in its past credentials. . . . Associations and interpretations, as they are inserted into the developing narrative, become true as they become familiar and lend meaning to otherwise disconnected pieces of the patient's life. The very process that allows the analyst to understand the disconnected pieces of the hour, when extended and amplified, enables the patient gradually to see his life as continuous, coherent and therefore meaningful."[20]

If the narrative is skillfully created and artfully applied, it can be a tool for influencing the client's behavior in the future. Thoughtful therapists will help create a narrative not simply to allow the client to assign blame (nor do they assume that once a believed-in narrative is created, the client's problems will simply disappear), but rather they will help create a narrative that holds lessons for the client's present and future actions and behavior.

Some have criticized Spence for overstating his point. Surely, the information provided by clients about their own histories cannot be totally distorted by the lenses it must travel through in therapy. If the narrative has any meaning for the client must it not resonate with the facts of the client's life? Leonard Shengold, author of *Soul Murder: The Effects of Childhood Abuse and Deprivation*, charges Spence with mounting an "assault on historical truth" and idealizing the narrative. "For him the . . . search for the 'real past' should be abandoned—the making of a narrative is all. The analyst's task is to be a superior novelist of the psyche."[21]

In a normal therapy setting, where the patient's initial memories of her childhood are assumed to contain the truth of her past, one could indeed assume that for the narrative to have a "good fit," it would have to more than less correspond to memories of her life. But in some therapy settings—recovered memory therapy prime among them—the client's pretherapy memories are assumed to be *false* or even to represent the exact opposite of the patient's real childhood. A patient who talks glowingly of her parents and upbringing can be suspected of hiding a dark past. Recovered memory therapy is an illustration of the ultimate outcome of Spence's notion of narrative creation, for the therapist not only helps build the narrative but helps to build the evidence for that narrative as well. In recovered memory therapy, the client's initial memories don't even have to go through the lenses of therapy: if those memories don't provide evidence for the abuse narrative, they are simply ignored.

*   *   *

To illustrate how therapists, through their interpretations, can build any number of stories that the patient can come to believe in, consider the case of Miss F.T., which was published in Robert Langs's influential work *The Techniques of Psychoanalytic Psychotherapy* along with the case's subsequent reinterpretation by Charlotte Krause Prozan in her book *Feminist Psychoanalytic Psychotherapy*.

According to Langs's account, Miss F.T., a young woman from a family of two sisters, came to therapy because she had a tendency to act out and showed a moderate character disorder. As in most therapy settings, the information from which Langs constructed his interpretation came out of F.T.'s description of her past, her dreams and fantasies, and the events in her current life. During therapy F.T. told Langs of childhood memories that included an accidental fall, a vaginal infection, trips during summer vacations during which the whole family sometimes shared a single hotel room, catching her leg in the spokes of a bike, and of being easily bruised. She recounted that she felt somewhat neglected because her mother worked while she was growing up. She remembered that her father had always wanted a son and that she, of the three sisters, was the one who shared his activities and worked with him on his job. She recalled her childhood wish to own toy guns. She also recalled seeing her mother's bloody menstrual pads as a child, and believing at the time that her mother had been damaged while being penetrated by her father. She described a fair amount of sexual activity during college. As the therapy progressed, she also reported dreams that included having sex with famous male singers and another where she sleeps with a movie star. She related other dreams as well: one in which she is sitting in a movie theater with a monkey scratching her head, one of her aged, senile grandmother, and another in which she sees herself as a shoe salesman with three pairs of shoes, two brown and one blue.

In addition to this material, she and Langs discussed three significant experiences from her current life. These included her mother having surgery, her sister getting married, and her own reaction to the news that Langs planned to take a vacation. At hearing the news that Langs would be leaving town, F.T. became "depressed and angry, thought of stopping treatment, and dreamt of sleeping with an old boyfriend."[22] She subsequently dreamed that she and her sister were having an affair with an older man, someone the age of Langs.

From this mix of fantasy, dream, memory, and behavior, Langs began to piece together a narrative of F.T.'s life. Both F.T. and Langs agreed that the dream of being a shoe sales*man* might connect with her desire to fulfill her father's wish to have a boy. The memory of her desire to own a toy gun furthered Langs's belief that F.T. might be experiencing penis envy. Langs suggested to the patient not only that she might have wanted to be a boy but that "as a child she had probably seen her father's penis—possibly when they had traveled and shared a room."[23]

This narrative seemed to strike a chord in F.T. In subsequent sessions she reported a fantasy of being a popular male singer and also reported a dream in which she "wanted her own set of balls." While this part of the analysis seemed to be confirmed, Langs wrote, "nothing more was said about the possible primal scene experiences and seeing her father nude."[24]

After F.T.'s mother became ill and she reported the dream about the monkey in the movie theater, Langs offered another "reconstruction." Langs intuited from the clues F.T. had provided that she had once witnessed her parents having sex.

According to Langs, F.T. at first denied having a memory of seeing her parents having sex, only recounting the times when the family had slept in the same room on vacations.[25] However, as with Langs's first belief about penis envy, evidence was soon discovered that substantially affirmed his suggestion. In discussing the interpretation, Langs recounts, "the patient suddenly, but vaguely, recalled waking up herself one time— away with her parents—and hearing movement of some kind." In subsequent sessions, she revealed seeing her sister in bed with a boyfriend as well as having had fantasies of her parents having intercourse, which upset her because she linked it to their constant arguments.

Finally, "a dream of a cold, gray forest with felled trees led to memories from early childhood when Miss F.T. shared a room in a cabin with her parents; she had awakened during the night to noises there too. Other even earlier similar experiences were then recalled, as were the nightmares that accompanied them."[26] In her last session, F.T. reported recalling a childhood fantasy of an alligator hiding under her bed. She also remembered another scene from a hotel room she shared with her parents in which "something small was getting large. She thought of a penis, of her mistrust of men, and of her fantasies that her father had done something to her mother. Fantasies of having had a penis, of her father having bitten it (and her mother's) off, and impulses of revenge-in-kind against her father, were all in evidence."[27]

By the end of therapy, both narratives offered by the therapist—that F.T.'s problems stemmed from penis envy and from witnessing a "primal" scene between her parents—were confirmed through fantasies and newly discovered memories. In addition, these narratives seemed to hold great meaning for the client. As Langs notes, F.T.'s "functioning much improved," as did her acting out. The reconstructions offered appear from Langs's account to have had the effect of giving the patient a greater understanding of her behavior, history, and fantasy life.

But were these narratives built in therapy historically true? Or were they narratives created because Langs brought the idea of "penis envy" and "primal scenes" prepackaged to the therapy setting? Could other narratives be made from the same material?

Prozan, in *Feminist Psychoanalytic Psychotherapy*, answers this question for us. In her reanalysis of the case of F.T., she proposes that penis envy may have been an inappropriate diagnosis and that the patient had found the diagnosis meaningful only because she desired to please Langs. "Miss F.T.'s improvement in therapy is due to some very good work," writes Prozan, "but may also be because she has finally been able to please a parental figure by giving her analyst what he wants, a patient who conforms to his diagnosis of penis envy. . . . What better way to please her Freudian analyst than to comply with his wish that she confirm his ideas about her problems?"[28]

Guided by her feminist perspective, Prozan offers several other interpretations that she feels might have better suited the case. The fact that her mother worked while F.T. was growing up and that she wanted to own toy guns could signal, according to Prozan, that she did not feel close to her mother, and desired a special closeness to her father. The

fantasy of being a boy, therefore, would not be literal but symbolic of
F.T.'s longing for recognition from her family. Prozan suggests that such
an interpretation would "encourage memories of loneliness and sadness
that could be therapeutic."[29]

Taking clues from other bits of information relayed by Langs, Prozan
offers still other possible theories. From the memories of sharing hotel
rooms with her parents, Prozan suggests that F.T.'s father may have been
enjoying a harem fantasy and her mother may have unconsciously been
"triumphing over the daughters, acting out her own old oedipal rivalries."
From the anxiety of witnessing these scenes, Prozan believes, the patient
may "create distance through anger-provoking behavior."[30] As for the
alligator under the bed, Prozan suggests it might be symbolic of F.T.'s
angry feelings toward her mother or that it could have been a fantasy
manifestation of the verbal fights she witnessed between her mother and
father.

At the end of her multiple-choice reanalysis of F.T.'s life, she offers
another, more comprehensive, theory:

> I propose the possibility that Miss F.T. was sexually molested as a child,
> possibly by her father, and that this is repressed and has not come up in
> treatment because her analyst never thought of it and never asked the
> proper questions. The clues are all in the material.
>
> 1. A childhood vaginal infection. This is not normally caused by mas-
> turbation, Langs's explanation for it.
>
> 2. The abundance of dreams and fantasies repeating the theme of sex
> being a dangerous attack on a woman and damaging her.
>
> 3. The visual image at age six of something small getting larger. There
> is no way a girl of six would know of penile engorgement by hearing or
> even seeing her parents having intercourse (likely under covers) in a dark
> motel room.
>
> 4. The crocodile terror, combined with the fantasy of the father biting
> off her penis. This could be the result of forced oral copulation in a sexual
> assault on her.
>
> 5. The clawing monkey causing bleeding on her head could represent
> displacement from the vagina and a concealment of the perpetrator, pos-
> sibly a hairy man. . . .
>
> 6. Promiscuity, also common in molested girls.
>
> 7. The occurrence of older men in her dreams and primal scene mem-
> ories and deviates might actually be screen memories of her own sexual
> assault.

8. The wish to own a toy gun. This could reflect anger at her molester, and an attempt at mastery of her fear and mistrust of men, as well as her fantasy of revenge.[31]

By offering several possible sources for F.T.'s problems—including a story of sexual abuse—Prozan perfectly illustrates Spence's and Viderman's contention that the narratives created in therapy are arbitrary by degrees. Unintentionally, Prozan exposes the fact that none of the fantasies, memories, or other details offered by F.T. in therapy, considered together or separately, have a single unshakable meaning. Because of this, there can be no empirical basis for choosing between Langs's construction or Prozan's. Both Langs and Prozan are forcing onto the patient their preconceived narratives, which have been formed by their different ideologies. By combining different details and viewing them from different perspectives (feminist vs. Freudian, for example), the therapist creates one of any number of interpretations, none of which necessarily has any true correspondence to the patient's past. Each narrative reflects the agreed-upon mythology of the therapists' respective camps.*

What decides which interpretation is offered? As Prozan herself admits, the choice of which path to take often comes not from what a patient tells the therapist, or even the ideas of the individual therapist, but from larger forces. "In 1973 and before, analysts were looking for penis envy. In 1990, we are looking for sexual abuse. It is true, now as then, we are more likely to find what we are looking for—the subjective component of our scientific investigation. It is common for therapists today to see a great number of women patients reporting sexual abuse because that is what they are reading about and hearing about on radio and television. . . . Patient and analyst are living in the same culture, and are being formed by similar trends. They may collude in what they believe is an accurate diagnosis of the patient's problems. But because they are both culture-bound, the truth may elude them both."[32]

This statement seems a rather devastating admission. Psychotherapeu-

---

*The assumptions that any of the details offered by F.T. necessarily have deep meaning at all, or that they can be added up to expose a hidden force that has shaped her life, are concepts peculiar to psychotherapy. Could the memory of being afraid of the alligator under the bed have come from having watched a nature film or from a storybook? Could the desire to own a toy gun have come from envying the next-door neighbor's toy collection? Could the dreams recounted be a result of the brain's randomly firing synapses during sleep? It seems that while therapists diverge radically about the meaning of these sorts of details, the only thing they agree on is that they are meaningful.

tic fashions, not being based on science, are formed by the culture and
what groups of therapists decide among themselves. Because directions
are determined by loose consensus, psychotherapy is extremely susceptible
to the winds of the current zeitgeist. To Prozan's credit, analysts rarely
willingly admit that they are often simply "finding" what they expect.
Unfortunately, Prozan does not take her own reasoning to the next step.
If she is right that F.T. capitulated to Langs's analysis because of her
desire to please him, are we to assume that the same dynamic would not
be present if another therapist had offered the theory of repressed abuse?
If social forces supposedly pushed Langs to an incorrect diagnosis, what
evidence is there that current social forces would not be just as misleading
for Prozan's interpretation?

In all likelihood F.T. would have come to accept any one of the
narratives offered by Prozan as true if it was presented convincingly. Just
as she conceded to the diagnosis of penis envy and the suggestion that
she witnessed a primal scene involving her parents (later in therapy offering dreams and newly discovered memories to confirm both suggestions), it's quite possible that had she been treated by Prozan, she would
have found equal meaning in any one of her interpretations, including
the suggestion that she had been molested by her father. To paraphrase
Prozan's own assertions: *What better way to please a recovered memory
therapist than to comply with her wish that she confirm her ideas about
her problems?*

What is missing in Prozan's text is not only an admission of how social
forces and therapeutic fashion could engender the creation of a false
abuse narrative but also an understanding of the pressure within therapy
circles to *never* question the reality of such a narrative. While Prozan
admits that social forces often determine the substance of the therapist's
interpretation, she does not offer the obvious corollary that those same
forces can influence how the therapist and client *react* to that conclusion.
Considering the current beliefs surrounding memories of abuse, the interpretation is more than just one possible path, it is a one-way highway.
If patients come to believe that they might have been abused, the same
social pressures that determined that diagnosis will press for beliefs to be
treated as true and accurate memories. As we will show, questioning the
validity of abuse narratives created in therapy is not tolerated within the
recovered memory movement.

Prozan gives no consideration to the obvious differences between
her interpretations *in the consequences of being wrong*. If a therapist is
mistaken about the diagnosis of penis envy, or about the patient having

witnessed a sexual scene between her parents, the potential damage to the client who believes these false narratives is inconsequential compared to the damage done to a client coming to the false realization that she was sexually molested by her father. Believing that you wanted to be a boy as a child or that you witnessed a "primal scene" would most likely have the effect of coloring your perceptions about your past. Suddenly believing for the first time that your father raped you, however, would force you to entirely rewrite your childhood and in all likelihood destroy your relationship with your parents. Those who have had their lives damaged by recovered memory therapy will surely be stunned by Prozan's offering up of an abuse narrative as simply one in a series of plausible diagnoses for a patient like F.T. By offering a history of abuse along with several other imaginative interpretations, Prozan seems to suggest that any of a number of narratives might have engendered confirming memories and proved equally effective in F.T.'s treatment. That she would offer this insight for a patient she never met shows the confidence certain therapists have in their insightfulness.

*   *   *

Spence's book, which was published in 1982, does not directly address recovered memory therapy, but his criticism seems remarkably prescient. It is hard to imagine a therapy that could more effectively illustrate the pitfalls inherent in the creation of narrative truths. In recovered memory therapy there is often not even the *assumption* that a patient is free-associating or that the therapist is attempting to listen with "evenly hovering attention." Because in many cases the patient and therapist have agreed that the patient's initial symptoms indicate abuse, they have also agreed that the purpose of the therapy is to uncover the memories hidden in the subconscious. Talk-therapy techniques, which can give clients a broader understanding of what makes them who they are, are used in the case of recovered memory therapy to simply remove what are believed to be "extraneous" factors and to focus only on the suspected hidden abuse. There is only one story created in recovered memory therapy—that of a patient as abuse victim—and it is forbidden to suggest that this narrative is anything less than identical to historical truth.

If, as Spence suggests, thoughtful psychoanalysts are akin to artists who create for the patient an "aesthetic experience," what can we compare recovered memory therapists to? To extend the metaphor, therapists who narrow their clients' lives into narratives of abuse are like propagandists.

Instead of creating a narrative that speaks to the deep truths of a patient's life, they funnel all information to one inevitable story: a history of being sexually abused as a child. Like propaganda, it is a narrative that has no depth or complexity. Remarkably, even the flat abuse narrative created in recovered memory therapy has explanatory powers. As with A. G. Britton, who came to believe that all her adult problems were caused by infantile sexual assault, believing all your problems are the result of events that were entirely out of your hands can bring a certain amount of relief and sense of understanding. To believe the reports of the therapists, clients often attest that the pain in their lives suddenly makes sense and that they are glad they faced the horrible truths hidden in their past. "Even though it was traumatic for me to realize that everyone in my family abused me, there was something reassuring about it," recalled one un-identified woman in *The Courage to Heal.* "My life suddenly made sense."[33] Therapists encourage clients to believe that their repressed mem-ories are at the root of every problem in their lives—all their pain, all their anxiety, every life tremor. Unfortunately, patients do not understand until it is too late the cost of coming to believe the repressed-abuse story.

While recovered memory therapists believe that the more hours they spend with a patient focusing on memories, the more truth about the client's past they will uncover, the exact opposite is often true. While during the initial therapy sessions patients may indeed think about mem-ories and experiences that they have not thought about in a good long while, the amount of real memory available is finite, and the amount of detail that can be confabulated or imagined or wished is open-ended. The longer the memory-retrieval process goes, therefore, the more of the latter elements will be incorporated into the memory belief. Considering the pressures and distortions inherent in the long-term-memory-retrieval process of recovered memory therapy, it seems likely that the patient's true recollection of the past will be better in the first set of sessions than at the end of treatment.

   While a therapist, conscious of the problems of memory retrieval, may be able to maintain the core veracity of a client's recall over the course of therapy, recovered memory therapy—by its very nature—does not concern itself with this problem. Some therapists ignore the influential factors surrounding the techniques they use, as they ignore the well-known tendency for subjects to confabulate and rewrite their memory to fit the perceived beliefs of the questioner. Within the recovered memory world, the longer and more intense the process is, the better. Recovered memory therapists pursue hidden memories for years like archeologists using dynamite. For months or years they blast away at what they believe are the barriers to memory, unaware that their process destroys the fragile treasure they claim to seek. While this mistake is not new to the field of psychotherapy, recovered memory therapists make it in the most egregious fashion.

CHAPTER THREE

Symptoms of Pseudoscience

If you think you were abused and your life shows the symptoms, then you were. If you don't remember your abuse, you're not alone.
—*The Courage to Heal*[1]

To entice patients and book buyers, the self-proclaimed experts of the recovered memory movement offer lists of "warning signs"—disorders and behaviors that are supposedly directly caused by having been abused. Mimicking the medical profession, the therapist labels the problems that the client presents as "symptoms" and tells the patient that there exists solid proof that the symptoms are the direct result of certain experiences. By authoritatively putting forward the idea that certain disorders are direct consequences of sexual abuse, therapists justify their predisposition to hunt for memories the client has no knowledge of and prime the patient with the expectation that they will be found. If the patient has symptoms that resulted from abuse, the logic goes, searching for them would be the only appropriate course for the therapy.

"Do you find many characteristics of yourself on this list?" reads the first sentence of E. Sue Blume's *Secret Survivors*. "If so, you could be a survivor of incest." In the left margin, in front of each "characteristic," there is a line drawn so that readers can check the items that apply to them. Here are some of the symptoms listed:

- Fear of being alone in the dark . . . nightmares, night terrors . . .
- Alienation from the body . . . poor body image
- Gastrointestinal problems: gynecological disorders . . . headaches; arthritis or joint pain.
- Wearing a lot of clothing, even in summer . . .
- Eating disorders, drug or alcohol abuse (or total abstinence) . . . compulsive behaviors
- Phobias

- Need to be invisible, perfect, or perfectly bad
- Suicidal thoughts, attempts, obsessions
- Depression (sometimes paralyzing); seemingly baseless crying
- Rigid control of one's thought process; humorlessness or extreme solemnity
- Adult nervousness over being watched or surprised
- High risk taking ("daring the fates"); inability to take risks
- Boundary issues; control, power, territoriality issues; fear of losing control; obsessive/compulsive behaviors (attempt to control things that don't matter, just to control something)
- Guilt, shame; low self-esteem, feeling worthless; high appreciation of small favors by others
- Pattern of being a victim . . .
- Abandonment issues
- Blocking out some period of early years (especially 1–12), or a specific person or place
- Feeling of carrying an awful secret; urge to tell, fear of its being revealed; certainty that no one will listen; being generally secretive . . .
- Feeling crazy; feeling different; feeling oneself to be unreal and everyone else to be real, or vice versa; creating fantasy worlds, relationships, or identities
- Denial: no awareness at all; repression of memories . . . strong, deep, "inappropriate" negative reactions to a person, place, or event; "sensory flashes" without a sense of their meaning; remembering the surroundings but not the event
- Sexual issues: sex feels "dirty"; aversion to being touched, especially in gynecological exam; strong aversion to (or need for) particular sex acts . . . compulsively seductive or compulsively asexual; must be sexual aggressor or cannot be . . . prostitute, stripper, "sex symbol," porn actress . . . crying after orgasm
- Pattern of ambivalent or intensely conflictive relationships
- Avoidance of mirrors . . .
- Desire to change one's name . . .
- Limited tolerance for happiness; active withdrawal from happiness, reluctance to trust happiness ("ice–thin")
- Aversion to making noise (including during sex, crying, laughing, or other body functions); verbal hypervigilance (careful monitoring of one's words). . . .[2]

This list, which is a compilation of unrelated, sometimes fleeting perceptions or emotions along with indicators of well-recognized emotional disorders, is common in the movement. As we will show in the following chapters, these lists are important not only because they lead patients onto a path to find repressed memories, but also because some of the symptoms are often said to be memories themselves. In addition, when survivors look for proof that the beliefs created in therapy are real memories, they are again directed toward the symptom list with the admonition that the memories must be real because they display the symptoms that indicate the presence of repressed memories.

These "warning signs" are sometimes presented in the form of vague questions such as these in *The Courage to Heal*: "Do you feel different from other people? Are you afraid to succeed? Do you find yourself clinging to people you care about? Do you feel alienated or lonely? Do you have trouble feeling motivated? Do you find that it is hard to trust your intuition?"[3] The authors give no hint how to analyze one's response to these questions. In several cases the questions are so broad that it is not clear whether the positive or the negative response would signal a history of abuse.

Other popular books on the subject include these symptoms: marrying too young, substance abuse, dropping out of school, lack of career success, general feelings of dissatisfaction and confusion, and physical symptoms such as headaches, asthma, heart palpitations, stomach pain, and dizziness. According to magazine advertisements for the therapy, the following symptoms can also indicate having repressed memories: "mood swings, rage, depression, hopelessness, anxiety, low self-esteem, relationship problems, irritable bowels, PMS, obesity, and parenting problems."

The "Symptom Checklist" in Renee Fredrickson's book *Repressed Memories* includes sixty-three statements, including: "I startle easily . . . I do some things to excess . . . I am preoccupied with thoughts about sex . . . I space out or daydream . . . I neglect my teeth . . . I often have nightmares . . . Certain foods or tastes frighten me or nauseate me . . . I feel a sense of doom, as though my life will end in tragedy or disaster."[4]

Not surprisingly, identifying with the often-quoted symptom lists is the reason patients first come to recovered memory therapy. In *Escaping the Shadows, Seeking the Light*, by Connie Brewer, "Fred" tells of his first clue to his hidden abuse while listening to a Christian radio talk-show program on the topic of repressed memories. "Strangely, I identified with many of the symptoms that she described. I too had few childhood memories, and had great difficulty forming and maintaining intimate relationships. Shame and low self-esteem dominated my life. I also learned that many victims don't even remember their abuse until they are well into their adult years. I wondered if this was true of me."⁵

Even considering the almost remarkable all-inclusiveness of these lists, some authors reassure readers that they are only partial. "It is not a complete list, by any means," Fredrickson writes. "It would be impossible to identify all of the things that can remind you of child abuse, so you need to think through any unusual reactions you have." Patients are encouraged, in this way, to view any troubles or abnormalities as signs of abuse.

Before cataloging a litany of symptoms, including apathy, lack of interest in sex, and headaches, John Bradshaw wrote in a magazine essay that "If you identify with five or more [symptoms], yet have no memory of incest, you might try an exercise. Accept the theory that you were sexually abused, live consciously with that idea for six months in context with an awareness of the traits you acknowledge, and see whether any memories come to you."⁶ Others are just as straightforward in encouraging patients to accept their connections between certain traits and abuse. In *Repressed Memories*, Fredrickson puts it simply: "If you have some of the warning signals, you probably do have repressed memories. You are unlikely to be the exception to the rule, no matter what your denial is telling you."⁷

Therapists often portray their ability to see abuse where the client knows of none as an example of brilliant intuition and diagnostic virtuosity of the highest order. Some therapists, for example, brag that they can tell at the very outset of treatment that the patient has a hidden history of trauma. "Within ten minutes, I can spot it as a person walks in the door, often before they even realize it," said family counselor Brenda Wade on CNBC's program "Real Personal" of her ability to identify victims of child abuse. "There's a lack of trust . . . there's a certain way that the person presents themselves [sic], there's a certain body language. . . ."

Therapists who take on the role of detective—keenly deducing a history of abuse from telltale clues—are glorified in the movement's writing. "Women usually do not make an immediate incest connection," write Carol Poston and Karen Lison in their popular book, *Reclaiming Our Lives*. "What she probably knows at the time is that she has migraines or that she feels out of control of her life. . . . The perceptive therapist sees incest as the central fact and the other issues as spin-offs."⁸ Therapist Douglas Sawin's ability to spot patients with hidden histories of abuse led him to tell Stephanie Salter of the *San Francisco Examiner* that he helped all of his fifty weekly clients to uncover repressed memories and that "not one walked in my office and said, 'I'm a survivor of incest.' "⁹

Professionals writing in clinical journals exude similar confidence in their ability to connect symptoms with a history of incest. Elaine Westerlund wrote in the journal *Women & Therapy* (Winter 1983) that therapists "may suspect an incest history before the client is able to confirm one." In the *American Journal of Clinical Hypnosis* Maggie Phillips, Ph.D., reviews the case history of Janet, a thirty-four-year-old woman, who came into therapy complaining of "a type of paralysis that seemed to occur when she reached a certain level of achievement in each of several different job positions." Further, she described difficulty with close relationships, little sexual satisfaction, and panic attacks. Based on these symptoms, "both Janet and her therapist believed that she had experienced some kind of early childhood abuse. . . ."[10]

Even psychiatric nurses have been encouraged to learn the signs indicating histories of incest so they can spot patients with repressed memories. Mark Greenfeld writes in the *Journal of Psychosocial Nursing*, "Nurses who could recognize symptoms indicating that incest had occurred and who could promote disclosure in a gentle, therapeutic manner would have a considerable positive impact on these clients."[11]

In analyzing the symptom lists, one is first struck by their all-inclusiveness. It is safe to say that any adult reading these lists could identify with a cluster of indicators. Who, after all, does not have headaches, nightmares, "relationship problems," or can't sometimes deeply identify with the feeling of being "different from other people"? We all, once we have reached the age of those in recovered memory therapy, are sometimes filled with a sense of "doom," if only because of a growing understanding of our own mortality. Nor is it at all uncommon to feel "alienated" from a body that collects creaks and ailments, and ages all too quickly.

The case could be made that these authors, wanting to sell more books, and therapists, hoping to find more converts, have intentionally created symptoms that would spark some level of recognition in everyone but at the same time exclude no one. A cynic might accuse these authors of intentionally using what are sometimes called "Barnum" statements; that is, observations used by fortune-tellers and con men that sound specific to the individual hearing them but actually describe a large percentage of the population.

In identifying these lists as Barnum statements, however, one would have to assume that these writers and therapists are willfully trying to mislead people. While it is true that the lists exclude no one—and therefore have the potential for gathering many clients and book buyers— it is probably incorrect to say that this was their primary motivation. One could argue that the lists are so forthrightly nonspecific that they were clearly not created by con artists. Notice, for instance, how Blume continually points to both extremes of a certain behavior as symptomatic. "Must be the sexual aggressor *or cannot be*"; high risk taking . . . *inability to take risks.*" Or, "feeling oneself to be unreal and everyone else to be real, *or vice versa.*" These statements are so transparently general, they fail as good Barnum statements. Fredrickson's assertion that *anything* can be an indicator of sexual abuse would be the equivalent of a Tarot reader informing the client, after carefully examining his cards, that he has led a life during which events have taken place.

A more likely—and more disturbing—possibility is that these authors and therapists believe these lists to be legitimate diagnostic indicators of past abuse. This possibility is more troubling because, if true, it shows how vulnerable the recovered memory field is to pseudoscientific reasoning.

To understand the seriousness of the mistake these therapists have made, one must first understand the two assumptions that underlie their lists. The first, and most obvious, assumption is that the disorders listed have shown a causal relationship with childhood sexual abuse. As we will show, creating this sort of cause and effect connection between child abuse and adult disorder is methodologically extremely difficult in patients who have always known that they were abused as children. The second assumption these therapists make is that they can safely work backward from one symptom, or a constellation of symptoms, to the inference that a patient has experienced a particular type of trauma where the patient has no knowledge of having been abused. While these two propositions seem similar, determining a hidden cause from the presence of a given symptom is an order of magnitude more difficult to accomplish in a methodologically sound manner than identifying which symptoms might be the result of a known event.

To show how difficult it is to work backward from symptom to a specific type of trauma, it is important first to understand the difficulty of making a much simpler connection between trauma to known-symptom. By examining the decade-long debate over the question of whether eating disorders—in particular bulimia—result from sexual abuse we can illustrate the difficulty of connecting a history of abuse with a specific disorder.

Ever since bulimia was accepted as a specific disorder by the American Psychiatric Association in 1980, researchers have looked for its cause in societal pressures, stress, chemical imbalances, and patients' personal

histories. Some have suggested that bulimia, which primarily affects adolescent women, is linked to biological factors related to depression.[12]
Others offered the idea that women with the disorder have a biochemical
malfunction, by which their bodies fail to release the hormone that brings
on the feeling of satisfaction and fullness after eating.[13] Still other researchers suggested that our culture's message that thinness is synonymous
with strength and beauty was the root of the problem.

Many theories surrounding patients' personal histories have also been
offered, including growing up in families with dominant mothers and
distant fathers.[14] Overly protective or rigid families have been seen as a
possible cause of eating disorders as were families that used the child to
defuse arguments between the parents.[15] Other researchers noted that
adolescent girls who showed a pattern of perfectionism and an abnormal
desire to please seemed to manifest the disorder more often.[16]

In the late eighties, at the same time that the ideas surrounding recovered memory therapy began to surface widely, therapists and researchers began to offer the theory that eating disorders were a result of the
patient's having been sexually abused. A number of studies were published
purporting to show that patients with bulimia reported high rates of sexual
abuse. This work was sufficiently convincing for many recovered memory
therapists to accept as fact the idea that sexual abuse sometimes causes
the victim to manifest eating disorders. From this proposed correlation,
many therapists also thought they could work backward from the disorder—assuming a history of abuse in those clients with bulimia. Often
found in the literature of the recovered memory movement are confident
statements such as this from a psychiatric social worker: "I would automatically suspect sexual abuse in someone with an eating disorder."[17]

"The relatively new programs designed to treat anorexia and bulimia
are filled with incest survivors," write the authors of *Reclaiming Our
Lives*. They note that along with obesity, eating disorders are "endemic
among survivors."[18] With similar assurance, Harvey Schwartz wrote in
the *American Journal of Psychiatry* that awareness of the high incidence
of sexual abuse among patients with bulimia can "alert clinicians to the
origin of patients' self-destructiveness and orient treatment toward the
necessary remembering and working through."[19] Testifying before a New
York legislative committee, psychologist Patricia Singleton stated confidently that it was "increasingly being recognized" that 90 percent of
patients hospitalized for eating disorders had been abused as children.[20]

However, examining the studies on which these statements are based,
the connection between bulimia and a known history of sexual abuse
proves to be far from an established fact. Drs. Harrison G. Pope, Jr., and

James Hudson of Harvard Medical School reviewed the major empirical studies that purported to link child abuse with the manifestation of eating disorders.[21] All were retrospective studies, with six basing their comparisons on control groups of either nonbulimic psychiatric patients or women in the general population. In analyzing these studies they discovered a number of errors and methodological problems that made the connection, at best, ambiguous.

One of the studies, for instance, purported to find a significant difference in the reports of sexual abuse in the histories of bulimic and nonbulimic patients admitted to an adolescent treatment unit.[22] Bulimic patients and anorexic patients were compared with adolescent patients with non-eating-disorder problems. Hall and partners reported that 50 percent of the bulimic patients and 50 percent of the anorexic patients told of being sexually abused while 28 percent of the other patients gave such histories. This difference would indeed have been significant had it not been for one methodological misstep. They did not match the control group with the eating disorder group for gender—a mistake of particular importance because it is generally accepted that women are more often sexually abused as children than men. Once adjusted for this error, Pope and Hudson found the significantly different rate of abuse in the eating disorder group disappeared. In other words, sexual abuse was no more likely in the life histories of eating disorder patients than it was in the histories of other patients.

Remarkably, a second study that compared patients diagnosed with eating disorders to three groups of patients with panic disorders, schizophrenia, and multiple-personality disorder, respectively, made the same mistake. By not insuring that the control groups were matched for gender, the slight increased rate of sexual-abuse histories among the bulimic and anorexic subjects became meaningless.

Hudson and Pope also reviewed two other important studies that used as control groups not other psychiatric patients but women from the general population. The first study, by G. W. Stuart and partners, compared bulimic patients to "supernormal" women. These supernormal subjects were required to have never sought psychiatric treatments and even to have no first-degree relatives with psychiatric diagnoses. The results showed that 50 percent of the bulimic patients reported sexual molestation as opposed to 28 percent of the supernormal control subjects.[23] Pope and Hudson point out that the flaw in this study is the use of supernormal women as the comparison. They illustrate this point by asking the reader to imagine a medical study that compared the prevalence of smoking by patients with rheumatoid arthritis and a control group of age-matched patients screened to show no medical illness of any type. Because, as the surgeon general reminds us, cigarette smoking can be hazardous to one's health in many different ways, the medically super-normal group would most likely have a lower number of smokers than normal (compared to the population at large) and therefore a lower num-ber of smokers than the group of arthritis patients, leading to an untenable connection between smoking and arthritis. To say that the Stuart study offered a meaningful comparison, one would have to make the case that those with histories of child abuse were not more likely than the "su-pernormal" women to seek therapy. Considering that the supernormal women were required to have no history of mental-health treatment, Pope and Hudson concluded that the researchers may have excluded some nonbulimic women with histories of child abuse.

The last controlled study they reviewed proved methodologically sound. In this study, by S. E. Finn et al. and published in *International Journal of Eating Disorders*, the researchers took a different tack from the other studies. Instead of beginning with a group of bulimic women, they began by selecting two groups, one of sexually abused women and one of nonabused women.[24] They then compared the two groups for histories of eating disorders. They found no significant difference, or even a trend toward a significant difference, between the abused and nonabused women as far as their reported histories of bulimia or bulimic behavior. Finn and researchers suggested that the perceived connection between sexual abuse and bulimia may be an "illusory correlation." Considering that eating disorders and histories of abuse are common complaints (par-ticularly among women seeking psychiatric treatment), a high rate of co-occurrence would be expected by chance alone. From their view of these and other studies, Pope and Hudson concluded: "Current evidence does not support the hypothesis that childhood sexual abuse is a risk factor for bulimia nervosa."

The researchers took their review of the literature a step further by reviewing several anecdotal and uncontrolled studies as well as some large studies that focused solely on the prevalence of child abuse in the pop-ulation at large. Comparing the rates of childhood sexual abuse in the general population to the rates of abuse among bulimics interviewed, Pope and Hudson found that the percentages of bulimics reporting abuse fell within the range of the general population.

This was surprising, considering that Pope and Hudson identified sev-eral possible ways the study of bulimics might have been skewed to find higher rates of abuse. One such factor was that many of the sample populations of bulimic women were interviewed on multiple occasions, while most of the control groups (and all of the samples from the large surveys focusing solely on sexual abuse) were interviewed only once. "Given that a patient may not reveal a history of sexual abuse until she or he has formed a trusting relationship with a therapist . . . it seems that the single-interview populations might find lower rates of abuse than studies of bulimic patients in treatment, even if the two rates were actually the same."

Pope and Hudson also noted that it is common for psychiatric patients to search their lives for explanations for their current behavior. Therefore, "bulimic patients, particularly those who become aware of the sexual abuse hypothesis, may be more likely to remember and/or report child-hood sexual abuse than control individuals who have less impetus for effort after meaning."

The idea of effort after meaning becomes more problematic if it can be assumed that some percentage of a given bulimic population in therapy has come to believe they were abused when they were not. Considering that people with eating disorders are often put on a search for their hidden memories,[25] there exists the distinct possibility that the correlation be-tween eating disorders and abuse might become a self-fulfilling prophecy.

What is important to remember is that even if researchers proved that those who were abused as children stood a slightly higher than normal chance of developing a eating disorder—which has yet to be done con-clusively—it still could not be assumed that someone with an eating disorder suffered from abuse.

In their review of empirical studies conducted on the long-term effects of childhood sexual abuse, researchers Angela Browne and David Fin-kelhor attempted to summarize the studies that tried to identify the af-tereffects of abuse. "Adult women victimized as children," they write, "are more likely to manifest depression, self-destructive behavior, anxiety, feelings of isolation and stigma, poor self-esteem, a tendency toward revictimization, and substance abuse." In addition they note that difficulty trusting others, sexual maladjustment, and avoidance of sexual activity have also been reported.[26]

Browne and Finkelhor note that all the studies share one common problem: the difficulty of effectively disentangling the effects of the abuse from other factors. "One of the most imposing challenges for researchers is to explore the sources of trauma in sexual abuse. Some of the apparent effects of sexual abuse may be due to premorbid conditions, such as family conflict or emotional neglect," they write. "Unfortunately, these questions are difficult to address in retrospective long-term impact studies, because it may be difficult or impossible to get accurate information about some of the key variables (for example, how much family pathology predated the abuse)."

The correlation between abuse and specific problems, as Browne and Finkelhor note, is not strong enough to be predictive. That is, from the information in these studies, one cannot predict with any certainty that a person who has been abused will likely manifest any given symptoms, or any symptoms at all. Despite this, some therapists continue to market the idea that sexual abuse—seen or unseen—can be identified as the primary cause for their patients' problems.

Let's assume that Browne and Finkelhor's summary of the available research—that abuse has shown a correlation with serious, albeit general, mental disorders and distress later in life—is correct. How can this conclusion be applied to the treatment of patients? First of all one must consider that while "disorders" such as depression, poor self-esteem, feelings of isolation, and self-destructive behavior seem specific, they are no doubt among the most common types of mental-health problems. They are the equivalents of a medical patient complaining of a headache, lacking energy, running a fever, or feeling generally sick. Unfortunately, Browne and Finkelhor's conclusion tells us little more than that sexual abuse may be damaging to the victim's mental health. Making specific predictions about what those problems will be, if such problems are caused specifically by the abuse act, has so far eluded science.

It is also possible that biological predispositions are the true root cause of the problem and that the social disruptions and stresses of incest, dysfunctional family life, or trauma may only precipitate a biologically given potential. This bio/social model has by no means been eliminated. Its implications are that the biological vulnerability needs to be treated in its own right and that additional attention needs to be directed at disentangling the developmental and behavioral consequences of the unfortunate event. Treating only half the problem would guarantee failure.

So, even if we were to pretend for the moment that the lists provided in the popular books on repressed memory therapy were made up only of the disorders that loosely corresponded with ones identified in empirical studies (such as depression and sexual dysfunction), it would still be a gross mistake to assume that one could work backward from these symptoms to a specific experience. If one cannot make a strong correlation from cause to known symptom, one certainly cannot work the other way. That is, even though some of the disorders listed can result from abuse, it does not mean that someone with these symptoms can be expected to have experienced abuse. Depression, self-destructive behavior, anxiety, feelings of isolation and stigma, poor self-esteem do not result only from child abuse but from a large number of experiences, chemical imbalances, genetic factors, behaviors, or combinations of these factors. That is, you can say that all people who have bullet wounds have been shot, for the reason that bullet wounds result from only one possible event. You cannot say that because many people with brain tumors have headaches, most, or even many, people with headaches have brain tumors, for the equally obvious reason that headaches are a result of any number of different causes.

Unfortunately, it is precisely these elementary methodological and logical mistakes that the repressed memory experts are making. Remember Blume's question at the beginning of her book: "Do you find many characteristics of yourself on this list? If so, you could be a survivor of incest."

This mistake can be seen throughout the recovered memory movement both in the popular-psychology books it has produced as well as in its most respected journal articles. After surveying sixty-eight women admitted to a private psychiatric hospital, Jeffrey Bryer et al. concluded in an article in *The American Journal of Psychiatry* that "victims of childhood abuse continue to experience long-standing negative consequences of abuse." The women who identified themselves as survivors of sexual abuse reported, among other disorders, behavior that included depression, psychotic thinking, anxiety, and compulsive behavior. While this finding seems reasonable, the authors went a step further in their conclusion. Noting their belief that patients often repress or suppress memories of abuse, their article suggests that "these long-standing negative consequences could be used to aid in the identification of patients with a history of abuse."[27]

Geraldine Faria and Nancy Belohlavek came to a similar conclusion in their article in *Social Casework*. "Because of [patients'] conscious or unconscious resistance to disclosing the incest, these victims are difficult to identify. The problem may be completely overlooked unless the therapist is alert to signs which suggest a previous incest experience and is willing to raise the issue with the client." These signs included "guilt, negative self-image, depression, and difficulties in interpersonal relationships."[28]

In *Social Casework*, Jill Blake-White and Christine Madeline Kline state in the first line of their article on treating adult victims of incest that "Clinicians are becoming increasingly aware that female clients who exhibit anxiety, depression, and sexual dysfunction may have been victims of incest as children." The writers then offer therapists a number of techniques designed to "elicit a response that confirms the clinician's suspicion that the woman had an incestuous relationship as a child."[29]

The questionable reasoning of "seeing through" the presenting symptoms to the hidden history of abuse carries another danger. If the client's complaints (whether they be sexual dysfunction, depression, or anxiety about work or personal life) are seen only as symptoms of another hidden problem, they are likely to be ignored in favor of giving attention to the pursuit of abuse memories. As Carol Poston and Karen Lison write in *Reclaiming Our Lives*, "not many women bring up incest immediately as the 'presenting problem,' . . . she usually feels there are too many other pressing issues she must deal with first." A committed recovered memory therapist will focus on memories of abuse and not allow the patient's focus on her current problems to derail the course of therapy. They warn that "a woman and her therapist may see the same body of facts from totally different perspectives."[30]

The logic of working backward from these commonplace symptoms to the hidden histories of abuse further breaks down when one considers the influence of the therapist in defining and labeling the patient's behavior and the distortion of the patient's self-reported history. Research in the medical field has long shown a tendency on the part of the patient to distort his or her true symptom history to fit the perceived expectation of the physician. In their criticism of reliance on patient reports, Lloyd Rogler and colleagues, in the *Journal of Nervous and Mental Disease*, noted that over a century of studies have shown the fallibility of human memory in this respect. They concluded that "the continuing use of retrospective lifetime symptom reports suggests that this literature has been largely ignored."[31]

It appears highly questionable that patients can accurately respond to a question such as, "Have you ever experienced two weeks or more during which you felt sad, blue, depressed, or when you lost all interest and pleasure in things that you usually cared about or enjoyed?" According to Rogler et al., this is due not only to unintentional fabrications and forgetting but to "myriad" factors "not the least being the type of symptom episode being recalled and the current mood of the respondent at the time of recall." They warn that "Questions prefaced by the phrase, 'Have you ever . . .' are assuredly not likely to produce what the retrospective requirement intended."[32]

In addition, as much as the mental-health profession has attempted to mimic medical doctors in attributing precise meaning to symptoms such as depression, anxiety, and sexual dysfunction, they remain nothing more than general categories and ones that everyone can attest to having experienced to some degree. No one, it is safe to say, has a trouble-free sex life or a life absent of troubling fears or sadness—no doubt this would be particularly true of those who seek therapy. What turns sadness into depression or garden-variety fears into "anxieties" is the joint judgment of the therapist and the patient. While a medical doctor may make a small interpretive leap in diagnosing a patient with gout after examining the foot, hearing the patient describe sensation, and finding uric acid crystals in the joint fluid, the symptoms that lead to the leap—the swelling, pain and tenderness, and lab results—are not a matter of unlimited interpretation. Considering the added interpretive step in therapy—that is, of the therapist helping the patient define the symptom—the logic of using these symptoms as indicators of any specific experience becomes highly speculative and unreliable.

The relevance and use of the symptoms becomes most suspect after both the therapist and the patient agree that the patient manifests one, two, or several symptoms from a recovered memory symptom list. Once the therapist and patient begin to scour the patient's history, looking for other behaviors on the list, it's likely that they will be able to construct a history that includes many of the items. Studies have shown that therapists tend to remember and report the symptoms and facts supportive of the hypothesis and to forget the facts that point to other possibilities,[33] and there is nothing to indicate that the client is not similarly influenced by the "knew-it-all-along" effect of looking back over one's life for clues after a conclusion has been reached.

There is not even the appearance of controlled studies to back up most of the dysfunction touted by recovered memory therapists as indicators of abuse. We have found no satisfactory explanation why, for example, neglected teeth, arthritis, feelings of ambivalence, headaches, heart palpitations, avoidance of mirrors, desire to change one's name, or humorlessness are believed to be signs of having been sexually assaulted as a child. We can only assume that evidence for these connections came from either the author's intuition or an accumulation of therapists' anecdotes. These symptoms appear not to be based on findings of empirical research published in any reputable journal. Rather they seem to exist only because of a word-of-mouth agreement among recovered memory clinicians.

The overall tone of these lists suggests that they were compiled with Ellen Bass's admonition in mind: "If we waited for science, we can forget the whole thing."[34] As far as the anecdotal collection of symptoms, what the list makers have apparently done is to interview women with either memories of sexual abuse or claims of repressed memories, and listed the problems they were struggling with in their lives. The problems that repeatedly came up in the interviews were assumed to be indicators of sexual-abuse histories. There is no indication that control groups were surveyed to see if some of these same symptoms would be found in similar percentages in the general population. Do women with histories of abuse neglect their teeth to a greater extent than other women? Do they avoid mirrors more often? Without knowing the prevalence of these disorders in a population compared with the women with histories of abuse there is no way to correlate the symptoms to the abuse. Assuming that one could work backward from these "symptoms" to hidden memories is absurd.

The all-inclusive nature of these lists of symptoms gives us some insight into the world of recovered memory therapy. There is the assumption within these circles that childhood sexual abuse, particularly incest, is omnipresent; it is assumed to be the cause of nearly any disorder. Only information affirming that abuse is the root of psychological or physical disorders is allowed within the echo chamber that passes for professional discourse. Other information, including all challenges to these assumptions, appears effectively filtered out.

Within the recovered memory community, abuse is assumed to be the defining experience in a person's life. Patients are encouraged to view themselves not as complex individuals with free will and the strength to shape their lives, but as one-dimensional creatures who share a single defining experience—sexual abuse. "The long-term effects of child sexual abuse can be so pervasive that it's sometimes hard to pinpoint exactly how the abuse affected you," reads the opening of *The Courage to Heal*. A page later, Bass and Davis quote one woman as saying: "As far as I'm concerned, my whole life has been stolen from me. I didn't get to be who I could have been. I didn't get the education I should have gotten when I was young. I married too early. I hid behind my husband. I didn't make contact with other people. I haven't had a rich life."[35] The lives of these patients are in essence reduced to the sum of their abuse— imagined or otherwise.

Believing that a strong correlation exists between sets of symptoms and a history of abuse is the first mistake of recovered memory therapy. It builds the therapist's confidence that his or her subsequent search for hidden memories—a search that often takes years—is valid and justified. Believing that the therapist can connect certain behaviors and disorders with specific types of events, the way a doctor connects symptoms with the disease, is the critical first step for the patient as well. "I must have been abused, for I show the symptoms," the patient comes to believe. Unfortunately, the patient, who has come to the therapist for help, is not likely to contradict the therapist if she is convinced that the therapist has superior knowledge of the cause of her problem.

The almost cavalier way some therapists diagnose patients as having been victims of abuse shows an arrogant disregard for the complex nature of behavior and the current limited ability of science to understand the complex motivations for behavior. Stunningly confident statements such as "if you think you were abused and your life shows the symptoms, then you were," from Bass and Davis, are the norm within the movement.

The problems and disorders on the lists often become clues that provide a starting point for the memory search. Karen Claridge of Texas A&M University, in the journal *Psychotherapy*, recommended that "When the client's symptoms suggest a history of trauma, but there is no memory of it, useful information should be available by questioning the client about past intrusive experiences. . . . These 'reminders' provide a way to start the memory process, by suggesting where it is headed. . . . [The clients are told] 'If we could talk about what has set off strong feelings for you in the past, we might be able to get some idea of what your memories are all about.' "[36]

Faced with a tidal wave of evidence, even the recovered memory movement's experts have begun to grudgingly admit that some therapists show an unseemly predisposition to find abuse no matter what disorders their clients present. "Therapists . . . sometimes fall prey to the desire for certainty," writes Herman in *Trauma and Recovery*. "Zealous conviction can all too easily replace an open, inquiring attitude. . . . Therapists have been known to tell patients on the basis of a suggestive history or 'symptom profile' that they definitely have had a traumatic experience. . . . Any expression of doubt can be dismissed as 'denial.' In some cases patients with only vague, non-specific symptoms have been informed after a single consultation that they have undoubtedly been the victims of a satanic cult."[37]

By taking no time to analyze or discuss how this sort of "zealous conviction" could affect the patient or, for that matter, how the profession should deal with this problem, Herman leaves the reader with the impression that it is a problem of little importance. The space this issue is given in her book is little more than what is quoted here. Ellen Bass, coauthor of *The Courage to Heal*, has given similar passing acknowledgment to the problem. Asked on a national CNN talk show last year if there were therapists who were suggesting to vulnerable people that they had hidden memories of abuse without any evidence of it, Bass responded, "Absolutely true, but the number is very minuscule. . . . Certainly I wouldn't want to defend the entire therapist population, because there are therapists who are not competent and who make a great many mistakes. But there are so many more perpetrators than [there are] therapists who implant memories."

The movement's own literature contradicts Bass's assurance (and Herman's implication) that the problem of therapists who are predisposed to find abuse is minimal. The message that there are only a very few "bad" therapists out there who are determined to search for hidden histories of sexual abuse, is demonstrably wrong. As evidence grows of therapeutic abuses, this concession (that a few "bad" therapists are making horrible mistakes) will undoubtedly become more commonly voiced. The casual nature of these types of statements by those who have created the movement is troubling. Bass and Herman appear less concerned with exposing or rooting out these bad therapists than with distancing themselves from responsibility for errors made by these unnamed practitioners.

Unfortunately, for those promoting recovered memory therapy, the trail of evidence is now too long and detailed. For Herman, Bass, and the other leaders of the movement, laying off responsibility on a few bad apples for the increasingly obvious mistakes made in therapy is no longer possible. As we will show, when they indict those few bad therapists—those who have made a "great many mistakes," and have fallen prey to "zealous convictions"—they indict the entire field of recovered memory, including themselves. They have unwittingly participated in the creation of a mad-hatter universe in which the therapist can discern events in the client's past that the client has no knowledge of herself. In some instances, logic seems to take wing and flutter away. In his article for *Lear's* magazine on how to tell if you have hidden memories, John Bradshaw noted one *symptom* of having repressed memories of abuse was not having memories of being abused. Bradshaw found it necessary to reassure readers with this chilling statement: "If you don't remember being abused it doesn't *necessarily mean that you were.*"[38]

CHAPTER FOUR

Creation of the Abuse Narrative

Finally, I realized the size of the problem. Millions of people have blocked out frightening episodes of abuse, years of their life, or their entire childhood. They want desperately to find out what happened to them, and they need the tools to do so.

—Renee Fredrickson, in *Repressed Memories*[1]

Depending on the technique, the time devoted, and the inclination of the therapist, recovered memory therapy can result either in the creation of a single scene of abuse or an enormously complex series of events that are believed to cover years of a client's life. Perhaps the simplest way therapists create a "memory" is by *declaration*. As the symptom lists have expanded to include nearly any disorder or anomaly in the patient's life, the definition of what a memory is has similarly blurred. After undergoing six months of therapy with only a vague feeling that she had been abused, one woman discovered that she had "been remembering all along. Not in the way we do as adults—in a neat sequential, narrative package. My memories came to life in the way I had experienced the events as a child: in symbols, body problems, emotions that seemed to come from nowhere."[2]

Convincing a client that she has a memory of abuse can be a simple two-step process. First, the therapist assures her that a symptom is a reliable indicator of abuse. Then he or she proceeds to change the client's definition of memory so that the indicator can be defined as a memory. All this process requires to succeed is a modicum of faith in the therapist's greater knowledge of human behavior and the manifestations of memory. Confused or swayed by the therapist's jargon, the patient can be completely unaware that she has been put on a logical merry-go-round on which the speculative evidence for the diagnosis also functions as the disease itself.

In assuring survivors that they will be accepted into her survivor seminars even if they lack memories of abuse, Laura Davis attests that our cultural conception of memory is too limited. "You feel like a scared child. . . . You get violently nauseated whenever you smell bourbon on someone's breath. You have an anxiety attack whenever you go back to your hometown. You hate it when your father hugs you. You have nightmares and can't sleep without a light. . . . When you get a message, you start sobbing uncontrollably. These are all memories."[3]

Renee Fredrickson, in *Repressed Memories*, identifies several other types of memories besides what she calls normal "recall memory," including imagistic memory, body memory, acting-out memory, and what she labels "feeling memory." "Feeling memory," Fredrickson explains, "is the memory of an emotional response to a particular situation. . . . [It] is often experienced as a flood of inexplicable emotions, particularly around abuse issues. A sense that something abusive has happened is a common form of a feeling memory. Some survivors will say, 'Yes, I think I was sexually abused, but it's just a gut feeling.' These clients are experiencing a feeling memory about being abused, even though at the moment they can recall nothing about their abuse."[4] With the advent of the all-inclusive symptom list, and the predisposition of many therapists to look for repressed memories, such gut feelings or vague suspicions are not hard to come by. At this point, it is difficult to imagine that many adults in America who feel the need to consult a therapist have not been exposed to the theories of the recovered memory movement—ideas that might be sufficient to predispose them to the belief that sexual abuse is at the bottom of their problems. In addition, nowhere in the literature do recovered memory experts distinguish between gut feelings that preexist the patient's exposure to recovered memory therapy and the intuition that emerges after reading recovered memory texts or after learning of the therapist's suspicions.

With similar ease, the patient's artwork and nightmares can also be classified as "memories." According to Fredrickson, "Dreams containing an explicit act or theme of sexual abuse need to be carefully scrutinized. In my clinical experience, these are always repressed memory dreams."[5] Later she quotes a patient who had painted a picture of a group of robed figures surrounding a small child. "This is a memory," the patient declares. "I painted it months ago, and it never bothered me. Then last week I saw it again, and all of a sudden I was really scared of it. After I stared at it for a while, I realized that this scene really happened. I painted a memory even before I knew it was a memory!"[6]

Considering the powerful position of the therapist, particularly to define terms, symptoms, and behaviors, it is not at all surprising that a patient would probably believe declarations about the nature of memory as confident as those from Davis and Fredrickson. In the client's eyes the therapist often has authority similar to doctors. Those who have come to therapy because they believe therapy can help them are predisposed to believe that therapists can interpret and define problems and behaviors, just as a medical patient is inclined to believe that a doctor can interpret the shadows on X-ray negatives. When a therapist tells a patient that her artwork, emotions, or physical symptoms are actually a type of memory of abuse, the presumption is strongly in the therapist's favor. The creation of this sort of abuse belief requires no coercion, complex influence, or thought-reform procedure. All that is necessary is that the client believe and trust the therapist.

The relabeling of dreams, artwork, or feelings as memories is not simply a picky debate of semantics. As we have noted, anything declared a memory of abuse within the literature of the movement becomes sacrosanct and unquestionable. Memories of abuse are said to be something that cannot be created or fantasized. If a patient comes to label a feeling or dream as a memory of abuse, it is likely the therapist and patient will come to believe that this new "memory" constitutes solid proof of the patient's victimization.

This changing definition of memory is particularly troubling if one considers the likely expansion of such a theory. What if the client's gut feeling was not just that she was abused but that she was abused by her father? What if a dream not only contained images of abuse but scenes of murder and sacrifice? It seems clear that Fredrickson, Davis, and others are willing not only to allow dreams, feelings, and artwork to be labeled memories, but to allow the *content* of those dreams and feelings to be labeled as accurate memory as well. A dream, then, can not only tell you that you were abused, but who abused you.

Almost any problem or behavior can be seen as a symptom of abuse, just as most any problem, behavior, or perception can be said to be a memory of abuse. If the client accepts these two suppositions, the therapist has effectively created the abuse belief in the patient's mind by fiat. In Fredrickson's construction, it's hard to imagine what form of perception, thought, or emotion might *not* be labeled a memory. While the new definitions of memory seem a willful blurring of the distinction between recollection and imagination, one must again resist the impulse to accuse therapists like Fredrickson of intentionally attempting to convert the widest possible audience to the idea that they were victims of sexual abuse. The willingness to label anything a memory can, however, be viewed as another illustration of the single-mindedness of these therapists. The disheartening truth is that a significant portion of practitioners in the mental-health industry believe these new types of memory to be valid. Their willingness to confidently state their new beliefs about memories, without offering any scientific proof, is not surprising considering that for a hundred years many of the theories surrounding talk therapies have rested on similarly unsupported speculations. The fact that their patients eventually come to *believe* their definitions of memory is the only evidence clinicians possess for the validity of those definitions. Because the theories of psychotherapy often defy scientific confirmation, authors promoting recovered memory seem comfortable not offering any—even when the subject in question (like memory) might lend itself to such analysis.

The creation of what Fredrickson calls "imagistic" memory is more troubling and more difficult to explain than the simple redefining of memory. From the descriptions of recovered memory patients, these types of memory-beliefs clearly go beyond the simple relabeling of already existing behaviors, feelings, or perceptions. Often in recovered memory therapy patients report clear and detailed mental pictures of the abuse they believe they have suffered. In *Escaping the Shadows, Seeking the Light*, a woman identified as Dawn describes recovering a minutely detailed memory of being molested as a three-year-old. Working with a therapist, she learned to write herself questions with her right hand and then allowed "Dawnie," her "inner child," to answer in letters by writing with her nondominant hand. The appearance of her left-handed writing, a childlike scrawl, helped convince Dawn that she was truly in contact with a child personality which lived within her. She recounts that "In February of 1988, after three and a half years of therapy and support groups, Dawnie felt safe enough to reveal to me what had happened to me when I was three years old. It took me another year and a half of single flashbacks to put all the pieces together. In the arms of a close friend I told the story as if it were rolling on film before my eyes. It was late at night. I woke up and had to go to the bathroom. . . . Being only three, I couldn't reach the light switch so I started jumping, hoping I could somehow flick it on in the middle of one of my jumps. Suddenly I heard footsteps. They were loud, hard, and fast. I felt my chest tighten, and my heart started to pound faster. The footsteps stopped and the light went on. A tall man was standing before me with a yellow towel wrapped around his waist. . . . The smell of alcohol was heavy on his breath." She goes on to describe in detail how this man, who she believes was a boyfriend of her mother, orally raped her. Afterward she says, "I was too scared to cry. I was too scared to make a noise of any kind. All I could think of to do was ask the dark to be my friend. I went back into my room, crawled into my bed, and draped the sheet up over my nose, leaving just my eyes and forehead uncovered. I was in shock, I had no one to take care of me."[7]

This remarkable level of detail is common among recovered memory patients. Dawn's belief not only includes great visual precision, such as the color of the towel, but also other impressions such as smells, emotions, and an impression of how a three-year-old might perceive the scene. This detail is equally specific for the moments of molestation as well as the moments leading up to and away from the trauma. Other survivors have recounted dialogue heard when they were infants or the exact descriptions of the rooms where they believe the molestation took place. Often these detailed descriptions are not just for one event but for many. Sometimes they are events believed to span decades.

The experience of patients such as Dawn obviously cannot be explained as the relabeling of feelings, dreams, or artwork as memories. While a therapist can convince a client to relabel an existing feeling or symptom as a "memory" in only a few sessions, helping the client to create a detailed pseudomemory of abuse can take much longer. The literature of the movement mentions a dozen or so techniques to discover previously hidden memories of abuse. They include those mentioned above (dream interpretation, art therapy, and nondominant handwriting) as well as hypnosis, free association, Amytal, guided imagery, age regression, "group work," gestalt therapy, psychodrama, storytelling, and body massage. As diverse as they sound, these methods have more in common than it would at first seem. Critical to the effectiveness of all these methods is the power of the therapy setting to change, mold, and sometimes create beliefs.

For some therapists the process of building the abuse belief only begins with the client expressing a desire to find hidden traumatic memories. This of course requires that the patient acknowledge that she was abused before any memories appear. Carol Poston and Karen Lison in *Reclaiming Our Lives*, for example, advise clients after entering therapy that their next step is to "acknowledge that something terrible happened," and to accept that they were victims of childhood sexual assault.[8] Once the client is convinced that she shows the signs of abuse, the search for memories can take years. Laura Davis's workbook on the subject illustrates how belief in the abuse often comes long before the memory. Users of the workbook are first asked to write on topics that include "Assessing the Damage," "Picturing the Effects," and "Preparing for Change," all before they are given instruction on how to find their memories.[9]

If the client is unfamiliar with the possibility that she possesses hidden memories, the therapist will often suggest and explain the possibility quite early on in treatment. Prominent recovered memory theorist John Briere, in his book on child-abuse trauma, states confidently that "little can be hurt and, ultimately, much may be gained if the therapist shares with the client his or her suspicions regarding the client's childhood experience."[10] He goes on to provide a script for how this might be done, complete with a blank space left for the therapist to insert whatever symptom he or she believes to be the result of the abuse. Briere's script is a striking example of what therapists believe to be a nondirective introduction to the idea that patients were abused in their past.

"It sounds like some of the problems you describe have been around for a long time, maybe since you were a child. There are many ways that you could have ended up with these difficulties. I want to share with you one of my guesses about this. It seems to me that when you talk about————, one of the ways that people have that kind of problem is if they were hurt somehow when they were kids. I know you don't remember anything happening like that, and maybe nothing like that did happen. It is possible, though, that your childhood has something to do with this. That's why, if it's okay with you, I want us to explore your early memories and feelings now and then during therapy, so that we can see where————might have come from, and why it's still here now."[11]

In view of this advice, Briere's warning that "obviously, however, it is not appropriate for the clinician to inform a client authoritatively that he or she was abused as a child and is repressing it"[12] seems curious. Briere is apparently oblivious to the possibility that the procedure he recommends would be the most effective way to implant just such an idea. If a therapist were to insist that a patient was abused, before the client was indoctrinated with the theories surrounding the recovered memory therapy, the patient might recoil from such insistence. However, for a therapist to offer his or her suspicion, as Briere recommends, the client does not need to express immediate belief or disbelief. Briere's tactic of assuring the client that it is normal to begin therapy with no memories of abuse allows the therapist and patient any amount of time necessary to marshal evidence that might confirm the suspicion. As Briere himself writes, "Since the client by definition denies that any abuse transpired during childhood . . . the repressed survivor is liable to see therapy as a power struggle if, from her perspective, the therapist tries to convince her of something that she 'knows' is false. Because this fundamental disagreement between client and therapist is potentially disconfirming [of the client's] sense of reality, the therapist is advised to 'tread softly' with such individuals."[13]

If the client initially rejects the possibility that she holds repressed memories of abuse, this "denial" can be used as evidence confirming the therapist's suspicions. In a section entitled "Cracking the Denial" in *Beyond Survival*, author Maureen Brady quotes one survivor remembering the start of his treatment. "The first time my therapist suggested that I was a victim of sexual abuse, I grew rageful and told her she didn't know what she was talking about. I reminded her that I came from a good, loving family. . . . I was so angry and upset with the very idea that I could be a victim of incest that I even rearranged a book in her office to avoid having to see the word incest. . . . It was after rearranging the book and returning to my chair in her office that I found myself chuckling over what I had just said and done, begrudgingly conceding that an alcoholic in treatment behaving as I had would certainly be labeled as in denial. This painful concession was the first step I took toward acknowledging the possibility that my therapist perhaps was right."[14]

Once the therapist notifies the client of his or her suspicion, or the client expresses the desire to find her hidden memories, the process of helping the client imagine scenes of abuse can begin any number of ways. Commonly, according to the literature, the hunt for memories begins with the therapist and patient focusing attention on one of the physical or emotional symptoms the client has brought into therapy. "The patient's present, daily experience is usually rich in clues to dissociated past memories," writes Judith Herman in *Trauma and Recovery*. "In addition to following the ordinary clues of daily life, the patient may explore the past by viewing photographs, constructing a family tree, or visiting the site of childhood experiences."[15]

E. Sue Blume, in *Secret Survivor*, recommends patients begin with what she describes as unexplained emotional responses or "sensory flashes." "A number of my clients reported a similar, mysterious experience: when faced with a particular combination of environmental stimuli, they would get what they all called 'the feeling.' No amount of direct attention to the problem ever uncovered what was going on. It wasn't until we approached the experience indirectly, by working on the incest . . . that we uncovered the real meaning of these 'sensory flashes.' For Pattie, it was a picture frame; for Delores, the color yellow; for Laura, a toy rocking horse or Mickey Mouse cartoons. These images, which can be of smells, colors, textures, or specific visual images, fill up their senses, blocking their ability to see any other part of the picture."[16] According to Blume, these sensory flashes become the outer edge of a jigsaw puzzle that, once filled in, will reveal a picture of the incestuous experience.

Karen Claridge, in her paper on the subject in the journal *Psychotherapy*, advises that clients be encouraged to relate their current physical or emotional problems with possible scenes of abuse. "When asked, 'What do you notice most about your body right now?' the client might suddenly realize that she felt pain that she could associate with a place and an emotion from the past." Any emotional reactions past or present might also be a starting point. Claridge advises that the client be asked "specifically about experiences that triggered feelings of panic, terror, or rage, which seemed out of place; events that left them suddenly confused or disoriented; and any other experiences that met the operational definition for intrusive experiences. The question was [then] asked, 'If these experiences hold the pieces of your memories, what sort of memories do they suggest to you?' [The client's] suggested possibilities tended to be very similar to the memories that later began to emerge."[17] When asked to identify any intrusive emotional reactions, a client identified as "Sue" answered that she felt angry every time she heard an older man talking nicely to a little girl. Answering the question of what those memories might "suggest," Sue responded that she might have been sweet-talked into an isolated place with an older man, then forced to perform sexual favors for him.

Claridge's treatment method encourages the link of any current event to a scene that might have an element of abuse. It is unlikely that a patient involved in a lengthy, abuse-focused therapy would fail to recognize what type of memory these "experiences" were intended to "suggest." Claridge unself-consciously reports that the subsequent "memories" that develop in treatment often mirror the client's first guesses. That Claridge gives great weight to a client's momentary speculation about what type of abuse certain feelings might "suggest" is illustrative of the inevitable nature of the therapy. Within therapy, nothing is considered random or unimportant. Because Claridge has clearly invested in the recovered memory mythology which assumes that all actions and behaviors are shaped and caused by deep psychic forces, she does not stop to ponder the possibility that her patient's guess as to what certain feelings might suggest might be just that: a guess.

Other less obvious starting points are also suggested by Claridge. Asking the client what she was most aware of at any moment, she writes, might also lead to the beginning of a memory. "The prominent thing in the client's awareness was often something that seemed trivial." She illustrates this point by describing a moment in therapy in which Sue lost her train of thought.

> She apologized and asked the therapist what they had just been talking about. The therapist suggested they return to that later, and asked, "What are you most aware of right now?" Sue said, "Oh, it's nothing. You just moved your hands and the movement distracted me." The therapist persisted. "What do you notice most about my hands?" As Sue focused her attention on the therapist's hands, a faraway look came over her face, and she said very slowly, "It's the fingernails—the shape of your fingernails." When the therapist asked what about the shape of the fingernails was having an effect, Sue shuddered and said, "I was hoping you wouldn't ask that. My grandfather's fingernails look like that." As she recalled her grandfather's hand, she felt fear and revulsion. . . . The recovery of this fragmentary memory led Sue to suspect that her grandfather might have abused her.[18]

This is an excellent example of the memory-creation process in midcourse. While Claridge believes she has helped her client find deep meaning in her momentary loss of concentration, there is another more plausible explanation for the scene. This possibility is that Sue, caught briefly distracted, finds herself forced to offer a plausible explanation for why she was daydreaming. Although Sue first explains that she had simply been distracted, the therapist's second question, "What did you notice about my hands?" clearly communicates to Sue that the therapist believes she is on to something. While Sue could insist that she was just bored or daydreaming, by going along with the therapist's suspicion, she can both seek her therapist's approval by being awed by her insightfulness as well as avoid her therapist's annoyance that she let her thoughts drift. Sue's response to her therapist's demand for more information is particularly telling. "I was hoping you wouldn't ask that" implies both that Sue expected something more would be asked and that she had already thought of the only type of response that would prove appropriate to the therapy. The selection of the grandfather as a likely abuser in this exchange could be a matter of chance (his fingernails might indeed have looked like the therapist's) or it could have been the result of his having been singled out in earlier sessions. The direction of the narrative being created seems, however, inevitable.

The starting points for memories don't even have to come from inside the patient's mind. McClure, in *Reclaiming the Heart,* recommends that patients who have not yet uncovered their memories continually expose themselves to information about incest and seek out the company of other survivors. "Activities that may help are: Reading books (especially about other women's stories). . . . Attending lectures and groups. . . . Going to movies." Two movies suggested are *To a Safer Place: A Story of Healing of Incest* and *Breaking the Silence*. McClure cautions that the movie watching should be done with care because "visual stimulation is so powerful and able to cut through your mental defenses, watching movies sometimes propels you back in time. If, during or after the movie, you find yourself feeling like the little child who was being hurt, use it as an opportunity to get in touch with those feelings."[19]

Bass and Davis, in *The Courage to Heal*, concur that memories often start by hearing or watching the stories of other patients. "As the media focus on sexual abuse has increased, more and more women have had their memories triggered. . . . Often women become very uncomfortable when they hear another survivor's story and realize that what's being described happened to them."[20]

Another way to begin the process of building "memories" is to write imaginatively about one's own life and family history. Bass and Davis suggest readers "Take an event in your family history that you can never actually find out about. . . . Using all the details you do know, create your own story. Ground the experiences or event in as much knowledge as you have and then let yourself imagine what actually might have happened."[21]

In *The Sexual Healing Journey*, therapist Wendy Maltz suggests a series of exercises for patients feeling "stuck." Maltz directs patients to "spend time imagining that you were sexually abused, without worry about accuracy, proving anything or having your ideas make sense. As you give rein to your imagination, let your intuition guide your thoughts. . . . Ask yourself or have a support person or therapist ask you these questions: What time of day is it? Where are you? Indoors or outdoors? What kind of things are happening? Is there one or more person with you? Male or female? What types of touch are you experiencing? What parts of your body are involved? What do you see, feel or hear? How do you feel emotionally? Angry, scared, excited, confused?"[22] Once the patient reflects on answers to these questions, Maltz recommends that the therapist proceed by asking: "Who would have been likely perpetrators? When were you most vulnerable to sexual abuse in your life? Why would it have been important for you to forget what happened?"

Maltz is far from the only recovered memory expert who openly suggests that the process of discovering sexual abuse begin with the patient out and out *imagining* the abuse. Using a focal point that can be anything from a dream fragment to a body sensation, Renee Fredrickson describes what she calls "imagistic memory work." "Seat yourself comfortably and take a few relaxing breaths before you begin the actual work. Most people prefer doing imagistic work with their eyes closed. Outside stimulation is kept to a minimum, and you can focus all your attention on your internal reality. . . . Whoever is guiding the memory will ask questions to help you picture or sense what is happening in relation to that focal point. If nothing surfaces, wait a bit and then give your best guess in answer to the questions. If you feel resistance or skepticism, try to go past it. *Whether what is remembered around that focal point is made up or real is of no concern at the beginning of the process* (emphasis added)."[23] It should also be noted that without informing the reader, and perhaps without realizing it herself, Fredrickson describes a procedure that is quite capable of inducing hypnotic trance and an accompanying increase in the client's suggestibility.

In the end, as long as the therapist is intent on finding memories of abuse, and the client is similarly motivated or at least open to the idea, it doesn't much matter whether the therapist uses the patient's artwork, fantasy life, emotional reactions, physical symptoms, or imaginings to build the abuse belief. When examined, each of the procedures can be used to effectively convince the client that her current reactions, feelings, or imaginings are linked to a history of abuse. In all of the methods, the two important variables are the patient's emotional investment in the therapy and the therapist's confidence that these supposed pieces of memory (or indicators of memory) are valid. Retrieving a "memory" of abuse in recovered memory therapy is as easy as imagining that abuse. Getting the client to believe that image of abuse often requires much more effort than went into its creation.

"My memory is beginning to return. I am starting to have real memories of the sexual abuse I suffered as a child, and I now know it was you who abused me," a therapy patient named Penelope wrote to a longtime friend of her family. "I have finally gotten to the bottom of this . . . and I can now tolerate real memories of your crime."[24]

How Penelope came to this belief is explained at length in Charlotte Krause Prozan's book *The Technique of Feminist Psychoanalytic Psychotherapy*. While the primary technique that builds the abuse belief in this case was Prozan's interpretation of her patient's dreams, the case illustrates how easily evidence to substantiate the abuse narrative can be found or created if the patient is willing and the therapist is predisposed to the project.

Penelope began treatment in 1976 with no memories of having been sexually molested in childhood. The idea came only after Prozan read an article that reported high rates of sexual abuse in delinquent girls. Although her patient was not a delinquent girl, but a grown business-woman, Prozan remembers that because of the article she had a "new idea to think about" but "still had no indication of sexual abuse in Penelope's case." Even though over the course of most of the treatment her patient was unable to remember any abuse, Prozan became confident that abuse had taken place. Despite worries that her patient might end up accusing an innocent man, Prozan says, "I nevertheless continued to have faith that we were on to something."[25]

In no small part, this faith came from Prozan's conclusion, after twenty years of piecing together clues, that she herself had been sexually molested at the age of two. Of her own experience she writes, "I have the utmost confidence in the knowledge of what happened, even without the actual memory, and this personal experience was a great help to me in my work with my own patients who struggled with memories of sexual abuse. The work is like putting together a huge jigsaw puzzle of 1000 pieces. You start with one piece and very gradually other pieces fit. Starting from the outside, you build the frame and then fill the picture. Years later you have assembled all but the final few pieces in the center, and those pieces are nowhere to be found. The other 995 pieces fit together, so the picture is quite clear except for that missing part at the center, the precise mem-ory, which has been lost because it was so horrendous. . . . Those mem-ories of terror and rage are gone forever, and perhaps it is best that they are, so that you are never forced to live them again in memory."[26]

For her patient Penelope, the first puzzle piece came over a year into therapy, with the interpretation of a series of dreams in which she imagines herself pursued by rats. That Penelope had reported an infestation of mice in her apartment is mentioned only briefly by Prozan: it seems such a mundane explanation for the dream is not the stuff of psychotherapy. During free association Penelope connects the dream of being bitten on the wrist by a rat with a tight handshake of a longtime male friend of her mother's. Later she reports the dream of having a penis and feeling a pressure on the back of her neck that she associates with forced oral copulation.

From these clues Prozan determined that her patient was sexually molested when she was a girl by the family friend with the uncomfortable handshake. Although Penelope at first "strongly resisted" the interpretation, Prozan did not give up. There is no small hint of pride when she writes, "It would take another thirteen years of work before the realization and acceptance of her sexual molestation would be a certainty for Penelope."[27]

During the last weeks of therapy, Penelope has a dream that she later labels a "memory" of the abuse. According to Prozan's account, this relabeling of a dream as a memory is as close to a recollection as Penelope ever accomplishes during her entire fifteen years of therapy. Nevertheless, during these many years, Penelope joins a sexual-abuse-survivors support group and submerges herself in the literature of the recovered memory movement. At her therapist's suggestion she reads magazine articles about incest and tapes television documentaries on the subject. Most importantly, during these many years, Prozan would analyze "literally hundreds of dreams," discovering and identifying for her client an abundance of clues to support the belief that her patient was abused as a child. Over and over, Prozan proclaims her own importance in directing Penelope's therapy toward supposedly repressed memories of sexual abuse. Early on in her description of the therapy, Prozan writes proudly that "Were it not for my knowledge of dream interpretation, I might never have known that Penelope had been sexually abused as a child."[28]

Prozan's keen knowledge of the meaning of dreams allowed her to interpret a nightmare of a VW bus crashing into a house as an indication that the suspected molestation likely consisted of anal sex. Animals who at first appeared playful but turn dangerous are interpreted by Prozan as symbols of the perpetrator's genitals. A dream in which Penelope saw herself setting fires is also identified as an indication of the sexual abuse, because fire "can have a sexual meaning as an intense feeling." (As evidence for this, Prozan cites the song "Smoke Gets in Your Eyes.")[29] In addition, dreams with any explicit sexual content were easily interpreted to add weight to the sexual-abuse narrative.

Often she ties the dream material to reactions and experiences in her patient's current life. Describing one session, Prozan combines Penelope's discomfort experienced during a gynecological examination with a dream of being bitten on the hand by three purple dogs. From her notes, Prozan re-creates the exchange:

Therapist: Was there something last night you were trying not to think about? You drank too much and then you overslept this morning, nearly missing our session.

Patient: It was a beautiful day and I was feeling so good all day. I did have an appointment with the nurse practitioner at Kaiser [hospital], but it was good, my Pap smear was OK and we discussed menopause. But the speculum, I never felt so uncomfortable. I couldn't wait until it came out. The speculum felt like rape. But why did I dream about hands? [Referring to the dream of the dogs.]

Therapist: Your hand may have been forced to stroke his penis, or your hands may have been held back so you couldn't protect yourself. . . . The purple dog—dogs aren't purple. You pretend it was nice like in all your dreams where animals start out nice and then change to dangerous.

Patient: Yes, purple could be a penis, the change of colors could be frightening to a child.

Therapist: This dream is tied to the feeling of being sexually molested at your (gynecological) appointment and helps to reconstruct the molestation (during childhood). He (referring to the believed abuser) stimulated you and then had you fondle his penis, perhaps making reference to petting an animal, then he raped you.[30]

If this featured exchange is any indication, it seems Prozan had no trouble explicitly suggesting her interpretation directly to Penelope. Explaining her insistence, Prozan writes, "It is clear that I am encouraging the patient's associations to her molestation by making formulations in which I connect the material from the dreams to possible scenarios. One might criticize this approach as a kind of 'leading the witness,' but this is not a courtroom. In trying to retrieve memories in psychoanalysis or psychotherapy, the role of the therapist is to tie together material and attempt reconstructions."[31] Here, as elsewhere, Prozan takes for granted the speculative conclusion that the molestation in fact occurred—despite her client's inability to remember, and uncertainty that she was molested. After all, as Prozan reminds the reader, "The phenomenon of not remembering should neither disqualify the patient from being believed nor serve to discourage the therapist from pursuing the work, but is in itself a *symptom* indicative of a severe traumatic experience (emphasis in the original)."[32] Lack of memory for a trauma, then, is evidence that it occurred.

As for who Penelope's perpetrator was, the focus never goes off the family friend who made at least the one mistake of squeezing Penelope's hand too tightly. Identified as F in Prozan's account, this man helped

Penelope's family in the years after her father died when she was a child. According to Prozan, both she and Penelope were concerned for a time that F might not be the right man. "We reviewed every other man in her life—her father, other friends of the family, her uncles, her grand-father—but what distinguished her memories of F from the rest was the ever-present feeling of anxiety when she thought of him."[33]

As an agreed-upon termination date for treatment approaches, Pene-lope finally begins to express more faith in the interpretation that Prozan has been offering her for well over a decade of her life. Often, after Prozan creates a connection with the abuse, Penelope will make statements such as "How deprived I must have felt," or, "I must have suffered—how terrible."

For Prozan, however, the progress is distressingly slow. She writes, "I feel like we're in the bottom of the ninth with one out. There is not much time left, and there is still much resistance and clearly more incest-related material on which to work. I am feeling some pressure to get the job done by the deadline." This pressure, she says later, was "to achieve a certain progress in relation to the memories of her sexual molestation before termination of the treatment."[34]

Finally, in December 1990, Penelope reports a dream that will become critical to the belief about her history. The dream is of being shot by a man. "I struggle to get up. A friend comes and peers down at me and says, 'Oh, but look at you, you're badly hurt, you're covered with blood.' I look at my chest and there are great globs of blood. I realize I'm really hurt. I say to a man standing there. 'You may as well shoot me.' I'm seriously hurt. The bullet goes in the left side of my neck, it penetrates—then stops. It's lodged in there. I'm not dead."

In response to this dream, Penelope offers an interpretation of her own. "I had the realization when I woke up that I quite possibly was literally raped. . . . Remember that dream of the van driving into the back of the house? I never thought of it, but you mentioned the possibility of anal rape. I've gone from that image to it being a direct penetration of my body, the bullet penetrating my neck."[35]

But even with this dream, Penelope expresses doubt and has to be reassured by Prozan, who tells her, "You still have resistance to accepting that such a terrible thing really happened to you. The resistance shows in the dream. You deny that you are badly injured. You try to get up. It takes a friend to tell you are badly injured, as I keep telling you." (Nothing, of course, is made of the interesting detail that the blood she was covered with, while frightening, looked "phony" and "not real.")

Over the next few sessions, Penelope and Prozan invest a measure of certainty and emotion into the meaning of the dream. In another session two days later Penelope cries when describing what the dream has come to mean to her. "This was the first dream in which it's clear to me that there was penetration," she says, sobbing.

> Patient: The bullet went inside my body, there's no question about it. That's pretty horrible for a child to experience. Just like the end of the world. . . . The pain, the invasion, the taking at will—to do that to a child—what a great shock.
> Therapist: Especially when it's someone you had trusted.
> Patient: I was deeply wounded.
> Therapist: Physically and emotionally.
> Patient: In the dream it's physical, but I was feeling the lack of desire to go on. . . . That SON OF A BITCH! It's totally his fault! He made me feel that way. It's almost more than I can tolerate when I read about it. What if I kill him? I'm afraid to stop therapy, I might lose control.[36]

To further invest in the importance of the dream, Penelope tells the story to friends and co-workers, as well as to her sister and mother. Finally, she becomes convinced enough of the meaning of the dream to write the accusatory letter to F himself. "You cannot hurt me anymore," she writes. "The crime you committed has had terrible effects on me for years, but I am now healing, and going beyond the pain and anguish I have had to endure. . . . From now on, the secret is out, and the shame is on you."[37]

For Penelope to have concluded that she was raped and to have accused F based on Prozan's long, relentless influence is a triumph of recovered memory therapy's ability to create an abuse narrative out of any grist. While other recovered memory therapists might have guided the client to imagine the trauma, or worked to define vague feelings into a story of abuse, Prozan used her interpretations of the client's dreams to build the narrative. Because Penelope's eventual belief that she was raped by F grew primarily from Prozan's interpretations of her dreams, in judging the veracity of the final belief it seems reasonable to begin with the validity of these interpretations.

The idea that dreams have deep or specific meaning is speculative, and is not limited to therapy. Over time, and in various cultures, dreams have been seen as windows not only into the past but to the future and to spiritual realms as well. However, it is perhaps in psychoanalysis that the idea that dreams carry deep meaning has grown to its most extreme and bizarre form. In some therapy offices, dreams not only have meaning, but *specific* meaning. They are seen as carrying coded messages from the all-knowing unconscious, which are then translated by the therapist. Because the symbolism and hidden meanings can be so oblique (a purple dog becoming a penis), the interpretation of dreams is perhaps the clearest example of therapists using a tool that can only confirm the therapist's suspicions.

Despite Freud's assurances, there is no indication in the considerable literature on the subject that certain symbols, images, or themes found in dreams have any specific meaning. The meaning of a dream of being bitten by a rat, or for that matter witnessing the crash of a VW bus, depends almost entirely on the context that the therapist decides to put it in. These images could be viewed as an illustration of hidden impulses or fantasies, and not necessarily illustrative of the client's history at all. Those who believe that they can make a one-to-one match with the symbolism in a dream and an experience in the past have perhaps not considered the magnitude of the difficulty of the task they are undertaking.

"Finding a match not only depends on the ingenuity of the observer; it also depends on what might be called the size of the search space," writes Spence of matching dreams with historical events in *Narrative Truth and Historical Truth*. "If we keep searching for an event that will correspond to a particular dream image, we are bound to come up with a plausible match if we continue to look long enough; and yet the time taken up in the search or the size of the search space are rarely mentioned in a report of the match. . . . Associations may go back to childhood. Considering the possible number of incidents covered in the patient's lifetime and the multiple ways in which they can be structured, we begin to see the near-infinite range of possibilities."[38]

Indeed, if we were to include in this formulation the idea that matches can include things *not* remembered, as Prozan insists, the range of possibilities becomes truly infinite. If the memory that the dream indicates has yet to be discovered, the therapist can propose literally any experience. That Prozan discerned an experience of sexual abuse is hardly a surprise considering her own belief that she was sexually abused as well as her interest in the literature on the topic, which gave her "new ideas to think about" during the early treatment of Penelope. As Prozan herself admits, what a therapist looks for—and therefore is more likely to find—is determined in no small part by larger societal currents and concerns.

The number of connections that a therapist might make from a dream to a client's past remains infinite only until the first interpretation is uttered. Once the connection is made, in this case between the dream of the rats, the firmness of F's handshake, and the possibility of having been molested, the field of other possibilities largely disappears. From this point, the therapist and patient have two options. They can dismiss the interpretation as being off the mark or they can tentatively begin to build evidence for its adoption. Because Prozan's recounting of the therapy in her book presents a fait accompli, the reader has no way to judge if any other interpretations suggesting different causes for Penelope's problems were offered but abandoned.

For whatever reason, this interpretation resonated with the pair, and over the course of the treatment they found, mostly in Penelope's dreams, evidence of its validity. Some of this evidence, for example, Prozan's interpretation of the dream of the VW bus crashing being an indicator of anal rape, seems to the nonpsychoanalytically inclined to be pure fancy. Prozan, however, seems assured that the cumulative interpretation of these dreams is nothing less than clear and obvious. In Penelope's case, there is no indication that other possible interpretations were offered, nor is any suggestion given that a multitude of interpretations might exist.

While Penelope apparently never had a dream specifically about child abuse, she did dream of explicitly sexual or violent situations. While it is impossible to know with certainty the exact source of these dreams, one obvious possibility is left out of Prozan's suggestions to her client. Prozan never mentions to the reader, and apparently never offers to her client, the possibility that the source for her sexually explicit dreams might be the years of focusing on the topic of molestation and violation *in therapy*. Indeed, many times during therapy Penelope reports having had dreams about having sexual relations *with Prozan* in the therapy office and elsewhere. That these dreams clearly had their source in the therapy setting makes it likely that other dreams were sparked by the topics *discussed* in therapy.

All in all, if, as it appears in Prozan's recounting, Penelope's belief about her abuse at the hands of F relied primarily on indicators found in her dreams, the conclusion seems wholly speculative. Considering Prozan's confidence, it is interesting to wonder whether the content of Penelope's dreams was at all integral to her interpretation. Critical to the process of recovering memories of abuse is not the weight of the evidence, but predisposition to find the evidence, and the patient's devotion to the process. In this case, it seems, both factors were present in force.

In tallying up the benefits of Penelope's treatment, the results look grim. At the end of treatment her behavior, including her smoking, drinking, and binge eating, still troubles her. She has exited fifteen years of therapy possessed with only the hope that things will soon get better. At the end of therapy she writes letters to both her sister and her mother, telling them of her last revelation in therapy. She writes to her mother that "[I] now have the chance to permanently stop smoking, to lose weight and stick to my beloved swimming." To her sister she says, "The days of being fearful and ashamed are over! The days of being powerfully angry are now and the days of increased good health and a chance for happiness and a family of my own are straight ahead."[39] After fifteen years of therapy, Penelope is forty-nine years old.

For the reader who might be wondering just what good came out of all those years of work, Prozan tosses in a final note about seeing Penelope six months after the termination of treatment. During their meeting Penelope tells of having a horrible falling-out with her sister over the abuse allegations. Despite this further problem in Penelope's life, Prozan manages to salvage some evidence from the meeting to show that all their work together improved her patient's life. In her last sentence about Penelope, Prozan writes, "She looked better than I had ever seen her look. She had on a very attractive outfit, had lost 30 pounds, gotten contact lenses and a becoming new hairstyle. If I had seen her on the street, I would not have recognized her."

The reader nearly chokes on the obvious question: *That's it?* Penelope is single at forty-nine, estranged from her sister, and saddled with the idea that all her problems were caused by an anal rape at the age of nine—an experience for which she has only a dream memory. And in defense of this outcome Prozan offers the equivalent of "But she looks great." It would of course be unfair to ask whether these modest improvements—the losing of weight, the donning of an attractive dress, the new hairstyle, the purchase of the contact lenses—might have been accomplished *sans* fifteen years of psychoanalysis? After all, there is no way to know what Penelope's life might have come to without her decade and a half of treatment. Whether therapy actually made her life worse is an open but ultimately unanswerable question. One thing is for certain: the evidence that fifteen years of treatment substantially improved her life is nowhere to be found in this account.

Throughout the literature of recovered memory therapy there are many stories of therapists sticking to their abuse interpretations for years until their clients finally come to accept them as true. Like Prozan, therapists proudly write of how they insightfully detected a history of sexual abuse by analyzing their clients' present problems and then steadfastly overcame denial and disbelief. Patients also write of being confronted with such an interpretation and spending agonizing years in therapy and abuse groups before coming to believe the abuse narrative. The story of her treatment written by Noelle in *Growing Through the Pain: The Incest Survivor's Companion* is one such account. According to the book's editor, Catherine Bronson, Noelle's story is of special importance because she gives a "detailed account of what it feels like to not remember incest trauma. . . . For those who don't remember, [Noelle's story] will be particularly useful in validating experiences and overcoming the tenacious grip of denial."[40]

Noelle entered therapy at thirty after divorcing her first husband and feeling that she needed help and advice on her relationships with men and with work problems. While, according to her own account, she had enough work and relationship problems to keep most therapists occupied, the therapist she went to quickly saw that these problems were a "disguised presentation" of another, deeper problem. After six months of treatment, her therapist announced to Noelle: "I think you were sexually abused as a child, and I think you know who did it, too." The therapist explained that he knew that she had been sexually abused by her father, just as a hunter knows how to read the tracks of an animal. "You don't have to see the animal to know it had been there. . . . I can see the tracks throughout your life—the monster has been there."[41]

Noelle, like many patients, at first reacted angrily to the interpretation, telling her therapist in no uncertain terms that he was wrong. The therapist used her negative reaction as the first bit of evidence to prove his theory. According to Noelle, he told her, "Well, if it's not true, then why is it upsetting you so much?" To this Noelle responded, "Well, if that's real, then nothing else can be real, and I don't know what is real."[42] Months later, after she was finally convinced to consider the interpretation that she was abused, she allowed her therapist to discuss the possibility "hypothetically." "At this stage, my therapist and I started trying to relate what I now know are 'recurrences' to the original incest trauma," Noelle writes. "When things happened to me that seemed 'crazy' or 'weird,' we would talk about them in terms of how they might be an expression of the incest."

While Noelle remembered her childhood as rather joyless and difficult, the idea that her father could have sexually abused her contradicted all she knew and felt about him. Although he was strict, Noelle writes of feeling great love for him and an assurance that if she ever was truly in need or danger he would do anything to help her. She also believed her father to be a man of virtue and honesty. "I saw him as a superman, a man of grand ideas and integrity against a corrupt and dirty world. . . . I was always Daddy's special girl. I felt I was special. I felt that if something ever happened and I needed him to save my life, he would." To accept the idea that her father had abused her, she not only had to break down this fantasy father, but also recast many of her childhood and adult memories to fit the abuse narrative.

The remarkable thing about this process, which took the next five years, is the stark, black-and-white nature of her recast memories. She came into therapy believing that she had been a "smart, wonderful child," and remembering being told that she was always smiling and happy. At the end of the therapy she came to believe that she grew up in a "concentration camp," where there were "no good times to offset the bad." In the end, she believed that she "had pretty much left home emotionally at the age of three and lost my mother and father, lost my childhood, lost everything."[43] Any smiling she remembered, she came to believe, had only been of "embarrassment, or apology."

Noelle and her therapist reworked every part of her past and current life to conform to the abuse narrative. Her feelings of awkwardness about her body during her teen years came to be seen as feelings of "shame" that she connected to the incest. When her father had shown concern over self-destructive behavior during her childhood, he was motivated not out of love, she discovered in therapy, but only because her behavior reflected on him. When she was punished for staying out late as a teenager, for instance, her father was not showing concern for her but only for himself. "He couldn't care less that his child was being destroyed." A memory of her father trying to help her when she was sick became just an example of how "I was not allowed to feel pain; I was not allowed to hurt."

According to the narrtive created in therapy, Noelle's childhood life outside of the family was also deeply affected by the incest she had suffered. When she was home sick, her teachers would talk about her in front of the class. "I remember once, in the eighth grade, my teacher took the opportunity of one of my absences to lecture the whole class on all my faults and what was wrong with me. I was hounded and persecuted, with nowhere to go."[44]

The success she had in college and in her subsequent career was also viewed in the light of the incest. She became a top student in college only to bolster "my almost nonexistent self-worth." At work, the incest manifested itself in Noelle becoming a perfectionist and being plagued with the constant feeling of inadequacy. At one point she describes a moment of confusion and panic after being asked for her opinion about a project. "Why had I gotten so confused?" Noelle asked herself. Once in therapy she found the answer: "That was a form of dissociation for me. In situations like that with a man in authority who expected me to know something, I would dissociate badly. Of course, the connection would be the abuse; it's real clear now. It was not at all clear until I remembered."

Her social life was similarly redrawn to conform to the incest narrative. She adopted the idea that she had often dissociated during parties and social gatherings. While she had acted like she was having a good time, looking back she realized that her real self had "crawled off into a very dark place, put her head down on her knees, and just sat there waiting for it to be over." Looking back over her life, she became aware that she never understood how to act around people and had always felt different from others. Her pretherapy belief that she had often enjoyed sex became viewed as nothing but a "fantasy" that she had created.

As her therapy progressed, Noelle found that literally any anomaly or problem in her life could be somehow connected with the abuse narrative. Her childhood fear of the movie *King Kong* was explained by the "association with the abuse—the big monster, little person, making strange noises and flailing about." Fainting during her first communion was also explained by the connection with the abuse because it consisted of a man wanting to put something into her mouth. The claustrophobic panic she experienced driving through an automatic car wash was also later explained in therapy. The blue cloths which scrubbed the car were later associated with the blue curtain in her abuse dream.

In another connection, Noelle describes how it took several years of therapy before she realized how her mother was complicit in the abuse by her father. Her mother encouraged her father's abusive behavior, Noelle came to understand, by never cooking enough food for the family. Because her father was served first, Noelle believes that her mother was trying to "teach me that my job was to 'do without' for my father's sake."

Dreams she remembered were also reinterpreted to become evidence for the abuse story. In her recurring dreams of spiders she and her therapist found two different clues for the abuse. "Because of their penis-like legs, I've always thought [the spiders] were representations of the male genitals I saw while being abused. Then, in a therapy session, my therapist suggested that maybe, since I was abused in the basement, and spiders tend to live in the basement, perhaps I really saw spiders while I was sexually abused . . . that made a lot of sense to me."[45]

Noelle's confirmation that she had been abused came in a dream in which she saw herself as a little girl of three being forced to perform oral sex on her father. Unlike Penelope, there was no metaphoric interpretation necessary. Noelle simply accepted this part of the dream as a memory. "When I woke up, I was screaming and crying hysterically and I could not stop crying or get myself composed for six hours. . . . I went to my therapist, who for five years had been working on getting me to recognize the sexual abuse by trying to show me the ways in which my current experience contained elements of the abuse. I went to him and I said, 'You can break out the champagne now, you were right . . . I never believed you. I wanted you to be wrong, but I can't deny it anymore. You were right.'"[46]

In Noelle's treatment, the actual dream "memory" of abuse is much less important than the manner in which she changed her entire life story so that it fit. Bronson aptly describes the process Noelle and other patients have gone through. "Because they have no prior consciousness of [the abuse], the emerging memories threaten to shatter their sense of reality. It feels like trying to force in a piece of a puzzle that doesn't fit, and in the process breaking apart the whole puzzle. . . . An effective and less traumatic way to overcome the denial is to examine the past behavior and identify the dysfunction created by the incest, gradually adjusting the picture so that incest, rather than appearing as something alien and new, is seen as something that was there all the time."[47]

This process of "gradually adjusting the picture" not only led Noelle to redefine most of her life, but also to cast off all responsibility for her pretherapy decisions and behaviors. Over the course of reframing her life, Noelle came to believe that she had "dissociated" much of her past and current life. In her current life she became vigilant for moments when she daydreamed or lost her train of thought or found herself confused, labeling these too as evidence for her dissociative disorder. Looking back on stressful incidents she handled poorly, she blamed her newly understood tendency to lose concentration. Noelle determined that the effect of the abuse and dissociation was so pervasive that until therapy she had no true understanding or control of her actions. "I was not in control; I did not know what I was doing. I was so confused and dissociated most of the time, I didn't have any idea what I was doing. . . . I had no awareness of my behavior. I had no connection to the abuse I had suffered. It was automatic behavior. . . . I think I was dissociated for the first twenty years of my life, at least twenty years."[48]

During five years of therapy, everything that she believed to be in order had to be redefined as only an illusion of order. It was only "on the surface [that] everything looked right." Her memories, her opinion of her parents, her sex and social life, her career and relationship with her daughter—all ceased to have meaning in their own right but became mere reflections of the trauma she had suffered as a child. Once the narrative was fully imposed on all aspects of her existence, she viewed her pretherapy life as only one of darkness. "All I knew was that the world was an overwhelming, disappointing place" where "every relationship was unworkable." Once she believed the narrative, she came to believe that her life fitted "beautifully with the profile of an incest victim."

Unfortunately, but not surprisingly, despite Noelle's commitment to readjusting the picture of her life so that the incest puzzle piece could fit, she has not become happier or less troubled over the course of therapy. At the writing of her story, nearly six years into therapy, she reports feeling "sexually dead," and not even being able to "imagine experiencing sex again and liking it." While she has had to abandon friends who made the mistake of questioning her abuse narrative, Noelle herself has been plagued with doubts about her memory. While she has times in which she feels like everything in therapy "must be a big mistake," she has become convinced that if the incest memories were not true, she would be truly crazy for having believed them.

The process of viewing her life as a reflection of the incest narrative continues. Noelle believes she is still not fully aware of how abuse affected her life. "Every day," she writes, "brings new revelation." During the process of writing her story of therapy for *Growing Through the Pain*, Noelle experienced new "flashbacks" of her father trying to rape her. Lately, she has been fighting off strong impulses to kill herself.

Through it all, she has faith that her nearly six years of work will eventually make her into a happy and healthy person. "I thank God that I had a therapist who knew what he was doing, who was there for years and years when I was in denial, and who knew a disguised presentation when he saw it. I hate to think what would have happened to me if I hadn't had him."[49]

CHAPTER FIVE

Investment in Belief

Picture an elephant. Imagine an apple. Now spend a moment visualizing an image of being sexually assaulted by one of your parents. It is an often distressing trick of the mind that it will create any event regardless of our desire to visualize that event. What separates an imagined image from a memory image is not a simple matter, for even imagined events are themselves largely built from memory. Our ability to imagine an elephant would be impossible if we didn't have a memory of having seen an elephant or a picture of the creature. Similarly our ability to—or more precisely, our inability not to—imagine a sexual assault by a parent would also come from an amalgam of memories. To create this image we might use recollections of our parents' physical appearances and of ourselves as children. We might place the scene in the memory of our childhood room. To create the action of the scene, we might use memories of other people's descriptions of sexual assaults or of abuse scenes depicted in books or movie dramas. In the end, all the pieces of the imagined event would have something of the weight of memory.

Our innate ability to distinguish between memory and imagination is a precarious and, at best, an imperfect mechanism. Because recovered memory therapists believe that all clients are initially "in denial" about their abuse, there is no assumption that clients possess the ability to apply this mechanism at the start of treatment. Indeed, it is assumed that this mechanism works against therapy—automatically misclassifying any and all memories of abuse as imagination. Recovered memory therapists assume that the mechanism that separates memory from fantasy can only result in "denial" of the reality of abuse memories.

Faced with the first visualization of abuse, be it a brief mental image, a dream, or a piece of artwork, at the beginning of therapy, patients often attest that the image does not feel like a memory. At the beginning of the therapy, at least, the mechanism that distinguishes between memories and imagination often clearly tells the patient that what has been arrived at is not an historical event. Because this initial denial is assumed to be the patient's pathological unwillingness to face reality, clients are encouraged to overcome it. There is virtually no mention within the movement of cases in which this initial denial has proven to accurately represent the patient's history. Within the literature, denial is *always* overcome, and patients inevitably learn to accept the reality of their abuse.

"Denial is the art of pretending not to know what you know," writes Renee Fredrickson. "Denial is overcome only by patients' growth in the opposite direction. . . . Survivors with very little denial can move through therapy fairly quickly, even if their abuse was massive. On the other hand, some survivors struggle for years simply to acknowledge that they were abused. . . . You have some control over your denial. If you have a strong denial system, you can work on dismantling it with a skilled therapist."[1] Bass and Davis refer to any "denial" the patients experience as just a "necessary stage" of therapy.[2] "Believing doesn't happen all at once," they warn. "It's a gradual awakening."[3]

Authors sometimes go to ridiculous extents to prove that beliefs built in therapy are always real. Disbelief itself is not rational, according to Fredrickson. "You may be convinced that your disbelief is a rational questioning of the reality versus unrealitiy of your memories, but it is partially a misguided attempt to repress the memories again."[4] Not only is disbelief irrational, but the presence of "crippling disbelief" is proof that the memories are real: "The existence of profound disbelief is an indication that memories are real."[5]

Bass and Davis instruct counselors never to let the client's belief slip. "You must believe that your client was abused, even if she sometimes doubts it herself. . . . Your client needs you to stay steady in the belief that she was abused. Joining a client in doubt would be like joining a suicidal client in her belief that suicide is the best way out. If a client is unsure that she was abused but thinks she might have been, work as though she was. So far, among the hundreds of women we've talked to and the hundreds of women we've heard about, not one has suspected she might have been abused, explored it, and determined that she wasn't. . . . No one fantasizes abuse."[6]

There are many techniques available to the therapist that effectively destroy the patient's ability to distinguish between imagined events and memory. It is testimony to the difficulty of doing this that the recovered memory literature often spends more time explaining methods of convincing the patient to believe the visualizations than it does detailing the methods of creating those images. Because Fredrickson believes that "denial" works against therapy, she recommends that patients simply put the question aside by accepting that their abuse was real for a period of time. "You will find it helpful to decide that your memories are real for at least a year. This decision allows you to look at them with some amount of continuity, without constantly going back and forth between belief and disbelief. . . . You will not get a sense of recall with your memories, but after enough memories, debriefed enough times, you will suddenly know your repressed memories are real." In *The Courage to Heal*, one patient describes using a sort of abuse mantra to convince herself that her memories of the abuse discovered in therapy were real. "I would walk around saying, 'My family abused me.' I had to say it a lot to really believe it. My first year and a half was spent just accepting the fact that I had been abused."[7]

Often, to convince patients that their memories are real, therapists point to the very pain and psychological torment their new beliefs have caused. Lynne D. Finney, author of *Reach for the Rainbow*, was convinced of this logic in her own therapy and went on to apply the reasoning with her own clients. "While memories of my own abuse were coming back, I repeatedly asked my therapists whether I could be imagining the scenes of my abuse and torture which seemed so bizarre and unbelievable. My therapists were astonished by this question since I always seemed to ask it when I had just experienced violent emotions after a new memory. They emphasized how hysterical I was and how much pain I felt and asked how I could possibly deny what I was feeling. And each time I would be temporarily convinced, only to be plunged into doubt by the next gruesome revelation. . . .

"When a survivor asks, 'Am I making this up?' I reply, 'Even if you could have made up the event, could you have made up your intense feelings?' The response is always 'no,' but the uncertainty continues. We all wonder why we do not immediately feel an inner certainty about what we are experiencing. The answer is really very simple. No one wants to believe that such horror could have occurred. Our minds naturally protect us from information that is too painful."[8]

This argument has hit home for many survivors, for it can often be heard repeated by those attesting to the accuracy of their new beliefs. As we argue throughout this book, the pain patients suffer during their therapy is without a doubt real. No one—not the patients, therapists, parents, or critics of recovered memory therapy—questions that this therapy is an intensely difficult and painful experience. That the pain of therapy is real should not be accepted, however, as an argument that the memories uncovered are accurate. One's emotional reaction to a mental image memory need not correlate with the truth of that image but rather only to whether one *believes* that visualized event to be true. In trying to convince clients that emotional reactions indicate the reality of the believed-in image, recovered memory therapists have created yet another piece of defective circular reasoning: if patients believe in the abuse narrative, they will experience emotional pain. That pain can then be used as evidence for the validity of the abuse, which bolsters the belief.

Using similar reasoning, patients questioning the stories of abuse can be directed back toward the symptom list for confirmation. In the same way that symptoms are often defined as memories, they can also be used as evidence that memories must be true. "The hardest part was accepting and believing that it really happened," Bass and Davis quote one survivor as saying. "Being in the group really helped. I was able to see other people who have gone through sexual abuse, and my symptoms were similar. I have all the classic symptoms of sexual abuse."[9]

Often, in convincing their patients of the veracity of their newly recovered memories, therapists intentionally confuse denial of child abuse at a societal level with denial on a personal level. Some argue that acceptance of the reality of child abuse on a societal level requires that we accept the reality of child abuse in each individual case. Arguing that Freud's theory that women only fantasize sexual abuse has led society away from an acceptance of the reality of abuse, Christine Courtois instructs therapists in her book *Healing the Incest Wound* not to question any stories of incest. "In order to conduct effective incest therapy, the therapist must absolutely accept that incest occurs and that children are used and exploited by their adult caretakers. They must continuously counter the personal tendency to defend the adult at the expense of the child or to otherwise deny, discount, or dismiss the survivor's story. They must also abandon those theoretical formulations and positions which reinforce denial. . . . Only through acceptance of the abuse experiences and their abreaction can the trauma be mastered and the incest wound healed."[10]

She is quite right that Freud's formulations did a huge disservice to women with real memories of child sexual abuse and gave many an excuse to ignore the issue for most of this century. But to accept and address the reality that incest *does* occur in our society does not mean that one must accept that incest occurs in all cases where it is suspected. Is it not possible to accept "absolutely" that incest does occur in our society, while at the same time remaining concerned with abuses in therapy and the potential for the therapeutic creation of false memory beliefs? To accept Courtois's position, one must not only ignore the growing number of recovered memory critics, but also the many patients who have come out of therapy telling of coercion by their therapists.

Courtois's flawed logic is often cruelly used to counter the patients' doubts that their memories are real. Implicitly or overtly, therapists sug-

gest to patients that society is split between those who believe memories
of abuse and those who deny that sexual victimization occurs. Suggesting
to patients that they must accept their memories because society has long
denied the reality of child abuse is the ultimate confusion of the slogan
"the personal is political," and an unfair burden for someone confused
about his or her own past.

To fully appreciate the power of a recovered memory therapist to change
a client's beliefs in this regard, one must analyze the tremendous investment patients make in the therapy. The unspoken therapist-patient
contract confers great power to the therapist. It has long been noted that
for psychotherapies to work, the patient must believe in the power and
status of the therapist as a healer. "The success of all methods and schools
of psychotherapy depends in the first instance on the patient's conviction
that the therapist cares about him and is competent to help him,"[11] writes
Jerome Frank in *Persuasion and Healing*, emphasizing later that "the
psychotherapist's success depends in part on the patient's image of [the
therapist] as the possessor of healing knowledge and skills.[12] At the beginning of therapy, the patient often believes that the therapist is not only
a healer but also an emotionally healthy, self-confident, and successful
professional. The patient, who is at least demoralized or troubled, often
finds herself drawn to the figure of the therapist. Much of the curative
power of talk therapy comes from the therapist's carefully exploiting his
or her power over the client. Because clients seek the approval of the
therapist, the therapist's expectations about how the client will behave
can have a dramatic impact on the client's actions. If the client is not
mentally ill, but rather suffers from mundane troubles, such as simple
demoralization, confusion, or anxiety, it is possible for the therapist to
persuade the client to change her behaviors and in doing so effect substantial and long-lasting improvement. If the therapist uses his or her
influence to do nothing more than convince clients to repeatedly attest
they are happy (as recommended in *The Power of Positive Thinking*), the
positive effects of therapy will likely be short-lived.
    Even considering the substantial influence the therapist wields, there
is considerable evidence that the dependence that recovered memory
patients develop on their therapists is much greater than it is in other
therapy settings. Again and again in the literature, recovered memory
experts recommend that patients seek, and that therapists forge, extremely
close emotional ties in therapy. "When you work with a good counselor,
you should feel understood and supported. You should feel warmth between you and your counselor. And that should happen early in the

therapy process," write Bass and Davis in *The Courage to Heal*.[13] They
note earlier in the book in a section directed at counselors, "Not only
does the adult woman need your sincere caring, but the child within her
is also hungry for heartfelt nurturing . . . don't be afraid to love your
clients. . . . All the techniques, all the methods, are really just tools to
channel the love. It's love that heals."[14] Another popular book on recovering memories describes the therapist's job as to "devote his or her
full attention to you during the course of your session. In doing so, the
therapist is in effect providing the parenting that was missing during your
childhood. . . . A big part of the incest survivor healing process is to
experience being in a safe place and in a relationship where it's safe to
have feelings, where you are believed, where you feel hope."[15]

Philip Kinsler, writing in the journal *Dissociation*, offers the idea that
treating survivors of severe abuse constitutes a "special relationship" that
has "goals different from those of traditional therapies." He emphasizes
that work with such clients "requires a different degree of engagement
and availability than does a traditional therapy." This heightened engagement can be achieved, he writes, by holding therapy sessions two or
three times a week and being available for the patient after "normal"
hours. Most tellingly, he recommends "Allowing extremely strong attachments to form towards the therapist," explaining that "through availability, real caring, and deep engagement, without either inappropriate
limits or under-involvement, we teach that it may be possible to trust
some of the people some of the time. . . . By our caring, we help teach
our patients their worth as real, lovable human beings."[16] According to
Kinsler, a good recovered memory therapist should become something
of a kindly parent—loving, available at all times, and listening when
others do not. From a book about multiple personality disorder, Kinsler
quotes a patient who writes: "We [referring to herself and her various
personalities] have an enormous need both to be loved and to love. . . . It
took our therapist a long and painful time to accept a careful expansion
of boundaries of the therapy relationship to meet those needs. She has
added some mothering-type stuff and some friendship-type stuff, when
the primary needs of therapy allow them, and we have thrived on it."

Therapists should be loving, and—above all—never question or downplay abuse narratives. "The old style of psychoanalysis in which your
therapist is totally detached in the therapy relationship is not good for
[adult surivors]," writes therapy patient Catherine Bronson in her book
Growing Through the Pain. "We need a more interactive therapy in which
we receive therapeutic validation and nurturing. If you don't feel you are
getting that, find another therapist. If you hear your therapist say, 'What

really happened? Are you sure?' . . . or if you feel the incest issues are being dismissed in any way, those are red flags that tell you to leave. What you should hear from your therapist are things like . . . 'You will learn to be cared for; you deserve it.' "[17]

We will not debate here the many dangers of this heightened emotional involvement in recovered memory therapy. We point it out only to note the likelihood that the heightened level of "warmth," "love," and "friendship" would increase the patient's emotional dependence on the therapy, and, in doing so, increase the vulnerability of the patient to direct and indirect forms of persuasion.

This heightened bond and increased dependence on the therapist is not the only reason a patient might invest in the recovered memory treatment. Judging from the movement's literature, spectacular benefits await those willing to put their faith in the theory of recovered memory. "At the end of her trip through her memories, she will emerge more serene than she had ever thought possible," Renee Fredrickson predicts of a client described in her book *Repressed Memories*. "Self-defeating behaviors and troublesome feelings will cease to plague her."[18] According to Mary Beth McClure, in *Reclaiming the Heart*, recovering memories of your abuse will allow you to discover and "reparent" your inner child. "Reaching the wounded child within, learning how to play and how to trust your inner voice or intuition. Having an energized core self comes from 're-parenting' yourself and discovering a state of self-love. This is the basis for allowing love into your life and developing the capacity for intimacy."[19] By doing so, she writes, it is possible to break the chains forged by the abuse and find a new depth and richness to life never known before. "Survivors have become excellent therapists, sensitive doctors, ground-breaking reporters, perceptive parents, compassionate friends. Other survivors have developed psychic abilities from their sensitivity," according to *The Courage to Heal*. "Deciding to heal, making your own growth and recovery a priority, will set in motion a healing force that will bring to your life a richness and depth you never dreamed possible." The book quotes many survivors attesting to the wonders of their life after treatment. One gushes: "For the first time I'm appreciating things like the birds and flowers, the way the sun feels on my skin. I can read a good book. I can sit in the sun . . . for the first time I feel alive."[20]

The pamphlets given out at support-group meetings repeat this message. One handout, entitled "The Twelve Promises," assures members that once they find their memories, they will "intuitively know how to handle situations which used to baffle [them]," and that their "whole attitude and outlook on life will change." The twelfth promise assures group members that they will "Suddenly realize that a loving spiritual source is doing for [them] what [they] could not do alone."

The more of the literature one reads, the more these women and men begin to sound like religious converts giving witness to the joys of salvation. It becomes unclear sometimes whether these therapists and groups are offering secular healing or a sort of quasi-religious deliverance from a difficult world—deliverance that rests upon one's faith, not in a deity, but in a therapist and the validity of recovered memories. There is, of course, no one who would not desire to have the package that recovered memory therapists purport to offer: a loving, caring friend/parent (in the form of the therapist), deep spiritual understanding, and the opportunity to become perceptive and compassionate (not to mention the possibility of acquiring psychic abilities). Promoters of recovered memory therapy who deny that therapists are creating false beliefs in patients often argue that there are no "secondary gains" to uncovering repressed memories of being abused. They ask, in essence, what a patient could possibly hope to gain by coming to believe she was abused. They should perhaps reread the movement's literature, keeping in mind the perspective of someone coming into therapy. We would argue that if one were to look at the treatment *retrospectively*, the pain of acquiring such beliefs would indeed outweigh the benefits. Unfortunately, a patient at the beginning of therapy doesn't have the advantage of this perspective. As these quotes from recovered memory books plainly show, for a patient at the start of therapy, the path offered by recovered memory practitioners seems to lead to substantial rewards.

Perhaps the cruelest way recovered memory therapy bonds the client to the treatment is by promising to provide a surrogate family to replace the one destroyed during therapy. This is often necessary regardless of whether the parents are deemed the abusers. *The Courage to Heal* includes an extended section on how and why to break off all connection with the "family of origin." Bass and Davis write, "It is painful to make a break with your family, but it is even more painful to keep waiting for a miracle."[21] The miracle appears to be the hope that the family will embrace the survivor's new memories.

Even family members who were not believed to be abusive should be avoided, according to McClure in *Reclaiming the Heart*. "In some unusual cases, family members can be a source of support, but this is the exception not the rule. . . . The power of family rules is very strong; there are usually unspoken instructions in incestuous families to 'go unconscious' and deny what the rest of the family doesn't see." McClure makes one exception: "However, family members who have been in therapy or are in their own recovery may be able to lend you valuable support."[22]

According to Elaine Gil, in her book *Outgrowing the Pain*, "when you give up the wish for the parents you hoped for, you can make room for the real people in your life." She goes on to note that "in addition to giving up the wish, you must also say good-bye to the ghosts of the parents you did have."[23]

Renee Fredrickson, as she often does, provides the most outlandish construction of this idea. In *Recovered Memories*, she charts an extended family tree with forty-one bubbles representing family members through three generations. Inside each of the bubbles is one of three letters: O for offender, D for denier, and V for victim. Within this family tree there are 13 offenders, 7 victims, and 21 deniers. In these family systems, according to Fredrickson, there are no other roles besides those of offender, victim, or denier. "Sexual abuse is always intergenerational, and everyone in a sexually abusive system takes on one of these roles. . . . When we look at the extended family chart, the number of potential abusers is shocking. Victims are growing up in family networks riddled with offenders who are protected by a cadre of deniers."[24]

In its cruelest lie, recovered memory therapy purports to provide replacement for all that the client is asked to sacrifice during therapy. The therapist is portrayed as the good, caring parent the patient never had, and her fellow survivors are promoted as a new family. This claim that therapy can provide a replacement for a family is the grandest promise that recovered memory therapy makes—and one that is pervasive in the movement. "Self-help groups can offer more than information, support, understanding, and acceptance," writes J. Patrick Gannon in *Soul Survivors*. "Self-help groups offer a sense of belonging that was probably not available in your family . . . these groups can become your surrogate family."[25]

"One of the best and most constructive ways for someone to take a big leap forward on the road to recovery from childhood sexual abuse is to join a therapy group specifically for abuse survivors," recommends Kristin Kunzman in *The Healing Way: Adult Recovery From Childhood Sexual Abuse*. [Groups] are a chance to experience what it is like in a safe family environment where family members are respected and protected."[26]

Mike Lew, in *Victims No Longer*, writes that many survivors decide "that, since their biological families are incapable of providing the needed support, they will create their own 'families.' . . . The new families may be made up of other incest survivors who have decided to learn how to support each other." Lew brags that some of the recovery groups that he has led have spontaneously turned themselves into "healthy functioning families."[27]

This belief that recovered memory therapy can provide a family is reflected in the writings of survivors as well. Writing about going back to her mother's funeral, one survivor wrote, "I could not depend on my family for [safety]. In the last year, people in my programs had become my real family. Some of them sent cards and flowers, and many kept me in their prayers."[28] Bass and Davis quote another survivor claiming to have "evolved past" her family.

These surrogate families that therapists encourage have an important role to play in the process of influence and belief change. By shifting the patients' attachments away from family and friends outside of therapy, the therapist effectively increases control over the patients. The principal lesson learned from the study of systems of influence is that peer-group influence is always the workhorse of the system. When therapists integrate patients into survivor-group "families," they effectively immerse them in a social system in which peer approval is granted when the patient conforms to the group's central value: that abuse "memories" recovered in therapy are always valid. Doubt of one's own abuse beliefs is frowned upon; doubt of anyone else's abuse beliefs is absolutely forbidden. Patients integrated into these groups quickly learn that their social survival and recognition of their newly claimed identities depend on silencing doubt and offering expression of belief.

Regardless of whether the patient had true cause to flee her real family (and even regardless of the current national debate over what constitutes a family), we should still question whether therapists should be explicitly offering clients the promise of creating a social structure as important and pervasive as a family. One could argue that creating such an important structure should not only be outside the scope of therapy but, more importantly, is far beyond the ability of the mental-health profession as it currently stands.

Indeed, reading the descriptions of what these new "families of choice" provide their members, one feels the authors straining for material. Mike Lew describes the "healthy functioning family" that he helped create "going out to dinner and inviting one another to coffee. They send each other notes and make phone calls. Group members have provided active support during intimidating life situations, such as accompanying one another to medical and dental appointments."[29] Describing what happens in the groups that can provide the "positive family dynamics" that the patient lacked as a child, Kunzman says that patients "can talk about how [their] childhood family operated and almost always find other group members who understand and sympathize. . . . Therapy groups can be a great place to give and receive caring touches and hugs."[30] Gannon's "surrogate families" offer survivors a place where they can be themselves "without fear of being judged, rejected or criticized . . . no one will criticize you or invalidate your point of view."[31]

From the available descriptions, it appears that what therapy is offering is an idealized and paper-thin version of a family. While we would not argue that all biological families possess some inalienable moral manifesto, the responsibilities and activities of what would reasonably constitute a family in any true sense of the term certainly go beyond what these therapists describe. In the therapy family, supreme emphasis is put on unconditional caring and unqualified acceptance. While no family would be complete without elements of caring and acceptance, this is certainly not all a family provides. In addition, it doesn't seem reasonable to view the role of any long-term family as solely a provider of "affirmations." Because the family is the social institution most charged with shaping beliefs and with inculcating socially responsible attitudes, why should we assume that all caring within a family be unconditional or that all acceptance be unqualified?

The emphasis on unqualified support goes to the heart of the distinction between a true family and what these therapists describe. Real families could be expected to provide a sense of belonging and support even during periods of strife within the family or within the social structure surrounding it. One of the most remarkable things about family structure is that it usually survives times of bad feelings and anger. One wonders what would happen to these therapy families if there came a time when criticism or conflict within the group were necessary—as they often are within a family. If the unqualified acceptance temporarily evaporated, would these people still be sending each other notes and holding each other's hands at dental visits? Would the bond between these people survive wars, famines, or holocausts?

And when these groups fail to fulfill the promise of becoming the loving family, will the client blame the therapist for offering a false promise? In all likelihood, the failure of the therapy group to become a true family would be perceived by patients as a failure on their part. Unfortunately, this further blow to the patient's self-image would likely increase his or her dependence on the therapist and the therapist's beliefs. While there is much anecdotal evidence that recovered memory clients fail to achieve the various nirvanas promised, there is no indication that therapists ever stop promising such rewards as new families and spiritual fulfillment.

There is another incitement to therapy which is even more disturbing and much harder to explain. Throughout the literature of the movement, the self-proclaimed experts on memory recovery glorify and sometimes glamorize the pain and suffering that they predict the patient will go through during treatment. In the *Courage to Heal*, for instance, Bass and Davis describe the "emergency stage," which they predict the patient will experience during treatment. This emergency stage will feel like "You walk out the door to go to work, and you fall on the steps and break your leg. Your spouse tries to drive you to the hospital, but the engine of your car blows up. You go back to the house to call an ambulance, only to find you've locked yourself out. Just as the police car pulls over to give you some help, the big earthquake hits, and your home, your spouse, your broken leg, and the police car all disappear into a yawning chasm. . . ."[32]

"Many women go through a period when sexual abuse is literally all they can think about," they go on to explain. "You may find yourself talking about it obsessively with anyone who will listen. Your life may become full of practical crises which totally overwhelm you. You may find yourself having flashbacks uncontrollably, crying all day long, or unable to go to work." During these emergency times, according to the book, it is likely that the recovered memory patient will become totally obsessed with the new abuse beliefs. Many women, they say, become suicidal, mutilate their bodies, and become unable to function in their daily lives. Some women go through the emergency stage for "several years."[33]

Often in the literature patients describe their self-mutilation and suicide attempts. "I've been suicidal many, many times and have been serious about it, but there is something in me that doesn't want to die," says a woman in *The Courage to Heal*. "I've slashed a razor down a vein, and the blood just spurted out, but I didn't die. I took twenty-eight meprobamate, which is a strong tranquilizer. Half of that should have killed me but I didn't die. I have a very strong will to live."[34]

The dramatic and grand way these distresses and self-destructive behaviors are described in the literature is troubling. It doesn't take much reading between the lines to see how Bass and Davis unintentionally glorify self-destructive behavior through the account of the woman who took an overdose of tranquilizers and cut her wrist. Clearly, the story does not emphasize the sad and desperate nature of the suicide attempt;

rather, it focuses on the patient's newfound proof—*thanks to the evidence of surviving the attempts*—that she has a superior "will to live." While almost all of the books, including *The Courage to Heal*, devote space to counseling readers against self-destructive actions, the descriptions of those behaviors often confer a badge of honor to those who have willingly hurt themselves. The patient was uncontrollably driven to these actions by the abuse, but she survived, the story goes, proving her inner strength.

Reading Davis's *The Courage to Heal Workbook*, one wonders whether the constant warnings about suicidal feelings might encourage the patient to focus on or draw out such feelings. She writes that "Most survivors have suicidal feelings at some point in the healing process. . . . If they didn't feel suicidal before they started to heal, the intensity of the healing process may cause them to contemplate suicide for the first time. . . . It is normal to have suicidal feelings as you deal with childhood feelings of terror and pain. When you experience the depths of your shame, it's likely that you will think about killing yourself." In one short page, then, suicidal tendencies are described as common, "normal," and "likely."[35] Survivors are instructed to "acknowledge the feelings" but not to kill themselves.

To help survivors acknowledge their feelings, Davis gives her readers the writing assignment to finish the following sentence: "When I am feeling suicidal I will" and then, "I will not." No doubt nonsuicidal survivors diligently working through this book of writing assignments would feel compelled to fill out this assignment as best they could. The specter of someone who has never considered suicide sincerely trying to finish the statement "When I feel suicidal" opens up the question of whether Davis's encouragement to "acknowledge" suicidal feelings might also set them in motion.

To counteract the stress and pain of the "emergency stage," Bass and Davis recommend that patients allow themselves to become obsessed about their memories. They also recommend that patients:

- Do as many nice things for yourself as possible.
- Drop what isn't essential in your life. Release the pressure any way you can. This means dropping unsupportive people, quitting activities, lightening your workload, getting extra child care. . . .
- Remember to breathe. Stay as connected to your body as you can. . . .
- Develop a belief in something greater than yourself. Spirituality can give you inspiration and strength.[36]

Davis, in her workbook, writes further that survivors should recognize that they are "no longer as capable or competent as you were before all this started." She goes on to tell those in the process of recovering memories: "Don't expect yourself to be able to handle things. Don't expect yourself to keep to your normal schedule, to have as much energy, or to be as productive. Don't expect to give much attention to your intimate relationships."[37] Most tellingly, Bass and Davis recommend, "Remind yourself that you're brave. This is a challenging, scary, difficult period. You don't have to do anything but live through it."

According to these experts, the difficulties of this therapy should not be overcome, but embraced. This acceptance of an inability to function even comes with rewards. For their failures to live up to their responsibilities, patients are encouraged to view themselves as courageous and to do "many nice things" for themselves. Implicit in this advice is the recommendation that patients ignore their pretherapy lives and retreat into the world of recovered memory therapy, where they will hear only support for the reality of their new beliefs and affirmations of their decision to focus only on recovery. Encouragement that patients drop other activities, abandon unsupportive friends, and cut down on their workload and child care seems a transparent recommendation that they make therapy the center of their lives. This is still another factor that could have the effect of increasing emotional investment in the recovered memory process.

The belief that recovered memory patients are so traumatized that they can't be expected to carry the burden of a normal life and must focus all their energy on living through the crisis seems to permeate the movement. Evidence that patients have pared down their lives and have trouble living with life's day-to-day demands can be found in the testimonies of survivors at group recovery meetings. At a recent meeting the authors attended, one recovered memory patient described not being able to walk down a busy street because of the potential that something she might encounter would trigger the surfacing of a repressed memory. Another woman who had recovered memories of ritual abuse took her allotment of time to explain that she had tried to "empower" herself that week by cleaning her room but had failed to complete the task. Still another woman described a confrontation with her boss, saying that it felt like a "revictimization."

Patients within the memory recovery movement receive encouragement not to overcome their problems through force of will but to surrender the will to the process. As Wendy Kaminer has noted in her broad critique of the adult recovery movement, it is an odd healing process indeed "that rewards people for calling themselves helpless, childish, addicted, and diseased and punishes them for claiming to be healthy." Those who embrace their sickness and become sicker are welcomed, "thus the search for identity is perversely resolved: all your bad behaviors and unwanted feelings become conditions of your being."[38]

In the glorification of the pain of treatment and the prediction that women in recovery will suddenly become unable to fulfill the demands of everyday life is a disturbing echo of another time. In *For Her Own Good*, Barbara Ehrenreich and Deirdre English write of a time last century when Western culture glorified illness and suffering in women. "Literature aimed at female readers lingered on the romantic pathos of illness and death. . . . Society ladies cultivated a sickly continence by drinking vinegar in quantity or, more effectively, arsenic. The loveliest heroines were those who died young, like Beth in *Little Women*, too good and too pure for life in this world."[39] Dr. Mary Putnam Jacobi observed of the trend in 1895 that "it is considered natural and almost laudable to break down under all conceivable varieties of strain. . . . Constantly considering their nerves, urged to consider them by well-intentioned but short-sighted advisors, they pretty soon become nothing but a bundle of nerves."[40] The recovered memory movement has revived this tradition of glorifying weakness in women and viewing them as illness-prone and self-indulgent.

From the description of the pain a recovered memory patient is expected to go through, it often sounds as if therapists are offering something of a death and rebirth ritual that requires that every support in the patient's life must crumble before she can rise from the ashes, renewed. The nirvana and understanding at the end of the treatment appears in the literature to be commensurate with the pain of the process. Unfortunately, women who do become dysfunctional or self-abusive, as predicted, are as likely to bond to it further. "If I had known anything could hurt this much or could be this sad, I never would have decided to heal," says one patient quoted in *The Courage to Heal*. "At the same time, you can't go back."[41]

CHAPTER SIX

Life with Father

Despite the claims of therapists, there is little glory in the painful process of recovered memory therapy. From our interviews and knowledge of those who have gone through this treatment, no patient has reached the promised nirvana. While the patient's prior doubts and questions about the narrative built in therapy can be overwhelmed by constant reinforcement from the therapist, the recovered memory literature, and the patient's community of fellow survivors, they don't appear to go away.

To explain the terrible momentum these therapeutic forces can achieve, we must turn from the therapists' writings and examine a story of a single individual subjected to this treatment. Jane Freeman's* story illustrates this momentum and also demonstrates how other siblings are often drawn into the debate over the past.

In 1988, Jane Freeman, a forty-five-year-old mother of two and an educational coordinator in a rape crisis center, sought therapy because she wasn't getting along with her boss.[1] Nothing Jane accomplished seemed to please her humorless supervisor. When Jane reported back from the seminars she often gave on the signs and symptoms of sexual abuse, her boss took every opportunity to point out how Jane had answered a question incorrectly or failed to fully cover a topic. For her therapist she picked Clark Parson, whom she had met several times at fund-raisers for the center. In their first session, Parson noted on his patient/inpatient form after the heading "Reason for Therapy" that Jane was "feeling overly criticized for her performance" at work. In the next entry, under "Relevant History," he noted, "Long history of being put on the defensive by her father's critical manner." Parson also wrote down that he planned only a short set of sessions, perhaps only one.

Jane had another vaguer reason for entering therapy that she didn't at first tell Parson, for it was not easily put into words. In her job, which she had held for less than a year, she was reading all sorts of literature on the aftereffects of sexual abuse and about how memories could be

---

*All the names in this story, including those of the therapists involved, have been changed.

repressed for years. To prepare for her public presentations, she referred to *The Courage to Heal* and *Secret Survivors* and many of the newsletters, brochures, and pamphlets that circulated through the center. She had a great respect for *The Courage to Heal*, and wrote in a review for a local paper that "the tone of the book is warm and personal and I haven't found a question this book couldn't answer." Jane learned from the literature she read that those victimized in their childhood often repress the experience until they recognize the symptoms later in life—symptoms that included low self-esteem, depression, feelings of shame, and anxiety attacks. Often, while she was listing off these symptoms in front of community audiences, she asked herself, "I wonder if I've been sexually abused?" The symptoms seemed to describe her pretty well. Thanks to the conflicts with her boss, she was definitely suffering from low self-esteem. Other things bothered her as well: she drank three glasses of wine most evenings, her heart often raced for no clear reason, and she had begun binging on gourmet ice-cream bars. In addition, sex with her husband had turned from unexciting to distasteful, and she came to hate the feeling of her husband's hands on her body. All in all, life had recently seemed like a round-the-clock job that she didn't like.

For two sessions Parson offered his new patient helpful advice on how to be more assertive at work, to stand up for her feelings and value her accomplishments. He also taught Jane exercises to help her relax and visualize peaceful scenes. He would tell her to imagine herself in an elevator. As she rode down from floor to floor, she would go deeper and deeper into a relaxed state. In this state she found it easy to vividly picture things in her head. After the first two sessions, Jane stopped therapy for three months and then came back when her life didn't improve much. Parson decided that Jane's problems at work were probably indicators of deeper problems with authority figures in her past. Since Jane had already mentioned that her boss's critical behavior reminded her of her father, Parson decided to focus his exploration there. Because Jane said she had few memories from childhood, he gave her a homework assignment to write a list of memories of her father—Parson believed that writing was one way to access information from the past. She came back with a two-page list of memories entitled "Life with Father."

For the most part the list was unremarkable, filled with some good memories and some painful ones. Jane remembered that her father had paid her one cent for every dandelion she could pull out of the lawn and how proud she was when she was able to save enough to buy a bicycle. She also wrote of the time when the family stove exploded, and when she stepped on a rake, and her father, who was a family doctor, cleaned and dressed the wound. She wrote about working together with her father on her algebra homework at the kitchen table. The only item that might be construed as sexual was that she recalled once, when she was very young, taking a shower with her father.

Because it was implicit in the focus of therapy at that point, Jane tried to focus on occasions when her father had unfairly criticized her. She remembered being spanked for stealing a sack of candy from the store. Once, when she had spilled a drink on the seat of the family car, her father had cursed at her. She also wrote that her father too often found fault in her personal habits. Whenever she picked up slang that he felt inappropriate for a young woman, he would correct her. The summer before she went to college, he was especially blunt about her table manners. Jane, who felt a little overweight, was worried at the time about leaving home and how she was going to fit in at college. At the dinner table one night that summer, her father told her that if she wanted to pledge a sorority, she would have to straighten up at the table and not let any food fall out of her mouth. Jane had been partially paralyzed during her difficult delivery, and the left side of her mouth often hung slightly open, causing some problems when she ate. Always self-conscious about this defect, and already worried about college, she ran crying from the room when her father berated her. Around the same time she missed several menstrual periods, and the doctor she visited explained that stress could interfere with her body's monthly cycles. In the writing assignment for Parson, Jane blamed her father's reproaches for her physical problems that summer.

When Parson read the document, he was struck by how few memories she had reported. Jane tried to think of more, but nothing came to mind. This seeming absence of memories made her think that something might really be wrong with her. Parson was also concerned about the mention of the shower scene and wondered whether Jane might have been sexually abused as a child. In that session they talked long and hard about her relationship with her father.

At the end of the second session, Parson asked a question that inexplicably panicked Jane. Referring to what Jane had written about her father, he asked her why she thought her father had been responsible for the disruption in her menstrual cycles. Hearing the question, Jane felt her heart race and suddenly wanted to run from the room. She felt sure that this meant something. As Jane would tell the story later, it was a combination of factors later that same afternoon that led to her first sexual-abuse image (which she learned to label as a flashback). Getting a glass of water at the kitchen sink, she suddenly held her hand up in the air and had a flash of a picture come to her head. She saw warm water coming down, and a small hand holding an adult penis. Immediately she identified the hand as hers and guessed she was perhaps four years old. The visualization lasted just an instant and it didn't include the face of the man. However, she felt sure the penis was her father's. She didn't react emotionally to the image. Standing at the sink, with the water running, examining her hand in the air, she thought only: "How strange."

In her next therapy session Jane told Parson about the freeze-frame image and asked him what he thought. Parson said that he didn't know for sure what the image meant, but encouraged her to continue writing and thinking about her distant past. He told her that they would find out what was behind the picture she had seen. Parson knew from his reading on the topic that it was common for people with traumatic pasts to have no access to the memories prior to therapy. Parson had read much of the popular literature of the recovered memory movement, including *Soul Survivors*, *The Courage to Heal*, and *The Courage to Heal Workbook*, but was mostly unaware of the scientific literature surrounding accuracy of recall. In recent years he had treated several patients who had also discovered previously unknown histories of abuse and felt adept at identifying the constellation of symptoms that trouble people who have been abused. While Parson did not immediately tell Jane that she had definitely discovered a repressed memory from her past, he had seen this same scenario in other patients he treated.

For the next month and a half Jane worked in and out of therapy on her memories, but nothing startling surfaced. They continued to work on the relaxation exercises in which she imagined riding down an elevator. Although Parson knew that there was not much of a difference between formal hypnosis and the relaxation exercises, they talked about the possibility of using hypnosis specifically to dig for her memories.

Six weeks after her first visualization, another disturbing picture popped into her mind when, one evening, she glanced into the bathroom and saw her husband standing over the toilet with his pants unzipped. She again saw a mental image of a child's hand touching a penis. For a second time she felt sure that it was her and her father. This time, instead of being in a shower, she saw the penis urinating. After this flash, the images came faster, perhaps one or two a week. Always they were triggered by something she saw or heard in her surroundings. One day when she was sniffed by a strange dog on the street, she saw an image of her father forcing the family dog to lick her genitals. On another occasion, while eating a chocolate ice-cream bar she visualized her father covering his penis with chocolate and forcing her to lick it clean. Some of the scenes mirrored the sexual-abuse literature she was immersed in at the time. Reading a book called *Spiders and Flies*, she began to feel anxious when she learned that sexual offenders sometimes put treats and coins in their pockets and then encourage children to reach in for them. Reading the passage, she was able to visualize a man's pants pocket and decided that the exact scenario had happened to her as a child. Over the course of months the scenes accumulated. According to Parson's notes, the scenes included oral genital contact, fellatio, voyeurism, and sexual intercourse with her father. Often the pictures came while she was having sex with her husband. These mental images, which she identified as memories, were sometimes nearly identical to what she was seeing and hearing at the time she had them. One day, hearing her husband react to his orgasm, she heard traces of her father's voice. Performing oral sex with her husband, she suddenly saw what she thought was herself holding her father's penis instead of her husband's.

She told Parson about each of these flashes and they discussed them at length and tried to discover the details behind the scenes. Guessing the ages for each picture, they created a time line for the abuse. As she talked over the abuse images with Parson, they began to have more structure and meaning. Discussing them, she found she could surround them with details they didn't have at first. The new images that were coming into her mind on a regular basis no longer seemed singular freeze-frames, but included action. Once, momentarily blinded by a light, she visualized a scene of her father taking her into his examining room and abusing her under the surgical light with a long medical instrument. In this image she not only pictured him standing over her with the silver tool, but also ushering her in and out of the examination room. The images became as clear as if she were watching a video on the television. As she worked over the scenes in therapy, she found she could rewind and play back particular parts of the dramas as one might on a VCR.

While her memories up to that point often included details about how her father had kept the abuse secret from her mother and the rest of the family, she began to receive new scenes that included her mother. While at first she believed that her father had kept their encounters secret from her mother and the rest of the family, she came to understand that her mother had known about the abuse and perhaps even encouraged it. Then came new revelations—her mother had not only known about the abuse, she had taken part. In one of these scenes, Jane saw her mother changing her diaper and her father instructing her mother how to orally copulate her. From what she can see of her body, Jane believed that she was less than one year old. In another vision, Jane is older and in bed with both her parents when her father teaches her how to touch and kiss her mother's body.

The knowledge that her mother had not only known about the abuse but had taken part in her sexual torture was particularly hard for Jane to believe. She and Parson worked session after session to transcend her denial both intellectually and emotionally. That is to say that once Jane came to accept that her mother was involved, she then had to work to *feel* the truth of the memories.

After the first dozen flashbacks, Jane's life fell apart. Most days she felt confused and overwhelmed. Her relations with her co-workers deteriorated. Her husband tried to support her but would later admit that he thought she might be going crazy. Her life was in "pieces on the floor," Jane said. On the advice of her therapist she joined a weekly group in which incest survivors could share their stories. She determined to pursue her memories and someday deserve the title of "survivor" of abuse. She left her job at the rape crisis center and found an administrative post at a manufacturing plant. Her job performance suffered because of her increasingly common anxiety attacks and flashbacks. In addition to the wine she drank every night, she began to take sleeping pills and anti-anxiety medication.

After several awful months, during which she continued to picture new scenes of abuse, Jane and Parson decided that it was time to confront her abusers. She compiled a long list of abuse memories, composed a letter to read to her father, and informed her mother and father when and where to meet her.

Conrad Bridges was approaching his eightieth birthday when his daughter Jane called and asked him to meet her at a therapist's office a few suburbs away. Tall and lanky, Conrad was a fit man for his age. Although his hearing was not perfect and his stamina seemed on a constant ebb, he managed to play golf every so often. His wife, Marybeth, was several years his junior, and a lifelong homemaker. Before they attended their respective conseling appointments, the couple both believed that they had managed to raise their children in a respectable way. With her five girls, Marybeth had been strict when it came to issues of manners and how to be ladylike. She took it as her personal goal to raise them to be "pure young women." "I took my job very seriously," Marybeth attests. "I was to raise them to be pure and to train them in various talents, develop their swimming abilities, their dancing abilities. It was a crusade of mine that those girls would be well brought up." She remembers Jane as the director of all the games among the children. She wasn't bossy, but seemed always to be organizing some activity or other. "She couldn't sing; she was good natured and well mannered," recalls Marybeth. "She had a sweetness all her own."

Conrad remembers not having as much time to spend with his family as other men might. As a doctor, his hours were long and sometimes unpredictable—although he indulged his passion for golf with two eighteen-hole games each week. Frequently he couldn't make it home in time for dinner, but he remembers fondly the times he did. To compensate, he tried, when he had time, to establish a one-on-one relationship with each of his children. When he had to drive three hours each week to a nearby city to get his tuberculosis treatments, he would sometimes pick one of his children to go along. He cannot remember any problems he had with Jane until the summer before she left for college and they had argued over her table manners. Looking back on that incident, he attests that he hadn't meant to be cruel. He knew Jane intended to go through sorority rush and recalled from his own college days that members of sororities and fraternities could be pretty mean about the way a person ate, talked, and dressed.

Both of the confrontations between Jane and her mother and father were carefully orchestrated by Parson. Both parents were told not to talk to their daughter while she read her statement informing them of the effects the abuse had caused throughout her life. When Marybeth listened to the first part of the list, she didn't understand what she was hearing. The descriptions of the sexual acts were like nothing she had ever heard—certainly nothing like she and her husband had ever taken part in. Masturbation and oral sex had little to do with their sex life over the years. "Did he put his penis in?" Marybeth broke in at one point and asked. At this Parson told her that she must stay quiet, and that abuse could certainly entail things other than intercourse. She was given a pen and piece of paper to write down her questions. As Jane continued down the list, the paper Marybeth held in her hands stayed blank. She was too stunned to write anything.

When Jane described the abuse scenes that involed Marybeth, Marybeth knew something was horribly wrong with her daughter's memory. The idea that she would have her daughter sexually please her was repugnant and horrifying. And performing oral sex on an infant? Even with a gun to her head, she believes, no one could have forced her to do something like that to her daughters.

Conrad was also given a piece of paper and a pencil at the beginning of his meeting with his daughter and asked not to respond until Jane had read what she had to say to him. She first read him a three-page statement that she had composed for the occasion. It began:

> A long time ago when I was a little girl you touched me in ways that you shouldn't have and you made me touch you in ways that you shouldn't have. What you did terrified and confused me. It was so awful that I repressed those memories for years. You helped me forget because you told me over and over again as I was growing up that I couldn't remember anything before the age of five. And I believed you because you were my father and the smartest man I ever knew.
>
> Now at the age of 45 I am beginning to remember what you did to me before the age of 5. I have been reliving those events the past few months, the scenes unfolding at unexpected times before my eyes much like a familiar old movie. It has been shocking, overwhelming and frightening.

She went on to list the scenes of abuse she had visualized and the problems those experiences had caused in her life. "Because you didn't want anyone to find out what you did, you did certain things to shut me up. Later you attempted to demolish my trust in myself through emotional abuse. You set up impossible, irrational tasks so that you could teach me that I could not trust myself to achieve. I could not trust my judgment to do the right thing because I was never right."

The statement ended by asking him to write her a letter explaining why he had abused her and to explain how he had gotten away with it without anyone else noticing. Conrad was confused by what he had heard. None of the strange and terrible things she said corresponded with anything he could remember. He wasn't allowed to deny the accusations or talk to his daughter because Parson announced that the meeting was closed shortly after Jane read her statement.

Later, Conrad and Marybeth tried to remember anything in Jane's childhood that might have sparked such thoughts. Marybeth remembered that the children sometimes slipped into bed with them when they had nightmares or when one of them was scared by a thunderstorm. She remembers allowing them to stay for a while but always putting them back in their own beds. She also remembers one time when Jane, who was perhaps twelve, had climbed into bed with her father one morning while she was caring for one of the babies. When she came back in the room, her husband was getting out of bed and going into the bathroom. There was a bulge in his pajamas. She knew that he often got an erection in the morning when he had to use the bathroom. Her mother felt Jane shouldn't be seeing her father in this state and scolded her, saying that she was too old to get into bed with her father. Conrad couldn't remember the incident.

At his eightieth birthday party a few weeks later all his daughters attended, but Jane kept her distance from her father. She had told her second-to-youngest sister, Tammy, of her new revelations and about the confrontation with her father. At the party Tammy urged her father to apologize to Jane even if he didn't remember what had happened. Perhaps with the apology, he could smooth things over and lessen the tension that was obviously growing between them. A few days later, Conrad drove out to his daughter's house to try to straighten things out. Jane came out on the front porch but did not invite him in. "I wanted to apologize," he said to his daughter. "I'm just here to say that I'm sorry."

Feeling that he was confessing to his crimes against her, Jane's heart raced.

"What are you sorry for?" she asked.

"I'm sorry that you have those thoughts in your head," he answered.

After the therapy confrontation, the scenes in Jane's head continued to grow worse. The abuse lasted long after she was five years old, she came to believe. Rubbing her body up against her husband's one night, a new image came to her of being forced to do the same thing to her baby brother when she was seventeen. This revelation was a blow: the abuse had continued until she had left for college.

As the visual images became stronger over the course of therapy, Jane began to experience waking hallucinations and often had trouble distinguishing between reality and what she would picture in her mind. Glancing at her male office partner at work, she would glimpse his penis hanging out of his pants. Looking twice, however, she would see that his pants were zipped. Another time, watching television with friends, she saw the man on the program rubbing himself as though he were masturbating. In the next moment she wasn't sure what he was doing. When she looked around at the other people in the room, she realized no one else had seen what she had. Eventually she couldn't have sex with her husband in the dark because every time the lights went off she could clearly visualize her father standing in the room, watching.

At the same time the visual images in her head began entering the reality around her, the images she believed came from her past began getting bizarre. In one scene she saw herself at the age of one, being forced to watch as her father rapes a dog. In another episode she is four years old, in her father's arms, at a stable. He carries her around the back of a horse and makes her insert her fist and arm into the animal's anus. This memory was so disturbing that it took her several weeks to excavate completely. Later she remembers having to do a similar act, only this time on her father. She also reconstructed a time when her father made her eat a bowl of her own feces, forcing her to chew twenty times after each bite.

How she managed to forget the abuse is a question that didn't seem to come up much in therapy. When the scenes first began to appear to her, Jane assumed that she had repressed each of these horrible instances separately and almost instantaneously. At another point she believed that she might have dissociated during the abuse such that the memories had never entered her consciousness but rather been recorded only unconsciously. However, the notion that the memories disappeared right after the abuse began to contradict her later stories. Some of the material found later in therapy—including one story in which she remembers thinking about the abuse "all the time" and another in which she reveals the incest secret to a childhood friend—clearly imply that she would have had memories of the abuse at the time it was taking place. The rationale for how and why Jane repressed these experiences slowly changes from one of instant repression to a repression mechanism triggered by her father's threats. As the more bizarre scenes surfaced, she went back to believing that she repressed the memories immediately. She would eventually attest that the abuse with the horse, for example, was wiped from her consciousness the instant after it happened. These contradictions apparently did not disturb her or Parson's faith that each of her visualizations were valid and accurate memories.

One after another, Jane's five sisters began appearing in the images of abuse. The oldest of five sisters and one brother, she remembered her father telling her to teach the other daughters the tricks of arousing and satisfying him. "I made them do it right," one entry read in Jane's expanding list of abuse scenes. "He would patronize me or get mad at me when I didn't do it right. I wanted them [her sisters] to do it right. I was responsible. I was the oldest. I instructed, taught because I knew how to do it. I showed them how. I see this. We're in bed naked, he's on his back. The little sister is masturbating him, but not well, so I show her. It was a crazy competition. We were supposed to compete, but daddy would decide who'd win."

Jane decided she had better call all her sisters together to discuss the matter. For the occasion she rented two adjoining hotel rooms. When they were gathered Jane informed them that she had been sexually assaulted by their father and read them a list of the memories she had uncovered. All the sisters, except for Tammy, who had heard the charges before, were stunned. Jane told them that she had confronted her parents and that their mother had said it wasn't abuse unless she and her father had engaged in actual intercourse. All the sisters were shocked that their mother would say something like this—not only because it was so obviously wrong, but that it seemed a tacit admission that some abuse had occurred.

None of the sisters, however, could recall their father sexually abusing them or anything about the episodes Jane described. Although disappointed, Jane was not surprised. She told them in detail of how long and difficult the process of finding these memories was and of how the knowledge initially came in still pictures—triggered by unexplainable anxieties—and only later turned into "full-blown memories." She explained the pervasive effect of the abuse, including her troubles at work and in her sex life, her frequent depressions, and her inability to cry or express emotions. She encouraged them to look again both at their current lives and childhood to see if there weren't events that might suggest that something happened.

One of the sisters, Meredith, said that she remembered a time when she was in the shower at about the age of twelve and her father had come in the bathroom and yelled instructions about how to wash herself thoroughly from head to toe. While he never opened the bathroom curtain, she remembered feeling awkward and embarrassed. She also remembered one time when she was sitting in a chair with her legs spread apart and her father had told her to put her legs together. Allison, the second-from-the-oldest, said that she had recently been bothered by the mental image of something large coming toward her face and the feeling of being smothered. At the time she was having emotional problems with her husband, and related the feeling to the fact that she didn't enjoy performing oral sex with him. Later she thought the feeling might be a memory of breast-feeding as an infant. Jane's revelations made Allison wonder if the suffocation might be related to something else. When it was her turn, Paula, the middle sister of the five, told the group a story she always seems to remember of a man asking a little girl to "play with his dolly," only it wasn't a dolly, it was his penis. The story seems to always have been with her but she did not know who the man or the girl were or whether she had been told the story, experienced it, or imagined it. Tammy couldn't remember any scenes, but told Jane that she completely believed that she was telling the truth.

Over the next months, all the sisters, especially Tammy, thought a good deal about Jane's new beliefs and their own memories from childhood. At the time, Tammy's marriage was crumbling and she wondered whether the problems in her life could be traced to traumatic experiences that she couldn't remember. She bought two books on incest survivors and found a therapist who seemed knowledgeable about recovering memories.

A few months later Tammy decided to take a personal retreat to explore her memories. She rented a cabin in the mountains, packed several books on repressed memories and child abuse, and took a long weekend. At the cabin she read and thought hard about her life. She called her sister to talk about her abuse memories. The two talked emotionally for some time about their childhood. Jane described the new abuse scenes she had recently pictured in her mind. Later in the conversation they spoke of their rooms and the toys they had shared. Tammy asked her sister if she recalled a storybook they owned about dolls coming alive to play. Jane had loved the book and had often wished as a child that her own dolls could magically come to life. While talking about the book, Tammy discovered that if she closed her eyes she could visualize the illustrations in the story with remarkable clarity. She described for Jane one picture she could see in her mind. In the story, when the dolls went out to play, they all got dirty and had to be washed and hung out to dry on a clothesline. In her mind, Tammy could see the picture of the dolls dangling upside down by their toes. Then something strange came into the picture: one of the dolls had a wooden stirring spoon between her legs. It didn't make any sense, Tammy thought: "that wasn't part of the picture." Then she got another, terrifying visualization. It was sort of a half image of a baby's chubby thighs and a wooden spoon handle coming toward them. Suddenly she felt a pain in her abdomen. In a panic, she described what she was feeling and seeing to Jane and suddenly the pain dissipated. It was a memory, they agreed: Tammy had also been abused. From the look of the baby thighs she had seen, Tammy concluded that she must have been about one year old. From the pain that accompanied the still image, the spoon she had seen must have been used as a sexual device.

As they discussed what Tammy had just experienced, Jane received a new vision of her own. In the picture she was four years old and her dad called her and her sister over to the kitchen table, where little Tammy, just one year old, lay on her back. Her father leaned over and kissed the child's genitals. Then he instructed the older sisters to hold Tammy down by the shoulders while he inserted a wooden spoon handle into her vagina. "I was there," Jane blurted out on the phone. "I saw what happened."

With confirmation from her sister, and no satisfactory confession from her father or mother, Jane decided to look into the possibility of suing her parents to help cover her mounting therapy bills and to receive compensation for the emotional turmoil she had suffered. Through her survivors support group she located a lawyer who had handled many of these cases. Upon meeting her, Jane immediately liked the lawyer, a kindly and fast-talking woman. The lawyer expressed every confidence in the accuracy and truthfulness of Jane's memories and explained that state law had changed only a few years previously so that those who didn't remember their abuse until they were older could sue the perpetrators. She told Jane that she had handled dozens of such cases and that most had settled out of court. She also mentioned to Jane that many survivors of abuse had found the legal process a valuable and important part of their healing. The lawyer had played a major role in the drive to change the state's legislation and had subsequently handled a number of lucrative civil actions.

Despite the promises from her lawyer, the lawsuit proved far from healing for Jane. Her therapist's notes are filled with references to the constant increasing anxiety. Jane's parents refused to settle or pay any money for crimes they didn't commit, or help pay for a therapy process that they were convinced was destroying their daughter. To further "empower" herself, Jane contacted a local newspaper reporter to tell her story. The three-layer bold-type headline read, DAUGHTER ACCUSES DOCTOR FATHER. Jane was quoted in the paper saying that she had remembered nothing about her childhood until she entered therapy, and that she was suing her parents as "part of my healing process" and on behalf of other survivors who lacked the money to bring similar suits. After reading the article in the morning paper, Conrad and Marybeth wrote a new will that excluded Jane.

Good news soon came from sister Paula. Her memory of the man making the little girl play with his penis had evolved since she told it when the sisters were together in the hotel room. Thinking it over again and again, Paula became convinced that the little girl must have been herself and that the man was most likely her father. While Paula's and Tammy's new beliefs helped in confirming Jane's memories, none of the three other daughters or her brother Matthew had been able to remember the years of continuous abuse that, Jane knew from her own visualizations, so engulfed their childhood.

During this time, Parson, Jane's therapist for the last year and a half, moved to another state amidst allegations of having had sexual relations with a patient. Asking other adult survivors, Jane found Donna Pearlman. Pearlman had helped many survivors of abuse uncover their memories and made a concerted effort to stay current with the quickly evolving understanding of memory and trauma. (Over the course of therapy with Jane, Pearlman would attend several seminars with the luminaries of the repressed memory, multiple personality world, including Renee Fredrickson, Walter Young, and Richard Kluft.) Pearlman's notes of her therapy sessions with Jane describe a troubled woman who she "feared was going crazy."

As the trial approached, Jane's beliefs in her victimization continued to expand. Her memories now included new perpetrators, including the family dentist and one of the doctors her father worked with. Jane's list now numbered over ninety different memories and involved every member of the family over the entire course of her childhood. In her new understanding of her childhood, her father's sexual appetite was insatiable and omnivorous. According to Jane, he was a masochist and sadist who practiced bondage, torture with surgical instruments, and all types of oral, vaginal, and anal sex. While watching or participating, Jane believed she had witnessed her father perform sexual acts with infants, girls and boys of all ages, women, male prostitutes, and several species of animals. In the history of sexual deviancy, he made de Sade look shy. The childhood of the Bridges children had been one long sexual-abuse nightmare and Jane felt she had been the only one who had worked hard enough on her memories to face the truth.

She became frustrated that her siblings had not sought therapy to find the memories that would confirm her beliefs. As she worried about their mental health, her own deteriorated. In the notes of her therapist, Jane reported becoming more and more "scattered" and felt that almost any conflict, fear, or emotional encounter made her dissociate. She and Pearlman worked hard to overcome her inability to cry but had little success. After she had a new series of flashbacks in which her parents tied her to a bed and abused her, she began to wonder if she had multiple personalities lurking in her subconscious. She knew MPD was common among women who came to believe they were abused as severely as she had been. Hiding alter personalities would explain why she had so few childhood memories, as well as her recently noticed tendency to lose concentration at stressful moments.

Jane's rage toward her father swept over to many other people in her life. She began to "see everyone as her father," her therapist noted, and realized how little she trusted her husband when he was around their daughter. She felt everything in her life was "100 percent" her responsibility. Although Pearlman counseled her on ways of relieving responsibility and how to recognize her wants and needs above others', stress seemed to mount. In a two-sentence therapy note, Pearlman summed up the state of Jane's life: "Anxiety re: marriage, difficulty concentrating at work. Lawsuit an ever-present stress." The next week Jane reported feeling suicidal. A few sessions later she described the urge to cut her hands. Pearlman notes that she helped Jane "Focus on allowing self to be self." At the following appointment Jane came in with bandages covering self-inflicted wounds on her hands.

At the nonjury trial Jane asked the court to award her $650,000 in damages and compensation for the pain she had suffered to pay for her past and future therapy. Over the course of the three weeks of testimony, the entire Bridges family testified, as did many therapists, memory and influence experts, and the family doctor. The defense even called in a veterinarian to tell the court what a horse's reaction might be if one were to stand directly behind the animal and force an arm into its large intestine. Of the five children besides Jane, three said that they could remember no abuse, while Tammy and Paula testified confidently that they too had recently come to the realization that their father had sexually abused them. Each day the court was filled with adult survivors from local therapy groups who had come to support Jane.

After the closing statements the judge would comment, "I left the courtroom without any clear feeling of the ultimate decision I would make." Eventually, based on the "more likely than not" standard used in civil trials, the judge awarded Jane $150,000. In his decision, he remarked that he had grave doubts about many of Jane's recollections but noted that the single memories of the two other sisters supported her contention that she had been abused. "I want also to tell you that there are doubts in my mind," he wrote in the decision. "There will always be doubts in my mind."

Because all of Jane's memories came about in the same manner, the decision to believe some and to doubt others surprised both sides. Jane took the decision more as a defeat than a victory. The $150,000 would hardly cover her therapy bills and lawyer's fees. When a reporter asked her what she thought of the decision, she burst into tears and sobbed inconsolably—she had, at least, regained her ability to cry.

In her most recent visualizations, Jane has noticed some disturbing symbolism that suggests that she might soon take the next step up the survivorship ladder. In one scene she watched her father put her into a coffin and close the lid. In another he makes her do something—she is still trying to picture what that something is—to the dead body of a young girl. Later she sees herself tied to a bed, naked in a strange place, watching as someone puts a snake on her stomach. In the scene her father's face turns ugly, like a monster. The coffin, snake, and young corpse convinced Jane that she probably possessed a whole new set of memories. She signed up for a therapy retreat and determined to follow these new dark clues. During an exercise where the participants were encouraged to express their anger by beating on phone books with rubber hoses, Jane lapsed into a trance. In this trance she let herself literally "step toward" the new memories. "I stepped forward to get closer to the memory," Jane remembers of the terrifying experience. "I was looking down at it and I could see it. It's dark and there's a big fire with people around it in masks and robes. They're standing around a child."

Hypnosis and the Creation of Pseudomemories

The stories that therapists tell in their journal articles and books invariably glorify the work of recovered memory therapy. In accounts of their own work they often tell of the hardships of being a selfless healer. The insights they gain through the daring explorations of their patients' psyches are always portrayed as profound. While the case histories reported by recovered memory therapists usually include a dramatic moment when the process of recovering memories stymies and the client's symptoms suddenly worsen, the stories almost invariably end with breathtaking breakthroughs. The therapist and patient overcome their uncertainty, push through the amnesiac barrier, and discover the horrible truth hiding in the patient's past. It is, of course, not surprising that the case reports written by therapists are self-serving, and we certainly do not suggest that they be dismissed for this reason. Therapists, in telling their stories and presenting their theories, have every reason to make themselves appear thoughtful, careful, and effective healers. Because of this, one would suspect that their own writings would be the least likely place to find evidence to support the theory that repressed memory therapists often tacitly coerce their clients into the false belief that they were sexually abused. It is a testament to these therapists' faith in their methods that it is just this source—their own publications—that forms a substantial portion of our evidence. The mistakes they reveal are particularly telling because, by exposing them in these formats, it is quite clear that these therapists don't consider them mistakes at all, but examples of their finest and most careful work. Often these therapists write of the power of hypnosis in breaking the barrier that supposedly separates the patient from unconscious repressed memories. Defined broadly as any intentionally or unintentionally induced trance state, the hypnosis can include Amytal interviews and age regression as well as relaxation and guided imagery exercises. In their enthusiasm for their work, recovered memory therapists often uncritically promote hypnosis as one of the most effective methods for finding memories of abuse.

Before examining the research on the relationship between hypnosis and memory, consider the story of Sue, which Dolores Siegel and Charles Romig published in the *American Journal of Family Therapy*. According to the paper's authors, Sue entered couples therapy with the fear that her fiancé, Jack, would break off the engagement. Sue's fear seemed well grounded in the fact that she had broken off her engagement with Jack not once but twice—each time only a week before the planned wedding. Sue also reported fears of the dark and difficulty sleeping alone. She also told of dreams, one of which was of sleeping in a crib and seeing someone about to tickle her. The authors also note that, "As she complained about her fiancé, she would periodically begin angrily to berate her father, then return to complaining about her fiancé. When this was pointed out to her, she was unaware of mentioning her father and insisted she had always had an excellent relationship with him.[1]

"These combined factors," write the authors about the information discovered in the first session with Sue, "led the therapist to suspect that this client had been sexually molested as a child and that her father was the likely abuser. Judging from her insistence that she had a fine and loving relationship with him, the therapist decided that an "indirect approach would be the wisest means to access memories of abuse." The key to this "indirect approach" involved hypnosis. In the second session the therapist put Sue into a deep trance and told her what was described as an "embellished" version of the following tale:

There once was a small kingdom with a powerful but friendly king who was well liked by his subjects. He was very pleasant and was willing to meet with almost anyone to talk about anything. He had a family of two sons and a daughter. . . . It was a happy kingdom, but something uneasy was going on in the castle. Like most kings, this king had a wizard who did what wizards do. The king loved his wizard, who was very wise and powerful. . . . The wizard was very loyal to the king, which was important because the wizard had a powerful secret word that would remove all the king's ability to rule if the wizard ever spoke it. If the word were ever said, the king would not only lose his crown, but his family would probably stop respecting and loving him, as would most of the king's subjects. Only the kind and the wizard knew about the magic word. Since the king loved the wizard and needed the wisdom and power of the wizard, and since the wizard was very loyal to the king, the king never feared that the wizard would say the magic word. They lived happily until one day the wizard wanted to visit other kingdoms to learn more and become a better wizard. This frightened the king because even though the wizard would make sure the king still ruled wisely, the king was afraid the wizard might meet someone and want to marry. The king was afraid the wizard would change loyalties to someone else and someday might say the magic word. The king and wizard had many arguments about this, and finally the king told the wizard to leave and return only when the king gave permission. The king even convinced himself that he had enough power to overcome the power of the wizard's secret word. Bitter words were exchanged, and the entire family felt much sadness as the wizard left, for you see, the wizard was the king's only daughter.[2]

Sue appeared greatly upset by the ending of the story. While she was still under hypnosis, the therapist suggested to Sue that she not remember the specifics of the story but that she soon might have many confusing thoughts about someone she cared for. Awakened from her trance, Sue was so shaken by the experience that she had to be driven home. In the next session, Sue revealed for the first time her belief that her father might have sexually abused her while she was a child.

What can be made of this account of therapy? According to Siegel and Romig's analysis, "This case demonstrates how the story that was told in trance allowed suppressed memories to enter the client's aware-ness. . . . The story gave her the option of choosing how to respond to her own experiences, which paralleled those of the fictional characters of the story. She chose to stop denying her victimization and approach her abuse directly, thereby setting the stage for therapy to begin." For the therapists/authors, this work was an achievement worth sharing with the professional community—a triumph of therapeutic technique over the client's "strong defensiveness."[3]

This clinical achievement illustrates the general attitude toward hypnosis within the recovered memory movement. Judith Herman, in *Trauma and Recovery*, touts hypnosis as a "powerful" technique to uncover lost memories of trauma. "In addition," she writes, "many other techniques can be used to produce an altered state of consciousness in which dis-sociated traumatic memories are more readily accessible."[4] These meth-ods include intensive group therapy and sodium amytal interview. As described by Renee Fredrickson in *Repressed Memories*, "Hypnosis is a structured process of relaxation designed to produce a state of dissociation. This induced state of dissociation facilitates your ability to get in touch with unconscious parts of yourself, such as feelings, awareness, or mem-ories. While in the trance state, you can tap into your imagistic memories and retrieve repressed memories of abuse."[5] To be fair, recovered memory therapists are not alone in their faith that hypnosis is a special conduit to memory. Clinicians have long been impressed by the apparent ability of hypnotized patients to vividly recall significant events from their distant past. As Fred Frankel, Harvard Medical School professor, writes in his essay "The Clinical Use of Hypnosis in Aiding Recall," "The notion that patients after hypnotic induction are able to recall considerably more of their past than when in the waking state has been universally viewed as a major advantage provided by hypnosis."[6] While many therapists have been aware of the body of research showing that recollections under hypnosis can be distorted or complete fantasies, this knowledge has been, for two good reasons, largely ignored. First, because therapists have no access to the literal truth of the client's past, trying to determine the validity of hypnotically enhanced memory (or any other memory, for that matter) becomes a difficult and distracting task. Except for memories that defy logic (for instance, where a Vietnam veteran patient "remembers" being killed in battle), the therapist cannot know for certain whether the event described happened or not. The second reason why therapists have largely ignored the question of the validity of memories is because recall under hypnosis can have a therapeutic effect *regardless* of its truthfulness. Simply put, therapists have been more concerned with the meaning of what is created in hypnosis than whether it is memory or belief. That is, if a Vietnam veteran lives out a fantasy recollection of being captured and killed by Viet Cong, the importance of his addressing and "working through" that deep fear he carried with him throughout the war can be valuable despite the obvious fact that the event never occurred. No therapist would dismiss such imaginings simply because they have no basis in reality—meaning is preferred over history. Although memories produced under hypnosis may be "fused or distorted," according to Frankel, because "the affects associated with the true or false memory are reflective of deep-seated wishes and fears, the negotiation or working through under reassuring circumstances is clearly relevant and helpful."[7]

This logic, Frankel knows, does not apply to the creation of a belief that a patient was sexually abused by his or her parent (or for that matter, a kindergarten teacher, neighbor, or priest). Any curative effect gained by a patient coming to falsely believe that her father raped her when she was young would certainly be outweighed by the psychological damage that fostering this belief would have in the long run. Unfortunately, many recovered memory therapists appear not only to assume "memories" found under hypnosis are always true, but are also unaware of the wealth of evidence indicating that the technique has shown a powerful tendency to blur the mind's ability to distinguish between the memory of a real event and a scene imagined in trance. Running counter to almost all evidence, recovered memory therapists often offer the idea that visualizations of abuse, whether recovered under hypnosis or not—cannot *not* be true.

In order to analyze the question of whether hypnosis is a special conduit to memory, it is first necessary to address what hypnosis is. Unfortunately, defining hypnosis is something of a quagmire. In his book *They Call It Hypnosis*, Robert Baker points out that those who study the topic can't fully agree that hypnosis exists as a definable and separate state of consciousness. Perhaps hypnosis can best be described as a state of focused attention on a specific set of mental images and thoughts with an accompanying restricted awareness of one's surroundings. Trance can perhaps be compared to the sensation of being so fully absorbed in the images produced from reading a novel that one loses track of time, tunes out surrounding sounds, and concentrates exclusively on the scene being created in one's imagination. The difference in a trance is that the images and sensations imagined are not taken from a book but from one's own mind and the suggestions of the hypnotist. Most researchers note that hypnosis allows the patient to set aside critical judgment, become more willing to accept suggestion and engage unselfconsciously in fantasy and role playing.

As for how hypnosis interacts with memory, much experimental work has been done. The primary problem of judging the accuracy of historical accounts in therapy (that neither the client nor the therapist has undistorted knowledge of the true historical event in the client's past is a hurdle that experimental researchers can easily jump. By showing test subjects movies, pictures, or lists of words and later testing them with and without the use of hypnosis, they can quite accurately determine the effects of hypnosis on normal recall. Experimenters have found that hypnotized subjects are more likely to give more correct *and* incorrect responses to the memory test than waking subjects given the same test. While the additional correct answers appear at first to show that hypnosis does have some special access to the memory, a further test shows this not to be true. When the nonhypnotized subjects are required to simply concentrate longer or to guess, their number of right answers rises to the levels of the hypnotized subjects.

Most importantly, several studies have shown that a hypnotized subject's confidence increases for both correct and incorrect answers. That is, while there is usually a positive relationship between confidence in one's memory and the accuracy of that memory at least in the short term, hypnosis lessens that relationship. Professor Peter Sheehan, of the University of Queensland, Australia, tested the extent to which hypnotizable subjects would adopt false memories of events they witnessed. He found that those people who were highly hypnotizable would often adopt suggested inaccurate details into their memories of what they witnessed. Summarizing the results of another study on hypnosis and recall, he concluded that hypnosis "does seem to be distinctively linked with the confidence or conviction that hypnotic subjects have in the accuracy of their reports. Regardless of the literal truth value of hypnotized subjects' memory reports, confidence is a reasonably reliable accompaniment of hypnotic testimony."[8] It appears that the apparent vividness of hypnotic recall can crystallize imagined events and give them the appearance of memory. Summarizing the relevant studies on the topic, the Council on Scientific Affairs of the American Medical Association published a warning that hypnotically refreshed memories could not be relied on. "Contrary to what is generally believed by the public, recollections obtained during hypnosis not only fail to be more accurate but actually appear to be generally less reliable than recall." The report, published in the *Journal of the American Medical Association* in 1985, went on to conclude that "in no study to date has there been an increase in accuracy associated with an appropriate increase in confidence in the veracity of recollections. Consequently, hypnosis may increase the appearance of certitude without a concurrent increase of veracity." Similar observations have led other researchers into hypnosis to define the state as one of "believed-in imaginings."[9]

Research scientists and others have also noted that under hypnosis subjects become increasingly willing to internalize suggestions from the hypnotist or the hypnotic setting. Canadian researchers Jean-Roch Laurence and Campbell Perry proved this neatly by suggesting a memory to twenty-seven highly hypnotizable subjects.[10] In the experiment, which was modeled after one done by world-renowned hypnosis expert Dr. Martin Orne of the University of Pennsylvania Medical School, they hypnotically "age-regressed" the subjects to a night the previous week and instructed them to relive their activities. They were then asked if they had heard a loud noise which had awakened them. Responding to the suggestion implicit in the question, seventeen of the subjects imagined hearing such a noise. After hypnosis thirteen of the total group told researchers their belief that the suggested memory had actually taken place. Half of these subjects were unequivocal, saying things such as "I'm pretty sure I heard them. As a matter of fact, I'm pretty damned certain. I'm positive I heard these noises." Others held strongly to their belief the event had taken place on the basis of reconstructing the memory.

One subject, for instance, said, "I'm pretty sure it happened because I can remember being startled. It's the physical thing I remember." Note also that the experimenters did not directly suggest the memory by instructing the hypnotized subjects to imagine hearing the noise. Rather, the experimenters merely asked a question as to whether the subject heard a noise or not. The subjects heard the question as a suggestion to imagine the experience.

The client's beliefs about hypnosis, as well as the information he or she gets from the hypnotist about the procedure, combine to form what Martin Orne termed the "demand characteristics" of the experience. As Orne describes the phrase, demand characteristics are the subjects' understanding of what behavior is appropriate or expected in a certain situation. It seems clear from the Laurence-Perry study that one such demand characteristic for hypnotic sessions is the underlying expectation that the subjects will glean information from the hypnotists' questions and include that information into the scene they are imagining. When the experimenter asks a question that suggests the presence of an additional element consistent with the scene already imagined, the subject can not only add that detail but often supplies additional details that incorporate that suggestion seamlessly into the story.

Whether the patient classifies what is envisioned during hypnosis as a memory or imagination also depends greatly on the demand characteristics of a given hypnotic session. If an experimenter tells a subject that what he will experience under hypnosis is memory, the subject is significantly more likely to identify what comes out of hypnosis as memory than subjects told otherwise. What happens to a person's belief in his memory under hypnosis in the end seems less a result of properties specific to hypnosis than several factors that surround the procedure. Hypnotists and therapists often lead their patients to believe, for instance, that under hypnosis they can activate parts of their minds that they cannot normally engage. With this expectation in place, a therapist can easily convince a patient that what she imagines or daydreams about under hypnosis is actually a hidden memory accessed by the magical hypnotic procedure. Therapists can quickly convince the clients, not only that a scene imagined during hypnosis is a memory, but that because the scene was discovered through trance, it is actually superior to the patient's normal memory. This dynamic goes a fair distance to explain the rapidly growing number of persons who genuinely believe that through hypnosis they have discovered memories of being abducted by space aliens or having lived in a past lifetime.

Through the therapists' own literature on the use of hypnosis in the recovered memory setting, we can clearly distinguish several demand characteristics. Because the recovered memory movement promotes itself by purporting to show a link between the patients' symptoms and the likelihood that they carry repressed memories of abuse, most patients understand exactly what the trance is intended to uncover *before it is induced.* Both current and former patients report that therapists often inform their clients before hypnosis that the procedure is intended to discover traumatic memories. In addition, because recovered memory therapists appear to unanimously agree that what is uncovered during hypnosis is memory and not fantasy, it seems reasonable to assume that they often communicate this second demand characteristic to their patients.

As an example of compliance with another demand characteristic, patients often willingly conform to therapists' expectations that they will relive their memory while acting out a child's personality. In response to this expectation, patients often display characteristics such as a high-pitched voice, which they feel is appropriate to a child of the age of the suspected memory. The fact that they do this role playing unself-consciously often adds confidence in both the patient and therapist that the memory being "relived" is real. However, while the effect often seems genuine, those patients who role-play child personalities do not behave like real children. As Robert Baker noted in *Hidden Memories*, "Hyp-notically age-regressed individuals behave the way they believe children of that age would behave." He notes that studies have shown that "age-regressed adults, when given the same cognitive and intellectual tasks as children of the age to which the subjects are regressed, usually outperform the children" and that "age-regressed subjects in no way act like real children. They behave like adults playing at being children."[11]

How a client internalizes suggestions while hypnotized, and whether the client does so willfully and knowingly, is a question at the cutting edge of the research into the properties of hypnosis and dissociation. Baker builds a compelling argument that hypnosis is simply a method to en-hance the client's suggestibility by appealing to the preexisting ability to imagine or fantasize. He offers the idea that the appearance of hypnosis—the client's acting out of the trance state—may itself be a product of the client's suggestibility. The fact that a subject willingly displays the signs of trance, therefore, is evidence only that he or she will probably be willing to accept further suggestion and manipulation. A hypnotized subject's willingness to perform illogical or even embarrassing acts is, for

Baker, not proof of being in an altered state but proof of the person's *acceptance of the suggestion* that he or she is in an altered state.

On the other end of the debate are those who argue that what happens under hypnosis is perceived as involuntary by the client. Professor Kenneth Bowers, of the University of Waterloo, Canada, finds some middle ground in arguing that highly hypnotizable individuals can respond to suggestion and fantasy with a lessened degree of what he calls "executive control"—meaning without much of a sense that they are intentionally responding.[12] He argues that the behavior, while willful (for it is clearly in response to the suggestion), can feel to the subject as if it happens largely without his or her intent.

In one of two studies Bowers cites evidence that highly hypnotizable subjects can react to suggestion with only a small degree of conscious will, researchers tested highly hypnotizable subjects and low-hypnotizable subjects on their ability to perform simple vocabulary tests while their arms were immersed in swirling ice water.[13] Predictably, in the first trials, both groups did worse on their vocabulary test when distracted by the freezing water than they did under normal conditions. Researchers then split the subjects into two groups and instructed one in methods of cognitive pain reduction while the other was given a hypnotic suggestion to reduce the pain. With their arms immersed, all the subjects were tested agian. While both pain-reduction methods (hypnotic and nonhypnotic) proved equally effective, those given the cognitive pain-reduction strategies suffered an additional drop in their vocabulary scores, as did the low hypnotizable subjects who were given the hypnotic suggestion. These results would suggest that for all three of these groups, the pain-reduction strategies required conscious attention that distracted them from the vocabulary test. The results of the last group—the highly hypnotizable subjects who were given the hypnotic suggestions—shows an *increase* in their ability to memorize and repeat words while their arms were immersed. Their hypnotic pain-reduction technique not only reduced their perception of the pain, but it seemed to free up mental resources that would otherwise have been distracted. The pain reduction seemed at once volitional (for it was in response to the hypnotic suggestion) but happening on a mental level partly distinct from that required for the vocabulary test.

In a second experiment pointing toward a similar conclusion, two groups of low- and high-hypnotizable subjects were tested for their ability to visualize imagery that was both neutral and fear-provoking.[14] To measure the results, subject's heart rates were monitored during the visualizations. They were also surveyed regarding the level of effort required to produce the images and the perceived vividness of those images. Researchers found that in both groups, and with both types of imagery, heart rate rose when subjects were asked to concentrate on the suggested imagery. (Because heart rate naturally goes up when one exerts effort to concentrate, this result was as predicted.) But while heart rate went up in all subjects, the highly hypnotizable subjects were less likely to *perceive* the effort it took to create the visualization. In addition, they reported the imagined scenario as significantly more vivid than did the low-hypnotizable subjects. The results become even more striking when examining the highly hypnotizable reactions to creating the fearful images. It appears that the *less* effort they reported in creating the disturbing mental pictures, the higher their heart rate went up. "In sum, for high hypnotizable subjects," Bowers concluded, "the less effort involved in generation of fear imagery, the more they experience it as frightening, and the more emotionally reactive they become."

This study seems to indicate that highly hypnotizable subjects can create imagined scenarios without the accompanying *sensation* that they are intentionally creating them. This result goes to the heart of how memories are created under hypnosis. If a patient has little sense of the fact that he or she is imagining a frightening scenario (while at the same time having a dramatic physiological reation to the feelings of fear), it is more likely that the patient would classify that scenario not as imagined, but as a previously hidden memory which has suddenly flooded conscious thoughts.

As with the study of memory, some recovered memory experts have argued that empirical research on hypnosis has little or no meaning for the practice of recovered memory therapy because memory of trauma is fundamentally different from other memories. On its surface, this argument makes a certain amount of intuitive sense. Memories of being awakened at night by a loud noise, after all, are not the equivalent of memories of being raped. It should be noted, however, that the research showing the suggestibility of hypnosis and its ineffectiveness in uncovering accurate memories has for years been applied to the question of whether hypnosis should be used in a criminal investigation—where victims and witnesses have often experienced trauma. Researchers have noted that when the subject of the memory is highly charged or the subject more motivated to remember—to identify a suspect of a crime, for instance—hypnosis may *increase* the inaccuracy of the memories retrieved. According to Bowers and Professor Ernest Hilgard, of Stanford University, research shows that hypnotically refreshed testimony should be corroborated independently: "In effect, this means that under hypnosis a person's associative networks are activated in a manner that is minimally or remotely tied to external reality constraints, and maximally responsive to a person's idiosyncratic mnemonic themes, imaginings, and fantasies. In other words, it is precisely under hypnotic conditions that we are apt to learn more about a person's idiosyncratic and imaginal contributions to memory reports, and less about the specific external events he or she is trying to recall." The overwhelming bulk of both the laboratory and field reports suggests that memories of witnessing or being victim to violent crimes are at least as susceptible to manipulation and confabulation during hypnosis as other, less disturbing, memories.

In addition, some researchers have indeed created in test subjects highly traumatic "memories." However, instead of building false beliefs about the subjects' childhoods (which would be grossly unethical), researchers convinced subjects that the "memories" they were to experience under hypnosis would be from previous incarnations. Using past-life ruse, experimenters managed to avoid the possible damage to the client of suggesting traumatic memory-belief for the person's actual childhood. Because past-life regressions tend to deal with traumas and death in a supposed former life, the technique dramatically illustrates that hypnosis can create believed-in "memories" of trauma.

In the most applicable study, Professor Nicholas Spanos and his colleagues at Carlton University, Canada, tested subjects selected for their hypnotizability to see whether they would conform to the suggestion of abuse in a past life.[15] Two groups of subjects were used. Before past-life regression, one group was told that people who lived in past times had much more abusive childhoods, and that the purpose of their past-life experience was to find out more about abuse suffered by children in previous generations. The other group of subjects was prompted with information that said nothing about child abuse. A series of questions was asked of the subjects during their hypnotically induced past-life fantasies, including: "Have you ever been abused by one or both of your parents?" followed by "Have you ever been abused by any other adult?" Those who said yes to either question were asked to elaborate. The responses were then rated for severity by two researchers uninformed of the purpose of the study.

The results were interesting for two reasons. First, there was no significant difference between the two groups in the number who reported abuse in their past-life fantasy. Eleven out of 14 in the abuse-prompted group said they were abused, as did 11 out of 15 of the group that was given no suggestion about the abuse. The researchers found, however, a significant difference in the severity of the abuse "remembered." The researchers concluded that the group that was given the suggestion that they were looking for abusive experiences "recalled higher levels of abuse when enacting their past-life identity than did the corresponding subjects in the [other group]." They concluded that "These findings are consistent with anecdotal reports indicating that clients in psychotherapy sometimes confabulate complex and extensive pseudomemories that are consistent with the expectations held by their therapists." The fact that there was no significant difference between the groups in their initial report of abuse is perhaps not so surprising when one considers that the questions themselves might have functioned as implicit suggestions. After all, a full three quarters of both groups confirmed that they were somehow abused in their past-life childhoods.

In three other studies reported in the same paper, researchers found that they could greatly influence the subjects' confidence in the truth of their regression memories by attesting to their own faith in the concept prior to hypnosis. When the hypnotist prepped the subject by suggesting that his or her trip to another lifetime would most likely be true, the subject would have a significantly greater likelihood of reflecting that belief after hypnosis. "Subjects with equally intense subjective experiences of a past life tended to interpret these experiences as actual incarnations or as fantasies, depending on the . . . context provided by the hypnotist."

Regardless of even this evidence, Herman's objection that memories retrieved in the laboratory are distinct from those retrieved in a clinical setting should, perhaps, not be dismissed so quickly. No one in the laboratory has ever attempted what we believe is happening in therapy settings. Like all good scientific tests, what the experiments surrounding hypnosis are clearly intended to do is establish unambiguous causation. This requires that the experiment be boiled down to very small, controllable variables. Done well, however, these experiments allow the researcher to say with assurance that one variable was responsible for changing another. To apply the results of these experiments to the real world requires careful extrapolation. While these experiments do not prove that complex memories of childhood can be implanted in patients, they do seem to prove that singular beliefs about memory can be influenced. While laboratory experiments have only intended to prove that a single subtle suggestion can be implanted and internalized, the potential for such influence in therapy is manifold. Directly or through questions therapists offer not one suggestion but thousands—each of which can build on the response to the preceding suggestion.

Indeed, there is evidence that what happens in therapy is a good deal more manipulative than even this would suggest. While laboratory experimenters seldom hypnotize their subjects more than once or twice, recovered memory patients are often hypnotized weekly for periods of months or years. While experimenters are careful not to influence the responses of the subject (excepting where such influence is part of the experiment), recovered memory therapists often show no such concern, blatantly suggesting histories of abuse, as in the case of Sue described at the beginning of this chapter.

The literature on the dangers of the use of hypnosis is not an obscure body of research that a reasonably competent therapist might have simply missed. Warnings about the suggestibility of a hypnotized patient, and the likelihood that he or she will classify what is imagined during hypnosis as memory, have come from any number of sources including the courts, the *Journal of the American Medical Association*, and prudent hypnotherapists.

Considering the mountain of empirical research on hypnosis and suggestibility, the case of Sue, outlined at the beginning of this chapter, becomes remarkable. To fully critique the case, we would first note that "suspecting" hidden abuse by the father with only the evidence of a dream and the verbal slip of saying "father" when she meant "fiancé" shows an clear predisposition to find such memories. Only in the world of recovered memory therapy would such details be immediately construed as adequate evidence to conclude that the father had sexually molested the patient. Just as disturbingly, the decision that an "indirect approach" would be the wisest means to overcome the patient's "strong defensiveness" seems an admission of the therapist's determination to find abuse memories regardless of the client's belief that she had a good and loving father.

The use of the story of the king and wizard during the hypnosis in the second session of therapy is profoundly troubling. Because the king in the story was concerned about the wizard getting married (Sue came to therapy because of her impending marriage), and because the story ended with the revelation that the wizard was the king's only daughter, it seems clear that the client understood that she was to identify herself as the wizard and the king as her father. From the grave consequences surrounding the "magic word" in the story, and the likelihood that the therapist had already explored the subject of sexual abuse, there is little doubt that Sue also understood that the "magic word" was "incest."

The author's assurance that "the story gave [the patient] the option of

COLLEGE OF THE SEQUOIAS
LIBRARY

choosing how to respond to her own experiences" stands in contrast with the singular focus of the tale. From this description of the fairy tale, there appears little room for choice. Considering the focus of the story and the research on the suggestibility of hypnotized subjects, it is clear this is a case of a therapist blatantly suggesting to a vulnerable and hypnotized client that she was sexually abused by her father. To publish the story of Sue's treatment as advice to other therapists shows a remarkable disregard of the widely accepted research into the use of hypnosis. The fact that these writers don't even mention the troubling issue of suggestion leads one to wonder whether these clinicians know of the applicable empirical research.

In other published recommendations for using hypnosis, the suggestions that the client will remember scenes of abuse are just as directed. In helping patients uncover repressed memories, therapist Donald Price recommends that hypnotized patients first be helped to visualize going down an elevator and entering a comfortable lounge, where they sit in front of a large TV with a videotape recorder. He then recommends telling the patients to "pick up a videocassette from the stack at the side of the chair. Our mind is very much like a giant video library. Take the tape that we need to review today. . . . Put the cassette into the VCR, and as the picture starts to appear on the screen [signal] yes." The client is encouraged to believe that the scene of abuse viewed on the imagined television in the imagined room is a real memory. Price goes on to explain that "as the person gets into the memory, I usually start talking in the present tense to help him/her be there now."[16] It is a leap of faith indeed to believe that despite the fact that the patient can vividly *imagine* riding down the elevator, entering the lounge, using the VCR, that what they watch on the television will be nothing more or less than a memory of actual events. While remarkable, this sort of direction is far from uncommon in the use of hypnosis by recovered memory therapists.

Not all recovered memory therapists give their unqualified approval to the use of hypnosis. Interestingly, those who object to the technique argue not that it can distort recollection and build confidence in imagined pseudomemories, but that hypnosis is *too* effective in uncovering repressed memories and may bring up memories that the patient is not yet ready to face. "The area [in which] I am most hesitant to use hypnosis, however . . . is in attempting to recover memories of abuse," writes Mike Lew in *Victims No Longer*. "Memories are blocked for a reason. They are hidden in order to enable the individual to survive a traumatic situation. . . . I question the benefits of dragging out memories before you are ready to deal with them."[17] While Herman uncritically touts the ability of hypnosis to uncover repressed memories, she recommends that it be attempted only when other methods have failed. "At these times, the judicious use of powerful techniques such as hypnotherapy is warranted." She hints of some discomfort with these "powerful techniques," warning that they "require a high degree of skill" and should be used carefully.[18]

Perhaps these warnings that hypnosis is too effective are a concession to the mountain of research showing that hypnosis is not an effective method of recovering memory and that it increases suggestibility. Because the literature on the dangers of hypnosis is so well known, Lew, Herman, and those who qualify their recommendations of hypnosis must know more than they are telling. It is possible that these warnings and qualifications are a way to discourage therapists from using hypnosis without throwing doubt on the validity of certain abuse memories.

Recently therapist David Calof took another tack. In an article in a magazine for therapists he suggests that those who criticize recovered memory therapy are setting up hypnosis as a straw man. Calof, who helps patients retrieve repressed memories, sometimes with the use of hypnosis, implies that therapists *already know* that the belief created under hypnosis can be false and use the procedure carefully. "[Critics unfairly suggest] that hypnotists don't know how undependable hypnotically refreshed memory can be. But, in fact, we know that hypnosis can distort memories by conflating them with *present* beliefs and feelings."[19]

Unfortunately, as we have shown, Calof's contention that recovered memory therapists know these facts is not supported by the literature of the movement. As we have shown, recovered memory therapists tout the use of hypnosis as an effective (indeed, perhaps *too* effective) way of uncovering memories of abuse. Within the published works of recovered memory therapists, Calof's warning is an utter anomaly. Statements like this one, written by Lynne D. Finney in *Reach for the Rainbow*, are, however, pervasive: "Memories retrieved under hypnosis are sometimes discounted by outdated therapists who say that hypnosis is unreliable because the hypnotist can put ideas in the subject's mind. That allegation is nonsense. Experienced hypnotherapists know that you cannot put anything in a person's mind that he or she doesn't want there."[20]

CHAPTER EIGHT

Two Cases of Hypnotic Story Creation

Two well-documented cases, one taken from recovered memory literature and one from outside the therapy setting, perhaps best illustrate how stories are created with the use of hypnosis. *Lessons in Evil, Lessons from the Light*, by therapist Gail Carr Feldman, unwittingly illustrates the troubling application of hypnosis through the story of her treatment of her patient Barbara Maddox. On the surface, this book seems simply another therapist's self-glorifying account of the wonders of recovered memory therapy. The jacket cover proclaims that it is an "unparalleled" work documenting the "depth of human evil and the transcendental power of the mind to heal itself." In the foreword, Carl Raschke, a professor of religious studies at the University of Denver and a promoter of the satanism scare in America, writes that this "is the first major book for a general audience to lay bare a broad context, into which is woven not only the life story of the survivor, but the challenges and professional anxiety of the therapist struggling to make sense out of what she has been told." Closer examination reveals that *Lessons in Evil, Lessons from the Light* does indeed prove to be a rather remarkable document—perhaps destined to be the Rosetta stone of the recovered memory debate. What makes this book remarkable is that Feldman uses transcripts of her tape-recorded sessions with Barbara as the basis of the book, which can be read as a therapist's confession of the manipulation of her patient. Feldman makes this confession unknowingly, seemingly unaware of how her techniques might appear to those who understand the dangers of hypnosis. She explains her therapy techniques with the self-congratulatory prose of someone proudly displaying her best handiwork.

The second case we will explore in this chapter is one of inadvertent hypnosis in a police interrogation setting. The tale of how sheriff's officer Paul Ingram learned to visualize and confess to crimes—some of which undoubtedly never took place and all of them entirely lacking any evidence demonstrating their occurrence—sheds a good deal of light on how memory belief can be created and internalized, even when the consequences of coming to believe the pseudomemories are exceptionally grave. Although Ingram's pseudomemories were created with the assistance of a clinical psychologist, the coercive interrogation setting cannot be said to fully parallel the coercive therapy setting. However, we feel the specifics of Ingram's story speak volumes as to how trance, combined with intensive questioning, can easily build believed-in "memories," and how the concept of repression can be used to convince someone that he might have memories of events that he never knew occurred.

According to Feldman's account in *Lessons in Evil, Lessons from the Light*, Barbara Maddox began therapy complaining of sexual problems with her husband and the "feeling" that her grandfather might have abused her. Barbara had no memories of being abused, however. In the first session, she also described growing up in poverty with an abusive mother, who made her do all the housework and cooking from the time she was six. According to Barbara, she lived a Cinderella nightmare, where her clothes came from the Goodwill once a year and her mother "enjoyed not giving [her] birthday presents or Christmas presents." In addition to her emotionally and financially impoverished childhood, Feldman learned that Barbara was having trouble with her seven-year-old daughter, Michelle. Barbara seemed to be "jumpy, irritable and always angry" around her daughter and feared she would become physically abusive toward her child. Barbara also told of her history of feeling suicidal. From these bits of information, all of which Barbara provided in her first session, Feldman came to this now familiar conclusion: "I felt certain that sexual abuse was the predominant issue."[1]

Considering the client's focus on her childhood poverty and her abusive mother, Feldman's certainty is troubling. Later in the book she admits that at the time of treating Barbara she was "counseling primarily sexual abuse survivors," an observation echoed by her husband's quoted complaint that "It seems like these sex abuse victims are the only people you see anymore."[2] After sharing her assumption that her client's unconscious held repressed memories of sexual abuse, Feldman goes on to describe what the coming therapy would likely entail. "Like all survivors, she would have to be helped to remember the trauma so that she could overcome the feelings of terror that were still attached to the repressed memories. No small assignment. It can take many years to help someone who has been abused from early childhood to unlock those traumatic memories. . . . Hospitalization could be required." When Barbara says that she would like to limit therapy to two years, Feldman worries that two years would prove an "impossibly short" time for therapy. "I had never treated a sexual abuse survivor who was able to complete treatment in that time." She then quotes an unnamed expert on sexual-abuse victims who said eight to fifteen years was a more reasonable time frame for such therapy.[3]

In her account of the first few sessions, Feldman continually refers to her patient as a sexual-abuse survivor, ignoring the fact that her client had shared no memories of being sexually abused, only her "feeling" that her grandfather might have molested her. She freely shares her suspicion with Barbara. In the third session, for example, when Barbara tells about her history of ailments—headaches, vaginal and kidney infections, and high blood pressure—Feldman tells her, "We know that memories of abuse are stored in every area of the body, so it's typical that survivors have lots of physical fears and discomfort."[4] Later she informs her patient of her "hunch" that Barbara's nightmares are not dreams at all but "flashback" memories. Despite Feldman's focus on the suspected repressed memories, Barbara repeatedly emphasizes her current problems, her failing marriage, and her inability to keep meaningful friendships. In her third session she tells Feldman: "I want to work on my self-image and sexuality." Several sessions later she again tries to focus the therapy on her present problems. "After [the last visit] I came up with three areas that I need to work on," she tells Feldman at one point. "The first is that I do have to become more comfortable with confrontation and expressing my feelings instead of holding them back; the second is I have to figure out what it means to be me, instead of always trying to please others; the third is I have to work on being able to be a sexual person."[5]

Through the first several months of therapy, Feldman seemed able to turn Barbara's attention toward her childhood, which is clearly where Feldman believed the source of Barbara's problems lay. During this time Barbara recalled a disastrous relationship with her mother, regular beatings, and a sexual assault by a gang of boys when she was seven. But these memories, Feldman apparently sensed, weren't horrible enough to account for her patient's problems. After months of therapy, during which Barbara mentions no memories of incest, Feldman suggests they try hypnosis to "help her access important memories." Feldman may have told her client, as she tells her readers, how she had "helped [other adult survivors] access their memories through hypnosis. . . . I could see the self-confidence evolving much more quickly by using hypnosis and getting right to those blocked memories."[6]

Feldman's confidence in hypnosis appears boundless, and is undiluted by any mention of the literature showing the technique's propensity to distort memory or engender confidence in imagined events. In her first hypnosis session with Barbara, Feldman establishes "ideomotor signaling," convincing Barbara that while she is under trance she will be able to communicate directly with her unconscious. She suggests to Barbara that her unconscious will signal "yes" and "no" by lifting designated fingers. A third finger will lift if Barbara's conscious mind is "not ready" to know the information. Once Barbara is put in trance, Feldman tells her: "Now, I'm speaking to your inner mind, your unconscious mind. It's that aspect of your personality that has always been with you. It knows everything about you."[7]

She then suggests to Barbara that she is traveling back through the "mists of time," to an "event or experience that is important for you to know about." According to Feldman, this exchange ensued:

> "How old are you?" I asked.
> "I'm five."
> "Where are you?"
> "In the church."
> "And what's happening there?"
> "Granddaddy takes the special knife. He says he's going to fix the cat. There's something wrong with the cat and he's going to fix it."
> The little-girl voice continues. "He's smiling now and ooooh" she whispers—"he sticks the knife in the cat and there's blood all over and on me, too." She fidgets uncomfortably. There's a long silence.
> I have the urge to fidget, too, but I stay still, trying to comprehend Barbara's grandfather's bloody activity.
> "He lied," the little voice said finally.
> "He lied?"
> "Yes, he lied. He didn't fix the cat. The cat's dead."
> "What do you do?"
> "Nothing. I'm real quiet. Grandma taught me to be real quiet. I never scream and I never cry. If I did, Granddaddy would hurt me."
> "What is he doing now?" I asked.
> "He's cutting the heart out. He says I must eat of the heart and drink of the blood."[8]

This is the first of many dozens of "Satanic Abuse" scenes that Feldman helps Barbara find through therapy. Over the course of the next year of therapy, Barbara discovers increasingly horrible scenes that she will learn to identify as memories. The scenes include being trapped under a dead body that falls out of a closet, made to sit in a chair and smell witches' brew for "days," being locked in a snake-filled basement for five days when she was three years old (during which time she was given no food or water but managed to stay awake and standing). Later she will uncover scenes during which she had to eat an eyeball, was sold into prostitution by her mother, and had to kill a baby and cut out its heart. At the climax of the therapy, Barbara comes to the belief that she gave birth to a baby who was sacrificed and eaten. According to the narrative created in therapy, Barbara did not repress these memories during or immediately after each instance of abuse but remained fully aware of the abuse during her childhood. According to the story, it is only at seventeen, when she starts to date her future husband, that she represses the memories, explaining, "I had to not remember what happened. So I forgot."[9]

The person who seems to have the most trouble believing in the memories of the satanic ritual abuse is not Feldman but the patient herself. After her first hypnosis session she says frankly of the scene in which her grandfather cuts open a cat, "I can't believe it. I must have made it up." Feldman does not pursue Barbara's concern, saying only, "I guess we'll have to wait and see how the rest of the story unfolds." After coming out of a trance in which she remembers having to inhale a witches' brew for "many days," Barbara says, "It's amazing to me that I remembered that. I never knew it. I can't believe I never knew all that."[10]

Barbara's mental health during treatment deteriorates, fulfilling Feldman's prediction that her patients usually get worse during treatment. Barbara begins therapy as a functioning woman, hoping to work on issues such as her sex life and "self-esteem." She soon becomes plagued by "terrifying images and physical symptoms." In addition, she describes not being able to sleep well and feeling "sad and angry all the time." During therapy she begins taking antianxiety pills and increases her high-blood-pressure medication. Barbara complains at one point: "I'm afraid I'm really crazy. I think I'm just losing it and I'm making all this up." Her inability to sleep and intense nervousness—symptoms not mentioned at the beginning of therapy—plague her throughout the treatment. Feldman at one point specifically recommends that Barbara *not* try to give up smoking or the several glasses of wine she drinks nightly, saying, "Now is probably not the time to try to give up addictions that help you manage your anxiety." The frequency of her treatments is increased from once to twice a week and then later to three times a week. At one point, Barbara talks of increased suicidal feelings. "I just want to be dead. . . . I have this feeling of just wanting all of this to be over. If I could only have some peace."[11] Feldman clearly believes "all of this" to mean the memories of abuse, but it could perhaps be read as referring to the therapy.

That same day, after putting Barbara in a trance, Feldman directly suggests her self-destructive impulses came from cult "programming." Feldman recounts the session:

> I had read enough by then to know that all survivors of sadistic cults have been programmed to kill themselves, and I had a hunch that Barbara was feeling the effects of that programming. . . . I became more direct in my questioning.
>
> "Do those in the clan ever tell you anything about killing yourself or hurting yourself?"
>
> "No. They never tell me to do that."
>
> "Remember who I am. I'm Gail and I've been chosen to help you. Please open your mind and let me know if you've been told to kill yourself."
>
> After a long pause: "Yes, I have. . . ."[12]

With this sort of insistence, it is horrifying but hardly surprising that in the next session Barbara comes in with her leg bandaged from self-inflicted burns. Feldman makes no connection that this new self-mutilative behavior starts the very session after she insisted to her hypnotized patient that she was programmed to hurt herself. Instead of proof of her client's suggestibility, Feldman tells Barbara, "Well, [the burning] tells us that you really are a survivor of extreme sadistic abuse."[13]

Feldman spent little time considering the possibility that the stories elicited from Barbara in therapy were anything but exact historical reality. "I 'knew' from the beginning . . . that everything Barbara told me was the truth," she writes of her feelings after the first hypnosis session. "How did I know? I'm not certain, but I knew." In a cruel turn, she muses that if these events weren't literally true, the only possible alternative would be that the patient was insane. "If none of the events occurred," she writes "these [satanic-abuse] patients know that the alternative is that they are indeed crazy. Otherwise, where would such bizarre and terrible images come from?" Later she restates this black-and-white dichotomy by claiming that those who question the stories of satanic abuse believe patients are "hysterical women . . . trying to get special attention."[14]

While she never directly addresses the possibility that the therapy's structure was largely responsible for the creation of the "memories," much of the book tacitly deflects that exact criticism. In melodramatic prose she often manages to put her reactions—as opposed to the patient's experiences—in the spotlight. Of her reaction to one hypnosis session she writes that her "rage imploded upon itself and dissolved into bleak sadness." At times she talks about being a "basket case" outside of therapy, constantly crying. During one winter she complains that the only place she had been "happy these past months had been on the ski slopes." That summer she complains of "not being able to look forward to" any of her normal activities, which include exercising to the Jane Fonda "Challenge Workout" video. Later she relates that her work with Barbara largely prevented her from enjoying a ten-day vacation, complaining that "Maui was colorless that summer." At another point she suggests that she is suffering from post-traumatic stress syndrome brought on by listening to Barbara's stories. (When asked on "Larry King Live" about how she discovered her client's history of satanic abuse, she said, "I wish I didn't ever see any of it.") By constantly focusing on the hardship of hearing Barbara's accounts of satanism, she puts distance between herself and any potential responsibility for those memories. "Why would I have helped create these stories?" is implicitly argued. "It hurt me to hear them."

Despite these oblique denials, there is, of course, a third source for these accounts beyond the possibilities that the stories were true or that Barbara was "crazy." This possibility is that the aggressive use of hypnosis, the structure of the therapy, and the subtle and not-so-subtle suggestions from Feldman led Barbara to create a series of pseudomemories that she was then encouraged to believe were real memory.

In her use of hypnosis, Feldman illustrates exactly how the factors surrounding the procedure can become all-important. Feldman expresses supreme confidence that hypnosis can "get right at" Barbara's "important memories," and there is substantial evidence that she communicated that confidence to her patient. Before the first trance session, both patient and therapist appear in total agreement that Barbara would soon discover the substance of the "memories" would be childhood sexual abuse. Further, because she has come to therapy to understand her problems, Barbara appears highly motivated as a hypnotic subject.

Going back to Feldman's account of the original trance induction, for instance, Feldman instructs the patient not to simply concentrate on her memories, but to *travel back through time*. Feldman's suggestion that Barbara act out a child personality is implicit in her first questions: "How old *are* you?" followed by "Where are you?" and "What's happening there?" Conforming to these clear suggestions, Barbara tells her story in the present tense, as if she were seeing the events unfold in her mind. At least on one occasion in therapy, Feldman encourages this role playing by acting out her own childhood personality. As for the satanic theme of the scenes reported, several sources present themselves. Before and during therapy, Barbara worked as a liaison with a children's psychiatric department of a mental-health center. In this capacity, during the late eighties she would undoubtedly have known of the day-care child-abuse cases, such as the one at the McMartin Preschool, in which rumors of satanism became widespread. Later in the book Barbara admits having heard teachers as well as people in the court system talk of rumors of ritual abuse.

While this might account for the genesis of the satanic-abuse theme, it does not account for the depth and detail of the gory stories that followed. After the second session of hypnosis, Barbara gives Feldman a book called *Michelle Remembers*, written by a therapist and his client and narrating the discovery of repressed memories of satanic abuse.[15] While Barbara is quoted as saying that she didn't read the book before giving it to Feldman, it is unlikely that she was unaware of its themes and at least of the details of the jacket copy. Feldman, for her part, reads the book immediately and rereads it later in therapy. She writes that she was "eager to understand what kinds of rituals the satanic cults practice," adding "*I had to know what to expect*" (emphasis added).[16]

Indeed, Feldman found in Barbara much of what she learned to expect from *Michelle Remembers*, for the parallels between the two books are remarkable. In hypnotic trances, both Michelle and Barbara "remember" participating in gruesome cult activity that included ritual murders and cannibalizations as well as more novel details such as incarceration in basements for days at a time. In both cases, interestingly, the floor of the basement was covered with snakes. Perhaps most strikingly, both Michelle and Barbara also "remember" that during the abuse they were comforted by, and communicated with, a mysterious white light that is identified as the spirit of Jesus Christ.

One need only review the accounts of the hypnosis sessions to understand how Feldman's new knowledge and expectations might have been incorporated into Barbara's story. While only bits of the sessions are transcribed in the book, there are several instances in which it is clear that Feldman, through questioning, suggests, in some cases insists, on aspects of the abuse belief. During the session in which she supposedly discovers that Barbara was "programmed" to kill herself, for instance, Feldman admits getting the idea from the literature she had been reading. Most importantly, she insists her patient adopt this detail even after Barbara answers that she had received no such instruction.

Considering her implicit and explicit encouragement, Feldman should be held responsible for the memories Barbara created in therapy. The evidence that she was complicit in the creation of her client's stories permeates the book. Whether she has applied the same procedure to other clients is an open question. However, while she claims that Barbara's treatment was her first encounter with a satanic-cult survivor, it seems a remarkable coincidence that many of her patients since then have told similar stories. While appearing on a TV show advertising her book, she said that she had treated *"only* a dozen ritual abuse survivors."

We certainly do not intend to argue that Barbara's stories are not true simply because of their severe nature, for humans are capable of supremely evil acts. Given the evidence provided by Feldman, however, it seems clear that Barbara's stories of satanic abuse are most probably not true. The regimen of hypnosis, prompting from Feldman, and Barbara's apparent willingness to accept suggestion make it likely that the two invented an elaborate fantasy world and labeled it as memory. While some may balk at this conclusion, they should first consider the dramatic ending of *Lessons in Evil, Lessons from the Light*.

During the later part of Barbara's treatment, Feldman writes of going to a new-age "Whole-Life Expo" and attending a workshop by Brian Weiss, the author of *Many Lives, Many Masters*. During the lecture, Weiss put members of the audience into trance in order to access their past-life experiences. After Weiss's instructions, Feldman found herself reliving a previous life as a Native American woman. "I was wearing moccasins. . . . I moved slowly around, gathering nuts. An immediate recognition of being 'one with nature' came over me. I was simply another living being on the earth, and the trees were my friends."[17] As she did when the stories of satanic abuse surfaced, Feldman feigns skepticism of her experience. She claims to have read every book she could find on the topic of past-life regression. Unfortunately, this research apparently includes no material critical to the phenomenon. As she did with her "research" of satanic-abuse stories, she seems to have limited the information she read primarily to that which confirmed the validity of past-life stories.

Around this time in the story, Barbara's mental health worsens. Her anger toward her daughter increases to the point where she feels like killing her. She describes a surge of anger she felt while watching her daughter spill a cup of juice. In addition, Feldman considers hospitalizing Barbara to prevent a feared suicide attempt. In order to justify what she does next, Feldman portrays herself as backed into a corner, and in the process appears to admit that the therapy to that point had not made her client happier or more functional but rather had brought her to the edge of self-destruction. Feldman tries to convince the reader that she was desperate to help her client and had no other choice than to hypnotically regress Barbara into a past lifetime.

As she did before age regression, before sending her patient on her "past-life experience," Feldman first indoctrinates Barbara to the technique's supposed effectiveness and validity. She tells her of Weiss's book, and of his "solid" reputation as a psychiatrist. After Feldman puts Barbara into a deep trance, she suggests that she not simply travel back through the "mists of time," but that she "float up onto a cloud and begin to drift back through time until she could look down on some part of the world and enter a lifetime." Responding to this suggestion, Barbara imagines herself as a little Jamaican girl named Denise, hiding under a porch. According to Barbara's subsequent vision, she was also abused during her Jamaican incarnation. She is hiding under the porch because she spilled "broth" on the floor of her "hut," angering her father into beating her. After she describes dying of exposure under the porch, she tells of floating in a white space with no ending or beginning, the "Place of Many Lessons."

The obvious connection between spilled broth and her anger at her daughter spilling the juice is not lost on Barbara, whose past-life experience had the effect of explaining her overreaction and anger toward her daughter. "My father beat me because I'd spilled broth," she says after trance. "I felt like beating Michelle because she spilled juice. This is just too amazing." In a dream a few nights later Barbara realizes that her daughter is a reincarnation of her past-life father, thereby further explaining her anger.

Recovered memory therapists often tell their clients that the emotional impact of a visualized scene provides positive proof that the memory is historically true. If we were to accept this assertion in Barbara's case, we would have to assume that the past-life memory was more true than her supposedly recovered memories of satanic abuse, for Barbara not only immediately finds meaning in the experience, but this past-life fantasy apparently cures her. "I don't have any anxiety since my past-life work," Feldman reports her as saying some sessions later. Her sex life, too, suddenly recovers, she is no longer angry at her daughter, and she even has overcome her fear of death.

From all indications, Feldman appears unconcerned that the past-life experience could throw doubt on memories elicited throughout the entire two years of therapy. Many therapists, including Judith Herman, recoil at the comparison of past-life regression (or space-alien-abduction stories created through hypnosis) and recovered memory therapy. Herman and others claim that to compare the past-life therapy to that of child-abuse survivors belittles the experience of child abuse. Through the work of therapists like Feldman, however, Herman's objections can be seen as nothing more than an attempt to shame critics into not exposing troubling and obvious parallels between the way recovered memories are found and the procedures that build other obviously false beliefs.

Brian Weiss, in *Healing Through Time*, also combines the past-life-regression and recovered-memory-therapy theories. Using the same hypnotic techniques, he describes helping a patient both uncover a "memory" of being molested by her father at the age of one as well as a "memory" of being a twenty-six-year-old who lived in the Dark Ages. "She remembered being a slave who was chained to the wall of the castle kitchen where she had constantly labored," Weiss writes. "In this lifetime, [she] had only been removed from her chains for one purpose—to be taken to a locked room in the castle to meet a man who used her sexually. [She] recalled feeling more disgust than any other emotion after these encounters, a disgust that was not dissimilar to her feeling of being abused by her father, who loved her."[18] The remarkable parallels between the procedures is perhaps best illustrated by Weiss's own admission that before he became the premier past-life guru, he routinely used hypnosis to uncover his patients' histories of sexual abuse.[19] At this point it should not surprise anyone that the most prominent figure in the past-life pseudoscience began as a recovered memory therapist.

Feldman, Weiss, and other therapists who combine the theories of past-life regression and recovered memory hypnosis illustrate what hypnosis researchers have reported for years: that the procedures, instructions, and suggestions that the subject receives, as well as the subject's own attitude and expectations, largely determine his or her belief in the validity of any scenes imagined while hypnotized.

For those in the recovered memory movement who claim to be serious academics and scientists, books like *Lessons in Evil, Lessons from the Light* must be troubling. At the same time that some recovered memory experts are attempting to create the appearance of a serious theoretical structure for recovered memory therapy, Feldman and other clinicians are effectively tearing the work down by helping clients believe they can talk with Jesus or by regressing them for help into previous lifetimes. However, it is thanks to published accounts of therapists as self-assured as Feldman that those outside the therapy setting can fully understand the excesses and coercive nature of recovered memory therapy.

Another telling illustration of the power of hypnosis to create believed-in imaginings can be found in the case of Paul Ingram. While to fully tell the story of the Ingram family would require a book of its own, some background is necessary to understand the context in which the extraordinary interrogation took place.[20] Until the end of 1988, Paul Ingram, father of two daughters and three sons, was considered an upstanding member of the community of Olympia, Washington.[21] Chairman of the Republican committee for the county, Paul also held the third highest civilian position in the sheriff's office. Raised Catholic and sent to seminary during high school, Paul converted to fundamental Christianity after he married. He and his family attended the Church of the Living Waters, where moments of religious ecstasy were routine. At services the sick were ministered to through the laying on of hands, and worshipers, including Paul, often spoke in tongues.

It was in an atmosphere of religious fervor, at a Bible camp his daughters attended in 1988, that the first child-abuse accusations were made against Paul. The original revelation that his daughter Ericka, who was twenty-one years old at the time, had been abused came not from Ericka herself but from a charismatic Christian speaker at the camp, Karla Franko, who believed she had the spiritual gift of healing and discernment. Praying over Ericka, who was unaccountably distraught on the last day of camp, Franko received what she believed was a divine message. "You have been abused as a child, sexually abused," Franko remembers announcing to Ericka. Deep in prayer, Franko then received another message from God. "It's by her father, and it's been happening for years."[22] Over the next months Ericka would begin to tell others that she was abused, and the accusations eventually made it to the sheriff's office. When questioned, Paul's other daughter, Julie, would also say that she had been raped during poker parties he used to hold at his house.

Although he had trained as a policeman, Paul had no experience with interrogations. The officers responsible for the proceeding—both of whom Paul knew and trusted—began by describing the accusations that had been leveled against him. When Paul denied any knowledge of the alleged crimes, the detectives told him that it was common for people to repress the memories of such crimes and that admitting the truth of the allegations would first be necessary for the memories to come fully into consciousness. Because of Paul's adamant denial of any wrongdoing, the focus of the interrogations shifted from asking Paul about his memories to inquiring about whether he truly knew who he was and whether he was capable of the acts his daughters had alleged. Paul's confidence in his understanding of himself and his past was especially vulnerable owing to his strong belief in the Devil's literal presence on earth and his power to distort the minds of men. When he was pressed to agree that his daughters would not lie about something so serious, Paul's confidence in his own memory of his life began to crumble. Eventually Paul changed his denial from "I didn't do it" to "I don't remember doing it." The detectives became confident that Paul was guilty and that it was only a matter of time before he would take the next step and admit to the crimes.

By convincing Paul that it was possible to repress memories, and by forcing him to concede that his daughters wouldn't lie about such a serious charge, by the end of the first day of the five-month interrogation process, Paul admitted that his daughters' accusations must be true— although he still reported having no memory of the crimes. He and the detectives had, however, identified telling symptoms, both in his daughters and himself, which suggested the allegations were true. In a taped portion of that afternoon's interrogation, Paul's quandary can be clearly seen.

> Paul: . . . I really believe that the allegations did occur and that I did violate them and abuse them and probably for a long period of time. I've repressed it, probably very successfully from myself, and now I'm trying to bring it all out. I know from what they're saying that the incidents had to occur, that I had to have done these things.
>
> Detective: And why do you say you had to have done these things?
>
> Paul: Well, number one, my girls know me. They wouldn't lie about something like this, and there's other evidence that would point out to me that these things occurred.
>
> Detective: And what in your mind would that evidence be?
>
> Paul: Well, the way they've been acting for at least the last couple of years [referring to how his daughters had been acting aloof] and the fact that I've not been able to be affectionate with them even though I want to be. I have a hard time hugging them or even telling them that I love them and I just know that's not natural. . . .
>
> Detective: . . . You don't remember going into that room and touching Ericka?
>
> Paul: No.
>
> Detective: If she says that happened, what does that mean to you?
>
> Paul: It means to me that it happened. My kids don't lie. They tell the truth, and that is what I'm trying to do.

Like recovered memory therapy patients, once convinced of the idea of repression, Paul became unable to confidently assert that he knew any of the salient facts of his own life for sure. If any troubling memory might be lurking in one's unconscious, it becomes impossible to assert with any assurance that something *didn't* happen in one's life. This left the door open for the detectives—assisted by Paul—to begin building evidence for a life history of which Paul had no knowledge. Because he believed that neither his daughters nor the detectives would lie about the evidence against him, he became willing to admit to anything but could supply no details of his own. This greatly frustrated the detectives. "You just keep copping out!" one of the detectives yelled at Paul later in the interrogation. "It's kinda like you're saying, I'll agree to whatever my daughters say and I'll give you that information—but I'm not gonna tell you anything more."

The following day, the detectives brought in Richard Peterson, a local clinical psychologist, to assist with the interrogation. When Paul asked, Peterson confirmed that it was possible to repress memories—even seventeen years of criminal activity. When the detectives again got angry at Paul's willingness to admit to crimes but his inability to come up with any details, Paul used his new knowledge of how the mind represses memory to insist that he was cooperating as best he could.

"I think it's just a matter of getting to the part of my brain that has this information," he said. "You've given me the pieces and they just haven't fit in yet. There is no doubt with me that this is my fault."

"Damn it!" one of the detectives responded, clearly displeased with Paul's claim that he couldn't access the information. "You're just going to sit there, aren't you. You're just going to sit there and say [mockingly], 'It's just too dark for me to see.' "

Because of his belief in the mind's ability to hide horrible events, Paul found it impossible to eliminate any possibility. When asked later if he had ever killed anyone, he said, "I can't picture it. I–I would have said no yesterday."

"That's playing games, Paul," one of the detectives challenged. "Convince me that you haven't [killed anyone]."

"I've got to convince myself first."

"You can't convince yourself that you haven't killed anybody?"

"Honestly, I can't," Paul said. "I can't deny anything I don't know. . . . If I don't know what I've done with my own kids. If I don't know that, I don't know what else is back there that I might have done. I honestly don't. I don't know what's going to be revealed to me."

During the first few hours of the second day of interrogation, the two detectives and Peterson played on Paul's guilt feelings and his fears for the safety of his daughters. They told him that Julie had said that she had been raped by some of his friends who used to play poker at his house, but that she was too afraid to name the other men who had raped her and she was in danger of being murdered by them. They convinced Paul that he might have to live with the responsibility for the murder unless he named the other men.

Eventually Paul was reduced to crying and praying. "O Lord Jesus, O Lord Jesus . . ." he repeated over and over. Peterson, picking up on his religious beliefs, tried a new tack.

"If you've ever been offered a choice between the Devil and God, it's right now," he said. "Choose life over a living death, a living hell." The interrogation quickly built in intensity. As Paul prayed to Jesus, the three interrogators bombarded him. "It's your responsibility as a father." "Come on, Paul." "It's important. It's got to come out."

When the barrage let up for a moment, Paul pleaded, "Just keep talking. Just keep talking, please."

"It's a clear and black-and-white choice between adherence to that living hell that you've been living and the cleansing absolution of honesty." Peterson clearly believed that the path through Paul's supposed resistance to telling lay in his religious beliefs. "You have to make that decision. No one can do it for you. You're alone as Jesus was in the desert when he was comforted."

"Father God," Paul was mumbling. "O Jesus, o Jesus, o Jesus . . . Jesus, Merciful Jesus help me."

After a few more moments, Peterson stopped the barrage. His voice was no longer challenging and threatening but had a soothing tone. "One of the things that would help you, Paul," Peterson said slowly, "is if you'd stop asking for help and just let yourself sit back, try not to think about anything. Just let yourself go and relax. No one's gonna hurt you. We want to help. Just relax." His voice continued to soften and slow down. "Just relax. Try not to think about anything. Ask yourself what you need to do. An answer will come, because I don't think you ever wanted to hurt your kids. I know you want to provide a life for your children that is not filled with pain. You can still do that."

This short speech was followed by a long silence. Paul sat with his eyes closed. One of the detectives finally said, "Why don't you tell us what happened to Julie, Paul—what happened at the poker games. . . ."

There was another long pause. This time Paul's voice broke the silence.

> Paul: I see Julie lying on the floor on a sheet. Her hands are tied to her feet, she's on her stomach. I'm standing there looking at her. Somebody else is on my left.
> Detective: Who is that person on your left?
> Paul: I don't know, I think maybe its Jim Rabie.*

*Rabie was a longtime friend of Paul's and a former sheriff's officer. His name had been mentioned earlier in the interrogation when Paul had listed who had attended the poker games.

Detective: Look at that person who's standing right there.
 Peterson: What does he smell like?
Detective: Yeah, what's he smell like? He's standing right next to you,
          Paul—all you have to do is just look to your left and there
          he is. Does he have any clothes on?
     Paul: I don't think so.
Detective: What's he doing to your daughter?
     Paul: He's getting down on his knees. Uh, uh it's leaving. The
          pictures are leaving.

   Paul's sudden ability to visualize the scenes that the detectives suggested
is troubling for several reasons. His description was in the present tense,
and he appeared to have no knowledge of the totality of the event he was
describing. Rather, he could only describe the visualization he was seeing
in his mind at that instant, as if he were seeing the scene for the first
time. These were just the first clues to the fact that Paul had slipped into
a trance state and was not remembering what had happened to him but
living the scenes in his mind. It soon became clear, for example, that
the detectives' questions virtually directed the scenes and that at their
request Paul could zoom in on details that the detectives asked about.
   When the "pictures" returned and began to roll forward, one of the
detectives asked if someone was taking pictures. Paul responded: "Uh,
pictures, is there somebody off to the right of me? It's possible, let me
look. I see, I see a camera." Often Paul describes the image of the scene
fading or leaving. For the periods of time that Paul can hold the "pictures"
in his head, he is also able to incorporate each of the questions he is
asked into the scene. For example, when Paul sees someone else abusing
his daughter, he is asked to describe the man:

     Paul: [Describing another person in his visualization] He's, he's
          big, he's husky.
Detective: Does he have any jewelry on?
     Paul: May have a watch on his right hand. A gold watch.
Detective: What time does it say?
     Paul: Uh, two o'clock . . .
Detective: Is there anyone else there?
     Paul: Uh, there may be somebody else on the other side of him.
Detective: Look! Look over there. Is there somebody else there?
     Paul: I think so, thinner build . . . I think I'm seeing Gary
          Edwards.
Detective: Is someone taking pictures?

Paul: Uh, pictures, is there somebody off to the right of me? It's possible. Let me look. I see, I see a camera!

Detective: Who's takin' the pictures?

Paul: I don't know. I, I don't see a person behind the camera. . . . I don't see the camera anymore. . . . Oh gosh, I don't know what else I see. I'm kind of losing it here.

In addition to his being able to read the time of a watch, Paul was supposedly remembering from a poker party that took place seventeen years previously. Several other statements indicated that Paul was displaying what is commonly referred to as trance logic. He described fleeting images that slowly evolved into faces of people he knew. After one suggestion he reported hearing his daughter speak, but in response to another suggestion a gag suddenly appears in her mouth. When he first sees the camera in the scene, it is not being held by anyone. Later he sees a "stick figure" that then evolves into someone he knew.

In examining Peterson's relaxation exercise, it becomes clear what happened to Paul in this highly charged setting. With the trance induction, Paul found he was able to relieve the stress of the interrogation setting by receding into a calm mental world. In this state he allowed his imagination to create scenes in his mind's eye that further revealed the intense pressure of the situation, because by describing his visualization, he was able to conform to the demands of his interrogators. Paul's first hypnotic experience was followed by many more. He learned how to focus his attention on the images of a particular scene and allow the questions of the interrogators to guide him. During these sessions he would sit hunched over, with his head in his hands, and close his eyes. The information that came out of the subsequent interrogations was just as troubling. Describing scenes of abuse, Paul described floating around the room or watching the scene from the ceiling. When someone in one scene pulled a gun, Paul's voice became filled with surprise and shook with fear. When one of these scenes flickered and faded on the third day of the interrogation, Paul said, "Boy, it's almost like I'm making it up; I'm trying not to. . . . It's like I'm watching a movie."

In between interrogations, while in his jail cell, Paul developed a procedure for adding to his recall, which he referred to as "praying on" a scene. This process incorporated not only what he learned from Peterson but also from the advice of his pastor, John Brayton, who often came to his cell to help Paul pray for his memories to return. Brayton told him that if he prayed prior to trying to visualize scenes, God would give him true images and that Satan would not be able to deceive him with false stories. Alone, Paul would sit on his bed in a comfortable position, relax, and close his eyes. He would then try to empty his mind of all thoughts by imagining drifting into a white fog. He would often drift off and feel himself floating in this fog for several minutes before he could access fragmentary memories of abuse and other crimes. Sometimes he could return to a particular scene that had already come up, and further develop the details over a period of these sessions. According to Paul, he was never able to fully control the subject matter of the images he saw in his mind. It was during these private "praying on" sessions as well as during his meetings with Brayton that Paul first developed images of his involvement in a satanic cult. Brayton was so convinced that Paul had fallen in league with the Devil that he performed a ceremony in which he attempted to cast the demons out of Paul's body. Combining his religion with recovered memory theories, Paul wrote in his diary shortly after the ceremony, "John thinks several spirits are in me yet, still in control of my unconscious. . . . [It] may take someone like John to guide me around my defenses."

As the memories developed, the Olympia sheriff's office soon believed that they were on to a large-scale child-abuse cult.* Because of his research into the workings of cults and cult-generated violence, the Olympia prosecutor's office contracted coauthor University of California, Berkeley, professor Richard Ofshe to provide advice on how to investigate this increasingly complicated and confusing case. While interviewing Paul, Ofshe began to suspect that Paul was not confessing to crimes he had actually committed but was self-inducing trance and imagining crimes suggested to him. To confirm his suspicion, Ofshe conducted an experiment. He invented and told Paul the story that one of his daughters and one of his sons had accused Paul of forcing them to have sex with each other while Paul watched. This accusation was entirely fabricated and

---

*The claim that Paul Ingram and his wife, Sandy, sexually abused their daughters for seventeen years and that Paul was the leader of a satanic cult that has murdered hundreds of babies lacks any evidence that might lead a reasonable investigator (or for that matter a judge or jury) to consider the story seriously. (For a fuller explanation of why this is, see Watters 1991, Ofshe 1992, and Wright 1994). After a massive police investigation— which included several large-scale excavations—no physical evidence was found. In addition, both Ericka and Julie Ingram proved wholly unreliable witnesses. Both had records of making abuse allegations at church retreats and both eventually claimed to be covered with scars from the satanic tortures they endured. Court-ordered examinations, however, revealed no scars. (Ericka still publicly maintains that she carries these marks.) Recently she has turned her accusations on the sheriff's officers who at first believed her. She has publicly claimed that they have refused to arrest the thirty doctors, lawyers, and judges whom she has identified as cult members and who supposedly continue their regular practice of sacrificing babies to Satan.

had no relation to any of the other accusations in the case. Asked if he could remember the event, Paul replied that he could not. Employing the vocabulary of Paul's "praying on" method, Ofshe instructed him to attempt to remember the scene. Paul closed his eyes and sat silently for several minutes and then said that he was beginning to see the scene that Ofshe had outlined. To ensure that his reactions would not influence Paul, Ofshe stopped him from describing the scene that was in his mind. Instead, he instructed him to return to his cell and continue the process of praying on the scene.

The next day, Paul had substantially filled out the story. That morning he reported that he knew which daughter and which son were involved. Again, other than naming the children involved, Paul was not allowed to describe the scene but was told to write a detailed description of the scene he had visualized.[23] Several hours later Paul returned from his cell with a three-page written statement describing the events he had successfully visualized:

> Daytime, probably Saturday or Sunday afternoon. I ask or tell Paul Jr. & Ericka to come upstairs & then we go into Ericka room I close the door and tell them we are going to play a game. I tell them to undress. Ericka says "But dad." I say, "Just get undressed and don't argue." From my tone or the way I say it, neither objects and they undress themselves. . . . Ericka is about 12 or 13, body fairly well developed, Paul is 13-14. . . . I tell Ericka to kneel and to caress Paul's genitals. When erect I tell her to put the penis into her mouth and to orally stimulate him. . . . When Paul has his orgasm I have Ericka hold his penis in her mouth and continue stimulation. I tell her to swallow the sperm but she runs to the bathroom and spits. I tell her to get back to the room and tell her the sperm is protein and wont hurt her

Paul then goes on to even more graphically describe forcing his two children to have sex and then having sex with his daughter. He ends by writing:

> I may have told the children that they needed to learn the sex acts and how to do them right. That it is important that each participant have a pleasurable experience. I may have had anal sex with Paul, not real clear. . . . We all get dressed. I ask, "Now you both enjoyed that didn't you?" Neither looks me in the eye, nor says anything. I say, "You might as well get used to it. We need each other, there's no reason to fight it."
> Paul Jr. goes downstairs. I go to my bedroom, perhaps to clean up. Ericka stays in her room. I go downstairs. Sandy [Paul's wife] and the other

children are down there. I go to Sandy in the kitchen and kiss her as if nothing has happened. Nothing is said about what just happened. . . . I'm not sure how often this type of activity occurred. I believe that I tell them to be gentle with each other. The ability to control Paul and Ericka may not come entirely from me. It seems there is a real fear of someone else. Someone may have told me to do this with the kids. This is a feeling I have.

The scene is remarkable for its detail. Paul not only describes the outline of what happened, but his thoughts and the reactions of his son and daughter. Presenting the written confession to Ofshe, Paul seemed almost proud of his memory work. He was confident that this memory was accurate and that the scene had taken place the way he said it had.

Presented with this obviously false confession, Ofshe tried to assess the strength of the beliefs and whether or not Paul's confession to the scene with his son and daughter was an intentional lie or a believed-in pseudomemory. Confronting Paul with the fact that he had made up the scene, Ofshe tried several tacks to force Paul into admitting that he had lied. Ofshe intentionally used a high-pressure approach to test the strength of Paul's beliefs. Paul was told that he would not be able to testify against the other men in the case—and thereby protect his daughters—unless he admitted that he had lied about the scene. During the confrontation, Paul became emotionally distraught. However, despite the pressure applied by both Ofshe and the detectives over several hours, Paul could not be shaken from his belief that the scene of forcing his children to have sex was as real as all the other scenes he had been able to remember through the interrogations and the method he had developed for accessing what he believed to be his blocked memories.

Paul's creation of pseudomemories holds several lessons that can be applied to recovered memory therapy. Once Paul had learned the process of repeatedly visualizing the scenes in question, he needed little encouragement, nor did he require any moment-to-moment suggestions to create his beliefs. The process was motivated by his own desire to find the memories in question and augmented by an environment in which his memory search was strongly encouraged. In addition, there is no indication that Peterson knew that he had managed to "relax" Paul into a hypnotic state. Without the tape recording of the interrogation, it probably would have been impossible to clearly demonstrate that Paul had been hypnotized at all, and the cause of the pseudomemories would have remained a matter open to dispute. The use of similar relaxation techniques is recommended in much of the recovered memory literature as an effective way to find repressed memories. Considering that relaxation techniques and formal hypnotic induction are virtually interchangeable, it seem worth wondering how frequently therapists unwittingly induce hypnotic states in their clients.

While to Ofshe the experiment proved that Paul had created a false memory, the encounter had a negligible effect on Paul's faith in the memories he was uncovering. Long after the experiment, Paul continued to use his praying on technique to uncover increasingly bizarre tales of child abuse and satanic worship. It seems that with a strong support structure and a client who adamantly believes that his or her newly built beliefs are memories, even the strongest negative proof can be ignored.

Eventually Paul learned to distinguish between his real memories and the ones that came out of his trance exercises. Much damage had been done, however. He had implicated many innocent people in his memories and in doing so destroyed the lives of at least two of his former friends. For nearly two years the town was rife with rumors of child-abuse rings and satanic activity. As for Paul, his realization that he had falsely confessed came after he had pleaded guilty to raping his daughters. He is now serving out a twenty-year sentence in prison.

CHAPTER NINE

Reason and Darkness: The Strange Stories of Satanic Abuse

This is a strange time, Mister. No man may longer doubt the powers of dark are gathered in monstrous attack upon this village. There is too much evidence to deny it. You will agree, sir?
—Reverend Hale, from Arthur Miller's *The Crucible*

The learned have their superstitions, prominent among them a belief that superstition is evaporating.
—Garry Wills, *Under God*

Therapists often find themselves forced to explain why, after the first series of recovered memories, the client's symptoms do not disappear as promised. The easiest answer is to presume that the abuse must have been more serious than originally thought, and that more repressed memories are hidden in the patient's unconscious. As the therapist pushes to find more hidden memories, the client, who is already trained in the process, often comes up with still more accounts of having been abused. A vicious cycle is established. When the new set of memories again do nothing to "cure" the client, most likely leaving him or her even more distraught, the therapist can again suggest that even worse memories lie in the unconscious. Once the patient and therapist become fully adept at the alchemy that turns imagination into memory-belief, the process often continues until the client's worst fears are forged into memories. What could be more psychologically damaging than being raped by one's father? Having to have his baby. What could be worse than having to give birth to your father's child? Having to kill the child. What could be worse than having to kill a baby? Having to eat the baby after you've killed it. What could be worse than all this? Having to do these things during ritualized worship of the Devil.

Accounts of satanic abuse are without a doubt the most disturbing stories to come out of the recovered memory therapies. By conservative estimates, about 15 percent of clients who uncover memories of abuse will eventually recall having been tortured by a satanic cult during childhood.[1] Some therapists report that half or more of their clients are survivors of such abuse.[2] The satanic cults that clients tell of during therapy seem to exist for the sole purpose of brutalizing children. Accounts of satanic abuse usually include the client's remembering ritual rapes, the murder of adults and children, and being forced to breed babies for sacrifice. Most often the cults described in these accounts have supposedly existed for generations and include dozens or even hundreds of members. A patient coming to believe such a story will usually believe that the abuse spanned all or large portions of childhood.

"Ritual abuse is a brutal form of abuse in which the victim is assaulted at every conceivable level, usually by multiple perpetrators of both sexes, over an extended period of time. The physical abuse is so severe that it often involves torture and killing. The sexual abuse is typically sadistic, painful, and humiliating. The psychological abuse relies upon terrorization of the victim, mind-altering drugs, and mind-control techniques. The spiritual abuse causes victims to feel that they are so worthless and evil that they can only belong to Satan, whose evil spirits further terrorize and control them," writes therapist Catherine Gould, in *Out of Darkness: Exploring Satanism and Ritual Abuse*. "These forms of abuse," she continues, "are perpetrated by a cult in a highly systematic way, utilizing ceremonies and symbols, in an attempt to indoctrinate the victim into the cult's antisocial, life-destructive belief system. Through an elaborate process of abuse and indoctrination, the cult attempts to gain absolute control over their victims' minds in order to transform them into members who will function in whatever way the cult demands."[3]

In a law enacted on January 1, 1993, the state of Illinois both helps to define ritual abuse and testifies to the fact that the threat is taken seriously by therapists and persons outside of the recovered memory circle. Public Act #87-1167, which itself reads like a witch's incantation, states:

(a) A person is guilty of a felony when he commits any of the following acts with, upon, or in the presence of a child as part of a ceremony, rite, or similar observance.

1) Actually or in simulation, tortures, mutilates, or sacrifices any warm-blooded animal or human being;

2) Forces ingestion, injection, or other application of any narcotic drug,

hallucinogen, or anesthetic for the purpose of dulling sensitivity, cognition, recollection of, or resistance to any criminal activity;

3) Forces ingestion or external application of human or animal urine, feces, flesh, blood, bones, body secretions, non-prescribed drugs, or chemical compounds;

4) Involves the child in a mock, unauthorized, or unlawful marriage ceremony with another person or representation of any force or deity, followed by sexual contact with the child;

5) Places a living child into a coffin or open grave containing a human corpse or remains;

6) Threatens death or serious harm to a child, his or her parents, family, pets, or friends which instills a well-founded fear in the child that the threat will be carried out; or

7) Unlawfully dissects, mutilates, or incinerates a human corpse.[4]

How widespread are these beliefs in the therapy community? A recent study indicated that over 12 percent of the American Psychological Association members surveyed indicated that they have treated one or more patients who had described ritual abuse.[5] Many of the respondents who had treated these patients told of treating dozens—and in some cases hundreds—of such victims. Some of the most prominent members of the therapy community have stated their firm belief that patients are often abused in this fashion. University of Southern California psychologist John Briere, who wrote one of the most widely used textbooks on child abuse, has written that adult patients "commonly" described "black magic or satanic rites, where the child victim is part of a ceremony involving desecration and sexual debasement. Examples of such activities include the child being forced to publicly masturbate with a crucifix; ceremonial gang rape by all (or a privileged few) of the male members of the cult; sexual contact with or dismemberment of a family pet; demands that the child drink blood or urine or eat vile substances; and ritualistic ceremonies where the child is stripped of clothing, tied to a crucifix or platform, sexually molested, and led to believe that she is about to be sacrificed."[6]

It is important to understand that implicit in these satanic cult stories is the idea that these cults have existed for years—sometimes generations—and have managed to commit strings of felonies without being caught. The two ideas that make this all possible are memory repression and the belief that victims of cults have been "programmed" into rigid obedience. The term "programming" refers to a mysterious process that can supposedly produce rigid patterns of behavior and Manchurian candidate–like obedience. Through programming, according to the mythology of the recovered memory movement, the cult gains near-miraculous powers of control. The true magic, of course, is how conveniently the "cult programming" theory explains away the obvious problems with the therapy. For those who wonder why memories of cult abuse aren't usually discovered until years into therapy, or why clients seem to become progressively more disturbed, or why the memories of cult abuse are often nonsensical, or perhaps why the patient committed suicide during the treatment, the answer is simple: the cult programmed the patient to behave this way.

As stories of such abuse continue to mount, many in the media have continued to report them at face value. The cover of *Ms.* in January 1993, for example, was an illustration of a snake wrapped around a baby. The headline read: RITUAL ABUSE EXISTS: BELIEVE IT. The article inside was a first-person account of a recovered memory client who believed that her baby-sitter and her own children had been sacrificed to the cult her mother's family belonged to.[7] Despite the magazine's urging to "BELIEVE IT," there is no indication that editors made any attempt to confirm the writer's story. Other media outlets, including television talk shows and many newspapers across the country, have been similarly uncritical of these beliefs.

Such stories of murder and rape have not gone unheeded by law enforcement officials. Police departments across the country have aggressively investigated stories of murderous satanic cults. They have questioned thousands of people, excavated for bones, and hunted high and low for ritual sites. Nothing has turned up that would indicate the existence of a widespread cult network. Even most promoters of recovered memory therapy admit that no compelling evidence of such cults has been found. Special Agent Ken Lanning of the FBI has looked into more than three hundred such cases and found no evidence that rings of child-murdering satanic cults exist. "Until hard evidence is obtained and corroborated, the public should not be frightened into believing that babies are being bred and eaten, that 50,000 missing children are being murdered in human sacrifices, or that Satanists are taking over America's day care centers or institutions," Lanning wrote in his *Investigator's Guide to Allegations of Ritual Child Abuse.* "While no one can prove with absolute certainty that such activity has not occurred, the burden of proof is on those who claim that it has occurred." Lanning concluded that it was now "up to the mental health professionals, not law enforcement, to explain why victims are alleging things that don't seem to have happened."[8]

Recently, some writings about the subject have attempted to portray therapists as confused recipients of satanic-cult stories told by patients. David Sakheim and Susan Devine, editors of *Out of Darkness: Exploring Satanism and Ritual Abuse*, write of patients who "present as cult survivors," and refer to satanic-cult information coming out of the therapy setting as "what our patients are disclosing." They set up the argument so that they can claim the honorable middle ground between "some clinicians claiming that every patient's story is true . . . and others claiming that every patient is delusional and [that] the rest of the field is merely too gullible."

"It seems likely that there will never be one single answer," they write in their most reasonable voice. "Patients will probably range from those malingering for secondary gain, to those who are delusional, to still others for whom descriptions of Satanism are screen memories, to those who have truly experienced ritualized abuse."[9] In attempting to set up the debate in this fashion, the authors seem to intentionally overlook the most troubling aspect of these memories. According to the movement's own experts, patients rarely if ever walk into therapy with the belief that they were abused at the hands of a satanic cult. It is only *during therapy* that these stories are painstakingly pulled out of the clients. Because they fail to mention this well-documented fact, the authors of *Out of Darkness* ignore the most probable source for these beliefs: the therapist and the therapy setting. Dr. Walter Young, the medical director of the National Center for the Treatment of Dissociative Disorders, notes that patients are usually unaware of these satanic histories before treatment: ". . . in most cases [patients entering treatment] have little idea of the presence of ritual abuse," he wrote in 1992.[10] As an example of the road a patient takes to belief in ritual abuse Young briefly describes his treatment of Anna, who came into therapy hoping to get help for problems in her marriage, including sexual difficulties with her husband. Over the course of treatment Anna gradually came to the revelation that she had repressed a rape during college. Because this new "memory" did nothing to relieve her problems, they continued to search for other repressed material, eventually determining that her father had repeatedly raped her over the course of her childhood. When Anna again failed to improve, Young continued his exploration of her unconscious, looking for even more disturbing material. When images of blood and figures in robes began to surface in her visualizations, Young began to suspect satanic abuse— a suspicion that was partly confirmed when Anna accidentally left a crucifix in his office. These clues, after five years of therapy, led to the discovery of her supposed satanic-cult history.

In a paper coauthored by Young and three other prominent clinicians in the field of dissociation, the authors wrote that of their thirty-seven satanic-abuse cases, nearly all had no knowledge of the abuse "until treatment began." Because most had no memories of their ritual abuse at the beginning of treatment, "most of the information and reports of childhood ritual abuse emerged gradually over the course of treatment."[11] Some therapists go even further, suggesting that any memories of cult activity that preexist therapy should be considered suspect. Dr. Bennet Braun, who has treated over a hundred ritual-abuse patients at his Dissociative Disorder inpatient unit at Rush Presbyterian, in Chicago, told an audience of therapists in 1992 that satanic-cult stories should be considered questionable if the client has them *before therapy*. "Any patient who has an investment in a ritual abuse history at the start of therapy should be suspect," he said, recommending that therapists carefully consider the validity of the stories if a patient "comes in saying that she was ritually abused, as opposed to [the therapist] having to pull the memories out of her."[12]

To blame these stories on delusional or malingering patients (and representing the therapist as only passive recipient of the information) ignores the obvious fact that the patients do not have these beliefs until they are well into treatment. In this debate, the polarization between those who believe these stories and those who think they are creations of therapy is understandable. Because the beliefs do not usually exist prior to therapy, it seems reasonable to assume that they are either true or a creation of therapy. Finding the middle ground in this debate is something like finding it between those who proclaimed the world flat and those who believed it to be round.

Like other recovered memory clinicians, the therapists who specialize in satanic-abuse stories first focus on vague feelings or intrusive images and slowly build evidence for the satanic narrative. In her book *Ritual Abuse: What It Is, Why It Happens, How to Help*, Margaret Smith, a researcher into satanic abuse, describes the "phases" of memory recovery for ritual-abuse victims. In the first stage, she writes, patients describe vague sensations of "anxiety and feelings of nausea or fatigue," a "numbing sensation throughout the body." "Many survivors are able to identify certain feelings that let them know a memory is surfacing," Smith writes. "One survivor described this initial sensation 'as a black presence coming over me.' "[13]

In phase two the "survivors get information or pieces of the memory without fully reliving the abusive experience." These pieces can come

from "visualizations," dreams, or "flashes in their mind of abusive episodes." It is these images that "often are the framework for an entire
memory."[14] In the course of asking questions exploring the possible basis
of the satanic stories, therapists not only provide the client with information about the therapist's suspicion but also innumerable chances to
confirm the satanic narrative. In the *Handbook of Hypnotic Suggestions
and Metaphors,* Cory Hammond, one of the leaders in the field of satanic-
cult abuse, suggests that therapists ask their patients a long list of items.
Certain items he provides are supposedly likely to "elicit a fear reaction
in ritualistic abuse victims." According to Hammond, satanic-abuse victims will be afraid of fire, knives, blood, dying, animals being hurt,
certain animals, eating certain things, coffins, being shocked, cemeteries,
snakes, and spiders. Sherrill Mulhern, a medical anthropologist at the
University of Paris who has been studying the MPD / ritual-abuse phenomena, has found that therapist-trainees at seminars are provided lists
of satanic holidays, an authoritative checklist of satanic signs and symptoms, and page after page of satanic symbols that they are encouraged to
use during interviews with clients suspected of having been abused by
cults. Therapists are further assured that "once they recognize the often
subtle satanic signs . . . they should feel free to probe the patient's memory actively for more hidden satanic material."[15]

Once the client fixes on one of these fears or comes up with an image
that might indicate satanic abuse, the therapist expands and shapes the
notion into a vivid scene by asking questions and giving specific or implied
suggestions about what the emerging memory might contain. Smith describes how the therapist uses these "pieces of the memory" to help the
client shape his or her vague feelings into the belief that they were abused
by satanists. "Once the client is in a relaxed state, the therapist usually
asks questions about the mental images the client is seeing, or feelings
the client might be experiencing. Often survivors see old abuse scenes
or remember the details surrounding an abuse episode. The therapist
then asks such questions as 'How did you get here? Do you hear any
sounds? Who is around you? What are you feeling?' Often these questions
prompt more images, which later result in a memory of an abuse scene
that includes all the feelings and sensations that accompanied the original
incidence of trauma." During this stage, she writes, survivors often work
with therapists "going over and over a specific memory until all emotions,
body memories and visualizations combine to create a complete memory
of an abuse episode."[16]

In a videotaped therapy session aired on "Prime Time Live," therapist
Randy Noblitt illustrated how this sort of questioning can help the hyp-

notized or suggestible client to create the story. Noblitt asked his hypnotized patient, identified as Vanessa, if any of her alter personalities
had attended a cult meeting within the last month. After Vanessa describes
cult members showing up for the meeting, Noblitt begins with his
questions.

> Dr. Noblitt: I counted twelve people who answered the door. There
> may be more. There may be thirteen. Thirteen would
> make a coven.
> Vanessa: Right.
> Dr. Noblitt: Okay?
> Vanessa: Oh, there was another name coming.
> Dr. Noblitt: What was that?
> Vanessa: Regina.
> Dr. Noblitt: Regina.
> Vanessa: Uh-huh.
> Dr. Noblitt: And that would make thirteen—
> Vanessa: Uh-huh.
> Dr. Noblitt: —by my count. That's a coven, right?
> Vanessa: Uh-huh.[17]

In Noblitt's and Smith's technique of questioning, we see how a therapist can shape and direct the emerging stories. As the images and scenes
are expanded, retold, and given more detail, they become easier to re-
classify as memories. "As the memory process continues, the images
become more solidified," Smith describes. "At the final stage of the
memory process, survivors know their memories are true as clearly as
they know their own name."[18]

As the questions asked by Smith and Noblitt show, patients uncovering
memories of satanic abuse are often expected to tell about the scene as
though they are experiencing it while they are describing it. When the
"memory" surfaces, the client is not expected to have knowledge of how
the scene will end. Therapists apparently believe that the memory surfaces
moment by moment. This makes it easy for the suggestions implicit in
the questions to be incorporated into the scene. Suggestions such as
Noblitt's that a thirteenth cult member is about to arrive are not likely
to contradict the substance of the imagined scene, because the patient is
playing out the scene as the question is being asked.

In an attempt to prove that they are not responsible for the creation
of beliefs, some therapists insist that they do not ask leading questions.
Walter Young warns, "It is imperative that therapists work cautiously and
judiciously when working with patients when they are in a state of dis-

sociation or under hypnosis to prevent the iatrogenic contamination of the patients' memories. Questions and directives should be open-ended and nonleading, such as 'What is happening now?' or 'Describe what you are experiencing.' " Memories that are elicited without leading questions "are more likely to be reports or facsimiles of actual ritual abuse."[19] However, while some therapists may indeed be careful to make their questions open-ended, in the end the distinction between leading and nonleading questions is moot. It is not simply the specific suggestions that create the scene but the overarching demand characteristics and expectations of the practitioners and the patients that predict the substance of the story created. With the mistaken assumption of recovered memory therapy in place—that abuse memories never before known can be viewed as if seen for the first time—*any* question the therapist asks about the scenes will likely help the client construct the story. Once the memory-creation process is put in motion, and the satanic-abuse scene is begun, it matters little if a therapist asks a nonleading question such as "Is anyone else there?" or a leading question such as "Can you see your father there?"

Many therapists suggest that the consistency of stories across the survivor community proves that some of the stories must be true. This argument is flawed at its premise. While stories told by patients of a given therapist are often strikingly similar, the accounts of satanism across the country appear to be highly idiosyncratic and share only obvious details such as cult members who wear robes, the practice of ritual sacrifice, and the use of props such as candles, daggers, and pentagrams. While these factors hardly result in a convincing argument, they nonetheless should be explained. George Greaves, the past president of the International Society for the Study of Multiple Personality and Dissociative Disorders, argues in a recent paper that he has found no single satisfactory explanation for the shared content of the satanic stories told in therapy. Patients could not simply be remembering things from their past knowledge of satanic activity (from popular movies and books), for "no single book or movie contains the material of even a single patient." Contamination and contagion between patients cannot be the source for the stories, because a therapist "can rather easily identify and trace such incorporations." The spread of urban legends cannot be responsible for spreading the details of satanic-cult stories because these stories do not fit Greaves's restrictive definition of urban legend. "Unlike urban legends . . . the stories are not brief . . . [and] there is no measure of fun or delight in them." Similarly, the spread of rumors cannot explain the shared details because they don't "have the normal properties of rumors."[20]

Greaves is quite correct in pointing out that no single source of material can explain the grist of the therapy-created stories, but he conveniently ignores the fact that nobody is arguing that these stories have such a shared beginning. However, if we added up the combined effect of all the individual sources that Greaves rejects, we would be quite far along in explaining why satanic-cult stories across the country have similar aspects. In setting up and knocking down his straw-man arguments, Greaves only begins to enumerate the ways in which stories of satanic cults have spread throughout the nation and the recovered memory movement. He makes little note of the fact that the stories of satanic-cult "survivors" have been told on innumerable talk shows, in hundreds of magazine and newspaper stories, and in dozens of popular books. In addition, he fails to weigh the enormous amount of information that has been spread through the survivor community through group programs, newsletters, and more informal channels. On some occasions even the experts of the movement are up-front about the massive amount of information that can be moved through the survivor/recovered memory therapist community. Frank Putnam, of the National Institute of Mental Health, has remarked, "There is an enormous rumor mill out there. Patients pick up stories, and therapists trade stories."

Even though the amount of information the patient can soak up from activities, literature, and people surrounding the therapy can be significant, these sources are barely mentioned in the recovered memory literature. If they are mentioned, it is to discount them as irrelevant. Brushing aside the possibility that groups of inpatients living together on the same hospital floor had shared their stories of satanic abuse with one another, Young, Braun, and their fellow clinicians wrote of their thirty-seven satanic-abuse patients that "the authors believe that there was minimal discussion between patients of their reports of satanic abuse, as patients tended to be secretive about this information and reluctant to share."[21] This casual assurance has not only been convincingly contradicted by patients in these situations (including the patient profiled in chapter 11 of this book, who was one of the thirty-seven), Dr. Braun, one of the paper's coauthors, has also admitted just the opposite in public. Talking about his satanic-abuse patients, he said to a group of therapists that "I will sometimes not put a new patient on my unit because they get too good an education too fast. I'll sometimes put them on another unit before they can get contaminated." Braun even bragged that thanks to the informal network of survivors across the country, he could ask about one detail of the cult and by the next day hundreds of patients would have heard about the question.[22] The assurance of Young and his fellow researchers that patients are naturally secretive becomes even more suspect considering that many of these patients participate in formal group-therapy sessions led by therapists and in which their satanic beliefs are specifically discussed.

It should be clear, however, that even if the satanic-cult theme is introduced into therapy from a source other than the therapist, it remains the therapist's responsibility if the patient subsequently comes to believe she has uncovered memories of satanic-cult abuse.

The primary mistake of the recovered memory therapists is not their investment in the satanic-cult belief, but the use of methods that coerce patients into reclassifying imagined events—whatever their content—as memory.

*   *   *

Psychologist Cory Hammond, who serves on the medical school faculty of the University of Utah and has been a member of a Utah state task force on ritual abuse, perhaps best illustrates the true depth of the satanic beliefs that have spread through the recovered memory community. By his own admission, he has consulted on suspected satanic-abuse cases across the country, spread cult-related information through the therapy community covertly, and, more recently, spoken on the subject to thousands of therapists at conferences. As for his credentials in the field, Hammond has published several books on the use of hypnosis, including the *Handbook of Hypnotic Suggestions and Metaphors*, which he edited. In addition to being a licensed psychologist in Utah, he is the founder and codirector of the Sex and Marital Therapy Clinic at the University of Utah and the abstracts editor of the *American Journal of Clinical Hypnosis*. He has served as both president and vice president of the American Society of Clinical Hypnosis and is a fellow of that organization. In 1988 he received the American Society of Clinical Hypnosis Presidential Award of Merit for Advancements to Clinical Hypnosis.

Although he claims to fear for his life, Hammond has taught his theories about satanic abuse across the country. The first time he broke his self-imposed silence on the subject was in 1992, at the Fourth Annual Regional Conference on Abuse and Multiple Personality Disorder. "I've finally decided—to hell with it, if the cults are going to kill me, then they are going to kill me," he announced to the audience at the beginning of his lecture.[23] After loud and lengthy applause from the hundreds of therapists gathered to listen, Hammond went on to describe the subterranean world he believed he had discovered. It quickly became apparent why he is afraid for his life.

According to what Hammond told his audience, the satanic cult that therapists are currently battling first began in this country after World War II. After the war ended, the U.S. government smuggled out of Germany a group of satanic Nazi scientists who had been conducting mind-control experiments in concentration camps. These scientists brought with them a Jewish teenager who had saved his own life by assisting these evil researchers in their work. They spared the life of this boy because of his knowledge of the Kabala, the work of Jewish mysticism that integrated well with the Nazis' satanic beliefs. Once in America, this Hasidic boy changed his name from Greenbaum to Green and continued to help in the mind-control experiments, which had been taken up by the CIA. With CIA funding and resources, Green and the Nazi scientists began torturing and brainwashing children on army bases across the country. But the experiments weren't simply to expand the intelligence community's knowledge of mind control. Apparently from the start, this work was directed at filling the ranks of an international satanic-cult organizaton. Eventually Green went to medical school and later took control of the experiments and the government-funded programming of cult victims. Currently, according to Hammond, the CIA is only the tip of the satanic iceberg: NASA, the Mafia, and many business leaders are also part of the diabolical satanic network. By Hammond's estimates, tens of thousands of persons have undergone this brutal programming.

Hammond does not balk from the grandiose implications of what he is saying. When someone at the seminar asked him what the satanic cult hopes to accomplish, Hammond proclaimed that it intends to create "tens of thousands of mental robots who will do pornography, prostitution, smuggle drugs, engage in international arms smuggling. Eventually, those at the top of the satanic cult want to create a satanic order that will rule the world." Further, he maintains that there is reliable evidence that the entertainment industry has already been infiltrated by this secret order. By producing horror films, these Hollywood satanists can send messages to members and at the same time ready the rest of us so that "when the international satanic order takes over, everyone will be desensitized to these things."

The cult's power over its victims derives from the ability to program children as they grow, so that they are absolutely obedient as adults. The programming, which Dr. Green supposedly oversees, begins at the age of two or three and continues throughout adolescence. According to Hammond, the procedure usually entails the child being strapped down naked to a gurney and hooked up to an intravenous supply of Demerol. The evil doctors insert a needle into the right ear and pipe in "weird, disorienting noise" into the other. The victim is forced to wear goggles that flash lights to control his or her brainwave pattern. Electrodes are connected to every part of the body to supply electric shocks at the programmers' command.

Once set up, the programmers ask a series of question and answers, using the electric shock to reinforce right and wrong responses. Sessions can last for three hours, with breaks every thirty minutes. With this system Hammond believes that the cult creates and programs alter personalities that perform a variety of functions unknown to the seemingly normal subject.

At the conference, Hammond described the intricate layering of these programs:

> Alpha represents general programming. Beta appear to be sexual programs such as how to perform oral sex in a certain way or how to produce and direct child pornography films or run child prostitution rings. Delta are killers. Delta-alters are trained how to kill in ceremonies and also do some self-harm stuff. Theta are psychic killers. This comes from their belief in psychic abilities including their belief that they can make someone develop a brain tumor and die. Omega are self-destruct programs which can make the patient self-mutilate or kill themselves. Gamma systems are protection and deception programs which provide misinformation to try and misdirect you. There are also other Greek letter programs. Zeta has to do with the production of snuff films. Omicron has to do with their association with Mafia, big business, and government leaders. You should go through the Greek alphabet [with your patients]. . . . These programs make a robot shell come down over the alter and make them perform acts in a robotic fashion.

Those who control these programmed cult victims keep a record of all the commands that activate different types of behavior in each member. "The programmers carry laptop computers," said Hammond. "They still carry records of everything that they did twenty years ago."

Hammond estimates that probably two-thirds of all those claiming to have been abused by satanic cults have had such programming. Those who claim to have been abused by these cults but show no willingness to confirm his programming story, he said, were also no doubt abused but by sects that had splintered off from the CIA/Nazi conspiracy. Hammond warns the audience that half of those formally programmed will not only be currently involved in the cult, but will be having their therapy monitored by cult informants.

While his belief in how his clients were programmed is remarkable in its details, it pales in comparison to the method he has developed to uncover and deactivate these programs:

> What I'm going to give you is the flaw in the system. Within the programs they have built in erasure codes which can consist of phrases or numbers. You can get these erasure codes from the patient. By telling the code back to the patient and abreacting the memories associated with those programs, you can erase programs. You should always ask the patient, "If I say this code, what will happen?" By speaking the erasure code you can give back to the host personality all the memories associated with those programs.
>
> Each program has backup programs with their own backups. Ask the patient how many backups there are for a program and if there is an erasure code for all the programs. So you should get the code for omega and all omega backups first.
>
> When you give the code and ask what the patient is experiencing, they will describe computers whirring, things erasing and things exploding and vaporizing. Below the alters, you have "Green Programming" named after Dr. Green. Below the Green Programming is Ultra-Green and the Green Tree. How deep does the programming go? Your guess is as good as mine.

As he explains this intricate system, it becomes unclear at times what is metaphorical and what real and whether Hammond concerns himself with this question. The metaphor of the mind as computer running a DOS program, for instance, seems so fully fleshed out that it is unclear if Hammond believes that the mind can react automatically to the recitation of "erasure codes." With other aspects of his theories, the line between metaphor and reality blurs. "[As you deprogram patients] sometimes robots will block your way," Hammond told his audience. "You can say to the patient, go around and look at the back of the head of the robot and tell me what you see. What they will see are wires or maybe a switch. I tell them to pull the wires or flip the switch and it will immobilize the robot. Then I tell them to look inside the robot and tell me what you find. Generally they will find several children. I tell them to remove the children and then tell them to vaporize the robot. They are usually amazed that this works." As indeed they should be.

During his presentation Hammond gave some hints as to how he developed these theories. He mentions that he didn't discover his first case of satanic-cult abuse until he had attended a conference in which he heard a case study described. He also mentions that several years into his work with ritually abused patients he "had some information dropped on his lap" by a mysterious source. While he didn't reveal this source, he implied that the information proved valid when he confirmed it with two of the three ritual-abuse clients. Hammond's therapeutic techniques for confirming are perhaps most telling. One method he described entailed first convincing patients that he could communicate with their "core" being: a part of the patient that is separate from all the alter personalities but could speak for all the alters as a group. Hammond communicates with the inner cores of his patients by establishing finger signals by which this core entity can answer yes and no questions. Of course the problem with this method is that all the information being unearthed comes from the therapist, not the patient. Since the patient is giving only yes or no responses, he can supply no detail, but only guide the story the therapist is creating.

Regarding his "nonleading" techniques for questioning patients, Hammond gives only one example. In explaining how he had confirmed that "patients from across the country" all know the name of his evil nemesis he says, "One of the ways I will ask the question to patients is: 'If there were a doctor associated with your cult programming, and that name was a color, what would the color be?'" Hammond offers the fact that many patients came up with the name "Dr. Green" as solid confirmation for theories. If this question is representative, and there is no reason to believe it's not, Hammond's interview techniques are far from evenhanded. On analysis, this question hardly qualifies as nonleading, for of the few colors that commonly double as last names—green, brown, white, and black . . . green is one of most common and perhaps most likely to be thought of as a color.

But even with the narrow set of possible answers implicit in the question, a wrong answer does not necessarily contradict the conclusion. Of the one patient who picked the wrong color, Hammond says he later discovered that Dr. Green had been training another doctor with that name at the time this particular patient was being programmed. In the same way he smooths over other possible discrepancies between patient stories. He explains, for example, that the Greek letters assigned to different activities were often changed from year to year to confuse investigators. In both the finger signaling and his modes of asking questions, Hammond seems to have rigged the system so that all information confirms his beliefs and all inconsistencies are explained away.

According to Hammond, other therapists have discovered the same programming. "When you start to find the same highly esoteric information from California to Florida you begin to understand that there is something going on that is very large and very well coordinated and systematic." Hammond is unclear as to how many other therapists have confirmed his suspicions or of what that the confirmation consisted.

While he mentions at one point that "many" therapists had independently confirmed his suspicions, several times during the presentation he repeats what appears to be a single story of another therapist treating a patient who told of alpha, beta, delta, and gamma "programs" with similar assigned characteristics.

There are several possible explanations for Hammond's claims of confirmation. The first possibility is that he has simply reinterpreted inconclusive information received from other therapists and reports it as solid proof. Considering Hammond's outlandish claims (such as his suspicion that satanists have taken over Hollywood) there seems more than enough reason to wonder whether Hammond has the capacity to judge and report information clearly and without bias. Another possibility is that another therapist (or therapists) had indeed found a similar story in another patient, but it was information that originated with Hammond himself. Considering the paths of communication between therapists and between patients, there is a good possibility that the information that Hammond had been covertly spreading throughout the therapy community about his theories had simply looped back to him. "For a long time, I have been telling a select group of therapists I knew and trusted the information I was discovering," Hammond admitted during his speech. "I would tell them to spread that information around but to not use my name. I would say, 'Here's what I've learned. Don't say where it came from.' Therapists have been very hungry for information."

Hammond implies that he was forced to spread information by unnamed rumor because he feared for his life. Regardless of this paranoia, it is not unlikely that his beliefs in cult programming were spread fairly widely among both patients and therapists within the recovered memory community. Considering this, it is possible that a few patients might have internalized these details and repeated them to their therapists. Because his own method of spreading information—telling people and instructing them to pass on the information without repeating his name—Hammond himself has eliminated the possibility that he could ever trace the information back to him.

As for evidence from sources outside the therapy community, Hammond appears unable to distinguish between evidence that would indicate the presence of satanists and the presence of the widespread *fear* of satanists. He proudly quotes a newspaper poll taken in Utah, for instance, that found that 90 percent of people polled in the state believe satanic-ritual abuse to be real. In answering a question as to what proof exists to connect the government with the conspiracy, Hammond notes that a friend of his has "tables of boxes" filled with declassified documents about mind-control research. Hammond doesn't seem to realize that newspaper surveys or boxes full of documents, in and of themselves, are not evidence of anything.

When he cites seemingly solid evidence, he does so in a manner that discourages follow-up. "When people tell you that there is no evidence for what I'm saying, that is baloney," Hammond said. "They have found the body of a child in Idaho. There was a case last summer of a murder in Detroit. You'll find that physicians are very involved in this. A couple of them have been nailed in Utah." To bolster those in the audience who may be wavering in their beliefs, he assures them that "people who believe ritual abuse is not real are either naive—like people who didn't believe in the Holocaust—or they are dirty." At this emphatic statement, the audience interrupted his presentation with applause.

In critiquing Hammond's work, one must fight the impulse to make fun of him. Using his own words, it would not be difficult to paint him as a ridiculous Don Quixote caricature. His theories must, however, be seen in light of their devastating impact on the patients he treats and their influence on the work of other therapists. Hammond's lecture, described above, was fully accredited as a continuing education workshop by the American Medical Association.[24]

If even one of these stories of an intergenerational, baby-sacrificing, cannibalistic cults proves to be true, it deserves a national spotlight much more intense than the Manson murders or the voodoo-related drug-ring killings in Matamoros, Mexico. If ten of these cults actually prove to be in existence, it will profoundly change our basic understanding of our society and our history. While ten such satanic cults would account for only a fraction of one percent of the total number of cults being described in therapy, it would mean that ten supremely evil organizations have so seamlessly woven into the fabric of our society that no one has noticed them until now.

While therapists often cite the Jim Jones cult, the Manson clan, and the murders in Matamoros, these parallels are hardly apt. Jim Jones's followers, the Manson clan, and the like were not believed to be upstanding members of our society until they committed the horrors they are known for. Manson and many of his followers had dozens of run-ins with the law before the Tate–La Bianca murders, and a congressional investigation sparked the Jim Jones suicide-massacre. None of these groups were able to kill without leaving physical evidence, nor were they able to select victims who were not missed by family and friends. None were able to commit monstrously criminal acts over generations. The stories coming out of therapy suggest the existence of a number of antisocial groups that have gone unnoticed because they maintain total psychological control over their members and official control over the locations where they operate. These are crucial distinctions. According to the belief promoted by many therapists, there are no signs to tell that many who appear to be normal law-abiding citizens are actually evil satanists who commit horrible crimes by night. They have escaped notice, according to the myth, by leading perfectly normal lives outside of the cult meetings and by having cult members assume key roles in the community, such as undertakers, doctors, and police officers, so that the crimes can be quickly and quietly covered up. Examining the implications of two survivors, Michelle Smith, as told in *Michelle Remembers*, and Jenny, as described in *Suffer the Children*, Professors Philip Jenkins and Daniel Maier-Katkin, from Pennsylvania State University, concluded that in order to accept these two stories alone, one would have to believe that sophisticated secret cults could "kill with impunity, and that no individuals from such a cult have ever betrayed its secrets or ever revealed its existence to a local church, police agency or newspaper." To believe even these two stories, they write, "calls less for a suspension of disbelief than a complete rewriting of the history of the United States and Canada."[25]

The accounts of satanic-cult abuse are the Achilles' heel of the recovered memory movement. With no supporting evidence, most reasonable people will eventually question the validity of satanic-abuse stories. The skeptical recovered memory therapist is stuck, for if he questions even a single account of abuse, he challenges the entire structure of the therapy and thereby jeopardizes his or her standing within the recovered memory community. In addition, as this quote from a twelve-step pamphlet shows, he also risks losing clients: "Look for a therapist who believes you. Any therapist who suggests that you are making up fantasies is not a good therapist. Leave him or her immediately. It's hard enough to face what happened without having someone undermine your own shaky belief." Within the movement, belief of a client's memories is not to be based on evidence or even plausibility, but on adherence to an orthodoxy. This orthodoxy states that all stories must be true.

Repressed memory therapy promoters are boxed into another corner. If they admit that these stories of satanic abuse aren't true, they would have to admit that their therapy methods have produced false accounts that clients have mistaken for memory. By doing so, they would call into question all memories, believable or unbelievable, satanic or not, that have been recovered through the very particular procedures of this type of treatment.

When asked on national television if he had any evidence for the theories he was proposing, Hammond said both that he shouldn't be responsible for proving evidence and that there probably wasn't any to find. "Basically, we're not going to find many, I don't believe, because the things that therapists hear all over this country are that morticians are involved in many cases, physicians who can sign phony death certificates."

As anthropologist Mulhern has pointed out, therapists and promoters of the scare often chide, or show a thinly veiled disgust for, those who ask for solid evidence that the cults described by patients exist. She quotes Dan Sexton, director of the National Child Abuse Hot Line: "I'm not a law enforcement person, thank God! I'm a psychology person, so I don't need the evidence, I come from a very different place, I don't need to see evidence to believe . . . I don't care what law enforcement's perspective is, that's not my perspective. I'm a mental health professional. I need to find a way to help survivors heal the trauma that they had as children and to help support other clinicians who are trying to help survivors and victims of this kind of crime."[26]

This argument that therapists should not be deterred by evidence, but should exist in a realm of belief, can be found throughout the movement. Although therapists justify their position as one that supports the patient's needs, it might just as well be seen as a position that frees therapists from any concern about reality and any need to be accountable for what they promote in their offices. Psychiatrist Roland Summit, author of "The Child Sexual Abuse Accommodations Syndrome," argued this point at a conference for therapists. "Because we see it clinically, we see something we believe is real, clinically, and whether or not our colleagues or the press, or scientists at large or politicians or local law enforcement agencies agree that it is real, most of us have some sort of personal sense that it is."[27] Sakheim and Devine, editors of Out of the Darkness, gave this same argument: "Therapists probably do best to lean towards the acceptance end of the skepticism continuum. . . . To hold a patient to rules of evidence will only inhibit the process of recovery. This is especially true since so much of the treatment is geared towards helping the patient to deal with his or her own skepticism and denial. . . . It does not help the process for the therapist to add to the patient's already profound distrust of his or her own perceptions."[28]

In Trauma and Recovery, Judith Herman instructs that "it is not enough for the therapist to be 'neutral' or 'non-judgmental,' " they should "assume a position of moral solidarity with the survivor. . . . The therapist has to remember that she is not a fact-finder and that the reconstruction of the trauma story is not a criminal investigation. Her role is to be an open-minded, compassionate witness, not a detective."[29] Sexton, in his address to the therapy conference, put it most strongly when he advised those who lacked the ability to believe these satanic-cult stories should bar themselves from working with patients who believe themselves victims. "If you don't believe this could possibly happen, do not work with this issue. We don't want you part of this because it is simply going to make the issue more confounded and more difficult."[30]

*   *   *

The comparison between the satanic-cult panic and the witch-hunts and satanic rumors of antiquity is inevitable. Stories of satanists secretly gathering to share in unspeakably evil deeds have been around for more than a thousand years. The parallels between the stories coming from therapy and these age-old beliefs have not escaped the notice of those who currently promote the idea that child-murdering satanic cults exist within our society. Instead of distancing themselves from the witch-hunts, several current promoters of satanic-cult stories have incorporated these ancient beliefs as evidence that current cult allegations are true and accurate.

In their attempt to "assist clinicians in considering as one possibility that [a satanic-ritual-abuse patient] is describing fragmentary or partially dissociated memories of actual events," Sally Hill and Jean Goodwin, from the Department of Psychiatry at the Medical College of Wisconsin, have taken the time to find parallels between the current accounts of ritual abuse and accounts of rituals which predate the Inquisition. In addition they compare two current stories of ritual abuse with historical accounts. "These [current] images [of satanic-ritual-abuse] seem so alien to normal experience," they write, "that both patient and therapist lack a framework . . . within which such frightening and often fragmentary images can be assembled, organized and understood."[31]

In finding similarities to satanic stories from the first millennium after Christ, Hill and Goodwin attempt to do their part in constructing that framework. "If it can be shown that certain satanic cult practices have been documented over many centuries," they promise at the beginning of the paper, "this knowledge could help therapists and patients deal matter-of-factly with similar material when it emerges in psychotherapy."

In the end they assembled a list of eleven elements of satanic rituals from history, of which seven correspond with modern therapy-inspired accounts. The eleven elements include "(1) secret nocturnal feasting around a special table or altar; (2) ritual orgiastic sex involving usual [sic] practices; (3) imitations and reversals of the Catholic mass, as the use of vestments; (4) ritual use of blood, semen, urine or excrement often connected with initiation; (5) sacrifice of fetuses or children involving the use of knives, cauldrons or fire and often including cannibalism; (6) ritual abuse of animals; (7) ritual use of torches, candles and darkness; (8) chanting, especially of names of demons; (9) drinking a drug or potion; (10) dancing backward in a circle or other ritual use of the circle; and (11) dismemberment of corpses and extraction of the heart."[32]

Goodwin and Hill's work suffers from one devastating and obvious flaw, and that is that they have no evidence to show that the accounts of satanic practices from a thousand years ago are anything more than religiously inspired rumor and hearsay. The two attempt to skate over this hole in their work by assuring the reader that they have considered this issue. "As with clinical data, there are many questions about the validity of historical data. To minimize these issues we will use only primary sources from before the Inquisition, that is, before A.D. 1200. The use of propaganda, torture and the seizure of property by the Inquisition so distort historical materials from that era that we have elected to discard them."[33]

They appear to be asking the reader to accept one set of accounts as trustworthy, for the sole reason that another set of information has proven untrustworthy. This is apparently intended to assure the reader that they have carefully discriminated between real accounts and false ones. However, despite this assurance, there is no indication in the paper that they did so. They supply no information as to why the reader should take pre-Inquisition accounts any more seriously than such accounts from any point in history.

Another researcher, in a rambling account of the history of satanism from 3000 B.C. to the present, has similarly revised history to marshal evidence for the current stories coming from therapy. To justify the parallels between modern-day therapists who use torturous abreactions to elicit stories of satanic-cult activity and sixteenth-century judges who used more conventional torture to extract similar accounts, Martin Katchem, a member of the Cult Awareness Network and a researcher in the field of dissociation and hypnotizability, comes to the defense of the witch-hunters. According to Katchem, the witch-hunts of the fifteenth and sixteenth centuries "make a different kind of sense than has previously been assumed.

"Witchcraft may well have been a constellation of actual political and organized criminal movements," he writes. "The idea that all who were accused of witchcraft were the victims of fanatical Dominican inquisitors using torture to extract confessions that would validate their preconceived notions appears to be a simplistic overreaction."[34]

Katchem redefines the Inquisition as a "police force." In his view they did not murder tens of thousands of innocent people but, rather, were only "attempting to investigate and bring to justice criminals, some of whom were not only criminals under the laws of the medieval Church, but under the laws of any modern society. The problems that the Inquisition faced, of reliability of evidence, overzealousness, and political pressures, are also problems of modern police forces and serious investigators of contemporary Satanism."[35]

That Katchem, Goodwin, and Hill are willing to take as evidence for modern satanism the accounts of satanism throughout history shows how willing those who promote the satanic-cult beliefs are to turn evidence on its head in order to further their own cause. There is no evidence, according to Professor Norman Cohn, Oxford University historian and perhaps the preeminent scholar on the subject, to suggest that Devil worshipers or witch covens—with magical powers or otherwise—existed in medieval times or during the Inquisition. Counter to Katchem's assurance that the witch-hunters were just police in another guise is the fact that witches were most often accused of crimes that could have no basis in reality. As Cohn documents in *Europe's Inner Demons*, witches were tried and executed for conjuring up demons, flying to far-off sabbat where they copulated with the Devil, cursing men to impotence, and putting spells on crops. In short, people were killed for performing manifestly impossible crimes.

In encouraging "researchers" to take evidence from questionable sources, like the book *Michelle Remembers* and confessions elicited by the Inquisition, Katchem suggests that "the facts must be separated from the theological beliefs of the writer. . . . The facts must be considered individually." If, then, *Michelle Remembers* contains accounts of literal appearances by Jesus Christ and the Devil, the "serious researcher" must not let these clearly sectarian fantasies shed doubt on parts of the book that could be real. Similarly, if a "witch" in A.D. 1200 was convicted of eating babies at a sabbath which she flew to, and at which she also copulated with demons who took the form of animals, we should also consider the baby-eating charge as a possibly provable fact—simply because it is the only part of the charge that is, in reality, possible.

Of course, these stories should not be given the benefit of such doubt. The supernatural is so intricately tied into satanic-cult myths that it is quite impossible and illogical to weed out true bits of information from stories that are for the most part obviously false. While scholars have often advanced the idea that there were indeed groups of heretics who worshiped the Devil, according to Cohn, once their evidence is examined it proves "wholly unreliable." "Each [account of plausible Devil worship cited] is accompanied by statements which are anything but plausible," he writes. "To understand why the stereotype of Devil-worshiping sects emerged at all, why it exercised such fascination and why it survived so long, one must look not at the beliefs or behavior of heretics . . . but into the minds of the orthodox themselves. Many people, and particularly many priests and monks, were becoming more and more obsessed by the overwhelming power of the Devil and his demons. That is why their idea of the absolutely evil and anti-human came to include Devil-worship, alongside incest, infanticide and cannibalism."[36]

The burden of proof that some piece of an otherwise impossible account might be true must be great indeed. Those who pick and choose plausible facts from fantastic accounts must tell us why we should consider some detail as possibly true if most of the story is obviously inspired by fantasy. As Cohn puts it, "Stories which contain manifestly impossible elements ought not to be accepted as evidence for physical events."

According to Cohn, a careful study of the witch-hunts "can in fact be taken as a supreme example of a massive killing of innocent people by a bureaucracy acting in accordance with beliefs which . . . had come to be taken for granted, as self-evident truths. It illustrates vividly both the power of the human imagination to build up a stereotype and its re-luctance to question the validity of a stereotype once it is generally accepted."[37]

Katchem, Goodwin, and Hill fail to emphasize that those writing about satanic cults throughout history have nearly always been self-proclaimed antisatanists warning of the perils of denying the doctrine of Christianity. The works they cite are those of religious zealots warning society about the evils of satanism. In this light, Katchem, Goodwin, and Hill are an interesting addition to this tradition. They warn of the evils and dangers of satanism, not to defend and promote a religious doctrine but to defend and promote the theories, practices, and therapeutic results of recovered memory therapy.

All shades of psychotherapy are to an extent insular and resistant to criticism. As Jerome Frank notes in *Persuasion and Healing*, practitioners of different techniques tenaciously hold to their methods no matter the evidence against their use. "One reason for the tenacity of all theories of psychotherapy, including psychoanalysis, is that practitioners elicit from patients material confirming their views." And because of shared theories, vocabulary, and similar clinical experiences, therapists with similar inclinations tend to associate primarily with each other, thus compounding the perceived validity of their procedures and eliminating sources of criticism. As Frank notes, for therapists to abandon their beliefs they would be in the difficult position of admitting that they were wrong. "In this conception, that the method may not work well and that the doctrine is open to question may paradoxically strengthen the analyst's dogmatic adherence to them as a way of stifling his misgivings. . . . For one of the best ways to allay self-doubts is to try to convert others to one's point of view, thereby gaining confirmation of its correctness from them."[38]

Supporters of recovered memory therapy and promoters of satanic-cult conspiracies have used many different tactics to discredit critical examinations, including accusing critics of blatant misogyny. In response to Carol Tavris's piece in the *New York Times Book Review,* in which she questioned many of the movement's books for their simplistic ideas, the editors of the book review ran three full pages of letters including this statement by *Secret Survivors* author E. Sue Bloom: "There is indeed the dramatic polarization Ms. Tavris describes and her essay places her directly on the side of the molesters, rapists, paedophiles and other misogynists—a side which she certainly should apologize for choosing." The promoters of recovered memory therapy have begun to claim that they are the targets of a "backlash" organized by a well-funded conspiracy of forces aligned against women and victims. To be inside the recovered memory movement now is to be in an echo chamber in which only information that confirms the effectiveness of the therapy and reality of repressed memories is allowed.

Another argument, directed less at defending the therapy than attacking the character of those who question such beliefs, has recently sprung up to counter the growing criticism. Some therapists and experts have objected to the questioning of an abuse narrative on the grounds that patients should have the right to remember their pasts in any way they see fit. On the television show "Sonya Live," *Courage to Heal* coauthor Ellen Bass emphasized, "It's very important that survivors who are listening to this show know that they have the right to trust themselves. Each survivor has the right and the ability to know and to name his or her own experience. That has to be the bottom line." After an accused parent called in to the show proclaiming innocence, Bass even conferred this right on those accused by their adult children, saying: "Everyone has the right to believe what they believe."[39]

Bass's implication is that those who question abuse beliefs that come out of therapy are infringing upon this right. At first blush, this idea has a certain appeal. If we all possess the inalienable right to pursue lives in the way we see fit, shouldn't we have a similar right to remember that life with equal freedom? Unfortunately, this new "right" relies on collapsing the distinction between fact and belief. In doing so, one eliminates the possibility of ever arriving at anything that approximates truth or reality. It substitutes for the question *What happened?* the ultimate psychobabble: all that matters is how you *feel*.

Considering the stakes involved in such memories, this "all-have-the-right" to their own memories "bottom line" becomes absurd. Ask the patients who believe they have recovered memories of being raped and tortured by their fathers during satanic rituals or the fathers who have been confronted with such accusations, and you will likely be told that the historical truth of the memory, not each side's right to believe whatever they want, is the true bottom line. The reason fact matters here more than belief about what happened should be obvious to most, even if it eludes Bass. If you form the belief that your mother and father were monsters, sexual deviants, torturers, or murderers, it will, in turn, determine everything about your relation with your parents. If the truth of these stories does not matter to Bass, it certainly does matter to the patients undergoing recovered memory therapy and those whom they learn to hate.

Bass's assurance that patients have the right to believe what they choose becomes more absurd considering how that right is steadfastly refused patients entering therapy. As we have documented, at the early stages of treatment, therapists assume that the patient's mind is clouded by repression and denial; the patient's sincere belief that she was not abused can be ignored or overcome.

Yet another argument therapists use to deflect criticism is to claim that any skepticism or disapproval is a sign that the rest of the world is sadly unprepared to see the horrible truths that they have bravely faced. Colin Ross, the current president of the International Society for the Study of Multiple Personality Disorder, ignores criticism of his treatment regimes by maintaining that it is a "pseudo debate" and "all political." "Basically what it is all about is that people don't want to hear about child abuse and people don't want to talk about it, and don't want their patients to talk about it."[40] By implying that they are morally superior—willing to face the truth when the rest of society stubbornly denies the abuse they are discovering—these therapists are attempting to shame the rest of the world into not questioning their theories or methods.

Hedging their bets, some therapists have argued that their work can be justified, *even if the stories of satanic abuse prove false.* "Even if we discover that no such conspiracy exists," write Sakheim and Devine, "we still need to develop ways to investigate and prosecute the criminal acts that do occur, as well as develop and provide treatment for the victims in such cases."[41] The idea that the battle that recovered memory therapy is waging against an imaginary satanic-cult conspiracy is a no-lose proposition is a truly pathetic piece of reasoning, for it ignores the damage the battle has caused. If we discover that satanic cults do not exist beneath our society, committing horrible crimes with impunity, then the recovered memory therapists are responsible for the destruction of the lives of thousands of patients and their families. In addition, to believe the satanic-cult theories offered by Hammond and many others requires that you give up the assumption your neighbor (or your doctor or the teacher who watches over your child) will act decently. If these theories are not true, recovered memory therapists can count themselves responsible for damaging not only individual lives and families but for tearing apart whole communities by eroding the trust that binds people together.

Even if we ignore the damage done, it would still be impossible to argue convincingly that society has made gains from the hysteria engendered by recovered memory therapists. Pursuing imaginary monsters requires that one ignore garden-variety evils. Who has time to make incremental improvements in our society when he or she believes a satanic cult is killing and programming our children at will? Conducting a witch-hunt against imaginary monsters does not increase our ability to face real problems and traumas, it does the opposite.

When listing reasons why we should accept the idea that murderous satanic cults exist unexposed within our society, therapists often repeat that many Americans initially denied that a Holocaust took place in Nazi Germany. This logic is sometimes offered to audiences in order to keep their minds open to the possibility that satanic cults exist, or to patients in order to help them maintain faith in the belief labyrinth they have created.

We would like to argue this parallel from a different perspective. The reasoning used to propagate and bolster the satanic-cult scare is the same sort of reasoning that is currently used by the so-called Holocaust "revisionists," who have, with growing efficiency, propagated the belief that it was a hoax. According to Deborah Lipstadt, who recently published *Denying the Holocaust: The Growing Assault on Truth and Memory*, those who deny that the Holocaust took place have achieved a veneer of academic respectability and have created a belief that relies not on evidence but on the constant quoting and referencing of others who hold the same beliefs. "They have academic conferences, and even a journal that looks respectable," she said during a recent interview. "Their evidence is a merry-go-round of cross-fertilization. One expert quotes another expert, who quotes another expert, who quotes another. The arguments go in circles. But they portray themselves as people who are exploring the truth. It's a cloak of respectability that often fools people."[42]

Lipstadt's thesis is that those who deny the Holocaust are just one of many groups rewriting history with no regard for evidence. This disregard of the provable is the ultimate dumbing down of the idea of deconstructionism: evidence has no particular meaning, only our *interpretation* of evidence has meaning. The growing acceptance of these groups and their theories, she believes, shows a fragility of reason within our society and dangerous relativism that makes it impossible to say that something is nonsense. "Reasoned dialogue has a limited ability to withstand an assault by the mythic power of falsehood, especially when that falsehood is rooted in an age-old social and cultural phenomenon," she writes in her book. "Mythical thinking and the force of the irrational have a strange and compelling allure for the educated and uneducated alike."[43]

Her indictment of "historians" who willingly make up evidence and ignore any fact that might counter their beliefs could just as easily be applied to therapists who promote the stories of murderous satanic cults. "Reasoned dialogue, particularly as it applies to the understanding of history, is rooted in the notion that there exists a historical reality that—though it may be subjected by the historian to a multiplicity of interpretations—is ultimately found and not made. . . . Even a historian with a particular bias is dramatically different from the proponents of these pseudoreasoned ideologies. The later freely shape or create information to buttress their convictions and reject as implausible any evidence that counters them. They use the language of scientific inquiry, but theirs is a purely ideological enterprise."[44]

This is the story of the recovered memory movement. The veneer of respectability that recovered memory therapists have managed to create, however, goes far beyond that which covers the work of Holocaust deniers. Hammond, Braun, and others with similar beliefs, continue to treat patients, train other therapists, publish academic books and papers, and maintain high positions in universities, hospitals, and their professional organizations. The prominence of these experts speaks to how deeply these beliefs have been accepted by large groups of practitioners, as well as to the inability of their professions to effectively expose and put a stop to their treatment methods.

Hammond, Braun, and others offer no compelling evidence for their wild theories but only clinical anecdotes, their impressive titles, and the constant reassurance that conclusive evidence will be coming shortly—if we only keep an open mind. Our growing willingness as a culture to throw history up for grabs—to believe anything is possible and therefore anything might be true—is the cornerstone from which the satanic-cult story is built. We are asked to deny reason in favor of belief.

While claiming the critics of satanic-cult stories are like those who initially failed to understand that a holocaust was taking place in Germany, these self-proclaimed satanic-cult experts miss the more obvious parallel between the Holocaust and their work: it is the arbitrary vilification of innocent people which allows holocausts to take place.

Multiple Personality Disorder:
The Creation of a Sickness

"Down with skepticism, up with awareness!"

—Text of a button handed out
at a conference for MPD therapists

The diagnosis of multiple personality disorder is tied up with the recovered memory movement because of the belief that childhood trauma causes children and young adults to "split" into new personalities. These personalities, recovered memory therapists believe, are created to live through the abuse so that the host personality can live free of both the pain of the attacks as well as any knowledge of the problem. "Virtually everyone who is diagnosed as being a multiple has been severely abused . . . as a young child," report Bass and Davis in *The Courage to Heal*. "To cope with this trauma, the child blocks the feelings and memories from consciousness and another self, the 'alter' personality, takes over and functions."[1]

Whether the therapist first hunts for alter personalities or for repressed memories seems to vary from therapist to therapist. Because MPD is considered an outcome of more traumatic sexual abuse, often the search for its symptoms does not begin until other therapies have proven ineffective or until recovered memory therapy is well under way. The average time in therapy *before* the multiple personality disorder is diagnosed is nearly seven years.[2] Often the searches for memory and alter personalities can happen in tandem. Recovered memory therapists believe that each alter personality can carry a set of abuse memories. Once a new alter is flushed out in therapy, he/she or it (some alter personalities are inanimate, such as a "cloud") is then expected to be able to tell of the events experienced by that alter.

In tandem with recovered memory therapy, the diagnosis of the multiple personality disorder has skyrocketed in the last ten years. As late as 1979 there were only two hundred cases of MPD in all of recorded medical history. In the following decade, the growth of the diagnosis kept pace with recovered memory therapy. Since 1980, thousands of recovered memory clients have been told that they harbor multiple personalities. Dr. Colin Ross, one of the most prominent promoters of the MPD diagnosis, believes that "One percent of the population fits the criteria for being a multiple personality."[3] Just in the United States, that would bring the number to over two million.

If one were to observe an MPD client after several years of therapy for the problem, one would have little doubt that one was witnessing a clear, specific, and distressingly severe disorder. Once the patient and therapist have both accepted the idea that the patient holds more than one personality, and that those personalities take turns surfacing and controlling the body, the actions the client displays are often breathtakingly bizarre. Watching female patients switch from a crying child to the personality of a menacing adult man in a brief moment, one can quickly rule out the idea that these patients are just good actors intentionally trying to deceive their therapists or the rest of the world.

A videotape of a group-therapy session led by Ross at his clinic in Dallas drives this point home.[4] The tape shows Ross surrounded by ten grown women sitting on the floor, all acting out their child personalities. One woman giggles as she tries to catch soap bubbles with her tongue, while another curls up sucking her thumb. They push their lips out when they talk and their voices are high-pitched and lispy. Later Ross asks one of the clients if she can talk to the Devil inside her. "This is Dr. Ross calling," he says to the woman, "can I speak with that part who calls itself the Devil?" Responding to his request, the client's eyes change from wide to narrow and her spine and shoulders stiffen. "Who has the authority to call on me?" she says, her voice now deep and angry. As the Devil personality looks around the room at the other women, who are still acting out their child alters, some begin to cry in fear. Soon they are all crying hysterically. Some of the women huddle together, sobbing and consoling each other.

The behavior illustrated by these women is just the tip of the iceberg for those suffering from MPD. According to the literature surrounding the diagnosis, patients will often produce dozens, sometimes hundreds of personalities. Some of these alters are expected to be of the opposite sex, while others can be animals. Sometimes these animal alters can speak, while others can only growl like a wolf, grunt like a bear, or howl like a rabbit in torment.[5] Another personality that is expected to emerge over the course of the MPD treatment is an alter intent on destroying the host personality through suicide or dangerous behavior. Often these personalities prove the sincerity of their threats by cutting or mutilating themselves or by attempting suicide. For these reasons, MPD patients often need to be hospitalized during their treatment.

When looking at the disorder from the perspective of a few years into its treatment, it is hard not to be impressed by the complexity and severity of the symptoms, as it is hard not to be impressed with the brave therapists who struggle to help their patients. Colin Ross, working with his roomful of highly disturbed women, for example, seems the very picture of a healer—compassionate and restrained.

However, to look at the disorder from the perspective of those well into therapy is to miss the most troubling aspects of the disorder: the process by which MPD is diagnosed and uncovered. The first surprise one gets when looking at the entirety of MPD is that neither the therapist nor the patient is aware that the patient has this severe and chronic disorder at the *beginning* of treatment. Even after the diagnosis is made, it may take a good deal of time before the patient begins to switch personalities in the manner displayed by Ross's patients.

One of the most troubling and telling facts of the disorder is that patients develop their most dramatic and debilitating symptoms only in the course of treatment. Therapists readily admit that at the beginning of treatment patients do not switch between child and adult personalities in front of them. Nor do they howl, growl, scream uncontrollably, talk in the persona of the Devil, or speak in strange voices that tell of a desire to kill the host personalities. One can see the remarkable disparity between the symptoms the client presents and the ones they later learn to display by juxtaposing the beginning and ending to the books that purport to help clinicians diagnose and treat the problem. Eugene Bliss, author of *Multiple Personality, Allied Disorders, and Hypnosis*, informs his readers at one point that the MPD symptoms can often go unnoticed by the patient or those close to the patient because the signs can often be subtle. But at another point in the same book he describes MPD patients as "literally living in another world," where fantasy and reality cannot be distinguished. "The Devil terrifies them; suicidal personalities frighten them; homicidal personalities are hidden or imprisoned; they sit in the lap of Mother Mary for protection. A rape at age seven is relived with all the anguish, anger and physical pain of the original event. One personality steals, another starts fires, a third solicits men as a prostitute, another slashes the patient's wrists. . . . A constant struggle is being waged with the patient between preservative forces and destructive ones."[6]

At the beginning of another book on the topic, Frank Putnam encourages therapists to suspect patients of MPD if they have some difficulty presenting a clear chronology of their lives, for example, being unable to remembering whether a particular event came before or after another event.[7] A hundred pages later, however, once he is past the section on how to detect a multiple and on to the description of the disorder, he writes, "Multiples . . . are 'unstuck in time.' The past and the present intermingle and follow each other in chronological confusion. Flashbacks, with their accompanying distortions of age and body image, send a patient hurtling backwards to relive trauma that seems more vivid now than when it actually occurred. . . . Time is discontinuous for multiples. . . . Reality testing is impaired by the lack of a firm 'now' against which to measure what is past and what is present."[8]

Why doesn't the clinician look for the severe symptoms described by Bliss and Putnam at the beginning of the treatment? The simple answer that everyone in the debate seems to agree on is that these symptoms, along with the alter personalities, are not present in the patient's behavior during the beginning of the treatment. This fact leads to two possible alternatives that are hotly debated. The first is that the client already displays these debilitating symptoms—but only *outside* of the therapy setting. MPD alters are said to rise up out of the unconscious and take over the patient's body without the request *or knowledge* of the host. The patient who denies being a multiple at the beginning of therapy is not lying, therefore, she just doesn't yet know that she displays the MPD behavior outside of therapy. Bliss writes that "Many patients' personalities remain undetected by clinicians and families until hypnosis uncovers teeming populations of them—in one case eighteen, in another fifty, and in a third more than a hundred. . . . The absence of confirmation by other people of manifest personalities does not eliminate the diagnosis. In some cases . . . what happens inside the patient's mind is not always evident to the casual observer."[9]

Again considering the severity of the symptoms patients display late in their years of MPD treatment, one wonders whether such a disorder could have gone unnoticed in the patient's pretherapy life. If the patient did indeed have eighteen or a hundred different personalities, many of which had totally different memories, attitudes, feelings, and behaviors (some of which perhaps consisted of being childlike, animal-like, or of the opposite sex), the indications of that disorder would be pervasive in the client's history. This idea that the disorder could lie hidden until therapy flies in the face of the experts' contention that switching between personalities occurs spontaneously and without the client's conscious will. As Bliss contends, the switching usually occurs when the patient encounters "stress with which he or she could not cope."[10] If the person had no control over her switching when faced with one of these stressful situations, how could this behavior have gone unnoticed? Even if the client somehow kept the knowledge from herself, any husband, friend, teacher, or coworker would surely have noticed and commented on the person's propensity to talk like a toddler for periods of time, or switch into the "dragon" personality where she could do nothing but roar.

The other possible explanation for the lack of observable symptoms at the beginning of treatment is that the symptoms *don't exist at the beginning of therapy*. As Dr. Paul McHugh, director of the Department of Psychiatry and Behavioral Science at Johns Hopkins Medical Institution, states concisely, this possibility leads to the conclusion that "MPD is an iatrogenic behavior syndrome, promoted by suggestion and maintained by clinical attention, social consequences, and group loyalties."[11] Evidence that MPD is a creation of therapy is mounting from a number of quarters, most conspicuously from former MPD patients themselves and from prominent members of the mental-health community who see it as another installment in a rich history of treatment-created behaviors.

The charge that MPD is a product of therapy is not made lightly. If true, therapists must take responsibility not only for the pseudomemories of abuse uncovered in MPD therapy process as a justification for the symptoms, but must also recognize their role in the creation of many of debilitating and dangerous behaviors that the clients learn to manifest. This is particularly troubling considering the prevalence of alter personalities who attempt suicide as well as cut, burn, and otherwise mutilate themselves.

The complaints that MPD sufferers bring to therapy are often the standard fare—depression, difficulty in relationships, vague anxieties.[12] Others have a long list of previous diagnoses acquired throughout years of mental-health treatment. Because they don't display the obvious signs at the beginning of treatment, experts write, great clinical skill is required to spot a potential MPD sufferer. According to Frank Putnam, "A clinician will not find MPD if he or she is not willing to look for it."[13] How long should this search take? A "lengthy period of intimate therapy,"[14] writes Putnam, is most often required before the discovery of the true MPD symptoms such as the switching among personalities.

Putnam describes a line of questioning he uses to uncover a variety of subtle clues through which he suspects clients of being hidden multiples. As other MPD experts also recommend, he first takes a chronological history of clients, starting from their "earliest memory" and working through their life, using their grade level in school as a reference. For a patient who may later turn out to be a multiple, Putnam often finds significant gaps in the patient's memory. He then goes on to ask the patient about her experiences of "being called a liar, of erratic school performance, of getting tests and homework that she did not remember doing, or of discovering she had taken a course she could not remember."[15]

Putnam also asks about nightmares or intrusive images, which he says are common to MPD patients. He also asks about flashbacks—which he describes as the experience of remembering an event so vividly it seems to be happening in the present. A therapist should not be deterred in his or her diagnosis by a patient who says that he doesn't have flashbacks, however. "A clinician may have to ask several similar questions to uncover the existence of this phenomenon in a patient," writes Putnam, noting that an "MPD patient who is having flashbacks may or may not admit to this experience."[16] What constitutes a display of one of these symptoms is left vague. Here again the therapist is given leave to hear whatever he or she wants to hear. As Putnam puts it: "It is important to listen carefully to what these patients say. They can be masters at appearing to say one thing while actually saying another."[17]

As with the symptom lists that lead therapists to suspect the presence of repressed memories, some of these supposed symptoms seem capable, if not designed, to include everyone. A sense of losing time—defined any number of ways—is a common experience. When daydreaming or focusing on some mundane task, such as driving, time often seems to slip by without the usual markers. Looking back over a month, or a year, or ten years, we often do not have a sense of a continuous flow of events and memories. This is not in the least abnormal. Indeed, Putnam's method of questioning clients about their pasts seems designed to show gaps and instill in patients the belief that they have huge and inexplicable holes in their lives. Asking clients to remember their earliest memory, and then working forward through their grade school years, shows a startling lack of understanding of how memory works. Confronted with a demand to list memories through our childhood, most of us would be startled to find that we are stuck for information—particularly if we are questioned about homework we did a couple of decades ago. The reason for this is not only that much experience is forgotten, but that memories are not organized in anything like a chronological fashion. Memory rises to consciousness by association, not by arbitrary demands for pieces of information. Patients who come to believe that they should be able to plod through their histories, listing experiences chronologically, could be easily convinced that they have huge amnesiac gaps. The anxiety produced by this sort of false realizaton ("My God, I can't remember what happened to me in the fourth grade") could be quite dramatic and do much to convince the client that she desperately needs the expert care of her therapist to return to normalcy.

According to the MPD literature, establishing the presence of vague MPD "symptoms" in the client is only the beginning of the process of bringing out the other personalities. Motivated by his or her confirmation of these symptoms, the therapist must undertake a number of procedures to attempt to bring out the disorder. "The clinician who suspects that his or her client may be suffering from MPD can make use of a number of strategies to confirm or exclude this diagnosis," writes Putnam. "The task of identifying and eliciting suspected alter personalities can be difficult and anxiety-provoking for both therapist and patient."[18]

According to Putnam, in the first part of this process of *eliciting* an alter personality, the therapist asks a series of directed questions. The patient is asked if she has ever "felt like another person." If this does not work, Putnam recommends asking if the patient ever feels like there "is some other part of yourself that comes out and does or says things that you would not do or say?" Do patients ever "feel as if they are not alone, as if there is someone else or some other part watching you?"[19] This technique is also recommended by other experts on the disorder. "It may happen that an alter personality will reveal itself to you during [the assessment] process, but more likely it will not," writes Stephen E. Buie, director of the Dissociative Disorders Treatment Program at North Carolina Hospital. "So you may have to elicit an alter. . . . You can begin by indirect questioning such as, 'Have you ever felt like another part of you does things that you can't control?' "[20]

With these questions, Buie writes, "You are trying to develop a picture of what the alter personality is like . . . at this point you may ask the host personality, 'does this set of feelings have a name?' . . . Often the host personality will not know. You can then focus upon a particular event or set of behaviors."[21] Putnam concurs: "If the patient makes a positive or ambiguous response to these questions, it is important to ask for specific examples. In particular, I am looking for either a name or an attribute, function, or description that I can use as a label to elicit this other part directly."

As with the symptoms that lead the therapist to suspect the disorder, most people could answer yes to some or most of these questions. Depending on the criteria for what would constitute feeling like another person (which is again left distressingly vague), we could all attest to times when we have embarrassed ourselves or experienced such intense emotions that—in retrospect—we appear a different person. A client willing to answer yes to these vague questions could quite easily skew certain memories to encourage this line of questioning. Clients hoping to please the therapist might tell of especially angry, sad, or happy moments in their lives—adopting the language and expectations implicit in the questions.

Patients' motivation for describing certain behavior or actions within the structure that the MPD therapist offers goes beyond simply wishing to please the therapist. A patient who abuses alcohol or hits her child, for example, may be desperately confused about why she behaves self-destructively or why she hurts the thing she loves the most. Confirming the therapist's suspicion by classifying these actions as those that feel like the behavior of another person—which may be true in retrospect—would not only be a step toward an explanation for those actions but would also give the client some sense of absolution for their consequences.

While these questions would do little to exclude the diagnosis in a given case, they most assuredly reveal to the client the course the therapist has chosen to pursue. If by this point the client hasn't yet discerned the therapist's suspicions, the experts recommend that the therapist confront the client with the diagnosis. "The first step is to make the subject aware of the problem,"[22] writes Bliss. "Making the diagnosis of MPD is not easy," concurs Bennet Braun, another leader in the field and director of a dissociative disorder unit at a Chicago hospital. "Once the diagnosis is made, the therapist must share it with the patient. . . . [Even] when the interpretation is properly timed and accepted by the patient . . . the therapist must be prepared for a cyclical pattern of accepting/rejecting the MPD diagnosis throughout the early and middle phases of treatment."[23] Unfortunately, thanks to the books and movies *Sybil* and *The Three Faces of Eve*, it is unlikely that any modern patient would have no conception of how MPD patients act. As far as all the current cases are concerned, they suggest that media attention given to the diagnosis has been so pervasive that it is likely that all patients would have some idea of the type of behavior that would confirm the diagnosis. Cornelia Wilbur, therapist to the famous Sybil, suggests not only that patients be informed about their diagnosis, but that they be given information about what sort of behaviors multiples manifest. She writes that, "A practical approach may be for the analyst to explain MPD and its effects," adding that "the patients should be encouraged to ask any and all questions they may have about their condition."[24]

To get the first personality to come out and take control of the client's body is the biggest hurdle in therapy. Both Buie and Putnam suggest that the therapist who suspects the client of MPD directly ask for a personality to step forward and take control of the client's consciousness. This can be done with or without hypnosis or trance-inducing drugs. "If the therapist strongly suspects that a patient may have MPD but has not spontaneously met a recognizable alter personality, there comes a time when he or she may have to ask directly to meet an alter personality. This moment is often harder for the therapist than for the patient. It can make one feel foolish, but often it is necessary."[25] In this way, Putnam and Buie recommend taking the information gained during the questioning to call up a personality. If a patient has often felt like a "different" person when angry, the therapist can ask to "talk directly to that facet" of the person. If you feel like a different person when you take long Sunday drives, Buie writes, the therapist should ask, "Can I talk to the part of you that is taking those long drives in the country?"[26] This moment in MPD therapy is critical. If the patient is motivated to cooperate with the healer, this sort of request to act out the "part" that takes long Sunday drives offers the patient an easy opportunity to step across the threshold into the bizarre world of MPD treatment. When the patient attempts to act out the Sunday-driver demeanor, the therapist is given his or her first opportunity to perceive the presence of an alter personality.

Putnam's warning that asking for an alter personality could be embarrassing to the therapist is a revealing comment. Considering the relationship that often develops between client and therapist, the client may be greatly motivated to act out the requested personality in order to save her highly respected therapist from looking foolish. As Nicholas Spanos, a critic of the MPD phenomena, writes, therapists are most often seen by clients as experts whose opinions should be "highly valued and whose suggestions are treated very seriously." Clients, for their part, are often sad and insecure, "with a strong investment in winning the concern, interest and approval of their therapist."[27] Considering this power balance in the relationship, it does not seem unlikely that the client may do much to confirm the therapist's daring MPD diagnosis.

Patients subjected to MPD therapy often tell of therapists who actively lobby for their patients to accept their diagnosis. One former patient, who calls herself Victoria, was surprised and unconvinced when her therapist first mentioned that she might have MPD. When Victoria told her therapist that the diagnosis did not apply to her, the therapist was not dissuaded. Her therapist began to convince Victoria by telling her that she had many of the "classic symptoms," such as losing time and hearing voices. She also suggested that Victoria "try on" the diagnosis for a time to see if it applied or not. To help her client find her alter personalities, she instructed Victoria to carry around a notebook to write down every time she lost track of time or heard an inner voice. During therapy she handed Victoria a set of index cards and asked her to write down names for a childlike personality and a suicidal alter. In addition, she put Victoria into a group-therapy setting with other people who believed they were suffering from MPD.[28]

There is even evidence within the MPD experts' own books of therapists actively trying to convince clients that they have the suspected disorder. One patient, profiled in Bliss's book, reports that Bliss had to actively convince her over a long period of time that the diagnosis was correct. The patient is quoted: "[Dr. Bliss] called my ways of being crazy multiple personalities, I found this almost impossible to believe. . . . I did not call myself by different names, nor did I have different wardrobes or lose memory of what I had done for a day or a week. I fought with [Dr. Bliss] so very many times over this."[29] The patient goes on to describe being "pushed" to give names to different emotional states and experiences. It seems clear from this description of treatment—published in his own book—that Bliss not only actively engaged in convincing his client that she had multiple personalities, but that he also coached her on the appropriate behavior by insisting that she provide names for her emotions.

At the beginning of treatment it appears that the therapist, not the client, provides almost all of the momentum directing the treatment toward the MPD conclusion. These methods of questioning, suggesting, and actively trying to convince patients (to the point of arguing with them) constitute blatant encouragement that the patients begin to manifest a symptom of a suspected disorder. In the eyes of some experts, like McHugh, MPD "diagnostic" procedures like those described above constitute nothing less than the "crudest form of suggestion."[30] Because the client is slowly introduced to these ideas over a long period of time, the process can not only be viewed as one that indoctrinates the patients into the MPD beliefs, but one that effectively weeds out those less willing to go along with the therapist's suspicions and speculations.

While many practitioners who specialize in the diagnosis deny that MPD behavior can be trained into their clients, they admit that individual alters are often created through the use of leading questions. Noting that MPD patients are highly hypnotizable and responsive to suggestion, psychiatrist Moshe Torem warns in the journal *Dissociation* that new "ego-states" can be created in response to suggestions imbedded in the therapist's questioning. He describes a therapeutic scene in which a new alter was drawn out of an MPD patient with twelve personalities who appeared sad and depressed to the therapist. "The therapist, observing this behavior, responds by saying, 'Who are you? You look so sad. . . . What is your name? . . . I don't think I've talked to you before.' "[31] Torem notes, quite correctly, that these questions communicated the therapist's expectation that he or she has found a new personality. The patient in this case responded by saying that her new name was "Sadie," a six-year-old alter personality responsible for carrying all the patient's sadness. These questions, which Torem points to as leading, appear nearly identical to the ones Buie and Putnam and others recommend to the therapist hoping to find the first alter personality. While Torem encourages therapists to replace directed questions with more oblique ones such as "How would you like me to call you right now?" this sort of semantic dance hardly solves the problem. For a patient steeped in the MPD belief, the difference between Torem's suggested question and the more direct "What is your name?" would likely be nil.

If, as is often agreed, therapists can create the thirteenth, thirty-seventh, or hundredth personality, what evidence is there to suggest they are not responsible for creating the first alter personality and, over the slow course of treatment, the entire series? We have found no reasonable answer to this question within the literature. Often MPD experts attempt to deflect criticism that they may have created a pathology in their clients by simply assuring the world that they know better. "To date the best argument against the iatrogenesis of MPD is based on extensive clinical experience,"[32] proclaim Ross et al. in a prominent paper on the subject. Apparently, then, only those with a huge investment in the idea that MPD is a real disorder can understand this "best argument."

Yet even with suggestions as blatant as those described by MPD experts, it is hard to imagine that they would be sufficient to convince a patient to act out behavior as bizarre as an alter personality, or, for that matter, to claim the amnesia that is often said to be present between the personalities. To fully understand how and why patients first begin to act out their hidden selves, we must first explore the close relationship between MPD treatment and the use of hypnosis.

Those who treat MPD are the first to concede that hypnosis is almost always used in the diagnosis and treatment of MPD.[33] Often hypnosis is introduced into the therapy setting in a nonthreatening way. A therapist might offer a hypnotic-induction procedure to help the client relax or to manage anxiety or stress. Richard Horevitz, writing in the *American Journal of Clinical Hypnosis*, provides these eight steps for MPD therapists:

(1) Suspecting the diagnosis; (2) confirming the diagnosis; (3) gaining the patient's acceptance of the diagnosis; (4) gaining access to known personalities and discovering others; (5) facilitating the switching process; (6) obtaining a description of the system; (7) facilitating co-consciousness; and (8) beginning to use hypnosis for investigative purposes. *Hypnosis can be of use in all of these stages* [emphasis added].[34]

Three case histories reported by Patricia Brassfield, which were also written up in the *American Journal of Clinical Hypnosis*, are standard examples of how MPD is discovered and encouraged through hypnosis. While one of these three patients (a therapist herself) suspected that she might be a multiple personality, none of them had any conscious knowledge at the beginning of their therapy of any MPD behavior. The author's comment that this is not unusual, considering that "most patients come to treatment for depression and suicide attempts with no suspicion in their mind that multiplicity was involved."[35] As Brassfield explains, hypnosis was used not only in "identifying the personalities," but also to "arrange for the personalities to work with each other or, in some instances, manipulate more difficult personalities. A hierarchy of control was established."

To deflect criticism that MPD is a hypnotically induced behavior, MPD promoters have published studies that purport to show that the disorder appears before hypnosis is employed and that some cases (usually a small percentage of the cases) were discovered and treated without the use of hypnosis at all. In a survey of American psychiatrists who treat MPD patients (48 patients in total), Ross et al. reported that hypnosis was used prior to the diagnosis in only 32 percent of these cases.[36] (They go on to note that hypnosis was used in 72 percent of the cases after diagnosis.) Unfortunately, for two reasons this study proves useless in addressing the question of whether hypnosis is the central factor responsible for producing MPD symptoms.

First, Ross and his colleagues fail to distinguish between the time of diagnosis and the first display of an alter personality. While the authors' intent was clearly to imply that hypnotic induction did not lead to the display of the alter personalities, it seems clear from sources quoted above that the diagnosis can be made long before the first alter appears in therapy. The clinician who decides that his patient is a multiple and then proceeds to hypnotize her to find the alters can still claim in such a survey that the hypnosis came *only after* he had made the diagnosis.

The second mistake is that these authorities do not acknowledge that hypnosis and trance states do not exist solely when the therapist induces them, but can be induced spontaneously by the client herself. As we noted in chapter 8, the trance may not be a specific state but rather a continuum in which the subject is able, in varying degrees, to focus attention on an idea or behavior to the exclusion of other factors. For those who are highly hypnotizable, there is often no need for formal hypnosis, nor is there any set of signs that are always present to indicate that the patient has entered trance. Evidence for the argument that multiples may be self-inducing trance in response to indirect suggestions from therapists can be found in the pro-MPD literature. All MPD experts seem to agree that MPD patients are excellent hypnotic subjects. One prominent MPD therapist even refers to them as "hypnotic virtuosos."[37] Most tellingly, two of the most prominent clinicians have directly suggested the mechanism by which patients switch personalities is self-hypnosis.[38] As Bliss states simply, "The crux of the syndrome of multiple personality seems to be the patient's unrecognized abuse of self-hypnosis. This unintentional misuse seems to be the primary mechanism of the disorder. . . . Personalities are first unwittingly created by self-hypnosis and later perpetuated by the same process."[39] While Bliss clearly intended to describe how and why the client creates and manifests alter personalities *prior* to therapy, the comment could just as easily be applied to our contention that the disorder is created *during* therapy. Bliss's statement so strongly mirrors our contention that hypnosis is at the core of the creation of MPD behavior that we would change it only slightly: the crux of the syndrome of multiple personality disorder is the *therapist's lack of recognition* of the patient's abuse of self-hypnosis. This unintentional misuse *in therapy* seems to be the primary mechanism of the disorder. Self-hypnosis does indeed seem to be the primary mechanism of this behavior.

The process of indoctrinating the client into the MPD belief system shifts into high gear after the first personality "appears" and after the diagnosis is accepted by the client. In their descriptions of how they "treat" the disorder once established, therapists provide a wealth of evidence that they encourage the development of alter personalities and behaviors. MPD authorities encourage therapists, for instance, to uncover and explore each personality before they attempt to integrate them again into one identity. In this process of exploration, therapists tell of blatantly directing and suggesting the client's behavior.

Several experts who write on the MPD subject repeatedly warn therapists that lasting integration of personalities cannot take place before each of the personalities receives a sort of individual therapy. Information must be obtained from each of the personalities, according to Braun. This includes the name of the alter, when the alter was created, why the alter appeared, where the patient was at the time the alter was created, and why the alter is currently present in the client's psyche. This information, once obtained, is only the beginning. "When history gathering has given the therapist an idea of the structure of the system," Braun writes, "then work can begin on the individual problems of each personality state."[40] This work requires, according to Braun, that the therapist "focus" on one personality at a time and explore its individual history and problems. Braun and others also recommend that the patient map out or chart her personalities. These charts should include the function of each personality as well as each personality's relationship with the other personalities in the group. In addition, Braun encourages his patients' personalities to talk with each other, either verbally or within their thoughts.

The therapists' influence over the MPD behavior is perhaps the most telling clue that they are not manipulating the behavior but creating and controlling it. A therapist's ability to call up different personalities, simply by asking them to come out, is one example of this control. According to the folklore of MPD, before therapy, the client's personalities have appeared only spontaneously—without the patient's knowledge—in response to crises or particular situations. In the therapy setting, however, the therapist's request becomes enough to elicit the behavior. The patient's supposed amnesiac barriers between personalities can also be breached at the therapist's command. If the therapist requests that the "host" personality listen in on an enactment of another personality, the amnesia that would supposedly otherwise block the enactment can be avoided.

Braun recommends that some personalities can be enlisted and trained to become therapists for some of the other personalities so that they can do "some of the therapy internally between sessions."[41] Another therapist, David Caul, puts his own spin on this theme by teaching his patients how to conduct "group therapy" sessions involving the different personalities of a single patient.[42] Once patients are taught how different personalities can be selected for this one-person group, Caul explains, the therapist can simply sit back and allow the patient to conduct the "group session." These recommendations are just some of the many indications of how bizarre and complex the MPD treatment process can become. The more one reads about the treatment of MPD, the more one sinks into a strange, Alice-in-Wonderland world where metaphor and reality cannot be distinguished.

Perhaps the most effective way therapists educate and train patients in the behavior expected of MPD diagnosis is to place them into real group-therapy settings with other MPD clients. Putting newly diagnosed MPD patients in this sort of surrounding would be the equivalent of giving them a crash course in the types of behaviors, repressed memories, and new alters that they should expect to experience during therapy. According to three experts in running such groups, "sibling rivalry" and "competition for dominance" are common to them. "Patients can and do use their Multiplicity 'skills' to compete for honors as the 'best' multiple personality patient in the group."[43]

So effective is the training patients get in these settings that in therapy groups that contain MPD and non-MPD clients, new converts can be gained to the diagnosis. Two therapists leading one group noted that two non-MPD patients began acting out the behavior once exposed to the other patients with the diagnosis in group therapy. Regardless of this persuasive evidence that these patients were learning the MPD disorder, they were allowed to stay in the group. To justify this decision the authors noted that they didn't want them to lose the feeling of group cohesion, adding that the other MPD patients asked that the new converts remain in the group.[44]

*   *   *

Drawing from a wide variety of sources, the current promoters of MPD often endeavor to give the impression that the disorder has always been with mankind. In stating that MPD is an "age-old disorder," Putnam writes that "the archetypes of MPD, Shamanistic transformation and possession states, lie as far back in time as religious belief and behavior can be traced."[45] Indeed, what these displays through history prove is that the human being has the ability to dissociate and role-play any number of socially appropriate sets of behaviors. These examples are not evidence for MPD, but rather evidence that the disorder might be part of a long history of highly hypnotizable and/or mentally ill people performing socially proscribed behaviors that clerics, shamans, doctors, and psychotherapists demand.

By looking back over history, it becomes clear that what subjects do during formal or self-hypnosis depends wholly on what others expect of them. As Drs. Martin Orne and Brad Bates of the University of Pennsylvania have noted, trance states (both self-induced and otherwise) have a long history of provoking strange behavior—but behavior that was always predicted by the healer in charge. Mesmer, who pioneered the use of hypnosis, would often gather his patients around a table covered

with iron filings. Upon his entrance, the patients would have apparent
seizures and throw fits so violent that they would frighten those witnessing
the event. The patients behaved this way because of the belief they shared
with Mesmer that the magnetic fluid in the body was rearranging itself
in response to his presence and the iron filings.[46] The mistake made by
Mesmer was to assume that the behavior his clients displayed was intrinsic
to their mental state and not influenced by cues from their setting. This
is a mistake that has been made again and again over the history of
research into hypnosis. Another researcher came to believe that his hypnotized clients had paranormal powers, including telepathy, and that
these factors were intrinsic to trance. Another prominent hypnotist of
his time came to the conclusion that catalepsy, lethargy, and somnambu-
lism were essential indications of the trance state. "Each investigator . . . insisted that his patients' behavior and experiences during trance
were intrinsic to the process," write Orne and Bates. "Each refused to
believe that the behavior subjects manifested upon entering trance was
a function of their own concept of how a hypnotized person should
behave. In retrospect, it is clear that each investigator was mistaken.
Afforded the luxury of historical perspective, it is difficult to overlook the
profound influence exerted by the belief and expectation of the hypnotic
subject of the hypnotic experience."[47]

The practice of exorcism in Catholicism shows the extreme malleability
of behavior in troubled and trance-prone people. When priests try to help
disturbed people by casting out spirits, their subjects often manifest symptoms predicted by the cleric—such as reacting violently to the application
of holy water or speaking in a deep and threatening voice. The kinds of
influence and expectations applied during an exorcism are quite similar
to those found in an intense therapy situation. In both situations, the
troubled person looking for structure and help will often acquiesce to the
intuition and expectations of the person attempting the cure.

Oddly, MPD experts are often the first to embrace these similarities.
Ross, in his book *Multiple Personality Disorder: Diagnosis, Clinical Features, and Treatment*, writes that the diagnosis of MPD and demonic
possession are much the same. Before listing the commonalities, he
describes demonic possession as a largely "culture-bound" process
through which the person must first learn what behavior is appropriate
for possession before they can display the signs. "This process may involve
identification with someone in the environment or the past, hypnotic
suggestion, or reinforcement by other people. The person then progresses
to a state of lucid possession, in which he believes that his thoughts and

impulses come not from himself but from another being inside of him . . . the person, under the influence of his culture, progresses to possession, which may be either lucid or somnambulistic, depending on how hypnotizable the person is, and the expectation of the culture."[48] Ross accepts as obvious the fact that the actions of the possessed individual are bound by the cultural cues he or she learns.

In describing possession as a culturally bound behavior reliant on hypnotic suggestion and reinforced by the clerics' expectations, Ross makes our argument for us: MPD has these exact same elements and can be viewed as precisely the same culture-bound construction. Remarkably, Ross appears to admit as much: "If the culture does not endorse the possibility of demon possession, then one would expect this process [leading to possession] to lead to a secular version of demon possession, which in our world is MPD."[49] Ross admits that, absent priests and culture-bound religious beliefs, the behavior specific to demonic possession vanished. Unfortunately—but not surprisingly—he does not offer the same logic in regards to therapists like himself, who promote the current MPD craze.

Examining the history of MPD, we find myriad clues suggesting that this supposed disorder is just as influenced by cultural cues and the healer's expectations as all the trance-related enthusiasm to come before. While the diagnosis has been around in some form for over a hundred years, it was not until the popular book *Sybil*, which came out in 1973, and the subsequent movie, that child abuse was offered as the cause of its symptoms.[50] It appears that it was through this popular story that the idea of childhood brutalization as the etiological factor explaining MPD was introduced to the general public and to the clinical practitioners throughout the United States. It was only after *Sybil* that therapists, often using hypnosis, began finding alter personalities and supposedly "repressed" abuse histories to match.

In a paper for the *British Journal of Psychiatry*, Dr. Harold Merskey examined all MPD case reports that predated the recent interest in the diagnosis in order to determine whether the phenomenon ever showed any indication that it existed on its own. He found that none of these cases—which span the last 110 years—"excluded possibility of artificial production."[51] In his examination of early MPD treatments, he found example after example of therapists suggesting to their clients, sometimes subtly and often overtly, that they displayed the alter-personality behavior. He concluded that "No case has been found here in which MPD, as now conceived, is proven to have emerged through unconscious processes without any shaping or preparation by external factors. . . . it is likely that MPD never occurs as a spontaneous persistent natural event in adults."[52]

To make the case that therapists suggest and encourage their patients to display the MPD symptoms is not to argue that those resulting symptoms are not debilitating, destructive, or truly felt by the patient. In our chapter on hypnosis we have mentioned research that points to the conclusion that hypnotically induced behavior can be perceived by the highly hypnotizable patient as nonvolitional. That is, the patient may become solidly convinced of the innate nature of her MPD symptoms. Once immersed in the behavior, the disorder becomes as real as the cuts and burns patients often self-inflict and the suicide attempts that are common among MPD patients and frequently successful.

The self-destructive behavior acted out by certain alter personalities deserves particular mention. Reading the literature, no MPD system of personalities seems complete without one or more alter who is given over to anger and intent on some dark purpose. Looking at the reports of self-mutilation in MPD behavior over the last decade, for example, Orne and Bates determined that the rate of such behavior rose from 21 percent to 48 percent in MPD patients. Considering that self-mutilation was rarely reported in the first cases of the disorder, Orne and Bates wonder why the rate of self-mutilation has more than doubled since it was first observed and reported only a decade ago. They conclude that "it is possible that the dangerous symptomology currently associated with the disorder, as well as the condition's unfavorable prognosis, is shaped by attitudes and convictions of those who treat it." The other factor that could be increasing the numbers of self-mutilation patients among MPD sufferers is the encouragement by therapists to look for MPD symptoms in patients already cutting or burning themselves. Orne and Bates point to the lead paragraph in a prominent article on the subject as one example:

> The high incidence of self-mutilation among patients with dissociative disorders in this study, particular among MPD patients, calls for increased vigilance among clinicians for evidence of dissociation in the patient demonstrating such behaviors. Further, the existence of self-mutilation should alert the clinician to the possibility of an abusive childhood history . . . the clinician should also consider the various dissociative disorders and search diligently for evidence of memory loss, which may not be immediately apparent.[53]

If this sort of encouragement is adopted by clinicians. Orne and Bates note, it is not unlikely that the next study will uncover self-mutilation in well over 50 percent of MPD patients.

If a personality is identified in therapy as self-destructive—imbued with the impulse to commit suicide or cut or burn him- or herself—what behavior must the client engage in to prove the existence and reality of that personality? Within the MPD literature we find tacit admission that behavior can be provoked through the process of finding and delineating among personalities. "The process of fragmentation and delegation, with an accompanying amnesia," Bliss writes, "allows these feelings to be amplified, so that even if the patient is only mildly depressed, the assignment of a suicidal personality to handle the melancholy may result in a suicide attempt."[54] While again Bliss is referring to patients' experiences *before* therapy, this statement is perfectly applicable to the sort of delineation and behavior labeling that is encouraged in therapy.

While the disorder is not real at the beginning of the therapy, there is little doubt that the patients are truly suffering as they come to accept the therapist's diagnosis. Examining the fad diagnosis of MPD, the cruelty of recovered memory therapy becomes particularly clear. Thousands of clients have learned to display the often-debilitating symptoms of a disorder that they never had. They become less capable of living normal lives, more dependent on therapy, and inevitably more troubled.

The fact that patients learn the debilitating and bizarre symptoms of MPD during therapy has not gone unnoticed by those close to the patient or by the patients themselves. "Don't you think it is odd that no one is getting better and that everyone wants to cut and kill themselves after they get into therapy with you?" one former MPD client reported asking her therapist. Of course therapists have a perfect excuse to deflect such questions. When confronted with this angry patient whose life had been destroyed by MPD therapy, the therapist responded by asking, "Which personality am I talking to now?"[55]

Colin Ross has a more bizarre counterargument for the growing number of people who suggest that hypnosis and overzealous therapists are at the root of the MPD phenomenon. Ross believes that the critics are dupes for the Central Intelligence Agency.

To understand this logic, one must first know that Ross believes that many of his patients were trained to be multiples as children by evil top-secret agents of the CIA. In a book proposal he has circulated on the subject, he promises to expose this "comprehensive and ongoing program," which has succeeded in creating "Manchurian candidates," which number in the "thousands or tens of thousands." Since the late 1940s, Ross explains, the CIA has systematically abused children in laboratory settings, using "hallucinogens, sensory deprivation, flotation tanks, electric shock, enforced memorization and other techniques," and that these "Manchurian candidates are being used by the intelligecne community on an ongoing basis for espionage and surveillance purposes and possibly for assassinations."[56]

Repeating his charge on a Canadian television program, "The Fifth Estate," Ross implied that the recent criticism surrounding the therapy of MPD patients was part of a conspiracy funded by the CIA to cover up what he was discovering. "If the dissociative field was starting to uncover mind-control programming that was hidden in the alters, naturally they wouldn't be enthusiastic about that happening," he said after explaining how the CIA creates MPD. "It would be necessary to have some sort of political strategy in place to counter that." According to Ross, this political strategy is to disseminate the rumor that MPD is "created in therapy, [that it] is not real, that it is [created through] hypnosis."

When reading the literature surrounding the topic of MPD, one sometimes feels the ground of reality crumbling away. Ross's CIA theory and Bennet Braun's belief that many patients come by their symptoms after being brutalized by international satanic-cult rings are two prime examples. Are these psychiatrists called to task by their professional organizations for the bizarre conspiracy theories they are foisting upon their clients?

Unfortunately, this subculture of clinicians appears to reward these beliefs. Within the last decade both Ross and Braun have served as president of the International Society for the Study of Multiple Personality and Dissociation—an organization that now boasts over three thousand professional members.

Therapy of
a High Priestess

We are not Gods. I can't say anything for sure. I can only judge
from my best ability, my experience, and knowledge.
                    —Psychiatrist Bennet Braun,
                         testifying in a child-custody hearing

Anne Stone's* story pierces the heart of the recovered memory debate
for several reasons. As an illustration of the harm that can be visited upon
one woman and her family, Anne's descent into therapy represents the
severe end of the spectrum. With her diagnosis of multiple personality
disorder, accompanied by her belief that she suffered torture by a satanic
cult, Anne represents the endgame outcome of recovered memory therapy: the "memories" she discovered in therapy were horrifying and complex as might be imagined and her treatment was as brutal as any that
has yet been documented. Some variation of Anne's treatment is currently
being repeated hundreds of times over in dissociative disorder units across
the country. While her experience exemplifies the most severe outcome
of recovered memory therapy, an equally important reason to profile
Anne is that many years of her treatment were spent under the care of
two of the nation's best-known experts on recovered memory therapy and
multiple personality disorder, psychiatrist Dr. Bennet Braun and psychologist Dr. Roberta Sachs. Sometimes coauthoring papers, both have
published widely, and Braun has led dozens of training seminars for
others in the field, while Sachs has starred in training tapes for future
MPD therapists. In the middle of the 1980s, Braun was the first to
establish an inpatient unit at Chicago's Rush Presbyterian Hospital for
those diagnosed with MPD and other dissociative disorders. In 1984 he
became president of the fledgling International Society for the Study of
Multiple Personality and Dissociation and now runs a twelve-bed unit

*The names of Anne Stone and the members of her family have been changed.

specializing in the treatment of MPD, at Rush North Shore Medical Center in Skokie, a branch of Rush Presbyterian–St. Luke's Medical Center. "Every MPD patient in the country owes a personal debt of gratitude to Buddy [Braun]," said Richard Kluft, director of the Dissociative Disorders program at the Institute of Pennsylvania Hospital. "All the [MPD treatment] units around the country followed the trail he blazed. . . . He's been a major player."[1]

Not only was Anne treated at perhaps the most prestigious clinic for MPD disorder, but she was, according to what Braun told her, his prize patient. He told Anne often that many of his theories about multiple personality disorder and his understanding of satanic-ritual abuse came largely from his work with her. When other doctors visited the unit, Braun would bring them to visit with Anne. When he presented lectures, he often brought her along. At one point Anne even agreed to accompany him onto a local television news program where she appeared, along with Braun, in a multipart feature story entitled "Making Anne Whole."

Because Braun's and Sachs's theories on recovered memories of ritual-satanic abuse and multiple personality disorder hold sway over so many practitioners, Anne's treatment by them deserves a close look. The following account of Anne and Anne's treatment, unless otherwise noted, is based principally on interviews with Anne and her husband. Where possible, her story has been checked against Anne's hospital records, Braun's and Sachs's writings, and other relevant documentation. Sachs declined to be interviewed, and Braun did not respond to repeated requests for an interview.

Like many recovered memory patients, the troubles that brought Anne to therapy, and eventually to Braun and Sachs, had nothing to do with satanism, symptoms of multiple personality disorder, or memories of child abuse.[2] On April 15, 1982, she gave birth to her second child, Steve, and because of the position of the baby, both Anne and Steve nearly died during the four-hour delivery. Once Steve was delivered it took fifteen minutes for him to begin breathing on his own. Due to the trauma of delivery, his right arm was paralyzed and he had to be rushed to the neonatal intensive care unit. Anne's pelvic bones were so wrenched that she couldn't stand or walk well enough to visit her newborn. When she finally did see her baby, he was so bruised from the delivery that, to her eyes, "he looked like he had been thrown out of a car window." Two weeks after the delivery she discovered that her doctor had pushed so hard on her abdomen during the birth that her gallbladder had ruptured. Anne had to go back into the hospital for emergency surgery.

Her inability to lift her new baby for weeks after the gallbladder surgery, as well as the mistaken expectation that the baby would be a girl, led to the ever-increasing feeling that she wasn't bonding with her new child. In addition, Anne grew intensely angry at the doctors whom she felt had botched the delivery. She also felt guilt for her sense of failure for not giving birth to a healthy and uninjured child. Anne believed a therapist might help her talk through these troubling feelings, and she made an appointment with a local psychiatric social worker recommended by her gynecologist.

From the end of spring through the summer of that year, Anne talked with this therapist about her postpartum emotional troubles, then broke off treatment in the fall because of the expense. Six months later, however, she returned to therapy because problems continued to plague her. Steve's birth haunted her. Anne faced the agonizing result of the delivery every day in her baby's slow and painful rehabilitation. Each day her husband, Joseph, would put Steve through a regimen of painful exercises designed to stretch and tear the muscles in her child's damaged arm so they wouldn't atrophy. If she could only do it over again, she felt, she would ask the right questions and take the action that would have saved her child so much pain.

Back in therapy with the same social worker, she began to have more troubling symptoms. For a time she feared she was pregnant again, although tests showed she wasn't. Her anxiety about Steve's physical and mental development escalated as did her anger toward the doctors who performed the delivery. She developed fantasies about murdering the doctors. When she told her therapist about these feelings, the therapist reported the story to the police. Sometimes, when she was depressed, the world seemed to slow down for days. At other times thoughts came to her mind rapid-fire. As therapy progressed, this cycle accelerated.

During this period Anne's therapist used various relaxation techniques to help her concentrate and talk freely in therapy. These techniques were similar to commonly employed hypnotic induction and allowed Anne to focus solely on the subject being discussed that day in therapy. She discovered she was quite good at losing herself in these waking trances. Anne already knew she was highly hypnotizable. At a county fair some years earlier, she had spontaneously fallen into a trance while watching a stage performer hypnotize several volunteers.

At the time her symptoms became more severe, a social worker who shared offices with Anne's therapist began treating a patient believed to be suffering from multiple personality disorder. After consulting with this other counselor, Anne's therapist suggested that Anne's mood swings indicated that she might be suffering from the same rare disorder. For several months Anne and her therapist discussed the possibility that Anne's mind hid aberrant personalities, which, unknown to her, surfaced and controlled her behavior. Anne and her therapist began to keep track of mood swings and watched carefully for memory blanks or any periods of time Anne couldn't account for.

One morning Anne woke up and greeted her husband in a childlike voice. "Hi," she said, "I'm Kathy Love." Though she stayed in this child character only for a brief moment, when she told her therapist about the incident, Anne remembers that she looked relieved. "She seemed to feel that she finally had an idea what was going on and that we were going to be able to straighten it all out," recalls Anne. "I was shaken. I remember wondering if I was going to start going crazy and breaking dishes like Sybil." Because of the belief that MPD results from early childhood trauma, the two abandoned the topic of Anne's delivery and her troubled feelings toward her son Steve and embarked on an exploraton of her childhood. Anne was certain that she was never sexually or physically abused; however, she did have memories that were troubling enough to draw the focus of the therapy. She recalled that when she was a young girl a neighbor she had known well had committed suicide, and she also described her baby sister's death and funeral.

For the next few months the appearance of "Kathy Love" remained an anomaly. But while no other personalities surfaced with distinct characteristics, such as voices or ages, she and her therapist began assigning names to Anne's various moods. They slowly identified different personalities, and Anne remembers becoming increasingly adept at switching from one to another. Describing the experience of switching, Anne remembers always knowing what she was doing, and always consciously deciding to shift personalities. As evidence that the switching was always of her own volition, Anne remembers that she was always conscious of when and where such displays would be appropriate. She notes that she never displayed any alter personalities around her children, at work, or in the company of strangers.

"When I took on a different personality, it wasn't as if I was trying to deceive anyone but it was more of a release," Anne explains of the experience. "In the beginning it was like a pressure valve. When I was another personality, I didn't have to be responsible for anything I said. I didn't have to be this mom who had been through this horrible delivery and had problems at work. I didn't have to be the person who was responsible for two kids and keeping this huge Victorian home clean. If

I wanted to be a sweet eleven-year-old girl, I could. I think I kind of got hooked on the escape."

At the time when her therapist diagnosed the multiple personality disorder, Anne had been in therapy for three years, and, while she had not found any relief from the symptoms, she had managed to care for two young children and hold down a job as a computer operator. With the advent of the MPD diagnosis, however, Anne's grasp on her life slipped. As her newly identified personalities became more distinct over months of therapy, her family and work life became more and more troubled. One night, after a confrontation with a male supervisor at work, Anne took an overdose of muscle relaxants and spent three days in the hospital. Hearing this news, Anne's therapist began looking around for a psychiatrist who specialized in MPD and could perhaps help with the treatment and prescribe appropriate medications.

Relationships with Anne's coworkers and supervisors at work deteriorated, and she seemed always irritable and anxious. When she started losing her temper with her boys and found herself one day violently shaking her older son, Mark, she decided it was time to go away to a psychiatric hospital and focus on getting better. As her life spun more out of control, she and her husband Joseph decided to sell their house in order to pay for more intensive therapy in a hospital setting.

Anne first tried the Menninger clinic, in Kansas, but when she arrived to check in with Joseph, several things bothered her immediately. Her husband was not allowed into any of the evaluation interviews and, worse still, they told her bluntly that she was not to refer to herself as "we" and she should avoid switching between personalities. This left her torn. The trusted therapist she had been seeing had taught her that living out her different personalities was the only way to heal. On the second day at Menninger, she asked her husband to take her home.

Anne felt miserable on the drive back, and had to stop six times to call and talk with her therapist. She felt as if inpatient treatment was her last hope, and it had turned into another dead end. Her therapist met with her when she arrived home at 11:30 that night. After the emergency session, Anne went home and, exhausted, opened that day's paper. Like a sign from God, there on the cover was an article about multiple personality disorder, quoting Frank Putnam, from the National Institute of Mental Health. Early the next day Anne was on the phone to him. After she recounted her disorder and desperate state, Putnam told her that she was lucky to be living in the Midwest because of her proximity to one of the preeminent experts on MPD—Dr. Bennet Braun. In trying to track down Dr. Braun, Anne learned of an upcoming conference on her disorder and quickly made plans to attend.

The conference proved a turning point in Anne's life. After meeting others who displayed multiple personalities, her feelings of desperation and isolation lifted. For the first time she could discuss and even joke about her strange behavior with others who seemed to know exactly what she was talking about. "It was like waking up and having something to live for," Anne remembers of the conference. "The hotel swarmed with doctors, nurses, and reporters. I was amazed. Through meeting other multiples, I realized that maybe I wasn't a leper."

Some of what she learned disturbed her. She attended one presentation on the possibility that MPD had a hereditary link. This information added weight to one of Anne's deepest fears—that her children would suffer because of her failings. Recently her son Mark had drawn a picture of a robot and then ripped the picture into pieces and had given each of the parts of the robot different names. This worried Anne so much that she carried the pieces of the picture in her purse, hoping someone at the conference could analyze her son's behavior.

At the suggestion of a doctor she cornered during the conference, Anne sought out Braun's colleague, psychologist Roberta Sachs. Anne managed to get Sachs's attention outside a conference room where Sachs had just given a presentation. As they walked through the labyrinth of hallways to Sachs's next meeting, Anne hurriedly described her therapy and behavior. She even pulled out the pieces of Mark's drawing. As they approached the door of the main ballroom, Sachs spotted Braun and waved him down. She quickly summarized what Anne had told her. According to Anne, with a few minutes' worth of knowledge about her case, she remembers that Sachs recommended to Braun that Anne be admitted to the Dissociative Disorders unit at Rush and, most shockingly to Anne, that her son Mark be hospitalized as well. Braun agreed.

"Sachs told me that my children were living in a 'psycho-toxic' home and that the drawing Mark had ripped up proved that he was suffering from MPD too and that he was trying to describe his problem with artwork. She said he couldn't make the picture if he didn't know what it was like to have multiple personality disorder. These guys seemed to know immediately," Anne says, snapping her fingers once. "Apparently, it was so clear to them. My head was just spinning."

Back working with her therapist at home, Anne had renewed confidence in her MPD diagnosis. While arranging her first formal meeting with Braun, she labored with her therapist to define, document, and explore the distinctions among her different personalities. By this point, she and her therapist had documented an alleged twenty-one unique personalities living inside Anne.

A few months later, after numerous phone calls and the seemingly endless exchange of insurance forms and questionnaires, Anne finally arranged to meet Braun, the expert she had faith could cure her problems. Thick fog descended on the Chicago area on the morning she and her husband drove to her appointment. As it became clear that they would be late, Anne became frantic. She'd come to believe that admission into the Dissociative Disorders unit at Rush Presbyterian was her last and best chance to find relief. Finally arriving at the hospital, she was told by a nurse at the reception area that Braun was no longer available. Anne was shaking and near tears. After a time, they convinced the receptionist to page Braun. "When he finally walked down the hall I was in a real emotional crisis. I was a mess," Anne remembers. "His first words to me were, 'This better be good because I was in a very important meeting.'" Anne felt that she had better muster every personality in her repertoire to show the seriousness of her case.

Throughout the day she met with Braun and Sachs several times. Sachs taught her how with the use of hypnosis she could communicate directly with her unconscious through finger signals. Sachs told Anne that because of the quickness with which Anne learned the technique, she was very excited about the prospect of working with her. By the end of the day, it was determined that Anne would be admitted for a three-month hospitalization and that Mark, whom no one at Rush had yet seen, should be considered for a six- to eight-week evaluation. In March of 1986 a slot finally opened on the unit, and Anne and Joseph again headed for Chicago.

On the morning of Anne's admission Braun met her in the hospital's lobby and asked about her history of child sexual abuse. When Anne told him that she had no history of any, he shook his head and said that there had to be, informing her that 97 percent of multiples had been abused as children. She told him about the suicide of the neighbor and of her sister's early death but assured him that she had not been abused. Anne remembers that Braun told her that she may not remember it now and that her memories were likely repressed in her unconscious and would come out during treatment.

Having seldom spent the night away from her husband during their years of marriage, the first weeks of therapy were difficult for Anne. In addition, she and Braun had an immediate disagreement over whether she should begin taking the tranquilizer Xanax and increasing doses of the heart medication Inderal. Inderal had not been approved by the Food and Drug Administration for the treatment of MPD, he informed her, but he felt it was critical to her treatment that she be part of the research he was conducting with the company that produced it.

After a few weeks of Anne's refusals to take medications, Braun warned her that if she didn't begin the program he would take her off the unit and send her to a state hospital. "He said he would put me in Chicago Reed Psychiatric Hospital, which had the reputation as a place of horrors. He spent long periods describing to me what I would experience at a place like that." Other nurses and doctors pressured Anne as well. Finally, Braun set a week's deadline for Anne to cooperate. By the time Anne was given the ultimatum, her son had been admitted to the children's unit, several floors below. A few days later, on Anne's thirtieth birthday, Braun took her down to visit with her five-year-old, Mark. She talked and played with her son while Braun watched. On the way back up to the adult unit, Braun asked if she had enjoyed the visit. She told him how much she missed her children. According to Anne, Braun suggested that if she went on the medication she could have more visits. She agreed immediately. Once they were back on the unit, Anne was immediately given a tranquilizer and her first small dose of Inderal.

During each day on the unit Anne was hypnotized several times. On a typical day a medical student, a psychiatric nurse, Sachs, and Braun would each spend an hour or more talking with Anne's different personalities. At the beginning of her treatment the interviews with the medical student often lasted for hours and not uncommonly she would spend much of the evening hours talking to him by phone. According to what the medical student told Anne at the time, Braun had assigned him the specific job of discovering her history of child abuse. Between the sessions, Anne would often talk with her roommate or spend time switching between different personalities. She soon learned that other patients were discovering histories of horrible abuse by satanic cults. During art therapy she watched other patients draw pictures of robed figures and strange altars. Once, Anne observed another patient take a red pen and violently mark all over her body. Her roommate told her stories of being ritually raped and of having to eat human flesh. Another patient showed her Polaroid pictures of a scene of ritual abuse she had re-created in a sand tray using small plastic figures. Perhaps most frightening, everyone, from the staff to the patients, continually implied that she would soon remember similar horrors.

One day, a week and a half after she had started the daily program of medications and hypnosis, Anne was sitting in her room, imagining herself in one of her different personalities, when Braun came to the door. He said he had just been down on the children's unit, talking with Mark, and now had a question to ask her. From the tone of his voice, Anne knew that it would be an important question. Braun asked her if she had ever in her life cooked and eaten people. Anne surprised herself by answering with one word: "Yes."

Anne remembers Braun "had a look on his face that said Bingo! He said to me 'That's what I wanted to hear,' and walked away." Anne was shaken and confused by her answer. She immediately picked up the Bible, opened it randomly, and read a verse that referred to a holocaust and offerings for sins. The verse, Anne felt, contained the message that she had answered Braun's question correctly. In the next therapy session, Braun told Anne that her confession to cannibalism was a breakthrough in her treatment. The drugs and hypnosis were starting to work, he told her, and the terrible, submerged parts of her past were starting to surface. All the moments in her past that she had probed in therapy—the painful pregnancy, the death of her sister, the suicide of her neighbor—were from then on abandoned as she searched for hidden memories of satanic abuse. At about the same time, she had another breakthrough during a session conducted by the medical resident. Toward the end of a three-hour hypnotic trance during which she was acting out one of her younger personalities, the medical student managed to "age-regress" her to a time when her father had taken her to visit him at the soft-drink plant where he worked. As she talked through the scene in a childlike voice, she visualized her father and his coworkers sexually abusing her.

As weeks and months passed, she uncovered scenes of abuse at an ever-increasing pace. The images involved satanic rites, including the ritual killings of people. Although these scenes were retrieved with all her therapists, Anne recalls that in the beginning, Sachs was the most unrelenting in her pursuit of such stories. At the opening of each session Sachs was quite specific about what she hoped Anne would remember that day. After hypnotizing Anne and asking her to assume one of her personalities, she would then help her picture a scene. If the scene was of an outdoor ritual, she might say, "It's a cool autumn night and you are outside in the dark. Can you see the stars?" When Anne would respond that yes, she could see the stars, Sachs would move onto the next detail. "There are leaves on the ground, can you smell the leaves?"

"Pretty soon I'd be able to smell the leaves," Anne remembers. "Then she'd ask something like, 'Look around and see if your mother is there?' And I'd look around and be able to see my mother. Then she asked me who else was there and if they were wearing hoods. So pretty soon I'd realize that they all were wearing hoods and robes."

The directed questions went beyond just scene setting. Once Anne had formed a clear image of a setting for a satanic ritual, Sachs might ask her if she could hear anyone screaming. If Anne could then imagine hearing a scream, Sachs would then ask her who that person was and whether he or she were going to be used in the ritual. Often she would lead Anne right up to the central act of the ceremony and then suddenly stop the leading questions. As the details crystallized in her mind, Anne's emotions would rise. Anne remembers, for example, Sachs leading her up to the moment where Anne saw herself with a dagger in her hand, standing over a pregnant woman.

"She'd say, 'You didn't want to be holding that knife, and you didn't want to do what you had to do,' " Anne says. "I would be very involved in this scene, and very disturbed by what I was seeing happening. I could smell, feel, hear what she was asking about and it all seemed so real. I'd get to the critical point of the ceremony and that is where she would stop. It was from that point that I was supposed to recover the memory of what I did." This technique, which Anne says Braun employed as well, left little doubt about where the imagined scene was headed. As soon as Anne recounted the details of what it felt like to stab the sacrificial victim, Sachs would begin asking questions again, leading Anne out of the scene and reassuring her that she had been forced to do the deeds she had done.

While the scenes with Sachs were often the most gruesome, each time she was hypnotized by Braun, the nurses, or the medical resident assigned to her case, she explored similar scenarios. These sessions were augmented by art therapy, in which she drew pictures of the abuse she had suffered. During each session she would "relive" a new scene or retell a scene that had already surfaced. Going through the process four or more times a day, so many scenes were created that she had difficulty keeping track of them. "If the scene didn't involve killing babies, it involved killing pregnant women, or being raped on an altar or raping someone else," Anne says. "Over and over. It's hard to imagine but you begin to become numb to the stories."

During the remainder of that spring and through the summer, the satanic-cult stories spilled out quickly and took shape. While some of the sessions involved specific scenarios, others focused on larger sections of her life, creating an overview of what had happened to her. They began to build a narrative that explained the cult's structure and Anne's changing position within the organization. Often it was just after a therapy session when, emotionally drained, Anne would have insights about the machinations and membership of the cult.

With Sachs, Anne remembers the sessions as brutal. Her pace for reliving the cult abuse was very fast and Sachs's demeanor, from Anne's perspective, seemed cold and cruel. With Braun, the scenes unfolded at a slower pace. His behavior during their sessions convinced Anne that he was a deeply caring physician who had her best interest as his top priority. The therapy sessions could take place at any time of the day. Oftentimes, Braun or Sachs would come in after midnight and wake her up before beginning the hypnosis. Because both Braun and Sachs might show up for their therapy rounds at any time, there was always a buzz among the patients about when the doctors were going to arrive and whom they would see first.

The therapy sessions were almost always held in her room. Braun would put a sign on the door that said THERAPY IN SESSION, take off his lab coat, and sit with her on the bed. To hypnotize Anne he would have her stare at a blank part of the wall and focus on the sound of his voice. He would tell her to let everything inside her mind go quiet and then instruct a particular personality to come forward. During the sessions, Anne remembers, Braun would often hold her hand, in an effort to comfort her, as he helped her describe the tortures she endured. At the end of the session he would sometimes kiss her on the cheek or forehead or lay her head on his shoulder and stroke the back of her neck. "He made it clear to me that I was really a special patient to him," says Anne. "He made sure that I understood that he was personally invested in my case."

While the memories evolved more slowly with Braun than with Sachs, they were just as emotional and psychologically painful. Braun explained to her that because her traumatic experiences were encoded into memory during times when she was frightened and emotionally overwrought, in order to access those memories it was necessary that she be in the same frightful state. With this in mind, Braun would sometimes take Anne to what was called the "quiet room" for an "abreaction session." In the quiet room was a bed equipped with leather restraints for the patient's arms, legs, and torso. Anne learned that Braun used the equipment in the quiet room to relive memories so terrible that an unrestrained patient undergoing the experience might injure herself or Braun. Walking into the abreaction room, Anne remembers intense dread that the memory she was about to experience was going to be something really horrible. Strapping Anne down, Braun would pad her wrists and ankles with towels to keep her from bruising or cutting herself.

After she was fully restrained, Braun would lay the ground rules: they would not stop the process until she had worked all the way through a traumatic memory. After inducing trance, Braun would specify the type of memory they would uncover. In one case the scene Anne "relived" was of being raped while tied down on an altar. "He asked me: 'Do you remember what it felt like to be out of control?' or 'Do you remember what it felt like not to be able to move your legs?' " Anne recounts. "Of course I could very much understand those feelings because it was happening to me as he was asking the questions. As confused as I was at the time, I knew this was wrong. I knew you didn't do this to someone."

Braun's questions, like those of Sachs's, suggested many details. While reliving the scene of the altar rape, Braun asked questions such as whether she could smell the alcohol on the breath of the person raping her. She had mastered the ability to immediately incorporate the content of the question into her memory. Once Braun would ask about a detail she would immediately imagine the detail.

The abreaction sessions in the quiet room particularly terrified Anne. Often when patients disappeared into the room, their screams could be heard up and down the hall. One patient had to be carried back to her room. Anne watched as Sachs held the exhausted and crying patient.

Despite the brutality of the treatment, Braun often appeared to share a good deal of the pain Anne endured. She remembers sessions in which he broke down and cried with her, and sometimes he would halt them, saying he couldn't stand to hear any more. At other times it seemed to Anne that Braun could not get enough of the stories they were creating. Several times while Anne was describing scenes of sexual assault, he excused himself, saying that he had become aroused.

Because of the gruesome nature of the cannibalism recounted in therapy, Anne began to have trouble eating and quickly lost weight. In what he told Anne was an effort to put her more in touch with her memories, Braun often played into her new aversion to food. According to Anne, one evening during dinner he asked how she knew the hamburger she was eating wasn't made up of human meat. On another occasion he asked her if the cottage cheese reminded her of anything, and if she had ever opened a human brain? While it is hard to imagine how questions like these might be therapeutic, at the time Anne believed that Braun was acting in her best interest. "If he said that asking questions like these was how he was going to help cure me, then no matter how horrible it was, I was willing to go through it," Anne says. "I believed he was trying to help me understand my past and get beyond it. I really trusted him."

*   *   *

In many respects, the satanic scenes Anne visualized were similar or identical to ones she knew other patients on the unit were coming up with. She learned that her family had for generations—since 1604—been involved in a satanic cult. She believed she had been raped and forced to cannibalize her own ritually aborted fetuses. She also believed she took part in the sacrifice of infants and adults. She began to recover cult stories not only from her childhood but from her adult life as well. While she had no "normal" memory of the experience, her recovered memories suggested that she had belonged to the cult up to the time she entered the hospital and her doctors began to suspect she might still be in contact with the organization by telephone and mail. As therapy wore on, they discovered her rank in the cult was elevated to "high priestess"—a position supposedly in charge of a nine-state region.

Even as she described the stories of her participation in the cult, Anne realized that they were inconsistent, contradictory, and often bordered on the impossible. While reliving specific scenes, characters and settings would often change in a dreamlike fashion. She described lit torches used as sexual devices, burial for days at a time, and having to eat parts of two thousand people a year. Her knowledge that she didn't get her menstrual periods until well into high school did not dissuade her from believing that she had been pregnant numerous times during adolescence. Her job as High Priestess, which she believed included frequent trips to other states, was supposedly managed without her husband's knowledge.

According to Anne, Braun continually helped her explain away the improbable nature of her new beliefs. To bolster her belief that she was able to eat parts of two thousand people a year, she and Braun theorized that the cult must have had a computer network and trucking organization responsible for distributing bodies. Where did the bodies come from? Some, they believed, were of homeless people, some were from nursing homes, and some were babies bred for sacrifice. At all possible points he would use her pretherapy memories to bolster her beliefs. The fact that she remembered not having regular periods until high school, for example, was proof that she had been pregnant off and on for the entirety of her adolescence. For details too fantastic explain away, Braun would simply reassure her that given enough time, the facts would all make sense.

As the other patients on the unit learned the story of Anne's status in the cult, they incorporated her into their own stories of abuse. Braun would tell her that other patients had seen her officiate at cult ceremonies where they had been abused. Anne said he even told her that another patient had shown him pictures of her taken while she participated in a satanic-cult meeting in another state. When she asked to see the pictures,

he told her that she wasn't ready. She also learned that another patient
had accused her of having killed and eaten the patient's child. Partly
because she was identified as a cult leader, and partly because she was
receiving a disproportionate share of attention from Braun, Anne began
to feel shunned by other patients. Conversations would stop suddenly
when she walked past, and people refused to sit by her at meals.

As her satanic rank grew, Anne's importance to Braun also appeared to
increase. Several times when he attended conferences to make presentations on MPD, she would accompany him. When reporters wanted to
talk with an MPD patient, he often asked Anne if she would be interviewed. During one conference, at Braun's encouragement Anne gave a
presentation on her history and the story of her treatment. During this
time she also appeared on the local television news series with Braun.

From Anne's account of her treatment, and from Braun's public statements at the time, there is a wealth of evidence that he sincerely believed
the satanic stories he elicited from his patients. Braun talked constantly to
Anne about his fear that members of the cult were out to kill him for the work
he was accomplishing. He told Anne how he bought his house through
a third party so that no public documents would contain his address, and
he also mentioned that someone had tried to run him off the freeway.

Many times Braun came to Anne for information about the workings
of the cult. Hypnotized into her High Priestess personality, she confirmed
or added weight to many of Braun's theories and suspicions. Often he
brought her get-well cards that had been sent to other patients and asked
her to interpret the cult messages hidden in the pictures and words. Colors
on the cards came to mean different satanic messages, as did the salu-
tations. She also analyzed phone numbers, dates, and bouquets of flowers.
Although she is not sure how she formulated these answers, Anne found
it easy to respond to Braun's questions: she would stare at a phone number
or a greeting card, and answers would just come to mind. Each new
interpretation would build on previous answers, creating a complex vocabulary by which they believed the cult communicated with its wayward
members at Rush Presbyterian.

In another series of sessions Anne envisioned a massive computer room
that controlled the satanic cult; they spent weeks trying to figure out its
location and the computer codes that could destroy the system. During
another session, Braun showed Anne a photograph of a man giving a
speech and said that he knew this man was a leader of the cult. He asked
Anne to identify the man's first name, saying that he knew she couldn't
tell his full name for fear of being killed by the cult. When Anne stalled,

he gave her two names and asked her to choose between them. When she guessed one of the names, he nodded and told her that she had confirmed his suspicions.

When Anne asked him why no one had found evidence of the satanic cult, Braun told her that initially no one had believed that the Holocaust was happening either. During a civil trial in California, when questioned about his beliefs in ritual abuse, he made a similar case: "How many people believed what the Nazis did, or what the Cambodians did? They could smell the burning flesh," Braun testified. "People weren't coming home anymore. But there was terrible denial. . . . People do horrendous things to each other."[3]

When Anne's belief had solidified, Braun called in agents from the Federal Bureau of Investigation. In the meeting she told the FBI everything about the cult. She named doctors and lawyers and politicians she believed were involved. By this time Anne and Braun's fantasy cult conspiracy included AT&T, Hallmark Greeting Cards, the CIA, and FTD florists. The Jerry Lewis telethon also functioned in the conspiracy, because Anne believed that the numbers posted on the pledge board were actually secret messages instructing cult members across the country. When the FBI failed to find the confirming evidence for Braun's theories, they, too, were linked to the satanic conspiracy. Months later Braun told Anne that he had narrowly escaped an assassin that the FBI had sent his way.

As evidence failed to materialize to prove Braun's theories, the conspiracy protecting the satanists grew ever larger. In 1988, while in the midst of treating Anne, he said confidently in a speech: "We are working with a national-international type organization that's got a structure somewhat similar to the communist cell structure."[4] Braun's fears of assassination, a testament to his belief in these stories, proved a strain on his marriage. His wife, Jane, described him as "paranoid" during this time. "He'd look over his shoulder, walk around his car before getting in," she remembers. "He couldn't enjoy a trip to Wisconsin because he saw a satanic symbol on the side of a barn."[5]

"When Braun would tell me the importance of the work we were doing, he made me feel very much like the pain I was going through was for a higher purpose," Anne recalls. She felt so strongly about what she was doing that even the possibility of going to jail didn't inhibit her from admitting to murders to the FBI agents. "While the process was so painful, I felt I really owed it to the world and to all the people I killed and to all the mothers who were grieving for their children who never came home. I felt I owed it to God to make things right."

Not surprisingly, her relationship with her mother and father during this time fell apart. She and Braun analyzed the content of their calls and letters and determined that her parents were giving Anne secret cult commands to kill herself. The fear that her parents wanted her dead, however, did not keep Braun from asking her to go to their house to collect baby pictures when the producers for a TV news show said they would be useful.

When her parents came to visit, Braun orchestrated an elaborate cloak-and-dagger scenario for the meeting. Because he didn't want her parents to see the dissociative disorder unit, he had Anne escorted across the street to the nurses' dorms by an armed FBI agent and large male nurse. Anne and Braun also decided that she should give her parents a secret signal (taking off a necklace) that she was still under the control of the cult so they wouldn't try to have her killed. The meeting was so strained, Anne remembers that it lasted only a few minutes.

As if the direction of therapy were not crazy enough, for a time Dr. Walter Young joined the staff. In addition to helping clients find repressed memories from their current life, according to Anne, Young often assisted patients in retrieving memories from past lifetimes. With Young's and Sachs's help, Anne had past-life memories of being a young British girl who died in a fire and then of being Catherine the Great. While Young was at Rush, Anne remembers he also talked about the possibility of holding a séance. The hope was that they could contact the souls of those whom Anne had killed and find out who they were so that they could document what had happened.

Her son Mark's life in therapy was similarly bizarre. Admitted at the age of five, he appeared so normal that Dr. Elva Poznanski, the child psychiatrist in charge of the children's unit, had to be convinced that he should be allowed into a psychiatric unit. The nurses who supervised Mark at the beginning of his treament confirm that he appeared to be a normal child. According to their notes, he showed no evidence of multiple personalities, demonstrated good verbal skills, was well adjusted, and slept and ate well. He underwent a battery of psychological and medical tests and scored within or above the normal range on all but one, in which he scored slightly below what was normal for his age.

However, not long after he was put in the hospital, new problems arose. Initially, his bad behavior appears to have developed in response to being separated from his home and his parents. Several times he physically tried to keep his father from leaving after his weekly visits. "Help me, help me," a nurse reported Mark screaming on one of these occasions. "Somebody keep him here." At the end of another visit, he tried to barricade his door so his father couldn't leave, saying, "Please don't go, Dad! When will you come back? A week is a long time." He also craved the attention and time of his mother, who would visit on most days. Often he would behave badly if—as often happened—one of her scheduled visits was canceled by Dr. Braun.

It seems clear from the nurses' records that Mark quickly picked up the notion that the nurses and psychiatrists paid more attention to him when he talked about anything violent. On several occasions nurses noted that Mark felt that he had to act out or talk of violent acts in order to get attention. One nurse wrote that Mark was "making more references to violence . . . and seeking attention for either talking about or wanting to do it so he can get basic needs met." Asked where he got the ideas for his graphic talk, Mark said simply, "It's on TV." After reluctantly returning to the unit after an afternoon spent with his father and brother, Mark told a nurse, "I'm going to kill myself." When the attending nurse asked why, he responded, "To make you happy."

In addition, he seemed to come to believe that his parents' visits were contingent on his behaving badly and describing violent fantasies. "I have to play wild games so my mother will come back," he was recorded as saying after one of her visits. "She won't come back unless I play wild games." At another point he said, "I don't want to behave. I have to be bad. If I was good, I wouldn't see my mom." One day when Dr. Braun had not permitted Anne to visit her son, Mark told a nurse that "The dinosaurs taught me all about dinosaurs and people and how to eat people." This statement no doubt earned Mark plenty of concerned attention, for he began to use the theme of eating people more often, at one point mentioning that he wanted to make "Barb stew" out of one of his teachers. This was apparently the clue that led Braun to ask Anne whether she had a history of cannibalism.

Although he showed no symptoms of multiple personality disorder at the beginning of treatment, the staff continually looked for signs that he might be harboring alter personalities. Rapid mood swings were noted in his files, as were any responses or actions that might indicate the disorder. One day he pointed to his reflection in a mirror and said, "I'm me." Apparently thinking that this was possibly a clue that he was displaying MPD behavior, the nurse asked if the person he was talking to had a name. Mark said that he was talking to his own reflection, and his name was Mark. At another point he used the pronoun "we" when making a get-well card for his mother. The nurse quickly inquired who "we" was referring to and he said that he meant his father, his brother, and himself.

Despite these clues that didn't pan out, the staff remained vigilant.

One nurse made a list of the different ways his voice sometimes sounded: "singsong," "loud," "conversational," "sweet," and "baby talk." In addition to this careful monitoring, Mark was subjected to a psychodrama exercise in which he was taught how to pretend to be a different person. Eventually he became more attuned to the demands of the MPD game and would sometimes switch into a "robot" personality.

Late in the summer of 1988, months into her treatment, Anne had the revelation that the cult was going to kill her younger son, Steve, on Halloween because she had been revealing the cult's secrets in therapy. Just shy of four years old, Steve was admitted to the hospital for his own protection. After Anne had substantially fleshed out her satanic-cult belief, she, Braun, and Poznanski held joint therapy sessions in which they tried to help the children "remember" the satanic abuse they had supposedly suffered. Anne remembers that Braun often prepped Mark by telling him that for his mother to get better and go home, he had to remember the bad things that had happened.

As Poznanski would reveal later, the satanic material from the boys "came out very slowly over the space of probably at least a year or year and a half." Eventually the children told stories depicting "cult activities with the mother and an uncle and an aunt." In one memory, Steve was put in a cage and lowered into water by his mother. In addition to this, Anne and Braun managed to convince Mark and Steve that they had helped their mother kill babies. With Braun's questions and his mother's encouragement, Mark came up with his own details about the rituals and evil acts he had allegedly committed.

To help her sons remember, Anne remembers using the same sort of leading questions that she learned from Braun and Sachs. Both boys quickly learned to agree to their mother's suggestions. Moreover, Anne and Braun created a board game in which the children would roll dice and move a marker along a path. The square they landed on would determine what type of memory they would talk about that day.

To convince Poznanski, who was skeptical of some of the stories Braun and Anne were eliciting from the children, Braun decided to provide proof. During a therapy session with Anne, her two children, the children's psychiatrist, and himself, Braun brought in a briefcase filled with handguns. The children's knowledge of how to hold and operate the guns would indicate that they had been trained by the cult. Braun passed out the unloaded weapons, one to each person in the room. Anne remembers that the stocks of the guns were too big for her children's hands, and the weight of the barrels prevented the boys from holding the weapons correctly. Anne tried to help her children out as Braun asked the boys to describe how they'd been taught to shoot babies. As the session progressed, both boys began to cry. The three adults took the hysterical children into the quiet room on the children's floor, but instead of consoling them or calming them down, Braun brought a set of handcuffs, which he encouraged the children to use on him, their mother, and Poznanski. The idea, as Anne remembers, was to show the children that they were in control, and to "empower" them. "The kids just lost it," remembers Anne. "The whole scene was just horrible."

From documents uncovered later at a custody hearing for the children, there seems little doubt that the boys' behavior and mental health worsened during their years of treatment. Dr. Poznanski, who initially had to be convinced by others that Mark should be admitted to the hospital at all, testified that after three years of "treatment" she had conclusively diagnosed him with MPD, and that both children had severe "disturbances." Described by a nurse at the start of his treatment as being "warm and appropriate and friendly with peers and staff," Mark was described by Poznanski three years later as incapable of "social niceties," and having trouble with "lying and violating the rights of others."

In summarizing Mark's treatment, one nurse wrote: "Due to the nature of this case, Mark has little knowledge of normal life experiences. . . . The hospital is so safe that Mark has been 'protected' from things most children experience. For example, Mark has never played tag, never gone trick-or-treating, never walked to school, never crossed the street alone, never ridden a bike, never gone to a friend's house."

In addition to this, the children were administered high doses of the heart medication Inderol and over the course of their treatment were given both the tranquilizer Xanax and the sleeping medication Halcyon. Most disturbingly, both children were convinced over the course of treatment that they had been sexually assaulted by their mother and that they had committed horrible crimes at her instruction. One can only wonder what it sounded like to the ear of these children to hear their mother and their mother's doctor describe their involvement in these gruesome cult scenes.

The road out of treatment for the family began partly because Anne's behavior and condition deteriorated. After trying to set fire to a comforter, she was transferred to an acute care unit and then to another psychiatric ward. One day, after assuming one of her little-girl alters, Anne found that she didn't want to regain her adult personality. She was warned that if she didn't snap into an adult personality by morning she would be moved off the unit. When morning came she was still acting out her child alter. As punishment she was sent to a general psychiatric ward of another hospital.

At the new unit she was treated like the other psychiatric patients, with no deference to her status as High Priestess or expectations that she would be switching back and forth between different personalities. While she still saw Braun regularly, her day was no longer filled with the constant rehashing of cult stories. No one woke her up after midnight to hypnotize her and to elicit gruesome tales. In fact, the care givers at the new psychiatric unit didn't seem much interested in satanic cults. Instead, they wanted to talk about the situation she was currently in, her loneliness and separation from her husband and children. Soon she was transferred to the medical unit and visited the psychiatric unit for only part of the day. As her sense of normalcy returned, the belief system that she had built under the care of her therapists began to show its first cracks.

Because the new hospital was not a long-term-care facility, Anne and Braun started looking for other hospitals that could take her and her children. Anne located a hospital in Georgia, but, according to Anne, problems arose when Poznanski became angry that Braun had planned the children's transfer without consulting her. When the children's psychiatrist refused to sign off on the transfer, the trip to Georgia was postponed, and Anne asked Braun to let her attend a local day psychiatric program. She and her husband rented an apartment in the area.

The professionals at the day program seemed appalled when Anne told them of the treatment she and her family had undergone at Rush. They stopped treating Anne as a patient and began treating her like an adult and a parent. Some of the staff advised her on how to retrieve her children from Rush. After a series of discharge dates for the children were set and then revoked, Braun, who had fallen out with Poznanski, began to counsel Anne on how she could work to get her children freed. In 1988, the dispute over the children's future ended up in juvenile court. Braun offered to testify as to Anne's fitness as a mother.

While her control over her life had increased, and she switched in and out of her alter personalities less often, at the time of the proceedings Anne still believed that she had been deeply involved in a satanic cult and had forced her children to perform horrible crimes. During the hearings, many of her therapy-created beliefs surfaced in testimony. On the stand, Anne, Braun, and Poznanski all testified to Anne's and the children's history of killing and eating people. Braun, for his part, maintained that while Anne had committed dozens, perhaps hundreds, of felonies, she was a fit mother for her children. By forcing her young children to kill people, he argued, Anne actually kept Mark and Steve from being sacrificed themselves—the act of a deeply caring mother. Even during their cult torture Anne had the best interests of the children at heart, he told the judge. Either the judge accepted this line of testimony or he believed the retrieved memories that came out of therapy were bogus, for in the end, he awarded custody of the children back to Anne and Joseph.

In December 1990, Anne took another critical step away from the treatment. She stopped taking the doses of Xanax, Inderol, Halcyon, and the other medications, cold turkey. For weeks her body went through terrible withdrawal. Joseph would hold her for hours at a time as she shook and perspired. It took months for her head to clear. Once off the medications, Anne stopped shifting among her different personalities. During therapy sessions she found it more and more difficult to go into trance.

Eventually her belief that she was the High Priestess of an international satanic order crumbled under the weight of its own improbability. In the summer of 1992, Anne went back to confront Braun. She told him that she no longer believed that she was the High Priestess of a satanic cult or that she had any alter personalities. Now that she was off medication, no longer undergoing regular hypnosis, and away from all the other patients, the stories about satanic-cult abuse sounded absurd and beyond belief.

Braun told her that she was the only one who was questioning these memories and that someday they would know whether the information he was discovering from his patients during treatment was true or not. As for the disappearance of her other personalities, he told Anne she was perhaps currently living in one of her alter personalities—one adept at functioning normally—but that it might only be temporary. He said time would tell if she would have a relapse.

"I told him that was bullshit. I told him that the problems I had were because of the hospital," Anne says emphatically. "I told him that he had done a terrible thing to me and my family."

In 1992, long after Anne left therapy, Braun gave an extended lecture on his treatment of patients believed to have suffered abuse at the hands of satanic cults. Given at the Midwestern Conference on Child Sexual Abuse and Incest, in front of several hundred mental-health professionals, this lecture provides much evidence that Braun still believes the stories he created with Anne and patients like her.

According to Braun, the patients whom he believes have truly been abused by a satanic cult are those who start therapy with no knowledge of that abuse.* The satanic abuse is more likely to be real, he said, if the therapist must "pull it out of them." From this statement it is not surprising that Braun was undaunted by Anne's initial claims that she had never been sexually abused, much less a leader in an international cult. For Braun, such initial denials were the norm.

As for the actual therapy, he confirmed that he often prescribes his patients a laundry list of drugs, including antianxiety medication such as Xanax, antidepressants, anticonvulsants, and massive doses of the heart medication Inderal. While he says there is as yet no evidence to prove its effectiveness, he sometimes prescribes doses ten times more powerful than the highest doses given to heart patients.[6]

Braun also told his audience that he often straps his patients down during their abreaction-memory sessions. Before these sessions, he said, he often works with the patients for over a week predicting what will happen during the abreaction session. "Often I'll have patients write in their journal what they are expecting,"[7] he said.

As for how abusive the abreactions can be, he said that patients often literally feel the sensation that they are describing, and that screaming and raging is commonplace. One patient imagined the experience of being whipped so vividly that welts appeared on her back. While he now limits abreactions to one hour, in the past, he said, they sometimes went on for nine. Braun also repeated to the audience what he told Anne about his belief that certain memories are easier to access if the patient achieves the same emotional state present at the time the memory was first encoded. "Information is best retrieved under the same physiological state as it was stored. The more different the stimulus, the less will be recalled." This is apparently one of his justifications for strapping his patients down and encouraging them to feel fear and pain.

Braun hedged a bit on how many satanic abuse accounts he considered authentic, suggesting that perhaps 5 percent of patients are "faking" their stories. Most of the information he gave the audience, however, was without qualification. "Satanic abuse is not a modern creation," he proclaimed, "it is as old as time and it is something to be reckoned with. I

*Braun has made the point that patients most often start therapy with no knowledge of satanic abuse in other forums as well. In the 1991 Southern California civil suit he testified: "Most patients come in not knowing anything about ritual abuse. It's rare that someone comes in talking about satanic ritual abuse." It is usually during psychotherapy, he said, that patients begin to describe tales of satanic abuse. Quoted in the *Los Angeles Times*, April 3, 1991. Part B, p. 1.

suspect that it has been with us forever." These satanic cults are funded, according to Braun, through "prostitution, drug sales, snuff films, and politics." The cult also earns revenues through contract killings, often carried out by the children in the cult. "Kids make great people to take internationally to commit a murder. How many people would suspect a ten-year-old to walk up to you on the street and blow you away?" he asked rhetorically.

He told the audience that children are often abused in day-care centers as a way of prepping them to join the cult. "You have to predispose the nervous system to this sort of behavior," he said. After the children are abused in day care, they are "then picked up in high school" and indoctrinated into the cult. The cult, he has come to understand, is networked with the Ku Klux Klan; neo-Nazi groups; the Mafia; big business; the intelligence community, including the CIA; and the military. He told the audience that he has developed twelve P's for those involved in satanic abuse: "Pimps, Pushers, Prostitutes, Physicians, Psychiatrists, Psychotherapists, Principals and teachers, Pallbearers [meaning undertakers], Public workers, Police, Politicians and judges, and Priests and clergies from all religions."

While Braun's inability to find any confirming evidence for a widespread cult organization has not caused him to abandon his beliefs, it has led to some interesting arguments as to how the hidden cult should be combated. After describing the dimensions of the problem, he said, "I caution people against panic. If there truly is an international organization, it has been around longer than we have. If it is running not only our society, but the world economy, then it has been doing it for a long time and neither you nor I are going to be able to change it."

Because of this, Braun says his hope now is not to stop the cult but rather to change the cult's attitude to the abuse of children. He hopes to do this by convincing the world that people are more loyal if they are treated nicely. "If you really want to control people, I truly believe that you can get it done a lot better with niceness than with fear and intimidation," Braun proclaimed to the therapists. "Out of loyalty, you can get a lot more done. My hope is by teaching loyalty and caring we can change the world at that level rather than try to compete with an organization that is better qualified to do what it is doing than we are organized to interfere with it."

Apparently, for Braun, it's all right if a satanic cult controls the world as long as it learns to gain power by being nice to children instead of abusing them. To ask whether such an international ring of evil satanists would be interested in such benevolent changes in their operation would be to enter the argument on its own bizarre level. It speaks to Braun's investment in the satanic-cult mythology that in the face of his inability to expose the cult, he has not abandoned his belief in it, but abandoned only the idea that it can be exposed and stopped. His line of reasoning illustrates how insulated from reality one can become within the recovered memory world.

There are hints that Braun has heard something of the growing wave of skepticism about his theories. While it does not stop him from stating his grandiose beliefs, he makes a point to warn therapists in the audience "not to jump to conclusions," and to take their time adding up the evidence. On rare occasions his statements about cult activities and history are prefaced with statements such as "patients tell me . . ." or "I'm told that. . . ." To prove that he does not believe everything said in therapy, Braun shared with his audience his new secrets for detecting the 5 percent of patients who are faking their stories. He claims some impostors can be spotted by their knowledge of general cult activity but lack of fine detail. Braun particularly suspects those who come to him with a preexisting notion that they were involved in a cult. These patients often tell stories that conflict with those told by the more than one hundred satanic-abuse patients he has treated. Of course, it is not at all surprising that the stories of patients who created their satanic beliefs in another setting would contradict the details of the intricate satanic world Braun builds with patients like Anne. Braun misses this obvious point: the stories he helped "pull out" of the patients conform to his preexisting beliefs because Braun *helped create those stories*.

While Braun's presentation came long after he knew that Anne had recanted her cult story, he continues to offer other therapists the theories they arrived at together. During his presentation, Braun talked about flower bouquets and showed slides of greeting cards. Using interpretations he and Anne developed, he illustrated for his audience how the cult was sending messages to his patients. "Pink flowers mean suicide, red means cutting." Braun listed these meanings matter-of-factly, as if reading down a list. "Red roses or white baby's breath means bloody suicide. Pink roses mean hanging. Blue is death by suffocation. Yellow is silence or fire. Green means go ahead and do something. If the card is signed 'Love you,' then that is a danger signal." While many of his interpretations emerged from his work with Anne, Braun failed to mention to his audience that the patient upon whom these interpretations relied no longer believed them.

Braun also shared several methods for determining the veracity of the stories he hears. One favored method he calls the "rule of five," that is, if he hears a similar detail about the workings of the cult from five different persons, he accepts that there is "probably something to it." Unfortunately, according to Braun, his rule of five was truly effective only early in his work with satanic-cult victims. Only stories he heard before 1987 were assuredly uncontaminated by the publication and release of *Michelle Remembers*. As he explained: "I think of information I have heard about satanic abuse before and after 1987 in different categories. The reason why I feel comfortable with the information I received before 1987 because of the publication in mid-1987 of *Michelle Remembers*. The reason that has meaning to me is that I really worry about the contamination effect."

Among patients today, according to Braun, information spreads phenomenally quickly. "I could ask a question about a cult and a patient would say, 'That sounds familiar to me. I'm going to a survivor group tonight and I'll ask about it,' " said Braun. "At the meeting ten more people have the detail, and when they get home—these people have tremendous phone bills—by the next morning five hundred people in California alone have heard about it. I'm not kidding." Because of this dissemination of information, he said, a therapist couldn't even apply a "rule of five hundred" to assess the truthfulness of a story. The contamination effect is equally dramatic among professionals, according to Braun. After telling another therapist a story that he heard in therapy, he said, within a week he had heard that there were three cases in existence. By tracing back the story, he learned that all three "cases" were different versions of his story. He determined that as the story was passed from therapist to therapist, some heard it from more than one source, and, because the stories sounded slightly different, believed that they heard several confirming cases.

From what critics of the satanic-cult stories have found, Braun's statements about the effect of *Michelle Remembers* and the subsequent diffusion of satanic-cult stories is accurate—except for one crucial detail. *Michelle Remembers* was not published in 1987, as Braun told his audience, but rather seven years before, *in 1980.* *

---

*Unfortunately for Braun, it is not likely that he simply misspoke the date. Not only did he repeat twice that *Michelle Remembers* was published in 1987, but the context of the statement indicates that this is when he truly believed the book was published. Braun presents the book as a marker in his career, after which he noted that he could no longer take satanic-abuse stories on face value. It is clear that he believes the book was published after he started treating these patients, which was in 1985. If he had truly known the book was published in 1980 and had only misspoken himself, he would not have put the statement in this context.

Despite this error, the substance of Braun's statement—that information after the publication of *Michelle Remembers* is suspect—should stand. Because Braun admits that he began treating cult victims only in 1985, there was no time when he was working with these stories that wasn't, in his own words, "contaminated" by *Michelle Remembers*.

Braun's firm belief in the existence of this international satanic cult, as well as his willingness to bend evidence to his own end, has been demonstrated in other settings as well. Testifying in a civil trial in 1991 in which two women were suing their grandmother for supposedly making them take part in satanic rites, Braun made it clear that he believed the satanic stories emerging in therapy across the country. He claimed that he had encountered patients from different states who had never met but who corroborated each other's stories. He said that several patients who did not know each other have given him names and physical descriptions of other cult members. "Some of the stuff I hear is so bizarre it defies belief . . . ," Braun testified. "I didn't want to believe it."[8]

During his testimony, Braun seems to refer to Anne's treatment and that of her sons, implying that it had provided some of the most compelling proof of satanic cults in our society. According to a report in the *Los Angeles Times*, he testified that although the two boys had no contact with their mother during treatment, they told identical accounts of the satanic rituals they participated in together.[9] Not only is this account of the children's therapy contradicted by Anne's memory of the events, but also by Braun's own testimony given during the custody hearing in 1989. The transcript of that hearing is unambiguous on this point:

> Lawyer: You indicated that [Anne] actually brought things out of the children in therapy.
> Braun: That is correct.
> Lawyer: Now, was the mother essentially part of the therapy?
> Braun: Absolutely. I don't think [the memories] would have come out otherwise.
> Lawyer: Could you elaborate on that a little further?
> Braun: . . . The children would not say anything unless the mother would draw it out of them. . . . The major information that came out in this case has come out in the presence of the mother.
> Lawyer: So the mother has always been an integral part of the children's therapy.
> Braun: Absolutely.

From Braun's own mouth, then, it is clear that Anne's children did not independently confirm her story.* His testimony that the children had no contact with the mother during their treatment should not be discounted as an offhanded misstatement of the truth. He was, at the time he made the statement, under oath and testifying in a civil lawsuit that would have a profound impact on the lives of those involved.

No doubt, as the general public becomes more and more skeptical about the stories which Braun has helped his clients create, he will further distance himself from the responsibility for their creation. Perhaps the percentage of patients he says are faking will go up from 5 percent. Perhaps he will begin to qualify his statements about the cult with phrases such as "patients tell me" or "I've been told." In blaming the creation of the stories on the patients, however, Braun cannot escape one crucial fact: by his own admission, all but a few patients who came to believe these convoluted satanic conspiracies came into his care not knowing anything about being involved in such an organization. Because the stories were only discovered through his treatment, there appears only one possible logical source for their creation.

The idea that her personality of High Priestess or her cult "memories" were anything more than inventions of a horribly misguided therapy treatment is now laughable to Anne. In a remarkable effort of will, she has pulled her family back together and restarted her life. In 1993, Anne filed a lawsuit against Braun and Rush Presbyterian claiming negligence. In their answers to Anne's complaint, Braun and Rush Presbyterian each denied all allegations. As this book went to press, the parties were still involved in litigation. To continue to claim that abuse beliefs can't be created in therapy, the recovered memory experts have to ignore her story or claim that she is fallen back into "denial" of her abuse. In the face of stories like Anne's, it is remarkable that many supporters of recovered memory therapy continue to attest that no one has yet proven it possible to create false abuse belief in patients.

---

*The fact that Anne was intimately involved in drawing out the satanic stories from her children has been confirmed not only by Braun but by the children's psychiatrist, Dr. Elva Poznanski, in the same hearing. She testified: ". . . there were joint sessions between the mother and the mother's psychiatrist, Dr. Braun, and myself and the two children . . . they must have gone on for about a year and a half."

CHAPTER TWELVE

The Murder, the Witness, and the Psychiatrist

Of all the cases of supposedly repressed and recovered memories, the best-known is that of Eileen Franklin Lipsker, who according to her testimony uncovered a vivid repressed memory of her father killing her childhood friend Susan Nason twenty years earlier. Based on Eileen's testimony—and in large part on the testimony of San Francisco psychiatrist Dr. Lenore Terr, who schooled the jury in her particular theory of memory repression—George Franklin was convicted in 1990 of first-degree murder. For both the American criminal court system and the American public, the Franklin trial was a case of first impression. For the courts, it was perhaps the first time the theories and ideas surrounding recovered memory testimony were explained and used as evidence in a criminal trial. Through the confident expert testimony of Dr. Terr, a jury heard the first explanation of a theory surrounding how memories are repressed and why they surface.

The Franklin case has deeply influenced the national debate over recovered memory therapy. For many with only a passing understanding of the case, George Franklin's life sentence solidly confirms the assumption that memories can be pushed into the unconscious and stay hidden for decades. The trial and the jury's decision were covered widely by papers and television stations. Eileen told her version on "60 Minutes," in a popular book she coauthored, and in a television movie starring actress Shelley Long. Most recently, versions of the story have been retold in Harry MacLean's *Once Upon a Time* and in Lenore Terr's *Unchained Memories*.

It is safe to say that if the trial were to begin today, it would have a much different focus than it did in 1990. In attacking Eileen's testimony, the defense attorney for George Franklin, Doug Horngrad, tried to show that Eileen might be lying about her constantly changing recollection of the murder. While Horngrad explored the idea that Eileen might have uncovered the memory during hypnosis—as she originally told her brother—when he couldn't confirm this he didn't pursue the idea that her memory might have been built through the therapy she was undergoing at the time. MacLean, while illustrating Eileen's vacillating memory in *Once Upon a Time*, largely ignores therapy as the possible genesis for her accusation. Because of the importance of the Franklin case and the fact that an alternative explanation for Eileen's memory (besides the possibilities that she was lying or that she was telling the truth) has never been offered, we have reexamined the trial. Viewed with the advantage of three years' hindsight—three years that have provided a quantum leap in the understanding of recovered memory therapy—the murder trial of George Franklin proves a dramatic illustration of the problems and potential consequences of recovered memory therapy and the dangers of questionable psychiatric testimony concerning memory and repression.

*   *   *

In her recent book, Dr. Terr retold the best-known version of how Eileen first experienced her murder memory. One day in January 1989, while she was watching her daughter play, Terr writes, Eileen suddenly met her daughter's eyes:

> And at exactly that moment Eileen Lipsker remembered something. She remembered it as a picture. She could see her redhead friend Susan Nason looking up, twisting her head, and trying to catch her eye.
>
> Eileen, eight years old, stood outdoors, on a spot a little above the place where her best friend was sitting. It was 1969, twenty years earlier. The sun was beaming directly into Susan's eyes. And Eileen could see that Susan was afraid. Terrified. . . . She looked away from those arresting eyes and saw the silhouette of her father. Both George Franklin's hands were raised high above his head. He was gripping a rock. He steadied himself to bring it down. His target was Susan.[1]

Terr goes on to write that Eileen "knew nothing at all about the psychological defense of repression,"[2] emphasizing later that she had no idea what repression was all about. In this manner she portrays Eileen as an innocent who unwittingly unlocked a horrifying memory stored away in her subconscious. For the most part, Eileen herself told this same account of how the scene surfaced to her father's jury, and then again in her book and movie on the subject. By the time of her testimony, Eileen would not only depict the moment of the murder but also tell of watching her father rape Susan before he beat her to death.

What Terr fails to mention is that this well-known version of how Eileen came to her belief is not the only version, nor, in view of the totality of the evidence, is it the most likely. As MacLean writes in *Once Upon a Time*, Eileen herself initially told her brother that she had remembered the murder through hypnosis. Later, she told another sibling that she came to the memory during therapy, but not via hypnosis, while at another point she said that the scene appeared to her in a dream. In yet another recounting she said that the knowledge entered her mind through a combination of a dream and therapy.[3]

The facts surrounding Eileen's beliefs are much more complicated than Terr portrays them. During the year that Eileen became confident that she had witnessed Susan's murder, she was under the care of *two* master's-degree-level therapists, and was actively engaged in uncovering a string of supposedly repressed memories about her childhood. The two therapists testified at George Franklin's trial that they employed the idea of memory repression and recovery and that they taught Eileen about these theories.[4] Indeed, the record clearly shows that the visualization of the murder was not the first "memory" that Eileen had recovered while in therapy. Terr's assertion that Eileen knew "nothing at all" about the idea of repression is contradicted by Eileen's therapist Katherine Reider, who testified that they had discussed memory repression in the summer of 1988, when Eileen had recovered a memory of being digitally penetrated by her father. Reider testified matter-of-factly that she explained to Eileen that summer that it was indeed possible to repress traumatic material and find the memories later in life. Terr's account and Eileen's trial testimony also run counter to the testimony of Eileen's other therapist at the time, Kurt Barrett.

Barrett began seeing Eileen and her husband for marriage counseling in the spring of 1989. After a series of meetings, however, Barry stopped going, and Eileen continued with individual sessions. To better allow memories to surface, Barrett encouraged Eileen to relax, to take deep breaths, and to experience feeling safe. His techniques were fully capable of inducing hypnotic trance. Barrett, a practicing hypnotherapist, should have known this. They probed Eileen's memory of her childhood and allowed recollections and associations to float up at will. Barrett wasn't in the practice of drilling his patients with questions about a memory once it surfaced. Rather, after relaxing Eileen and helping her feel safe, he let the conversation drift with her associations, explaining later, "My purpose really was just to help her have those memories." Barrett also was in the practice of discussing the dreams of his patients and encouraging them to keep a notepad by their beds so that they could record nightmares or dream images right after they woke up.

One of Eileen's childhood experiences that came up many times during those sessions was her knowledge that her best friend, Susan Nason, had been kidnapped and murdered. Barrett reports that they discussed many details that she had always known about the murder, including the fact that Susan's ring had been crushed, most likely as she held her hand up to ward off the killer's blow. (Eileen's sister, Janice, had identified the crushed ring for the police.) "We were talking about her early life and how lonely she felt and that is when she told me about Susan's death," Barrett testified in court. "And that was in context with a lot of other memories about what her life was like, what it was like being in school and the isolation and loneliness that she felt. . . . My impression was that she had been raised in an abusive atmosphere. That there was a lot of anger, a lot of violence, alcoholism. And that had affected her quite seriously."

Over several sessions they talked over Susan's death, probing Eileen's current feelings about the crime and how it had influenced her as a child. Sometimes Eileen would get very emotional and cry when discussing this part of her childhood. During this time she began to report a series of images that she saw in her mind's eye. Barrett testified that Eileen had identified these visualizations as "pictures" that would flash into her mind. The first was an image of some clothes on a sidewalk, the second was of the victim's crushed ring, and then she talked of a visualization of riding in the family's VW van. According to Barrett, Eileen reported these still pictures as strikingly clear. "She said she felt disturbed about some things that were coming into her thoughts," Barrett testified of these initial visualizations. "And she told me some of the images that were coming into her mind. It was like they were strong images, but she didn't know if she was going crazy. . . . She didn't know how she could be having these memories. And that's what her disturbance was about."

It was immediately apparent to Barrett that the images were somehow related to Susan's death. As he testified later: "I assumed we were talking about Susan Nason when we were talking about the ring." When Eileen asked Barrett his opinion about whether it was possible to repress horrible experiences from consciousness and retrieve them later, Barrett confirmed what Reider had told her a year before. "I told her yes, it was possible and that it's not uncommon. It's a protective adaptive reaction to repress something that's overwhelming or powerful. . . . Everyone represses things."

The images forming in Eileen's mind were, according to Barrett, folded into the therapy dialogue, where they were analyzed. *

What is critical to note is that according to Barrett, Eileen's memories "developed" over the course of the therapy sessions and often during the encounter itself. With the relaxation exercises and the free-association techniques, these memories often became more detailed during their hour-and-a-half meetings. In recounting these images and the developing narrative during therapy, Eileen often became so frightened at what she was picturing in her mind that Barrett would have to calm her down and reassure her that she was not threatened by the events she was visualizing.

Barrett remembers that from June, when she initially visualized the first element of what was to become the crime scene, through July, Eileen worked both in and out of the sessions trying to sort out the meaning of her feelings, visualizations, and memories. He assured Eileen at the time that it "wasn't important . . . whether her visualizations were real or not," and that they could "sort that out later." In and out of therapy the details slowly cohered into a narrative. One day she came in and reported to Barrett that she had seen a flash image of someone hitting Susan with a rock—*but that she couldn't make out who the person was.* According to Barrett it was several sessions later, in a highly emotional moment, that Eileen revealed that she was finally able to see the face of the man who killed Eileen. It was her father's. . . .

Barrett's assurance that it "wasn't important" to know initially whether her memories were real or not can be found repeated in books of recovered memory therapy. Just as with subjects under hypnosis, Eileen was encouraged to unself-consciously produce mental images and thoughts with the maximum emotional impact and therefore greatest presumed therapeutic value. While Barrett assured his patient that they would later spend time questioning the truth of the images and thoughts, this apparently never happened. From Barrett's testimony it seems clear that he always treated these images as reflections of actual events, referring to them as "memories." In describing how he reacted to Eileen's descriptions of her mental pictures, Barrett remembers calming her down by assuring her that "it was just a memory." When Barrett was asked during the trial

---

*A recording of these therapy sessions would likely provide a keen understanding of this process and how Eileen eventually came up with her beliefs about the murder. Barrett not only didn't tape the sessions but took no notes, nor did he keep any other record of the sessions.

whether he thought the memories were true, he replied, "I believed her, yes." When asked whether he *ever expressed any doubt* to Eileen about the truthfulness of the memories, Barrett answered simply, "No, I didn't."

In assuring his client that it was not initially important to know whether her mental images were true or false, and telling her that they would address the question later, Barrett makes a false promise offered by many recovered memory therapists. Unfortunately, in recovered memory therapy, as in Eileen's case, later never comes. By the time the images, emotions, and other details have been crafted into a narrative, both the client and therapist have made a heavy investment in the validity of the story, and they have no reason to conspire to tear it down. The more meaning the patient takes from the narrative—the greater the sense of "Ah-ha! Now I understand"—the greater the likelihood that the patient and therapist further invest in the notion that they have uncovered the memory of real events. To review the narrative at the end of its creation would be antithetical to the process and to the very purpose of the narrative.

After Eileen was convinced that she had witnessed the murder, but before she testified, her "memory" continued to change dramatically, incorporating new details about the murder, which were duly reported in the press, and even more conveniently losing details that contradicted the physical evidence of the case. In Eileen's original report of the murder she had been wrong about its happening in the morning and wrong that it had taken place off a dirt road in the woods. She also incorrectly identified what Susan had been wearing. Virtually the only details she got right were that Susan had been killed with a rock and that her ring had been crushed—facts that she told Barrett she had known all her life. As the day of her testimony approached, Eileen's "memory" cleared on each of her mistakes as the details of the original police investigation came to light in the media. (MacLean, in *Once Upon a Time,* gives a chilling and detailed account of how Eileen's memory fluctuated until the moment she took the stand.)

The scene of her father's killing her friend was just one in a series of beliefs Eileen Lipsker came to and molded during her time in therapy. She also "remembered" sexual abuse from the age of three as well as witnessing her father's killing an anonymous woman. She visualized George Franklin burying a diary in which she said he confessed to the murder. Over the course of therapy she also pieced together the story that her father had brought her to a black man and held her down while the black man raped her. Later in therapy, the man in that memory turned white and took on the appearance of her godfather.

The role of her sister Janice in the affair reveals a great deal about why Eileen would finger her father in her recovered string of visualizations, as well as the dubiousness of her account. Janice, who loathed her father, had long suspected him of Susan's murder. In 1984, she had gone to the police with her suspicion, but the case was not pursued. In the course of attempting to get the police to investigate her father, Janice was questioned about George's activities on the afternoon Susan disappeared. Janice undermined her accusation by reporting that her father was at home in her company when Susan was abducted. In *Eileen's* original version of the murder story, Janice had been in the van when they stopped to pick up Susan, at which point George told Janice to get out. Unfortunately, Janice was already on record with a different story. To accommodate for this problem, Eileen's memory evolved, slowly removing the image of Janice from the scene. In a similar fashion, Janice eventually altered her memory of the day of Susan's abduction to conform to Eileen's story. After Janice spent a few sessions in treatment with Barrett, she was able to reremember that she had probably not gotten home the day of Susan's death until later. George's alibi for the critical hours when Susan disappeared was erased through psychotherapy.[5]

Weighing Barrett's account of the therapy process against Terr and Eileen's version, we must consider which of these stories is closer to the truth of the "memory recovery" process. One question to consider in answering this question is whether Barrett (or Reider) would lie about the events. Barrett testified confidently that he believed Eileen's memories were true. Because he believed Eileen, he certainly would have no reason to cast doubt on her story. Perhaps most telling, however, is the fact that Barrett's version fundamentally matches the original stories Eileen told family members about how she had uncovered the murder scene: variously, that she had uncovered the scene through dreams, in therapy, from hypnosis, and, in another version, as a combination of dreams and therapy. All of Eileen's original explanations may be correct. Barrett admits that Eileen's story did become clearer during the therapy sessions and that he did encourage his clients to use dreams as grist for the therapy encounter. As for the question of hypnosis, while Barrett—a practicing hypnotherapist—claims he never employed a formal hypnotic induction, the relaxation exercises he used can function as the equivalent. And because there is no specific state of hypnosis, but only gradations of being able to focus on mental images and to respond to suggestions, it is quite possible that Eileen was in trance during these sessions. That she became visibly frightened when the visualizations surfaced during therapy (leading Barrett to assure her that what she was visualizing was "only memory") might also indicate that she was in a trance state. The case of Paul Ingram, described in chapter 8, illustrates how trance can be induced spontaneously through seemingly innocuous relaxation procedures. Eileen may have realized that the process of relaxation in therapy was in her case tantamount to hypnotic induction. When she first changed her story to claim that she had not uncovered the memory during hypnosis, Eileen's mother remembers her daughter telling her that what she had undergone was only "light hypnosis."*

Considering Barrett's testimony, combined with Eileen's first account of how the "memory" was uncovered, a more likely scenario is that Eileen's visualization of the murder did not arrive one day in January 1989 while looking at her daughter. The evidence overwhelmingly suggests that Eileen *built* the belief six months later, during therapy sessions, at a time she was obsessed with her childhood and a year after her first therapist had told her of the mind's supposed ability to repress trauma. That she would focus on Susan Nason's murder as the subject of her memory search is hardly surprising, for, as Barrett testified, the two were already focusing on how Susan's death had affected Eileen. That she would select her father as the villain of the story is also understandable, considering that her sister Janice had long suspected him of the murder and had even reported her suspicions to the police. In addition, Eileen had already created a visualization during therapy of a scene in which her father sexually molested her. These facts, together with her lifelong memories of her father's physical abuses of his family, probably led Eileen to expect to find more hidden memories of evil deeds committed by George Franklin.

If this analysis is accurate, there is no more reason to believe that Eileen witnessed the murder of Susan than there is to believe any of the satanic-abuse stories, space-alien abductions, or past-life accounts that evolve through similar memory recovery processes.

In her book, Dr. Terr claims she carefully sifted the facts of the case to determine that Eileen's recovered memory of the murder was probably true. In considering the truth or falsity of traumatic memories, she wrote, one must employ "good detective work" and consider all evidence. If her

---

*It is interesting to note that Eileen's story changed after she consulted a criminal attorney who may have advised her that hypnotically refreshed testimony is inadmissible in criminal trials.

account is read without an understanding of the facts of the case, that is just what Terr appears to have done. She reports that the murder memory explained many long-troubling behaviors in Eileen's life—most notable was that Eileen had, during her childhood, pulled the hair out of her head, creating a bloody bald spot.

Taken by itself, Terr's story is an impressive account. With considerable storytelling acumen she marshals her facts to support her conclusion that Eileen Lipsker probably witnessed her father kill Susan Nason and then repressed the memory for twenty years before recovering it. Although the trial judge instructed Terr not to directly testify to her beliefs about Eileen's memory, this probably made little difference to the conclusions the jury drew from her testimony. Terr was so confident in her conclusion about Eileen's memory that she admits to molding her hypothetical illustrations and examples about memory so that the jury members would most easily intuit her testimony as a confirmation of Eileen's story. She also notes that after the trial she learned that a number of the jury members who voted to convict George Franklin were convinced by her testimony. "I learned something from that," she writes, "sometimes hypothetical [sic] are just as compelling as specifics. For concrete thinkers like me, that's a revelation."[6]

One might defend her story by arguing that she simply believed Eileen's final version of the "memory" recovery. But even given this benefit of the doubt, we still have to wonder why Terr largely ignores Barrett's crucial testimony regarding the creation of Eileen's narrative. Terr mentions Barrett only when she states confidently that Eileen was never hypnotized and to assure the reader that he "never attempted to confirm or deny Eileen's murder memories." Terr's omissions and mistakes regarding Eileen's knowledge of repression and her memory recovery prove exceptionally convenient for Terr's story. Because Terr largely ignores the testimony of Eileen's therapists, she doesn't have to distract the reader from the more sensational story that Eileen suddenly saw the murder one day while watching her young daughter.

From one point of view, Terr's account of Eileen's case can be seen as an illustration of how therapists can create compelling narratives out of a body of information elicited from patients. In Terr's adept retelling of the case, no fact she introduces is left dangling. All the information she presents—even including evidence that seems to run counter to her own theories—is explained away or turned around to add weight to her conclusions. In this instance we are fortunate to have the testimony of numerous others—most importantly, Eileen's therapists, as well as the careful reporting of Harry MacLean—against which to weigh Terr's account.

In explaining why Eileen recovered her memory at the time she did, for example, Terr teaches the reader of *Unchained Memories* that recovered memories often return when a "ground of comfort" is achieved in one's life. According to Terr, Eileen at the age of twenty-eight had achieved a sense of well-being and had learned "to relax and let up a little bit. . . . As Eileen's mind went on idle, so did the powerful inhibitions that had blocked her memories. The murder memory could now come forward. The ground was there for memory retrieval."[7] However, Terr's contention would probably come as a surprise to everyone who knew Eileen at that time.

According to the evidence, Eileen was far from emotionally comfortable during the time she was working on her new memories from childhood. "Eileen was trying to escape from this monster of a husband who she loathed," MacLean said when recently interviewed by the authors. "She was trapped in an emotionally abusive and loveless marriage. She had filed for divorce. When she tried to run off with the children, he had threatened to track her down, file criminal charges that she had embezzled money from the business that he ran. Eileen herself said that she was miserable at the time."[8] Terr clearly knew the facts of Eileen's life, for she was challenged on just this point during cross-examination. Defense attorney Horngrad pointedly asked Terr if a person filing for divorce, preparing to fight for the custody of her children, and under the threat of being charged with embezzlement would feel safe and secure. Realizing that Horngrad was describing Eileen, Terr backtracked, saying that feeling secure and relaxed was really only one reason that a person might be able to recover a traumatic memory. But although Terr appeared to concede in trial that her "ground of comfort," theory didn't apply to Eileen, she reinstates this idea in her book, where she could be sure no attorney would pop up and cross-examine her. Regardless of facts to the contrary, she appears to be willing to apply her theory about memory recover to Eileen's story.

At another point in *Unchained Memories*, Terr explains that because of Eileen's love for her father she has continued to find it difficult to face the memory that George not only fondled but raped Susan before murdering her. As proof that Susan was raped, Terr notes that there was sperm discovered in the girl's body.[9] Terr is wrong about this crucial detail. There was no sperm found in the body, for it was almost entirely decomposed in the two and a half months it had lain exposed on a hillside. Oddly, Terr herself writes that what the police found of Susan's remains was little more than mummified tissue and bones, only two pages before she contends that sperm was found in the body.*

In crafting a story with critical errors, omissions, and conclusions built largely on unconfirmed and at some points nonexistent evidence, Dr. Terr illustrates Donald Spence's contention that therapists often choose selectively from a large body of evidence in order to construct a compelling narrative. Terr's recounting of the Franklin case ties up most of the loose ends and leaves little for the reader to speculate about. However, with the number of questionable facts and the amount of essential testimony that she omits, we must consider whether her role as compelling storyteller eclipsed her role as a scientist, for instead of examining complicated facts and conflicting testimony surrounding Eileen's report of memory recovery, Terr sanitizes at every turn.

After combing through Terr's written account of the case, MacLean commented that Terr appeared to be "neither a journalist nor a scientist," adding, "She gives one version of the facts when there are very many possible versions. Not only does she not explore other versions, but she doesn't indicate to the reader that there *are* other versions. What she has ended up with is a tale—a good story. If the facts she reported in *Unchained Memories* are the basis for her conclusions about anything, then her conclusions have to be questioned."[10]

But Dr. Lenore Terr did arrive at conclusions about Eileen's memory, and those conclusions informed her testimony at a trial in which a person's freedom stood in the balance. According to Terr, her influential testimony regarding her theory of memory repression and recovery was a critical factor in George Franklin's conviction.

In explaining to the judge in the Franklin case why she wanted to call Terr as a witness, Elaine Tipton, the prosecuting attorney in the case, said that she intended to challenge the "myth" and "misconception" that an experience such as Eileen's would be impossible to forget. "I'm entitled to rebut that misconception, to explain how memory works, how trauma might affect memory, what are the factors that would contribute to repression versus nonrepression of the traumatic event, what might cause the retrieval of that memory, what the triggering process might include and

---

*According to MacLean, Terr makes several other factual mistakes, including her contention that Susan's body was found in a makeshift grave. Terr also writes that George Franklin drove an old hippie van. While he did drive a VW bus, it was only one year old in 1969 and a common vehicle for a young family. While this is a minor mistake, it shows how Terr seems to be willing to manipulate facts so that they add weight to her conclusions—in this case that George Franklin was a questionable "hippie" character.

what types of features would be consistent with the triggering of a real memory versus the confabulation of a false memory."

As Tipton hoped, Terr did indeed use her impressive credentials to put a scientific stamp of approval on the concept of memory repression and recovery. Not only did she testify that memory repression and recovery were well-accepted facts, but she also approved a hypothetical scenario that exactly mirrored the prosecution's portrait of Eileen. Asked by Tipton whether a child who witnessed a particularly violent event would repress that memory if it had occurred during a childhood that was generally violent and abusive, Terr replied, "My opinion is that such an event would very likely—probably, most likely—be repressed."

Because Dr. Terr is both a clinician and a researcher, we might well ask where this conclusion came from. Had she concluded from her empirical research that memories could be repressed, become inaccessible for years, and then revive in extraordinary detail? Or were the theories derived from other sources? In the prologue to her book, Terr makes a remarkable admission on this count. She writes that it was only in the summer of 1990, after interviewing Eileen, that the question of how adults might repress and recover trauma became a "new" topic of interest to her. The woman who "led me to a new interest in psychiatry came to my San Francisco office in the summer of 1990," Terr writes. "That woman got me to think about the memories that adults retain or recapture from early traumas. Her name was Eileen Franklin Lipsker."[11] So Terr appears to admit that it was only *a few months* before she testified in a murder trial that she began considering memory repression and recovery, topics on which she offered herself as an expert.

Where did the information for her testimony come from? In her "new interest" in memory repression and recovery, Terr describes a lucky co-incidence that helped her "tremendously" in boning up for the trial. That same summer, she was deluged with letters responding to her first book, *Too Scared to Cry*. "The letter writers had many things to teach me," she recalls. "They showed me what a wide array of defenses exist to keep adults from recalling the horrors they experienced as children. And they showed me what a wide variety of ways there are for memory to return." Some of the ways these memories return, she wrote, were "through dream watching, poetry writing, painting, keeping journals."[12] Terr's reliance on these letters received "over the transom" is troubling. Because the methods of memory recovery mentioned in them are widely employed in recovered memory treatment, it is quite possible that the psychiatrist was learning about memory repression from patients in various forms of recovered memory therapy. Terr doesn't mention that by 1990 recovered memory therapy had been practiced in various forms for well over five years. *The Courage to Heal* and several other books on the topic had long been on the market, and thousands of women already believed that they had uncovered repressed memories of abuse through a variety of questionable methods—some of which Terr lists. Nevertheless, Terr appears to have accepted the letters as valid accounts of memory retrieval and used them to inform her analysis of the Franklin case.

If Terr had limited herself to her empirical research on children's memories of trauma, her testimony would have likely destroyed the prosecution's case against George Franklin. Studying the twenty-six children who were kidnapped and buried alive in a school bus in 1976 in Chowchilla, California, she found that each child remembered the event even many years later.[13] Studying sixty children from Christa McAuliffe's hometown who watched live as she died in the explosion of the space shuttle *Challenger*, Terr again discovered that all of these children retained their memory.[14] Even her study of nineteen abused children under five years showed that nearly all remembered their trauma.[15] Interviewing this group of children an average of four and a half years after their trauma (incidents that she reports to have outside confirmation of), only four of the children did not tell Terr some memory of the trauma.* This study is particularly important because all of the traumatized children above three years of age who had suffered *repeated trauma* could remember and talk about it.

To account for Eileen's beliefs and the stories in the letters she received, Terr offered at the Franklin trial the novel theory that a single traumatic event—in otherwise nontraumatized lives—will last in memory while repeated events of trauma are more likely to be repressed. So the child learns from each progressive trauma how to forget negative experiences. Explaining Eileen's memory, Terr suggests that because George was sometimes drunk and violent (memories she never repressed), she had

---

*The four children who did not remember the trauma deserve a special look. Not surprisingly they include the two who were the very youngest at the time of the trauma. One child was six months old at the time of the event while another was seven months old. The two other children were two years and two years, four months respectively. That these children would not remember traumatic episodes when interviewed years later is perfectly consistent with the long-agreed-upon observation that small children forget most if not all the events from their years as toddlers. Terr herself comes to this conclusion in the paper: "2 and a half to 3 years appears to be about the time most children will be able to lay down, and later retrieve, some sort of verbal memory of trauma." She does not invoke some powerful repression mechanism, but points to the long-recognized phenomenon of infantile amnesia.

intuitively learned how to repress trauma. "These experiences," Terr explains in her book, "were probably frequent enough and awful enough to have allowed Eileen to develop the knack for automatic repression."[16]

Terr's theory, which she offered the jury, that single trauma would likely be remembered and repeated trauma would likely be repressed is truly remarkable on at least one level: it is a theory that would allow her to stay in psychological vogue without recanting her earlier research, which appears to argue strongly *against* the idea of massive repression. Repression occurs not from the shock of the event, Terr concludes, but because the child can anticipate the trauma and begin to dissociate from the experience by not encoding the memory. "A person will be less likely to remember because they've gone through a series of events," she testified. "The child, instead of being surprised by these events, anticipates the events. . . . Once a child begins to anticipate events, the child can actually use mechanisms to stop perceiving, even stop the input or stop the storage."

According to our reading of Terr's theories, the Chowchilla kidnappers abducted a school bus filled with children, none of whom had ever been beaten or abused or suffered multiple traumas. If, as Terr attests in Eileen's case, repression can be learned through the experience of having a drunken and violent father, it is remarkable that none of the twenty-six children, who ranged from kindergarten to sixth grade, had come from homes where they were subjected to physical or other traumas. (Using Terr's definition of what constituted trauma in Eileen's case, one wonders whether all of these children could be classified as having suffered only a "single traumatic event" in their lives.) Of the children who watched the space shuttle explosion, Terr managed *again* to find sixty who also had not experienced repeated trauma and therefore had no choice but to remember the disturbing event.

Her theory about why repeated trauma would be repressed is also troubling because it never seems to settle down. In her previous book, *Too Scared to Cry*, she explains that children who experienced repeated or long-standing trauma develop the ability to "deny reality" because they become "battle-weary." A child learns to make "his senses go numb and guard against thinking."[17] This of course makes good sense. The clarity of a memory of living through a bombing raid would, for example, be much more memorable if it was a singular event and not the 47th bombing lived through in a series of 110. This is not, however, due to repression but due to the simple reason that the 47th bombing is less novel and therefore less likely to be remembered in detail or retold or continually mulled over. Would the child forget that all the bombing raids happened?

Humans, including children, have the capacity to become accustomed and numb to the horrific. In addition, while it may be true that children learn ways of distracting themselves from repeated disturbing events, this would affect the encoding of the event and has questionable relation to the retrieval of the memory (that is, the retrieval of whatever was encoded). If a child were to experience a decade of repeated abuse, the traumatic events would of course blur together in memory and become less distinct as individual events. To offer this obvious fact as evidence suggesting that the decade-long series of trauma might be entirely lost from consciousness is nothing but fanciful.

While this is apparently where Terr's initial ideas about the difference between the recall of single and repeated abuse came from, in the Franklin case they took a different tack. She contradicts herself by writing that memory of repeated traumas is equally vivid, if not more detailed, than that of single trauma—the only difference being that repeated traumas can be pushed into the unconscious. As Terr explained to the prosecuting attorney in the Franklin case, repressed memories of repeated traumatic events are quite clear and don't "appear to undergo much weakening over time."[18] As evidence for this point, she points to the clear memories of the Chowchilla children—apparently not realizing that this seems to contradict her earlier theory that their kidnapping memories were so clear for the exact reason that they had *not* undergone repeated trauma, like Eileen, and therefore had not become numb to the terror. Terr never addressses this fundamental contradiction in her analysis of the case: if repeatedly traumatized persons are able to "stop perceiving" or stop the "storage of the events," why would it be normal for uncovered memories to be exceptionally detailed and vivid?

That Terr's empirical studies show little evidence to support the idea of the sort of massive memory repression Eileen Lipsker claimed did not stop Terr from confidently confirming the theories surrounding Eileen's story. Besides the letters she received in the summer of 1990, Terr also used anecdotal stories from her clinical work with patients and from other sources to bolster her testimony. She testified that she saw three or four patients a year who recovered memories that had been submerged for decades, including "a couple" of patients who had retrieved memories of being victims of satanic-cult abuse during which they watched ritual murders.

Terr did not limit her anecdotal stories to people she knew through her practice or even personally. For example, she testified that she knew the nature of a trauma that writer Stephen King suffered as a child. Terr told the jury the story of seeing the movie *Stand By Me*, based on a screenplay by King, which includes a scene in which some young boys run off a trestle to avoid being hit by a train. Watching the scene, she said, "I felt I was in the presence of someone who had been almost hit by the train. . . . It was so frightening." Terr learned later that as a boy King had a friend who was killed by a train. Terr's analysis of King's past goes beyond the unsurprising inference that his writing was informed by the friend's death. Dr. Terr claimed she could tell that King had *witnessed* his friend being killed—something that King himself denies.

"As some of you who like Stephen King know, he writes about mechanical monsters that just overrun people again and again. He's living under the influence of that terrible thing that he saw." Later, under cross-examination, she became more adamant about her insight into King's history. "As a child psychiatrist, I know that King saw [the friend's death] because I see what he produces. Everything in King is mechanical and terrifying, and he shows me time and time again what he's doing by—by mowing people down in the same kind of way. . . . One knows this—at least as a child psychiatrist—King can't stop what he does." To strengthen her assertion, Terr testified that she recently happened to overhear, while in a Hollywood coffee shop, King and some producers discussing making a movie. Terr remembered that the producers were telling King that he could kill only one character in his next movie and King saying, "I've got to kill more because it's really part of me. I've got to do it."

Using this evidence, Terr concludes, "The person who has been traumatized can't stop this kind of behavior. And the person may not be aware of why the behavior is linked to the trauma, but it's there and it has to be repeated." Terr is unrepentant that she used a scene from a movie and an overheard conversation as evidence for her "expert testimony." In *Unchained Memories*, she recounts this part of her testimony with no small hint of pride. She writes that through the illustration of King she was successfully able to "pose to the jury" the image of Eileen pulling out her hair. "The twelve people deciding George Franklin's fate needed to know that behaviors, especially if they are trauma-specific, confirm the gist of a memory."[19]

In an example from her clinical practice, Terr further illustrated how she can help discern the trauma from telltale symptoms. She told of a woman, whom she described as a spinster, who reached forty before she had her first lover. While in therapy, the patient began to describe having troubling dreams about being forced into sexual situations. In addition, Terr noted that the woman had been embarrassed that she had tried to perform an act of oral sex with her lover. "He was shocked and she was shocked," Terr said, "and she didn't know where this came from."

Terr and the patient apparently took on the task of trying to explain this history and behavior. In the end they were able to explain the woman's avoidance of men, her troubling dreams, and the oral sex act that had so embarrassed her, by determining that she had been forced to perform oral sex as a child by a group of strangers while at the beach in San Francisco. As Terr explained, "It appears that this woman had been forced into oral sex acts when she was a very small child, and that was the only kind of sex or romance or anything that she understood, and she had no memory of these events."

When asked on cross-examination how she could be sure that the conclusion that the woman came up with of being sexually abused while at the beach was historically true, Terr conceded that there was no corroborating evidence, but because of the symptoms, dreams, and behaviors she could tell that the story was true. Terr explained that the patient and therapist often have to go on a "mutually agreed-on hunch that this did indeed happen. And I use the word 'hunch,' but I really mean, in all probability this woman was sexually abused by a group of strangers down at the beach. And in all likelihood, she was abused orally because this is what she did to her boyfriend. . . . She and I both are quite sure that she was sexually abused by a group of strangers."

Terr went on to testify that through an examination of a "cluster" of symptoms and signs from a client's life, she can often discern what type of trauma the client experienced. In this way, she said, therapists are often "able to construct that the trauma was something sexual; that it was done by an adult; that it was done by a stranger adult; or that it was done by one adult in the family." From behavior and symptoms, she testified that she could "know that the child was there," and witnessed the suspected trauma. She said that psychiatrists, thanks to their advanced training, can identify symptoms and signs of past trauma and intuit the trauma—even when it is unknown to the patient. "When you are looking at the symptom, if you are a psychiatrist, you look to see if it's literally connected to the event."

Applying this method of identifying symptoms in cases of known trauma is benign, and perhaps even marginally therapeutic, even if it is not accurate, because the client comes to explain her behavior by connecting it to a single event or a series of events. When there is no question as to the nature of the trauma, the matter of whether these connections are true or not is not necessarily critical. However, as we have noted in chapter 3, to believe that therapists can have knowledge of an unknown event through an analysis of symptoms is a fantasy. Terr's notion that psychiatrists, because of their advanced training, can relate symptoms to a particular event is not accepted within the ranks of scientific psychology or scientific psychiatry. To allow this belief into a courtroom is, to put it mildly, dangerous.

At the trial, Terr claimed that for a psychiatrist to be able to confirm a particular type of trauma, the symptoms "have to be convincing. They have to be symptoms that are lined up with what happened and flow from what happened." In this statement she seems to be referring to Eileen's contention that for five years after the murder she pulled the hair out of one spot on the side of her head. In her book, Terr writes, "She began pulling out the hair on one side of her head, creating a big, bleeding bald spot near the crown." At another point Terr describes the behavior as "the bloody hair pulling all through her mid-childhood." Terr explains that "Most likely, young Eileen unconsciously set out to duplicate the horrible wound she had seen on Susan Nason's head. This behavioral reenactment provided internal confirmation for me of the truth of Eileen's memory."[20]

The self-mutilating behavior does indeed fit Terr's criteria that the behavior be specific and telling. However, she doesn't appear to have explored a more fundamental question: did the behavior indeed occur? This is particularly odd considering that Terr stresses that a psychiatrist addressing these questions must be like a good detective. Would a good detective have verified with Eileen's mother, or siblings, or medical records that such self-mutilation had taken place?

Until 1993, Eileen's mother, Leah Franklin, believed that her daughter did indeed see George kill Susan Nason. It was the sincerity in Eileen's voice that initially convinced her. Recently, however, after hearing Lenore Terr lecture on the subject of her daughter's dramatic childhood symptoms, Leah began to wonder whether something might have gone horribly wrong in her ex-husband's trial. Reading Terr's account of Eileen's childhood in *Unchained Memories*, she grew even more worried that Terr and the prosecution were working with many false assumptions.*

Because she was under subpoena as a witness, Leah kept herself ignorant of the testimony in the case during the trial. She is just now learning all that was said—and it has been quite a revelation. She became

---

*Leah, it should be pointed out, has no love for her ex-husband. During the trial, she testified for the prosecution, saying that George had been a physically abusive and angry father and husband.

so troubled about the alleged facts on which Terr based her conclusions, and on which the prosecution largely based its case, that she shared her concerns with the authors.

Leah is quite sure that Terr, if not other persons, was working with unfounded assertions—the story of the bleeding bald spot prime among them. Throughout Eileen's upbringing, Leah combed, cut, braided, or helped style her daughter's hair. It is safe to say that hundreds of times during those years, Leah had some sort of direct contact with her daughter's hair, not including the thousands of moments when she simply looked down at Eileen or patted her on her head. If Eileen had been pulling out her hair from the age of nine to fourteen, creating a large bleeding sore, Leah is sure that she would have noticed it. Not only did she not notice this "symptom," but no doctor, sibling, friend, or teacher ever mentioned it.

Some real detectives in the case apparently did look for corroborating evidence of this behavior. At the request of the prosecution, Leah found over forty photos of Eileen taken between ages seven and thirteen. Leah did not know, before or during the trial, of Eileen's supposed hair-pulling symptom, and didn't realize the significance of the photos. The photos, which she gladly showed the authors, reveal no indication of self-mutilation. Looking at some of the school portraits, Leah clearly remembers helping her daughter comb and style her hair the mornings the pictures were to be taken. "There was never any sign that Eileen pulled out her hair," Leah said when interviewed. "I'm sure I would have noticed if any of the girls had any sort of scalp problem during their childhoods."[21]

The prosecution team assured Leah that they would ask all the necessary questions and give all the information she provided to the defense. They also advised her that she wasn't required to talk to anyone from Horngrad's office. This advice was clearly a strategy to isolate Leah from the defense, and it worked. When a defense investigator called, Leah refused to be interviewed. While the detectives assured Leah that they would turn over all the material to Horngrad, they apparently did not follow through. According to Horngrad, the forty-plus photos showing Eileen with a perfectly healthy head of hair were never seen by the defense.*

In Leah's eyes, Terr makes another equally unfounded assertion about

*Because of the importance of the "bleeding bald spot" in the trial testimony, these pictures would, we believe, have qualified as exculpatory evidence. Being evidence that tended to show the innocence of the defendant—what is called "Brady material" in criminal law—the prosecution was obligated to provide these photos to the defense attorneys. Failure to provide the defense with Brady material could be grounds for a new trial.

another of Eileen's uncovered memories. In the book, Terr describes a time when Eileen was three and her father was anally raping her in the bathtub. "Leah walked into the bathroom and demanded to know what he was doing," Terr writes. "Somehow George slipped out of his predicament, life went on."[22] Leah was more than a little stunned when she read Terr's account: "The scene she described simply never happened. Neither of us ever bathed with the children," said Leah. "If I found him in that sort of situation I certainly would have remembered it. I probably would have killed him."

These anecdotes have led Leah to realize that Eileen's memory, and its evaluation by Terr, are fundamentally flawed. "I'm beginning to realize that a lot of what was introduced in this trial does not correlate with the facts as I know them," Leah said. "I'm beginning to realize that something doesn't fit. What I'm beginning to hear doesn't match reality."

Neither the defense team nor the reporters covering the case fully appreciated the fact that Eileen was undergoing recovered memory therapy at the time she came to believe that she saw her father murder her best friend. If George Franklin ever receives another trial, it will certainly focus more closely on what happened to Eileen in therapy. A new trial might help educate the public about the mistakes of recovered memory therapy as effectively as the first one misled it. With the knowledge that has been gathered in the last few years, Dr. Terr's confident testimony would today be challenged as speculation unsupported by science, her own empirical research, or the facts of the case.

CHAPTER THIRTEEN

Deaths in the Family

Avoid being tentative about your repressed memories. Do not just tell them; express them as truth. If months or years down the road, you find you are mistaken about the details, you can always apologize and set the record straight.

—Renee Fredrickson, *Repressed Memories*

The case of George Franklin has not been the only one in which theories of recovered memory therapy have been offered to juries. Over the last few years dozens of civil cases have been filed by those who believe that they have recovered long repressed memories of abuse. As the theories have gotten a foothold within the mental-health profession they have become increasingly applied to a variety of settings. The story of young Stephanie West deserves telling not only because it shows the ultimate damage these theories can cause but because it shows that the theories of recovered memory therapy are beginning to be used in the treatment of children. Because some therapists assume that children have the ability to immediately repress knowledge of sexual abuse, some have begun using the questionable memory-retrieval techniques in interviews with suspected child victims. Because the statute of limitations would not have run out on these supposedly repressed and recovered crimes, this new application of recovered memory treatment opens the possibility of criminal charges being filed against parents and others based on "memories" the child never knew they had until they met the therapist.

In 1991, at twelve years old, Stephanie West* was introduced to the frightening reality of death. At the beginning of that year her favorite aunt died suddenly, and only two weeks later, her grandmother was diagnosed with terminal cancer. Stephanie's reaction to these events would not have been obvious to someone who didn't know her well. Growing up a tomboy, among family not given to showing emotion, Stephanie had learned from her dad how to affect a tough exterior. She

*The names of Stephanie West, her family, and her therapists have been changed.

didn't cry or speak easily of her fears. Her mother, Barbara, however, saw signs that she was deeply saddened and disturbed. At one point Stephanie confided to her: "I'm afraid everyone is going to die and I'm going to be left all alone." Still, Stephanie seemed to be handling the traumas as well as might be hoped, or at least that's what her parents thought until they got the call from a security officer of a nearby Mervyn's department store. Stephanie had been arrested for shoplifting.

It was the first real trouble of any sort that Stephanie had ever gotten into. The elder of two daughters by six years, Stephanie had been an avid sports player since she could kick or throw a ball. The other young families her parents socialized with had mostly boy children, and Stephanie learned from a young age to hold her own in any competition or rough-and-tumble. Short and stocky, she played catcher on a mostly boys Little League team and goalie on an otherwise male traveling soccer club. Baseball was her first love, and by the age of eleven she could throw a hardball 65 miles an hour and play almost any position on the field. After seeing the power of her throwing arm, other teams quickly learned that you didn't steal second when Stephanie West was behind the plate. More than just a good player, Stephanie was the team leader. At catcher, she directed the positioning of the infield players and easily commanded the respect of her teammates.

It was through her passion for sports that she found communion with her father, Jeff, who coached Stephanie's team. By his own admission, Jeff was a strict father and demanding coach. He was a career navy man, and after he retired from active duty he took a civilian administrative job with the military. Prepping his players for a game, he would often tell them that if they didn't give 100 percent that they were cheating their team and themselves. Jeff encouraged his daughter's intense competitive spirit, and when he wanted to make a point with his team or with his daughter, he was likely as not to yell it. He remembers proudly how she once got into a scuffle defending one of her smaller teammates who had crossed a bully on the other team. When Barbara told him he should reprimand their daughter for getting into a fight, Jeff refused. Stephanie had done the right thing, he told his wife, she defended a teammate. One of Jeff's proudest moments was when his daughter was selected for the end-of-the-season all-star lineup. He had hopes that she might be the first female to pitch on a college baseball team.

As Stephanie grew older, Jeff found their communication off the playing field increasingly strained. If something was bothering his daughter, he would take her out for a cup of hot chocolate or a milkshake, but often he felt clumsy trying to draw out feelings. Stephanie drew back at these moments, and the conversation would turn easily to baseball.

Like most adolescents, Stephanie seemed intent on challenging rules around the house. Each night she had a fight with her mother over completing her math homework. She seemed to know just how obstreperous she could be before her father would step into the arguments. Even when her father joined the yelling, Stephanie sometimes didn't back down. Jeff tried to apply what he learned of discipline in the military to his house. He felt that if he stated the rules clearly, pointing out which lines could be crossed and which couldn't, he should be able to expect an amount of obedience from his children. Until Stephanie was nine, both Jeff and his wife sometimes spanked her when she disobeyed. When his daughter started showing signs of becoming a young woman, he stopped corporal punishment. He was, however, in the habit of flicking her on the cheek with his finger to get her to pay attention, and once, recently, he had kicked her in the backside with the side of his foot to get her into her room to start cleaning.

But even with these trials, Barbara and Jeff were proud parents. There were many signs that Stephanie was growing into a strong-willed and responsible woman. Each week, for example, she volunteered at the family church to watch the toddlers during services. When the other volunteers would talk among themselves, Stephanie prided herself on giving her full attention to the children. Visiting friends' houses for dinners or overnights, her manners always garnered rave reviews from the other parents. Whenever the school or Little League had a fund-raising drive, it was Stephanie who always sold the most candy bars or magazine subscriptions. She wasn't an aggressive or demanding salesperson but rather respectful and persistent in a way that charmed adults.

Unfortunately, as she grew, the politeness she showed others seemed to extend to her parents less and less. As Barbara and Jeff drove down to the Mervyn's department store to collect their daughter, they talked about how they should react. They guessed their daughter would likely be more angry than contrite, and they decided it was best not to be confrontational. When they saw her in the security office, her arms were folded and her eyes looked mean. The overalls that Stephanie had been caught trying to steal were ones that Barbara had recently refused to buy for her daughter, and for this reason, Stephanie was ready to blame her mother for the incident. Instead of getting angry or being drawn into an argument over who was responsible, Jeff and Barbara calmly told Stephanie that they were disappointed in what she had done. At home they sent her to her room. When Barbara checked on her later, she found that Stephanie had climbed out the window. She returned home three hours later.

Although Stephanie grew increasingly moody, the shoplifting incident seemed an aberration through the rest of the winter, spring, and summer of that year. In May she flew to Florida with her mother for a last visit with her grandmother, who died later that summer. As her seventh-grade school year ended, Stephanie told her mother that she was going to make school a higher priority in her life. She was a bright child, with a 135 IQ, and had always done above average in the school's special accelerated program for gifted students. Recently, she had heard that college admissions officers often examined school records back to the eighth grade, and she wanted to make sure she could attend the university of her choice. Stephanie had determined that year that she wanted to become a doctor, specializing in sports medicine. Barbara wasn't sure if she believed that college officials evaluated records back to eighth grade, but she wasn't about to question her daughter's new resolve. When Stephanie signed up for a summer course in advanced placement history, both her father and mother were skeptical that she was serious about the commitment. But as the summer wore on, she excelled, and never once needed reminding to complete her homework. She received an A-minus for the course.

At the beginning of the school year, death again touched Stephanie's life. One of her favorite teachers, who also volunteered as the adviser to the chess club she belonged to, collapsed and died of heart failure. Stephanie attended the memorial service and took to carrying the Xeroxed program for the memorial everywhere she went. At this same time Barbara noticed that Stephanie's behavior around the home took another downturn: she was always angry and agitated. When Barbara walked into the room, Stephanie walked out. On the few occasions during those weeks when she was able to talk with her daughter, she learned only that she was writing a report on a book entitled *Violence and the Family*. In the book Stephanie had learned that many types of verbal confrontations were as abusive as hitting. She began to redefine the yelling matches she had with her parents as a type of child abuse. That week, the day after a yelling match with her father, Stephanie told a teacher's aide that her father was verbally abusive and she was afraid to go home. Her father had recently quit smoking, she told the aide, and he was grumpy and angry all the time. The teacher's aide called the police and reported what Stephanie had said. When Barbara went to pick Stephanie up at school she saw her walking down the steps with two police officers. When they sat down with the school counselor, principal, and the policemen, Stephanie conceded that she was more angry at her dad than afraid of him. Impressed by Barbara's concern, the policemen recommended that the case not be pursued.

A week after that, Stephanie visited the nurse's office and pointed to a bruise on the side of her head, near her temple. When the nurse asked what had happened, Stephanie told her, "My dad slugged me." As she was required to do by law, the nurse called the Child Protective Service for the county and reported what she had been told. The nurse had also noticed scratches on Stephanie's arm which she at first said she had gotten from a fence but later admitted that she had inflicted herself with the point of a school compass.

The CPS investigator interviewed the family but dropped the case. The bruise on the side of Stephanie's head had not been inflicted by her father, the social worker discovered, but was the result of being hit by a soccer ball kicked at close range. Dozens of people had witnessed the event, and the referees even allowed a time-out to ensure that Stephanie didn't have a concussion and could keep playing. Even though Stephanie eventually admitted that her father hadn't hit her, the confrontation had seemed to further drive a wedge between Stephanie and her parents. Her moods were dark most of the time, and she answered questions with shrugs and seldom looked either of her parents in the eye. Once in a while Jeff could engage her in a conversation about sports, but the connection wouldn't last. The evening after reporting that her father had hit her, Stephanie hopped out her bedroom window and ran away. Barbara got a call from the mother of one of Stephanie's friends, telling her that her daughter was at their house and asking her if Stephanie could stay the night. Barbara thought about going and getting her daughter, but decided that they could all use a time-out from the tension in the house.

It was the scratches on Stephanie's arm, more than the false accusation, which worried Jeff and Barbara. They talked about what they could do if this sort of self-mutilating behavior got worse, and they began to look around for professional help. Barbara scheduled an appointment with a woman police officer who specialized in counseling troubled teenagers. A tough and no-nonsense woman to whom Stephanie seemed to respond, the officer laid out in clear terms that during their talk she would tolerate no defensive behavior. She expected to be looked in the eye and talked to in a clear voice, otherwise she might just remand Stephanie to juvenile hall—an option, she told Stephanie, that was within her power. After getting Stephanie's attention in this way, she talked to her for an hour, trying to impress upon her the serious consequences of her decisions and actions. When Stephanie told the officer that she didn't like the way her parents were trying to run her life, the officer tried to help her see the positive aspects of her family. "Many kids I see don't have parents who care about them," the officer said. "Everyone fights with their parents. But your parents care a lot about you." The officer told Stephanie that when she was a teenager she had many fights with her father, but now that he was gone, she would give anything in the world to spend just a few minutes in his company.

The officer's tough talk seemed to get through to Stephanie. As her mother watched, she could see her daughter's defiant expression soften. At the end of the hour, the officer asked if she had anything to say to her mother. Stephanie turned to Barbara. "I'm sorry, Mom," she said and began to cry. For a few days after that encounter, Stephanie's anger slackened and she talked more openly with both her parents. But soon there was another yelling match—over an issue no one can remember— and tension rose again in the West house. Stephanie told her parents that she thought they all needed to see a therapist. Although Jeff was resistant to the idea, Barbara agreed, and they scheduled an appointment with a local family and marriage counselor named Dean Graham.

Both Stephanie and her father found they liked Graham, and the first two sessions showed that the counseling could indeed open up communication. In the sessions, Stephanie's anger was directed mostly at her father. Stephanie complained to Graham that her father watched TV too much, was always grumpy because of his cigarettes, and never talked to her except to tell her to do something. "I want a relationship with my dad," she said, "but he doesn't understand me." Her father sometimes reacted sternly to Stephanie's criticism and other times admitted faults.

"I was able to establish an immediate therapeutic relationship with all family members and get them motivated for therapy," Graham later wrote. "Sessions . . . have focused on Stephanie's frustrations with her father's communication style," which he noted could be very "rigid, black and white, and intimidating."

The day of their second session with their new counselor, Stephanie received her first report card for her eighth-grade year, and found that she had made the honor roll. After the counseling session, the family went out to dinner to celebrate and then went to an arcade to play billiards—a game Stephanie particularly liked. Stephanie's mood was improved, and she seemed both proud of her school performance and looking forward to her approaching thirteenth birthday. Her mother had planned a large party with the children of several other families whom Stephanie had grown up with. But this upturn was also not to last. While they were celebrating at the arcade, Stephanie managed to steal her mother's automated teller card. Later that night, she walked to a teller machine and withdrew sixty dollars.

The next day, when Barbara figured out what had happened, she had her daughter pulled out of class and confronted her in the presence of the school counselor. At first Stephanie denied that she had stolen the card. When her mother told her that the bank had surveillance cameras and they could easily check who had withdrawn the money, Stephanie admitted her crime but steadfastly refused to say where the money had gone. Barbara was disturbed by her daughter's stubbornness. She told Stephanie that she would be grounded for the coming weeks and that her thirteenth birthday party would be scaled down to include just the immediate family. That night Stephanie hopped out her window and ran away to a friend's house. This time Barbara went and retrieved her.

Stephanie began to tell every friend and grown-up in her life how mean her parents were. "My dad's been impossible to be around since he gave up smoking," she told one teacher. "All my parents know how to do is yell at me," she complained to another. Her guidance counselor was getting so many reports of Stephanie's complaints that he finally had to strike an agreement with her that family dynamics would be discussed only with him or the school nurse. In the family counseling sessions she switched the focus of her anger from her father to her mother.

Stephanie's thirteenth birthday, on November third, was a sad affair. Because Stephanie had continued to refuse to tell her parents what she had done with the sixty dollars she had stolen, Barbara held to her threat to have a family-only party. Stephanie was given cards and allowed to pick what dinner her mother cooked, but she was given no presents. The next week, at school, Barbara got a call from the school nurse. One of Stephanie's teachers had noticed that she was hiding something on her upper left arm. Barbara said that she would come right away, and asked the nurse to examine Stephanie. When she got to the school, Barbara learned what she had suspected: Stephanie had made more cuts in her arm. This time, however, the wounds were not made with the dull point of a school compass but with a razor blade.

Barbara had talked with both the family's therapist and the school counselor about what they might do if Stephanie's self-mutilating behavior got worse, and they had agreed that if Stephanie became a danger to herself, putting her into a psychiatric treatment center would be one option. Talking with Jeff on the phone, Barbara felt they had no choice. Their daughter was hurting herself, and there seemed no way that they could reach her. "These are my issues," Stephanie had taken to saying when her parents expressed concern or asked her why she was angry, "it's none of your business." At the nurse's office she asked her daughter if she would be willing to spend some time at a hospital to figure these problems out. They could not only get the very best professional help, she told her daughter, but get a little distance and perspective from the problems that seemed to be getting worse so quickly. Stephanie agreed with a shrug.

Barbara drove her daughter straight from school to Southwood Psychiatric, an inpatient treatment unit that had been recommended by the therapist. While Barbara filled out the insurance forms, a nurse asked Stephanie a series of questions about her history. Stephanie told the nurse that she had never used drugs, or smoked, or been sexually active. The forms Barbara filled out specified a four-week stay, although the clerk at the admissions counter told her that four weeks might not be necessary. Their insurance would cover 80 percent of the $25,000 monthly bill. Barbara wasn't sure where the family would find the remaining five thousand dollars, but she knew that even if they had to pay in installments, it would be well worth the price if the doctors and trained staff could help her daughter.

Psychologist Janet Baker was the first psychologist to interview Stephanie the next day. Stephanie opened the interview by saying, "I have mood swings," and telling Baker how sore her hands were from punching the wall the night before. When she asked why she thought she was in the hospital, Stephanie said, "Because of my parents and what they do to me." She told this psychologist that she had recently been thinking of killing herself or perhaps killing her father and then herself. After talking with her for two long sessions, Baker wrote that Stephanie was a strong-willed young woman who appeared to vacillate between being "socially agreeable, sullen, passive and aggressive and contrite." She concluded:

> There are irrational and bitter complaints about the lack of care expressed by her family and of being treated unfairly by peers. . . . She may try to be obliging and submissive to others but she has learned to anticipate disillusionment and often creates the expected disappointment by provocative questioning and by doubting the interest and support that is shown by others. She employs self-damaging acts and suicidal gestures to gain attention and sympathy. . . . It is likely that this youngster will actively solicit and demand more attention and nurturance than may be called for. The fragile trust Stephanie feels in others is readily shaken, leading to demands, feeling sorry for oneself, and sometimes to tantrums or isolation. . . . It is doubtful that she will move easily once she has taken a

stand on any subject. . . . In other words, once she has made up her mind, she will not want to be confused with the facts.

Jeff and Barbara were told not to visit their daughter on her first full day in the treatment center in order to allow her time to acclimate to her new surroundings. On the next day they came to visit but were told that Stephanie was angry and didn't want to see them, and that the psychiatrist in charge was too busy that day to consult with them. The next visit, Stephanie again refused to see her parents. When Barbara and Jeff demanded to see the physician in charge, they had to wait an hour. When Dr. Daniel Farmer finally appeared, Barbara and Jeff asked him a long series of questions. What was Stephanie's frame of mind? Why wouldn't she see them and why couldn't the doctors insist that she talk with them? What was he discovering about Stephanie's behavior? Could they use hypnosis or truth serum to find out what was wrong? How did they plan to treat her? Had they done any biological analysis to find out if she had chemical imbalances? Openly annoyed with their questions, Farmer only answered a few to their satisfaction. Stephanie would see them when she was ready, he told the pair, and assured them that although he had prescribed an antidepression medication, the problem was not biological in nature.

In the hospital Stephanie found herself surrounded by troubled people of all ages. The doctors placed her into two group-counseling sessions which met once a day. One was for teenagers with troubles ranging from drug and alcohol abuse to violent and uncontrollable behavior. The second group she attended was for women who had suffered abuse at the hands of their parents.

Within a week of entering the hospital, Stephanie began telling the staff of a life history she had never disclosed to anyone else. In the group session for disturbed teenagers, she spoke of having an eighteen-year-old boyfriend whom she often had sex with, and that she was forced to have sex with a boy at a party a few months ago. In the following session she said that she was part of a street gang and that she liked to smoke cigarettes and marijuana and had both snorted and smoked cocaine. When her parents heard of these new revelations they didn't know what to make of them. Drugs? Sex? Gangs? Between baseball, soccer, and the handbell choir practice, her parents didn't see when she would have the time for these activities. Stephanie wasn't allowed out after dark unless they knew where she was, and that an adult would be nearby. They called her school counselor, teachers, friends, and other parents, but no one had any information concerning these stories. After calling the police to asked what sort of devices and clues would indicate drug use, they spent a whole evening searching Stephanie's room but found nothing. The next week, as the stories Stephanie told of her delinquencies became worse (Stephanie had told a new story about being raped at a gangland party), Barbara and Jeff began to believe that their daughter was engaged in some sort of bizarre one-upmanship in these groups. None of what Stephanie was saying corresponded to what they knew of their daughter. Her friends she brought home weren't delinquents but the junior high school's top students. Stephanie didn't belong to a gang, she belonged to the chess club.

They told the doctors at the hospital that they didn't think much of what Stephanie was reporting was true. The doctors, it turned out, had already arrived at a similar conclusion. From written reports of the hospital staff, the treating therapists agreed that Stephanie's stories of drug use and gang involvement were stories she was telling either to get attention from the staff or to fit in with the other teenagers on the unit. "She may have smoked some pot," wrote one psychologist who evaluted Stephanie, "but her appearance and weight suggest that she has not done much with cocaine or its derivatives, and her professed street smarts seem more imagination and fantasy than based on real experience."

Despite the false aspects of the life history she was telling, no one doubted the seriousness of her behavior or her continued threats to hurt herself. Several times she had tantrums so violent that she had to be wrestled to the ground by hospital orderlies and given strong doses of Thorazine. The doctors increased the doses of the antidepressant medication.

In the group she attended with women who had histories of child abuse, Stephanie complained that her parents always yelled at her when they wanted her to clean her room or do her homework and that they didn't understand her. She told the women that once her father had kicked her in the back and then she repeated the story that her father had recently hit her in the head with his fist and left a bruise. Stephanie was given *The Courage to Heal* and *Outgrowing the Pain: A Book for and About Adults Abused as Children*. From *Outgrowing the Pain*, an eighty-eight-page work filled with text and cartoons, she learned that emotional neglect—in which parents wouldn't "hug and hold" their children and were "generally emotionally unavailable"—was a type of child abuse as serious as other types of sexual or physical molestation.[1] She also read that "most adults abused as children have an initial period when they cannot decide if they fall into the 'abused' category. The reason for this is that adults usually have a defense mechanism called *denial* that protects them from anything that is too painful. Denial helps block out unpleasant and painful memories." *Outgrowing the Pain* urged "survivors" not to minimize the abuse they had suffered or to let their parents excuses or denials "interfere with the crucial task of accepting that the abuse did indeed happen and did indeed hurt you."

Barbara and Jeff were finally able to see their daughter at the first family-counseling session a week after she was admitted. The family had planned to meet their therapist, Graham, at the hospital and continue with their weekly counseling sessions. Barbara and Jeff brought their other daughter, Samantha, with them. The moment Stephanie walked into the room she unleashed a string of obscenities unlike anything they had ever heard from their daughter. "You've fucked up my life," she said, in part. "You don't love me. You don't care about me. You love Samantha more than me. I hate both of you." The yelling went on for over a minute. Samantha hid behind her father, tightly squeezing two fingers of his hand.

To try to end the tirade, Stephanie's mother reached across the table and grabbed her wrists. "Look at me," she yelled at her daughter when she tried to pull away. "We've got to start talking about these things. Talking is the only way we are going to work these things out."

"Fuck you," Stephanie yelled back. "These are my issues and I don't have to talk to you about anything." Breaking her mother's grasp, she stormed out of the room, slamming the door behind her. They called one of the hospital staff members into the conference room and asked her to bring Stephanie back into the session. The staff member told them that forcing someone to participate in a session was not the way they did things. "Can I go get her?" Barbara asked. She was told that she couldn't. Stephanie would have to want to talk with them.

Later, during a counseling session with one of the hospital psychologists, Stephanie reported that her mother had reached across the table and slapped her. The incident was reported on her treatment chart.

In the group she shared with women who were abused as children, Stephanie soon discovered other group members had suffered far more serious abuse than she had disclosed. Some of the women reported being repeatedly beaten and abandoned by their parents. Others were currently uncovering repressed memories of having been sexually assaulted in their childhood. They described having powerful flashbacks in which scenes of horrible molestation would suddenly appear out of their subconscious.

Sometimes these flashes would come to them during group sessions with terrifying emotional force. From *Healing the Pain*, she learned that people who had been abused often recovered their memories "like watching a movie in which scenes of your life suddenly appear. It may be the look in your mother's eyes when she first took a strap to you or your father's eyes as he put your hand on his penis. These flashbacks are your memories trying to push their way into your reality."[2] In *The Courage to Heal*, flashbacks were described in a similar manner: "[They] may be accompanied by feelings you felt at the time or they may be stark and detached, like watching a movie about someone else's life." One survivor is quoted as saying her flashback memories were like "viewing slides in a slide show."[3]

Stephanie began keeping a flashback journal in which she could write down any unusual body sensations or mental images. Shortly, she had her first flashback. Piecing the images together, she told her therapy group that she had uncovered a repressed memory of being raped by a stranger while she was on her way home from school at the age of nine.

In the middle of December Stephanie was moved to a residential treatment branch of the hospital. Barbara again had to fill out new sets of forms. This time the expected treatment term would be four months, at an expected cost of $60,000, $12,000 of which Barbara and Jeff would be expected to pay for. She told the clerk that the family didn't have the money. After consulting with her supervisor the clerk told Barbara that she wouldn't have to pay the $12,000 but only promise to pay it in the forms. If she filled out the forms, she was told, the hospital could bill the insurance company for 80 percent of the bill and the hospital would "absorb" the rest.

As Christmas approached, the weekly family therapy sessions with Graham continued to get more confrontational. More often than not, Stephanie would walk out of them. Her parents and Graham tried to draw Stephanie out, but nothing they said could shake her conviction that the world was against her. On Christmas Day her parents brought Samantha and a few close family friends to spend the day with Stephanie at the hospital. They successfully steered the conversation away from anything that might feed Stephanie's anger.

Two days after Christmas, the family had their first productive therapy session in weeks. Graham successfully kept Stephanie from becoming confrontational and Jeff from becoming defensive, and because of this Barbara wasn't forced to try to play mediator or choose sides. Graham encouraged the family to discuss issues without trying to prove who was on the right or wrong but rather as individuals viewing the same problem from different perspectives. Unfortunately, the progress in the session didn't translate to the hospital setting, where her status seemed tied to her stories of victimization and delinquent behavior. After the session Graham over heard Stephanie tell a hospital staff member that the family meeting had been another horror story, in which her parents assaulted her verbally for the entire hour. A few days later she reported that in the previous session she had seen Samantha with a bruise on her forehead. She said that Samantha had confided in her that her father had hit her. Although if they had checked with Graham they would have learned that Samantha hadn't attended any of the recent family sessions, the hospital staff reported the information to the Child Protective Service office and a new investigation ensued.

A few days later, on the night of the fifth of January, Stephanie became hysterical, pounding on the walls of her room. They physically restrained her and injected her with Thorazine. When that didn't calm her they increased the dose and then doubled it. That night Stephanie visualized a series of terrifying scenes that she believed were flashbacks to abuse she had suffered at the hands of her parents. During her group sessions she told of what she was discovering in her past. She had seen scenes of her parents taking turns beating her and her sister with sticks, pots, pans, and vases. She came to believe that her mother had left her alone for weeks at a time when her father was away on navy ships. During this time she also saw the first image in her mind of her father sexually touching her. Later she saw flashes of him beating and then raping her. Eventually she came to believe that the abuse happened every other weekend between the time she was eight and ten years old. With the new sexual-abuse charges, the hospital therapists quickly moved to make sure Samantha was protected from her parents. Stephanie was assigned a lawyer and hearing dates were set to remove her parents' custody rights. The new revelation of sexual molestation, severe beatings, and child abandonment were reported to the CPS investigators looking into the treatment of Stephanie's sister Samantha.

While the therapists in charge of the abuse group had reported that Stephanie often tried to get attention by acting withdrawn, with the new flashbacks, they noted, she became a productive and fully participating group member. "In the past the resident has sought attention by withdrawing from the group or acting sullen and depressed, this week the resident did not feel the need to do this in order to get the sort of attention she needed." In another report one of the therapists wrote that "The resident was able to express herself openly and honestly about issues of

suicidal ideation as well as conditions of hopelessness and helpless-
ness. . . . The resident has a clear understanding of the etiology of her
depression, which is mostly based on the history of her abuse and molest."
Nowhere in these notes is there any indication that these therapists considered the possibility that the visualizations were not based on real
experiences.

The new acceptance Stephanie found in her abuse group was offset
by the severe anxiety she began to feel about the CPS investigation of
her sister's care and the criminal and child-custody proceedings that had
been begun against her parents. In group session she talked of fearing
that she wouldn't be believed. In Stephanie's journals, however, she writes
of her fear that the legal proceedings would splinter her family forever.
After Stephanie told one of the psychologists that she felt the legal hearings
and investigations were moving beyond her control, the psychologist
noted in her treatment record that Stephanie should be kept informed
about all the investigations and legal actions against her parents, as this
would help her feel less "helpless and out of control."

On January 16 the CPS agents went to Samantha's school and took
her into protective custody. For Barbara and Jeff, the rest of the month
of January and February saw series of meetings with lawyers and investigators for the Child Protective Service agency. Upon hearing Stephanie's
new charges that she had been raped by her father, Barbara demanded
that a medical doctor examine Stephanie. The exam found that her
hymen was in place and normal for her age.

At the center where Samantha was being detained, interviewers used
"direct and indirect" interviewing techniques and anatomically correct
dolls to assess whether Samantha had been abused. In all her time away
from her parents, Samantha maintained that they had done nothing bad.
"I want to go home and be with my family and stay with them forever
and ever, even my sister, too," one of the investigators quoted Samantha
as saying at the time. On March 9 the West family was due in court,
where Stephanie would testify about her abuse. In advance of the hearing,
the CPS workers had filed a report that would recommend Samantha be
returned to her parents, but that Stephanie be permanently removed from
the family, and detained at a receiving home until a suitable foster family
could be found.

In the treatment center, Stephanie was becoming increasingly agitated
about the upcoming hearing. While the question of the custody of her
and her sister would likely be settled, her new memories had engendered
a criminal investigation against her father. The hearing would be the

first time she would have to repeat her new beliefs in front of her father. In her flashback journal—just five days before the court hearing—Stephanie wrote of the images she was seeing. "I saw my father touching me and he was trying to have sex with me and I kept saying no and trying to fight back but he kept hitting me and he said it would hurt but when I yelled he socked me really hard and I got knocked out." In the margin of the journal she reports that these images have been coming into her mind "all day and they're getting me really upset." In another flash "I saw my mom just keep hitting me and cussing at me and she wouldn't stop. She kept hitting me for a long time and by the time she was done I was bleeding and I bruised up really bad. Then she called someone and was telling them how bad I was and how her life was hell because of me."

On March 6, the night before Stephanie was scheduled to meet with her attorney, just three days before the hearing, Barbara got a phone call from the psychiatrist at Southwood in charge of Stephanie's treatment. There had been an accident and an ambulance had taken Stephanie to the nearby children's hospital. When Barbara and Jeff arrived at the hospital a few minutes later, a nurse told them that the doctors were working on Stephanie and that they would have to wait. After an hour they were allowed into the intensive care unit to see their unconscious daughter. Intravenous tubes curled from both arms and a machine near the bed was pumping air into her lungs. Before they could ask the doctor what had happened, they noticed the bruises around her neck. Stephanie had tried to hang herself in her room at the residential care facility. She had been found crumpled on the floor, the sash of a robe tied around her neck.

The next day the doctors ran a series of tests that gauged the level of brain activity and determined that, although her heart was still beating, Stephanie was dead. The doctors, not Stephanie's parents, made the decision to turn off the machines and allow Stephanie to stop breathing. Barbara and Jeff were barred from taking part in this awful decision because Stephanie was scheduled to testify about her recovered memory beliefs that her father had molested her.

Two years have passed since Stephanie's death, and her parents still ponder the terrifying momentum of the events of that year. Among all the documents and reports that they have collected surrounding their daughter's death is the journal in which Stephanie described the flashes and physical sensations that she had learned to label memories. Among all the descriptions of abuse one entry stands out. Just a few days before she killed herself, Stephanie wrote, "One of my fears is things aren't going to work out. It really seems that way because my parents are acting like they're mad at me. I want it to get better because I don't want my sister to be sad because she's away from my mom. I want things to work out because I want to go home after things work out."

Conclusion:
The Etiology of
Recovered Memory Therapy

A science that hesitates to forget its founders is lost.
                                      —Alfred North Whitehead
                                      The Organization of Thought

While recovered memory therapy may appear to have entered the American scene in the 1980s, the assumptions and ideas that have made the movement possible have been part of the very fabric of psychotherapy throughout this century. Many of the theoretical and practical mistakes committed today by recovered memory therapists were made by Freud a hundred years ago. Freud first put forward the concept that the unconscious is a world of its own—a place where memories, thoughts, desires, and instinct fight among themselves and attempt to control behavior. Much of our conscious life, Freud believed, was ruled by this underworld of forces. Although Freud's theories have been largely reworked by psychoanalysis, the terminology and his romantic conception of the mental-health healer have remained in the profession of psychotherapy and in our culture like props on a vacant stage. It is onto this stage that recovered memory theorists have walked. Without Freudian props and backdrops, recovered memory promoters would not likely have been tolerated or accepted by their professional peers, asked to give workshops, or invited to appear on national talk shows or write books for respectable publishing houses. Without the stage once lively with Freudian players, recovered memory therapy, if it had existed at all, would probably have been quickly identified for what it is—pseudoscience. Although their notions and methods lack scientific backing, recovered memory therapists for the most part did not have to prove that their theories were valid or even explain what they meant by "repression" or "the unconscious" because most people thought they already knew.

The year 1996 will mark the one-hundredth anniversary of Freud's presentation of his famous paper "The Etiology of Hysteria." In it he described using various techniques to elicit memories of infantile sexual abuse from all of the eighteen patients he diagnosed as suffering from hysteria. With this scant evidence he built the seduction theory—the notion that all neuroses could be traced to forgotten infantile sexual trauma. "If we have the perseverance to press on with analysis into early childhood," Freud wrote in the paper, "we invariably bring the patient to reproduce experiences which . . . must be regarded as the etiology of [the patient's] neurosis for which we have been looking. These infantile experiences are sexual in content. I therefore put forward the thesis that at the bottom of every case of hysteria there are one or more occurrences of premature sexual experience, occurrences which belong to the earliest years of childhood but which can be reproduced through the work of psycho-analysis."[1]

Freud later repudiated the seduction theory, deciding that the accounts of abuse from his patients could not be true. As he explained, his theory "broke down under its own improbability and [the patients' contradictory stories]; the result at first was helpless bewilderment. Analysis had led by the right paths back to these sexual traumas, and yet they were not true. Reality was lost from under one's feet. . . . Perhaps I persevered only because I had no choice and could not then begin again at anything else."

By the time Freud concluded that his patients' accounts were historically untrue, he had already proclaimed his method of psychoanalysis and claimed discovery of the cause of hysteria. He saved himself by theorizing that his method was correct, but that the truth it discovered was deeper than he had at first realized—the patient's unconscious lust for her father during her childhood. The stories of sexual contact did not come from repressed memories, he decided, but from repressed fantasies. What his method had discovered, he offered, was an unconscious realm of seething sexual desires in infants and young children. Freud then expanded this theory, suggesting that almost all forms of mental illness reflect the patient's unconscious desires and fears. "If hysterics trace back their symptoms to fictitious traumas," he wrote, "this new fact signifies that they create such scenes in fantasy, and psychical reality requires to be taken into account alongside actual reality."[2]

As Allen Esterson shows convincingly, the idea that Freud was a passive recipient of his patients' stories of sexual abuse has long been the accepted version of history. In *Seductive Mirage: An Exploration of the Work of Sigmund Freud*, Esterson quotes from half a dozen biographers and historians who tell virtually the same story—one that Freud himself repeated later in his career—that he at first believed the accounts of abuse and then later classified them as fantasies. This argument received the greatest recent attention in Jeffrey Masson's 1984 book, *The Assault on Truth*. Masson puts an additional spin on the story by suggesting that Freud changed his thesis largely because of pressure from his colleagues and Victorian society to ignore the reality of child abuse. Masson believed that Freud had been strong-armed into turning his back on the dark truth that he had discovered.

This story of Freud's early work pervades the literature of the recovered memory movement. "Freud was simply unwilling to believe that so many fathers—possibly including his own—could abuse their children," write Bass and Davis in *The Courage to Heal*. "Freud's new theory was obviously more palatable to society and to the patriarchal profession in which he worked . . . he substituted Oedipal Theory, thus turning the reality of abuse into a child's fantasy."[3] Supporters of the recovered memory movement have resurrected Freud's early theories of hysteria, holding his methods and discoveries as brave and groundbreaking work. In *Trauma and Recovery*, for example, Judith Herman writes of Freud's paper on hysteria: "A century later, this paper still rivals contemporary clinical descriptions of the effects of childhood sexual abuse. It is a brilliant, compassionate, eloquently argued, closely reasoned document."[4]

To praise Freud's early methods and results so unconditionally, recovered memory therapists ignore a troubling problem: the often-told story of Freud's passively receiving these abuse memories from his clients stands in sharp contrast to many of his own accounts of their treatment. As with recovered memory therapists, proof that Freud pressured clients to confirm his preexisting belief that all hysterics suffered abuse as small children comes from his own writing. Freud was quite open and revealing about this pressure, stating that the memories were uncovered against the patient's "greatest reluctance." In addition, Freud was clearly not counseling women who prior to therapy had memories of sexual abuse. "Before they come for analysis the patients know nothing about these scenes," Freud wrote, adding that the patients "are indignant as a rule if we warn them that such scenes are going to emerge. Only the strongest compulsion of the treatment can induce them to embark on a reproduction of them."[5] In another paper on the same topic he talks of using "the most energetic pressure" to overcome "enormous resistance." In a letter, Freud compares his methods to the pressure required to elicit confessions from suspected witches. "Why are the [the witches'] confessions under torture so like the communications made by my patients in psychological treatment? . . . I [now] understand the harsh therapy of the witches' judges."[6]

But even when patients acceded to his demands that they describe such a scene, Freud admits that they "have no feelings of remembering the scenes," and tell "emphatically of their unbelief." Judging from his own writings, Freud's techniques were brutal and unyielding. Simply put, he bullied his patients in order that they might confirm his theories and interpretations. This conclusion is inescapable, for Freud himself admits as much: "Having diagnosed a case . . . with certainty and having classified its symptoms correctly, we are in a position to translate the symptomatology into aetiology: and we may then boldly demand confirmation of our suspicions from the patient. We must not be led astray by initial denials. If we keep firmly to what we have inferred we shall in the end conquer every resistance by emphasizing the unshakable nature of our convictions."[7] As Professor Frederick Crews has written, Freud waited for evidence "that would permit him to put his trademark suppositions into play," relentlessly forcing his conclusion on his clients. He held to his interpretations "like a pit bull," notes Crews, only later taking the time to portray himself as having "gradually solved the case with all the prudent objectivity and uncanny astuteness of his favorite literary character, Sherlock Holmes."[8] Indeed, the conclusion that Freud was able to conquer resistance in every patient is also thrown into question by his own writing. Freud admits later that his presumptions about events in the patient's life "are not reproduced during the treatment as recollections, they are the products of construction." This admission leads to the likelihood that Freud came to his beliefs about the histories of some of his patients' pasts wholly without their assistance or cooperation. That recovered memory therapists like Herman should tout Freud's early work as "brilliant" and "compassionate" demonstrates how willingly these experts ignore the coercive nature of any procedure so long as the resulting memories confirm their beliefs. Herman makes no mention of the harsh nature of Freud's methods just as she ignores similar techniques today (and in doing so turns her back on the pain of women patients both past and present), for the apparent reason that the results confirm her ideological position. To tout Freud's early work as "closely reasoned" requires the same sort of blindness as Herman and others employ today to ignore current gross mistakes in therapy.

Freud's work proves a remarkable mirror to recovered memory therapy. His reports of overcoming strong resistance, and his willingness to ignore patients' testimony that their visualizations did not feel like the experience of remembering, are reproduced nearly verbatim in the literature of the recovered memory movement. Freud, like recovered memory therapists today, showed an unyielding determination to impose his unsubstantiated assumptions about human memory and causes of psychological disorders on his patients. He created a system of treatment that, as Crews notes, depreciated the "patient's self-perceptions as inauthentic," and seemed "ideally geared to assaulting the very selfhood of insecure female patients."[9] The figure of Freud that is finally emerging shows a man who manipulated his clients' beliefs about their upbringing to confirm his theories, a shameless self-promoter and a healer who blamed his clients for his own mistakes. All in all, Freud cut the very figure of a recovered memory therapist.

In the end, Freud made two unforgivable mistakes: coercing false memories from his clients, and then blaming the client for the creation of those beliefs. It is perhaps the latter mistake—the conclusion that almost all accounts of sexual abuse, whether produced in therapy or simply remembered, were the fantasies of his clients—that was his most damaging. By lumping all accounts of sexual abuse together and labeling them fantasy, Freud gave those portions of Western society impressed with psychoanalysis an excuse to ignore the reality of childhood sexual assault for much of the twentieth century.

Certainly, no portion of Western society was more impressed with psychoanalysis than psychoanalysts themselves. For them, Freud's conclusion that patients fantasized sexual encounters with their parents undoubtedly led to the twisting of thousands of honest reports of sexual abuse. Patients who told of sexual molestation they had known of all their lives were often informed that they had only fantasized the experience. Having accepted one groundless position, psychoanalysts now seem frighteningly willing to embrace another groundless extreme. Perhaps motivated by feelings of guilt over their long denial of the reality of child abuse, certain therapists appear ready to argue that all therapy-generated visualization of sexual abuse should be assumed accurate representations of the past. One analyst recently wrote: "For one hundred years we psychoanalysts have believed that incest really did not occur in our society, or at least not in the middle or upper classes, that it was just an Oedipal fantasy. During the last fifteen years we have learned that it does exist; and that it can cause severe pathology. . . . Perhaps the pendulum has swung a bit too far to the other side now. But only a little too far. Can we deny help to all the patients who actually have gone through abuse and who suffer? Can we say all is false memory? We cannot and must not do that."[10] Such arguments ignore the fact that no one is arguing that "all is false memory," and fail to make the elemental distinction between memories the patient has at the beginning of therapy and beliefs produced through the highly charged therapeutic encounter.

While the opinions of analysts may have been influential in our culture, the idea that all of society has followed Freud in his mistake is simply ridiculous. The reality of child abuse and the victimization of children has long been apparent to individual physicians, nurses, social workers, teachers, parents, and anyone with a commonsense understanding of human deviancy. The fact that this problem did not receive the attention that it deserved did not mean that it was unknown, nor does it mean that concerned caregivers were ignorant of sexual threats to children. The psychotherapeutic community has projected their own mistakes onto society as a whole.

Freud proves to be the father of the recovered memory fad for reasons that reach far deeper than his seduction theory. To adapt a concept offered by Thomas Kuhn, in *The Structure of Scientific Revolutions*, one could say that Freud created a pseudoscientific paradigm in the mental-health profession.* That is, unconstrained by any substantiated or agreed-upon body of data, close observations, or demonstrated effects, Freud proposed what appeared to be an impressive intellectual structure for the understanding of behavior. Kuhn explains that scientific paradigms are created and maintained when a set of theories so grips a discipline that the work of scientists becomes organized around extending and refining the ideas that form the paradigm. Founders of new paradigms, according to Kuhn, must offer theories "sufficiently unprecedented to attract an enduring group of adherents away from competing modes of scientific activity," but at the same time be "sufficiently open-ended to leave all sorts of problems for the redefined group of practitioners to resolve."[11] Freud's theories possessed both of these characteristics.

Freud believed—and promised his followers—that his intellectual brainchild would eventually explain almost anything that people did: from slips of the tongue to art, from the very development of civilization and on to the psychological basis of religion. As promoters of paradigms

---

*Kuhn's analysis of the conditions surrounding scientific revolutions presumes that the basic enterprise of science is empirical observation and analysis of phenomena, which includes data collection, analysis, and the empirical testing of theories. It would be inappropriate to unconditionally apply Kuhn's ideas to Freud's work because it did not involve empirically testable theory. However, because Freud's formulations functioned like a scientific paradigm, we have chosen to apply Kuhn's term.

routinely do, Freud attempted to apply his notions everywhere. Forcefully asserted, the basic postulates of Freud's theories take on the appearance of a huge and complicated machine with neatly intermeshing gears and cogs driven by a powerful engine. The sheer complexity of it defies critical analysis. The piece one studies is always connected to a dozen other parts, and it never becomes quite clear what the part being studied does or how it applies to the whole.

While Freud's notions functioned something like a paradigm, his theories were prescientific and based on no reliable empirical evidence. As in prescientific eras of other disciplines, his theories were accepted by consensus—not because of anything resembling empirical proof but because of his magnetism and the seductively broad nature of the ideas. No doubt it was the very arrogance and grandiose application of his theories that was appealing to intellectuals and mental-health practitioners who were happy to claim an understanding of what motivated people— even if they could not actually explain the workings of these theories, much less prove their truth or value. Those who adopted his theories and defended his assertions gained by association something of Freud's status, at least vis-à-vis the untutored. Recovered memory therapists in many respects have operated within Freud's pseudoscientific paradigm. In doing so they have become to the study of the mind and behavior what astrologers are to the scientific study of the stars and planets. They have engaged in an enterprise based not on science but on impressionistic insight, myth, metaphor, and the powerful persuasive nature of the therapy setting.

The many recent critiques of Freud's legacy are worth noting because they could just as easily be applied to a critique of the paradigm he established and therefore to the recovered memory movement. Professor Crews could just as easily have been profiling any number of recovered memory, satanic-cult, or MPD experts when he described Freud as a man who threw together his "magisterial-looking claims from various unacknowledged sources—some of them more folkloric than scientific— while passing them off as sober inferences from the data of his clinical practice. . . . Once having arrived at those claims, we see, he adhered to them with a blind, combative stubbornness—though not without willingness to expand the system on an ad hoc basis to encompass newly perceived difficulties."[12]

Although he specifically targets the practice of psychoanalysis, Crews might as well be addressing the problems of the recovered memory movement when he wrote that "the movement's anti-empirical features are legion":

They include . . . its casually anecdotal approach to corroboration; its cavalier dismissal of its most besetting epistemic problem, that of suggestion; its habitual confusion of speculation with fact; its penchant for generalizing from a small number of imperfectly examined instances; its proliferation of theoretical entities bearing no testable referents; its lack of vigilance against self-contradiction; its ambiguities and exit clauses, allowing negative results to be counted as positive ones; its indifference to rival explanations and to mainstream science; its absence of any specified means for preferring one interpretation to another; its insistence that only the initiated are entitled to criticize; its stigmatizing of disagreement as "resistance" (or in the case of recovered memory therapy "denial") along with the corollary that, as Freud put it, all such resistance constitutes 'actual evidence in favor of the correctness. . . .' "[13]

We suspect that one of Freud's motivations—and perhaps his key rationalization for his manipulation of his patients—came from his belief that he was revealing the dark truths of human nature for the first time in history. Motivated by his grand conception of his historical importance (which was perhaps fueled by his heavy cocaine use), his patients became a means to an end: that end being the confirmation of his brilliant theories. A similarly grandiose conceit has been adopted by many recovered memory therapists. The movement's literature shows that some of the prominent experts believe that they are not simply exploring the pasts of their clients but in the process exposing evil that has gone unnoticed throughout the history of patriarchal society and perhaps even unearthing a secret satanic organization that rules the world. What happens to the individual patient—and that patient's family—caught up in a movement with such a grand and noble cause?

Freud himself defined the model for the professional mental healer as something of an amalgam of genius, shaman, and life mentor. The romantic notion of the brilliant therapist supplying dramatic and transformational interpretations—offering insights like incantations over the client—has remained intact. This conception of the therapist's role has remained a draw for both would-be healers and for patients who are particularly vulnerable to the confidence exuded by such self-glorifying professionals.

In his own description of his work, Dr. Lawrence Pazder shows how some therapists help build this romantic ideal in their clients. Pazder, who recounts his counseling of Michelle Smith in one of the first recovered memory books, *Michelle Remembers*, explains to his patient that "before one can touch one's depths, risk that journey, an atmosphere, a contract, a relationship that is sufficiently trusting and safe is necessary. . . . Only then is the patient able to touch his core, to re-experience the past. . . . In my experience, true changes come only from depth experiences, from re-experiencing and reintegration. I like to describe the process as core realization."[14] Dr. Colin Ross writes in *Multiple Personality Disorder* that working with patients gives him a sense of communion with a "higher intelligence" in the universe. "The sense of a higher intelligence at work, evoked by the complexity of the [MPD] system and the vast quantity of information it organizes, stores, and accesses, provides the MPD therapist common ground with molecular biologists. Working with the MPD patient, one has a sense of being on the ground floor of the mind, looking directly at its basic structure, much as one must when studying DNA."[15]

It is this sort of arrogant self-appraisal—combined with a belief in robust repression and an all-powerful unconscious—that allows these therapists to assume that clients have little or no understanding of their own motivations or pasts at the beginning of therapy. The role of the therapist established by Freud permits therapists to dismiss a patient's pretherapy sense of self as hopelessly flawed, inauthentic, or clouded by the mind's own defenses. Patients often allow this to happen because they believe their healer possesses unique knowledge of all facets of human nature, including memory and symptomology, and has a near-magical ability to know their true past.

As a discipline becomes scientific, it becomes progressively more difficult to create sweeping grand theories. As knowledge develops through research, all-encompassing theories based on supposition or anecdote tend to be less marketable because they can rarely account for the ever-growing body of empirical evidence. As the standard for evaluation of a given hypothesis shifts, demonstrations and data replace demagoguery. Portions of the mental-health field are well along in making this shift.

For large parts of the profession, advances in understanding of mental illness and effective treatment is defined by the progress of scientific work. Since the Second World War, significant progress within the field has been made outside of the Freudian paradigm in two areas: the application of biomedical and genetic research to the understanding of major mental disorders and psychotherapy focused on rehabilitative activities. With the research advances made to date, some observers now predict a time when specific genetic predisposing factors for serious mental illnesses will be identified and their effects countered though biomedical intervention via drug or gene therapy. This will come only through the painstaking, expensive, and time-consuming application of science.

At the same time that the application of scientific method is starting to yield hope for one class of mental-health problems, the application of applied knowledge in the talk-therapy portion of the industry has also advanced. Psychiatrist Samuel Guze has identified rehabilitative-focused psychotherapy as a method based on "helping the patient better understand the presenting illness or problem and on developing approaches for minimizing the difficulties or disabilities associated with illness or problems."[16] As he notes, this approach requires no assumptions or grand theories regarding the etiology of the disorders, but rather focuses on the patient's individual circumstances. Patient and therapist endeavor to do nothing more or less than improve the patient's ability to function in the world by identifying troubling behavior and coping patterns and considering ways to improve them. "When such a process of psychotherapy is successful, the patient may feel better, suffer less disability, and cope more effectively." While this process would require the healer to apply some amount of impressionistic insight and persuasion, the treatment does not rely on these factors. In changing behavior, a psychotherapist can battle a mental disorder or deficient socialization in much the same way a medical doctor can battle high blood pressure by focusing on the client's amount of exercise, diet, and stress level. Patients in rehabilitative therapy are not asked to devote a large part of their lives and energy to the therapy or to join a political or social cause. Nor are they expected to lose the ability to function during therapy, become suicidal, redefine their histories or sense of self, disown their families, create new "families of choice," or come to any sort of mind-shattering therapeutic gestalt.

Dr. Paul McHugh of Johns Hopkins has proposed that there is something of a civil war within the mental-health field between romantics who rely on inspiration and myth, and empiricists who argue that practice in the mental-health field should be based on scientific observation and methodical study of patients. "The empiricists are winning because their approach has expanded, in a clear and gratifying way, our knowledge of mental disorders," he writes, adding that the romantics are losing because "as romantics will, they have become infatuated by their own thoughts. They claim to know things they never try to prove. They are charmed by novelty and ignore, even disdain, drab facts. More recently, in their thinking they have taken a nightmarish turn towards chaos that has caused patients and their families much suffering."[17]

The all-knowing therapist is disappearing, McHugh believes, just as "sexual metaphor and Greek myth are disappearing from psychiatric explanations." "In their place is an appreciation that mental life is as open to empirical assessment as are other aspects of the world. Empiricism prompts psychiatrists and patients alike to work with what can be observed and confirmed—emphasizing what we know and how we know it. It indicates how decisions for treatment are made, how their strengths are reviewed, and how their errors are corrected. It does not exclude inspiration but keeps it within bounds."[18]

While these trends are encouraging, neither recovered memory therapy nor the Freudian paradigm of psychotherapy will disappear soon. This sort of social change requires decades. The current reappraisal of Freud, combined with the impressive developments in biomedical psychiatry and rehabilitative psychotherapy, suggest that Freud's dead-hand grip on the mental-health industry is slipping.

While we would like to believe that recovered memory therapy is a last hurrah of the romantics, its widespread practice and public acceptance tends to counter that hope. In predicting the future (which is always a risky enterprise), one should consider the very real possibility that recovered memory therapy may become institutionalized within the therapy profession and become a constant presence in our society. While it would be hard to conceive of this outcome, we should remember that ten years ago no one could have predicted the current prevalence of recovered memory therapy, nor could anyone have guessed the number of patients and families that have been devastated. That the pseudoscientific ideas of recovered memory therapy could so easily have been the basis for new laws in over half the states in the Union speaks to how willing the culture at large is to accept these ideas.

While many in the mental-health field have identified recovered memory therapy as an inexcusable mistake that is causing enormous harm, there is, unfortunately, no regulatory body that can stop its practice. Some look to the huge professional associations in the mental-health field—including the American Psychological Association and the American Psychiatric Association, that oversee the various social work disciplines—and trust that they are protected from misguided or dangerous therapists just as they doubt that a large segment of the physicians could today choose to bleed patients with leeches as a cure for pneumonia. We suggest, however, that this trust is misplaced. Unfortunately, these organizations function less as regulatory bodies insuring the safety of the patients than they do as guilds protecting and promoting their membership. Dramatically different, foolish, and often damaging treatments have often been tolerated because the consequences of seeking an open debate would inevitably shake the public's confidence in the profession as a whole. It is probably unrealistic to believe that any committee called by these organizations will be able to take a strong stand on an issue, such as recovered memory therapy, which so divides its membership.*

In choosing to tolerate recovered memory therapy, the majority of the members of the major mental-health organizations are being irresponsible and foolhardy. Eventually the scandal caused by this treatment will likely damage the reputations of their professions in the public mind and diminish them as practitioners. Unfortunately, it is likely that only when the scandal reaches this magnitude that mainstream practitioners will realize that they must act to repudiate the dangerous techniques employed by some of their colleagues. By then, much additional damage will have been done to unwary patients and their families, and to the progress of these important professions.

It is interesting that the American Medical Association has been able to take a far stronger stand on this issue than the professions most directly implicated in the problem. Since the AMA principally represents physicians who practice specialties other than psychiatry, fewer of its members have a vested interest in ignoring the recovered memory epidemic. In June 1994 the AMA passed a resolution warning of the danger of creating false memory that is inherent in the techniques utilized by recovered memory specialists.

The use of lobotomies in the 1940s and 1950s is the best recent historical example of the unwillingness or inability of professional peers to regulate and restrain an unjustified and dangerous practice. The barbarous nature of this procedure is described by Elliot Valenstein in *Great and Desperate Cures:* "After drilling two or more holes in a patient's skull, a surgeon inserted into the brain any of various instruments—some resembling an apple corer, a butter spreader, or an ice pick—and, often without being able to see what he was cutting, destroyed parts of the brain." For a time lobotomy was very much in the mainstream of psychiatry, an "uncritical enthusiasm running rampant and causing great harm to des-

---

*Indeed, in 1993 the American Psychological Association deputized a panel to examine the recovered memory therapy dispute. Although some believed that this committee was formed because of complaints about the therapy, according to one source close to the committee the panel was requested because recovered memory therapists themselves sought the imprimatur of the organization for their methods, theories, and conclusions. With the panel's current composition, three scientists and three clinicians, two of whom practice recovered memory therapy, the committee is unlikely to take much of a stand.

perate patients."[19] Tens of thousands of mutilating brain surgeries were performed at the treatment's height, and in 1949 the healer who introduced the procedure, Dr. Egas Moniz, won the Nobel Prize in Medicine. For nearly a decade criticism of the procedure, while present, was given only in hushed voices. At the same time the operation was widely recommended by "distinguished psychiatrists and neurosurgeons, many of whom were affiliated with highly respected medical centers and universities." In addition, "magazines and newspapers, whose readers numbered in the millions, popularized each new 'miracle cure' with uncritical enthusiasm, while commonly overlooking its shortcomings and dangers." Those opposed to the procedure published very little criticism during the first ten years of its use, partly because of, as Valenstein concludes, a "long-established tradition that considered it bordering on the unethical to criticize in public another physician's treatment."[20]

Unlike those harmed by recovered memory therapy, these patients, in the main, were lost souls already confined to state mental hospitals— long given up as hopeless by their families and communities. The damage their doctors inflicted on them fundamentally limited their ability to seek redress. There was no constituency to advocate their interest and no one obviously harmed beside the patient. The social circumstances of the recovered memory epidemic, however, are quite different in these regards. The patients are primarily middle-class women with no major mental disorders. Apart from the troubles, problems, and worries that brought them to therapy, these patients were functioning members of society prior to treatment. Their mistreatment by recovered memory therapists has also resulted in a second tier of victims: middle-aged or elderly parents, family members, and other adults who are accused of heinous crimes. This second tier of victims has an interest in protecting their children who are being victimized as well as one in keeping their reputations, their economic security, and their freedom.

The allegations, civil suits, and sometimes criminal charges brought against these supposed child molesters have forced the debate over the validity of recovered memory therapy out of the consulting rooms and into the public eye. Because this therapy shatters lives and families, many of the world's leading experts have taken public stands on the scientific and psychological issues surrounding it. Patients who have publicly denounced their parents as monsters, and the outrage of the accused parents, have drawn much media attention. During the first years of coverage of this epidemic the media accounts tended to report only the patients' tale of molestation. Recently, the media have shifted their focus to the practices and theories of the therapy. The issue before the public today is whether recovered memory therapists are helping or harming their patients.

With no one willing to make much of a fuss, the practice of lobotomy continued for nearly twenty years. It can be hoped that the public nature of the debate over recovered memory therapy will bring about a quicker end to its practice.

As this debate continues, the damage done by recovered memory therapists will slowly become known. Suicides will be tallied, patients and parents will file lawsuits, and many stories of families torn apart will be told. The full accounting of the pain inflicted by these ill-conceived methods will, however, never be complete, nor will we know the good that could have been achieved in these patients' lives with the time, energy, and resources wasted.

One dimension of the damage done by recovered memory therapy that has not been discussed in this book is its economic impact on American society. Almost no serious attention has been given to this question from any quarter; perhaps this is because reliable information is difficult to develop. Although we can offer no solid estimate of what the total bill for recovered memory therapy comes to, our research has convinced us that hundreds of millions of scarce health-care dollars are being wasted. It is also obvious that more than half, perhaps as much as three-quarters, of the money funding recovered memory therapy comes from either insurance company or government sources. That is, funding comes from all of us and is removed from the finite pot of money through which medical care is paid for in the United States.

Many hospitals have founded dissociative disorder units in the decade of the rise of recovered memory therapy. These units undertake long-term treatment of patients classified as MPD and are often the setting in which the search for repressed memories is carried out. By streaming patients to an in-patient facility rather than treating them in office visits, it is possible to tap insurance policies for their vastly higher coverage limits for in- versus out-patient psychiatric care. Dissociative disorder units are profit centers for the hospitals that operate them.

In addition, throughout the country special facilities have sprung up to treat women undergoing recovered memory therapy on a residential basis. These treatment facilities are often set in attractive locations and advertise themselves in a fashion that puts a deceptive resort experience– like spin on the process of undergoing recovered memory therapy. It appears that these facilities are being promoted as a psychological version of the dude ranch—a memory ranch.

From what we have been able to learn, it is not unusual for a single hospitalized MPD patient to be the basis for over one million dollars in billing by the collection of psychiatrists, psychologists, social workers, and hospitals that treat her. We discovered one case in which the billing ran to $2.75 million. In another case, a woman was dumped into a state facility after she reached the million-dollar cap on her policy. The state facility discharged her in short order, after determining that she had no significant psychopathology.

Through its victim witness program, the state of Oregon, to choose another example, funds therapy for women who have been victims of recent sexual assaults and rapes, as well as for women who have come to believe they have uncovered repressed memories of being abused as children. On average, the state pays psychotherapists less than two thousand dollars for the treatment of a rape victim, while it pays out more than nine thousand dollars to recovered memory therapists engaged in the process of convincing a client that she was horribly sexually abused during childhood.

Recovered memory therapy, like lobotomy, illustrates the worst of all possible medical or psychiatric mistakes. Unlike useless treatments that merely do patients no good, the practitioners of this therapy harm patients and cause them to suffer. This need not happen. Tolerating recovered memory therapy harms us all because it diverts attention from problems that are real and may be solvable, and squanders funds dedicated to the care of people in need.

The large body of research on other systems of influence teaches us that the successful maintenance of new ideas and perspectives that run counter to long-held beliefs requires near-constant effort. That is, to maintain beliefs that contradict our established understanding of reality, we must be surrounded by a peer group and authority figures who help control the recurring doubts and reservations. Within the recovered memory movement this structure of support is precarious, for inevitably many patients discover that the therapy has not fulfilled the implicit or explicit promises made. While the literature of the movement counsels that patients cut themselves off from those who question the conclusions of the therapy, and limit their social lives to a small group of believers in which absolute belief in the reality of all memories is demanded, this vigilance will become an increasingly difficult burden. Many will likely realize that the identity of "survivor" is not the stuff out of which a fulfilling life and meaningful identity can be created. Increasingly, patients will discover that the abuse narrative has not changed their current problems (in many cases they will discover that their lives have become markedly worse), and that the therapy group has not lived up to its billing as a "family" of choice. With these realizations, patients will step back from the structure that restrains them from questioning their abusive narratives. The debate over this therapy will be conclusively settled, not in the pages of books or journals, but in the minds of those subjected to this treatment. If we are right about these beliefs, given time they will collapse on their own. The more frequently this begins to happen, the more likely the structure of the therapy itself will begin to show cracks, and the more likely an ever-increasing number of women and men will demonstrate the courage to reject their kind, compassionate, and incompetent healers.

Appendix: Three Papers

As we have noted, within the recovered memory movement there is a virtual absence of empirical research that might give weight to the idea of massive repression or provide validity to the processes by which the recovered memory therapist supposedly unearths memories. Three sets of researchers have come forward to attempt to fill this profoundly embarrassing hole. Two of the resulting papers attempt to show that repression is common to women who were abused, and the third, coauthored by Judith Herman, purports to prove that the majority of the women she studied were able to confirm their memories through outside sources. On analysis, these papers not only fail to show what they purport to show but, perhaps more important, attest to the poor quality of what is accepted as legitimate research in this segment of the mental-health community.

In the most recently released study, Linda Meyer Williams surveyed 129 women who had documented histories of having been examined as children for sexual victimization at a hospital between 1973 and 1975.[1] The abuse the parents of these children reported them to have suffered ranged from fondling to rape. The women, who were between ten months old and twelve years old at the time of their abuse, were interviewed seventeen years later. Williams found that forty-nine of these women had no memory of the event documented in the hospital records. "The finding that 38 percent of the women did not tell the interviewer about the child sexual abuse which was documented in hospital records . . . is quite astonishing," she writes of her work. From her results she draws a number of broad conclusions supporting the predisposition of recovered memory therapists to hunt for abuse. "Having no memory of child sexual abuse is a common occurrence, not only among adult survivors in therapy for abuse but among community samples of women who were reported to have been sexually abused in childhood. . . . The current findings . . . indicate that therapists should be open to the possibility of child sexual abuse among clients who report no memory of such abuse."[2]

However, if we look at her methods and results, the picture becomes much less clear. First, the fact that thirty-three of the forty-nine women who could not remember the specific recorded abuse freely told of other incidents of childhood molestation is not mentioned prominently in the paper. This leaves sixteen of the 129 women (12 percent) who both reported no memory of the specific incident as well as no memories of the other abuse in childhood. There is no reason to believe that normal forgetting wasn't the cause of their inability to recall their experiences. No one questions the fact that almost all experiences—especially those of young children—are eventually forgotten. Looked at in this light, the most dramatic conclusion of the Williams study might be that close to 90 percent of women abused as children know as adults that they were abused, although they may have forgotten one or more specific instances.

The fact that many people who know they were sexually abused as children forget a specific instance is simply not, however, evidence for a repression mechanism but only for the fact that traumatic memories can sometimes be forgotten. Williams's own numbers bolster this conclusion. For example, the women who did not recall the abuse recorded in the hospital records were just as likely to report other instances of abuse as the women who *did* recall the hospital event. This contradicts the theory of Dr. Lenore Terr and others cited in Williams's paper that children who become able to repress trauma are more likely to repress subsequent abuse. The finding that the women who could not remember the target event were just as likely to remember other abuse is compelling evidence that these women lacked any special ability to force disturbing events from their consciousness.

It is troubling that Williams doesn't examine the sixteen women with no memories of abuse (neither of the specific event nor of other episodes in their childhood) separately from the larger group of forty-nine who remember being abused but couldn't recall the target event. Because she doesn't tell the reader the type of abuse these women suffered (the abuse of the 129 women ranged from rape to nonviolent fondling) nor their ages at the time of their treatment, it is impossible to say conclusively why these memories were absent. There is no reason, however, to assume some powerful repression mechanism was responsible. Some of these sixteen women may simply have forgotten their experiences while others may not have wished to disclose any abuse memories to the interviewer. Since there is no control group (for instance, of children treated at the hospital for other reasons), Williams gives the reader no reason not to believe that garden-variety forgetting was responsible for those failing to remember the recorded event.

Williams also claims that her study has dramatic implications for the correlation between age and the ability to remember abuse. While the results show a predictable correspondence between age and recall (those who recalled the abuse were two years older on average than those who didn't), Williams purports to have found that nearly half of the women abused when they were under four years of age remembered their abuse seventeen years later. These findings would indeed have a dramatic effect on the assumption that very young children forget almost every experience (traumatic or not) were it not for a remarkable footnote in which Williams admits that: "Some of the 'memories' may be attributable to information they received from others later in life; however, this was not explored in detail in this interview." The fact that she made no effort to distinguish between abuse the subjects remembered and events they had learned of only through other sources throws the usefulness of the entire study into question—particularly in regard to the "memories" of those abused before the age of four. Using Williams's criteria, if these subjects had reported knowing the circumstances of their birth, she would have classified them as having "recalled" the event.

The Williams study is also interesting for some things it doesn't mention. Apparently, nowhere in the hospital records is there any indication that these young victims forgot their trauma immediately or shortly after it occurred, as many recovered memory therapists attest is likely. In addition, it appears that none of the women who remembered their trauma described retrieving their memories after decades with all the feelings and emotions of the original event (as is often described by recovered memory therapists). Because she does not document the recovery of any forgotten memories, Williams admits, in the end, that her study does not address the "validity of 'recovered' or recalled memories of once-forgotten abuse or the association of such memories with adult symptomatology." Williams proves only that traumatic events suffered by children can sometimes be forgotten. Despite its constant use by recovered memory therapists as proof of their assertions, this flawed study tells us little new about memory (because it doesn't distinguish memory and knowledge) and nothing about the repression mechanism as it is postulated by many of today's therapists.

In a paper titled "Self-Reported Amnesia for Abuse in Adults Molested as Children," researchers John Briere and Jon Conte more directly attempt to prove the existence of repression. The pair located 450 therapy patients who identified themselves as abuse victims and asked them whether there had ever been a time before their eighteenth birthday when they "could not remember" their abuse. Answering this yes or no question, 59 percent of the subjects reported that they had experienced such a time. From this result the two researchers concluded: "Amnesia for abuse . . . appears to be a common phenomenon among clinical sexual abuse survivors." As to how their empirical conclusions should be applied to the clinical setting, Briere and Conte write that "it is likely that some significant portion of psychotherapy clients who deny a history of childhood victimization are, nevertheless, suffering from sexual abuse trauma. . . . Thus the clinician who has some reason to believe that his or her client was molested as a child . . . may be well advised to continue to entertain that hypothesis during treatment, even in the absence of specific abuse memories."[3]

It doesn't take a social scientist to see that the survey question Briere and Conte used to draw their far-reaching conclusion is that flawed at its premise. The question ("During the period of time between when the first forced sexual experience happened and your eighteenth birthday, was there ever a time when you could not remember the forced sexual experience?") turns on the "could not." Patients are not only asked to remember a time when they did not remember something, but to have known whether, during that time, they could or could not have remembered the event if they had tried. Asking patients to remember a time when they couldn't remember something is a logical quandary. The question borders on the ridiculous, for it assumes the subject would have knowledge of the status of a memory during a period when that memory by the subject's own admission never came into consciousness.

Retrospective studies to determine past symptoms, as we have noted earlier, are difficult because of patients' propensity to redefine their experiences in terms of the questions the doctor asks. In assuming that patients would know what they could and couldn't remember over a period of many years, Briere and Conte's question takes this problem to an extreme and appears designed to maximize the chances that respondents will conform their answer to the perceived assumptions of the questioners. Because of the broad and ill-defined nature of the question, people with relatively continuous memories were likely to respond that they experienced periods when they *could not* remember only because they experienced periods when they *did not* think about the abuse.

Another obvious problem with the study is the likelihood that Briere and Conte's pool of respondents was composed in large part of recovered memory patients who, by definition, would classify their therapy-created "memories" as inaccessible during their pretherapy life. If the memories of abuse were not "discovered" in therapy but rather "created" in therapy, the patient would, of course, believe that she had been amnesiac for the material. This is to say that the survey is only valid if the recovered memories are valid. Briere and Conte offer no evidence to counter this problem, saying only that due to their "clinical experience" they "doubt that abuse confabulation is a major problem in abuse research." The validity of this supposedly empirical study, then, rests on the clinical assumption that patients are not likely to create histories of abuse in therapy. Now that there is evidence that therapists—infused with a false confidence in their ability to identify the symptoms of someone who was abused—can and often do create false memories of abuse in the minds of their patients, that assumption should no longer be allowed to stand unchallenged. That Briere and Conte further encourage therapists to hold to their abuse interpretations regardless of the patients' memories (or lack of memories) is likely only to make this problem worse.

Judith Lewis Herman and Emily Schatzow's paper entitled "Recovery and Verification of Memories of Childhood Sexual Trauma" is perhaps the most-often quoted paper in the recovered memory movement. In this study the researchers worked with fifty-three women in group-therapy settings and encouraged them to search for evidence that their memories of abuse were accurate. They conclude that "three out of four patients were able to validate their memories by obtaining corroborating evidence from other sources."[4] In reporting this result, Herman and Schatzow are, in fact, being modest. Because six of these patients (11 percent) made no attempt to confirm their abuse memories,it could be said that a full 89 percent of the forty-seven women who made an effort were able to confirm their memories.

This study, published in the prestigious *Journal of Psychoanalytic Psychology*, has had a profound impact on the recovered memory debate. It is cited often not only within the recovered memory literature but also in newspapers and magazine articles on the subject of recovered memory therapy. Herman's credentials as a doctor, her association with Harvard University, and her previous book, *Father-Daughter Incest*, gained her a national reputation. Her recent book *Trauma and Recovery* was hailed in the *New York Times Book Review* as one of the "most important psychiatric works to be published since Freud."

The first and most striking problem with applying the results of this study to the recovered memory debate is that it does not focus on women who supposedly repressed and then recovered their memories. Among the fifty-three women were three groups, those with no amnesia for their abuse (38 percent), those with "moderate" amnesia (36 percent), and those with "severe memory deficits" (26 percent). The vast majority of these patients, then, had at least some previous and apparently continuous knowledge of their abuse. Only fifteen of the fifty-three women had what Herman and Schatzow refer to as severe memory deficits, qualifying for this label if "they reported recent eruptions into consciousness of memories that had been entirely repressed, or if this kind of recall occurred during the course of group treatment." In reporting their results about clients who confirmed their abuse, Herman and Schatzow made no distinction between patients with previous knowledge of abuse and those who discovered that they were abused through therapy.

According to the researchers, nearly all the women who couldn't remember abuse on entering treatment were able to find their memories during these group encounters. The authors attest that "participation in the group proved to be a powerful stimulus for recovery of memory in patients with severe amnesia." It is worth wondering why, if these women were initially amnesiac for their abuse, they signed up to participate in therapy groups specifically for "incest survivors." That is to say, how did they know they were sexually abused by family members if they had no memories of these events?

The case report of one of the women with "severe amnesia" answers this question and sheds a great deal of light on the work of these two therapists. As described in the paper, Doris, a thirty-seven-year-old housewife and mother of four children, went to couples therapy with her husband because of sexual problems they were having. According to Herman and Schatzow, it was the marriage counselor who suspected the sexual abuse and referred Doris to one of their incest-survivor groups. For the first five weekly sessions, Doris said almost nothing and listened to the other group members tell of their memories of abuse. In the sixth session, Herman and Schatzow write, Doris began to "moan and whimper and wring her hands. In a childlike voice she cried, 'The door is opening! The door is opening!' " Fearing that her memories were returning too quickly, the therapist running the group "instructed [her] to tell her memories to go away and not come back until she was ready to have them." Doris was reportedly able to do this by talking to her memories— telling them over and over to back into her unconscious. In the three weeks following this session Doris was "flooded with memories" of sexual abuse lasting from the age of six to the age of twelve, including rape by her father and being forced to "service" a group of her father's friends while he watched. Doris also remembered becoming pregnant by her father and being taken to an underground abortionist.

According to the paper, Doris was among the group of five women who could not fully "confirm" their memories but received evidence that indicated the "strong likelihood" that they had been abused. This evidence consisted of a sister asking Doris at a Thanksgiving dinner, "Did Daddy ever try anything funny with you?" (It would of course be tragically ironic if Doris's sister was in therapy herself and attempting to confirm her own newly visualized repressed memories.) Herman and Schatzow do not explain how or why this question should be accepted as evidence for the validity of Doris's new belief that she had suffered through years of sexual assaults, forced abortions, and gang rapes.

Doris's case is also interesting because it shows that the researchers didn't distinguish between confirming evidence that existed before the repressed memories were discovered and evidence that came to light after the discovery. The evidence for the validity of Doris's recovered memories came two years *before* the memories themselves. Indeed, it may have been this very incident which started Doris on the road to recovered memory therapy. Doris's sister's comment appears to have been the trigger for Doris's anxiety attacks which, in turn, were the reason she went into therapy. Because recovered memory therapy often begins with the identification of a potential abuser, it is likely that the perpetrator identified in the patient's repressed memories would be someone suspected to be a pedophile through another source—perhaps in Doris's case her sister's question. However, if a given piece of information is what started the patient on the hunt for repressed abuse, it should hardly be considered confirming.

The questionable way memories surfaced for the women with severe amnesia is intricately tied to Herman and Schatzow's conclusions on the confirmation of these memories, but it takes a little digging to understand why. Reading a paper Herman and Schatzow wrote three years earlier describing their group-therapy methods, one learns that group members were pressured to achieve a preset "goal" during the course of the meeting. As they describe it, at the beginning of the ten or twelve weekly sessions, patients were encouraged to define personal objectives for the course of treatment. For many patients described in the 1984 paper this goal was the recovery of suspected repressed memories. From Herman and Schatzow's description of those patients, it is clear that they felt considerable group pressure to find abuse in their past and in so doing affirm their group membership."Women who wished to recover memories," they wrote in 1984, "were often preoccupied with obsessive doubt about . . . whether they belonged to the group at all," noting also that some women defined their goal for treatment by stating, 'I just want to be in the group and feel I belong.' "[5]

After the fifth session, Herman and Schatzow would remind their patients that they were reaching the midpoint of the therapy, in order to spur group members to "clarify their goals and begin taking action." This, no doubt, added to the pressure on the group members who had so far failed to find any memories or achieve their goal. (It is interesting to note that Doris began to report the surfacing of memories in the *sixth* session). Not surprisingly, the authors report that during this time the goals of the group members were often achieved in "chain reaction" fashion.

This sort of goal setting and group pressure has dramatic implications for the 1987 paper because it seems clear that the same sort of process was employed in encouraging patients to find "confirmation" of their abuse. "Participation in group therapy offered an opportunity for many patients to gather corroborating evidence of abuse," they wrote in the 1987 paper. "The groups were structured around the definition and achievement of a personal goal related to the abuse." The pressure to achieve the stated goal of finding confirming evidence by the end of the group sessions and the pressure to belong quite possibly had a significant impact on reports of "confirmation." It is not hard to imagine that the obligation these patients felt to achieve their goals, combined with pressure from the therapists and the group dynamics, might have affected the quality of what the patients accepted as "confirmation."

This leads to two other critical problems: Herman and Schatzow never clearly state what sort of evidence would qualify as confirmation, nor did they attempt to independently confirm the reports of the patients. They attest that 40 percent of the women obtained corroborating evidence from the perpetrator himself, from other family members, or from physical evidence, while another 34 percent confirmed their suspicions through the discovery that another child had been abused by the same perpetrator. Why did Herman and Schatzow not view any of this physical evidence for themselves or double check the stories by speaking directly to the source of the confirmation? It appears that the patient's preset goal was achieved by simply reporting to the group an account of having her memories confirmed. In addition, there is no way to tell what percentage of reports of confirmation came from the women who had continuous knowledge of their abuse over the course of their lives.

Cast differently, Herman and Schatzow's studies might be seen as illustrations of the power of group settings to elicit conformity from group members. However, in this light they would tell us nothing new. The conclusion that highly charged group settings are capable of producing conformity in belief is far from new or unsurprising and would add nothing to the literature on interpersonal and group influence.

Notes

INTRODUCTION

1. Herman 1992, p. 2.
2. Bottoms et al. 1993.
3. Valenstein 1986, p. 291.
4. Herman 1992, p. 9.
5. Gould 1981, p. 22.
6. Ibid.
7. Haaken and Schlaps, 1991.
8. Swink and Leveille, 1986.
9. Steinem 1992, pp. 157, 162.
10. Tavris 1992, p. 321.
11. Herman 1992, p. 9.

1. THE MYTHS OF MEMORY

1. The details of Christine's story were gathered through interviews with her mother, correspondence, and other written documentation. Some details have been changed to insure anonymity.
2. Bass and Davis 1988, p. 298.
3. Ibid., p. 289.
4. Erdelyi 1990.
5. McClure 1990, pp. 1–4.
6. Bass and Davis 1988, p. 42.
7. Lew 1988, p. 101.
8. Davis 1990, p. 204.
9. Fredrickson 1992, p. 24.
10. Clark 1993.
11. Bliss 1986, p. 133.
12. Westerlund 1993.
13. Briere 1989, p. 49.
14. Bass and Davis 1988, p. 22.
15. Singer 1990, pp. xi–xii.
16. Holmes 1990, p. 98.
17. Ibid., p. 86.
18. DSM III 1987, p. 395.
19. Erdelyi 1990, p. 4.
20. Holmes 1990, pp. 96–97.
21. Braun, B. Taped presentation given at the Midwestern Conference on Child Sexual Abuse and Incest, University of Wisconsin, Madison, October 12, 1992.
22. Loftus and Loftus 1980, pp. 409–20.
23. Brewer 1991, p. 5.

313

24. Steinem 1992, pp. 163–65.
25. Neisser and Harsch 1992.
26. Pynoos and Nader 1989, pp. 320–25.
27. Malmquist 1986, pp. 320–35.
28. Westerlund 1993, pp. 17–31.
29. Bliss 1996, p. 143.
30. Smith 1993.
31. Holmes 1990, p. 96.

2. EFFORT AFTER MEANING

1. Britton 1992, p. 188.
2. Frank 1973.
3. Kris 1955, p. 54.
4. Viderman 1979, p. 259.
5. Gannon 1989, p. 96.
6. Blake-White and Kline 1985, p. 402.
7. Brewer 1991, pp. 7–8.
8. Peterson 1991, p. 79.
9. Burpee 1992.
10. Guze 1992, pp. 69–70.
11. Ibid., pp. 20–21.
12. Ibid., pp. 22–23.
13. Spence 1982, p. 25.
14. Ibid., p. 32.
15. Ibid., p. 268.
16. Ibid., p. 31.
17. Viderman 1979, p. 269.
18. Ibid.
19. Ibid., p. 270.
20. Spence 1982, pp. 276, 280.
21. Shengold 1989, pp. 33–36.
22. Langs 1973, pp. 524–29.
23. Ibid.
24. Ibid.
25. Ibid.
26. Ibid.
27. Ibid.
28. Prozan 1992, p. 203.
29. Ibid.
30. Ibid.
31. Ibid., p. 206.
32. Ibid., p. 207.
33. Bass and Davis 1988, p. 80.

3. SYMPTOMS OF PSEUDOSCIENCE

1. Bass and Davis 1988, pp. 22, 81.
2. Blume 1990, p. xxvii.
3. Bass and Davis 1988, p. 35.
4. Fredrickson 1992, pp. 48–51.

5. Brewer 1991, p. 13.
6. Bradshaw 1992.
7. Fredrickson 1992, pp. 53–54.
8. Poston and Lison 1989, pp. 93–95.
9. Salter and Ness 1993.
10. Phillips 1993, pp. 241–48.
11. Greenfield 1990, p. 20.
12. Lehrman 1987.
13. Weiss 1988.
14. Boskind-White and White 1983.
15. Lehrman 1987.
16. Elkind, 1988.
17. Quoted in *Cosmopolitan* 1992.
18. Poston and Lison 1989.
19. Schwartz 1990.
20. Singleton 1992.
21. Pope and Hudson 1992.
22. Tice et al. 1989.
23. Stuart et al. 1990.
24. Finn et al. 1986.
25. Torem 1992.
26. Browne and Finkelhor 1986.
27. Bryer et al. 1987, pp. 1426–30.
28. Faria and Behlohlavek 1984, pp. 465–71.
29. Blake-White and Kline 1985, p. 394.
30. Poston and Lison 1989, p. 195.
31. Lloyd et al. 1992, pp. 215–22.
32. Ibid.
33. Arkes 1981.
34. Bass, E. Interview conducted by the authors, fall 1992.
35. Bass and Davis 1988, pp. 33–34.
36. Claridge 1992, p. 244.
37. Herman 1992, p. 180.
38. Bradshaw 1992.

4. CREATION OF THE ABUSE NARRATIVE

1. Fredrickson 1992, p. 15.
2. Britton 1992, p. 189.
3. Davis 1990, p. 206.
4. Fredrickson 1992, p. 92.
5. Ibid., p. 127.
6. Ibid., p. 154.
7. Brewer 1991, p. 63.
8. Poston and Lison 1989, p. 196.
9. Davis 1990, table of contents.
10. Briere 1992, p. 151.
11. Ibid., pp. 51–52.
12. Ibid.
13. Ibid.
14. Brady 1992, p. 168.

15. Herman 1992, p. 185.
16. Blume 1990, pp. 99–100.
17. Claridge 1992, pp. 243–52.
18. Ibid.
19. McClure 1990, pp. 29–31.
20. Bass and Davis 1988, pp. 75–77.
21. Ibid., p. 154.
22. Maltz 1991, pp. 50–51.
23. Fredrickson 1992, p. 109.
24. Prozan 1993, p. 307.
25. Ibid., p. 262.
26. Ibid., p. 207.
27. Ibid., p. 261.
28. Ibid., p. 260.
29. Ibid., p. 287.
30. Ibid., p. 267.
31. Ibid.
32. Ibid., p. 270.
33. Ibid., p. 264.
34. Ibid., p. 289.
35. Ibid., p. 300.
36. Ibid., pp. 302–3.
37. Prozan 1993, p. 307.
38. Spence 1982, pp. 155–56.
39. Prozan 1993, pp. 307–8.
40. Bronson 1989, pp. 30–31.
41. Ibid., p. 192.
42. Ibid., pp. 230–31.
43. Ibid., pp. 208–9.
44. Ibid., p. 93.
45. Ibid., p. 235.
46. Ibid., p. 207.
47. Ibid., p. 87.
48. Ibid., pp. 93, 195.
49. Ibid., p. 245.

5. INVESTMENT IN BELIEF

1. Fredrickson 1992, pp. 17, 224.
2. Bass and Davis 1988, p. 87.
3. Ibid., p. 91.
4. Fredrickson 1992, p. 161.
5. Ibid., p. 171.
6. Bass and Davis 1988, p. 347.
7. Ibid., p. 90.
8. Finney 1990, p. 28–29.
9. Bass and Davis 1988, p. 88.
10. Courtois 1988, p. 231.
11. Frank 1973, p. 165.
12. Ibid., p. 179.
13. Bass and Davis 1988, pp. 460–61.
14. Ibid., p. 352.

15. McClure 1990, p. 53.
16. Kinsler 1992, pp. 167–68.
17. Bronson 1989, pp. 224–25.
18. Fredrickson 1992, p. 21.
19. McClure 1990, p. xix.
20. Bass and Davis 1988, pp. 46–64.
21. Ibid., p. 305.
22. McClure 1990, pp. 51–52.
23. Gil 1983, p. 76.
24. Fredrickson 1992, pp. 83–94.
25. Gannon 1989, p. 239.
26. Kunzman 1990, p. 139.
27. Lew 1988, p. 177.
28. Brewer 1991, p. 135.
29. Lew 1988, p. 178.
30. Kunzman 1990, p. 139.
31. Gannon 1989, pp. 239–44.
32. Bass and Davis 1988, p. 65.
33. Ibid., p. 69.
34. Ibid., p. 48.
35. Davis 1990, p. 69.
36. Bass and Davis 1988, p. 68.
37. Davis 1990, p. 73.
38. Kaminer 1992, p. 26.
39. Ehrenreich and English 1978, p. 98.
40. As quoted in ibid., p. 97.
41. Bass and Davis 1988, p. 62.

6. LIFE WITH FATHER

1. All the information for this chapter came from depositions and other documents in the lawsuit which Jane eventually brought against her parents.

7. HYPNOSIS AND THE CREATION OF PSEUDOMEMORIES

1. Siegel and Romig 1990, pp. 246–56.
2. Ibid.
3. Ibid.
4. Herman 1992, p. 185.
5. Fredrickson 1992, p. 149.
6. Frankel 1993, pp. 954–58.
7. Ibid.
8. Sheehan and others 1991.
9. Council on Scientific Affairs 1985, pp. 1918–23.
10. Laurence and Perry 1983.
11. The two studies cited in Baker 1992 are Silverman, P. S., and P. L. Retzlafaff 1986. "Cognitive Stage Regression through Hypnosis: Are Earlier Cognitive Stages Retrievable?" Int. J. Clin. Exp. Hypnosis 34: 192–204, and Barber, T. X., N. P. Spanos, and J. F. Chaves 1974. *Hypnosis, Imagination and Human Potentialities*. New York: Pergamon Press.
12. Bowers 1991, pp. 155–76.

13. Miller, M. "Hypnotic analgesia and stress inoculation in the reduction of cold-pressor pain." Unpublished doctoral dissertation, University of Waterloo, Waterloo, Ontario, Canada, 1986.
14. Hughes, D. "Factors related to heart rate change for high and low hypnotizables during imagery." Unpublished doctoral dissertation, University of Waterloo, Waterloo, Ontario, Canada, 1988.
15. Spanos et al. 1991.
16. Price 1990, p. 344.
17. Lew 1988, p. 305.
18. Herman 1992, pp. 185–87.
19. Calof 1993b, p. 44.
20. Finney 1990, p. 185.

8. TWO CASES OF HYPNOTIC STORY CREATION

1. Feldman 1993, p. 14.
2. Ibid., p. 21.
3. Ibid., p. 15.
4. Ibid., p. 19.
5. Ibid., p. 33.
6. Ibid., pp. 36–37.
7. Ibid., p. 42.
8. Ibid., pp. 42–43.
9. Ibid., p. 258.
10. Ibid., p. 55.
11. Ibid., p. 230.
12. Ibid., p. 230.
13. Ibid., p. 235.
14. Ibid., p. 111.
15. Smith 1980.
16. Feldman 1993, p. 51.
17. Ibid., p. 207.
18. Weiss 1992, p. 112.
19. Ibid., p. 18.
20. For a fuller explanation of the case, see Ofshe 1992b, Wright 1993 and 1994, or Watters 1991.
21. Unless otherwise noted, all details of the Ingram case came from court documents or author interviews with the those involved.
22. Wright 1993, p. 67.
23. To confirm that Ofshe had made up a scene with no basis in reality, the daughter identified by Ingram as being part of the scene was subsequently asked if anything like what Ofshe had offered took place. She reported that nothing like the story Ofshe created had ever happened.

9. REASON AND DARKNESS: THE STRANGE STORIES OF SATANIC ABUSE

1. From surveys of the False Memory Syndrome Foundation.
2. Ross, Colin. Interview with authors, 1992.
3. Gould 1992, p. 207.
4. Smith 1993, pp. 2–3.
5. Bottoms et al. 1993.

6. Briere 1989, p. 128.
7. Rose 1993, p. 40–44.
8. Lanning 1989, pp. 62–83.
9. Sakheim and Devine 1992, pp. xii, xiii.
10. Young 1992, p. 251.
11. Young et al. 1991, pp. 182, 187.
12. Quoted from a speech given at the Midwest Conference on Child Sexual Abuse and Incest, held at the University of Wisconsin, October 12, 1992.
13. Smith 1993, p. 58.
14. Ibid., p. 64.
15. Mulhern 1991, p. 163.
16. Smith 1993, p. 64.
17. *Prime Time Live* 1993, from transcript.
18. Smith 1993, p. 64.
19. Young 1992, pp. 262, 254.
20. Greaves 1992, p. 61.
21. Young et al. 1991, pp. 81–89.
22. Braun, audiotape 1992, op. cit. A more complete explanation of Braun's beliefs on this subject can be found in chapter 11.
23. Hammond's comments were made at the Fourth Annual Eastern Regional Meeting on Abuse and Multiple Personality, June 25–29, 1992. Audiotaped copies of this lecture are available from Audio Transcripts in Alexandria, Va.
24. Victor 1993, p. 295.
25. Quoted in Best 1991, pp. 135–36.
26. Quoted in Mulhern 1991, p. 146.
27. Ibid.
28. Sakheim and Devine 1992, p. xvii.
29. Herman 1992, pp. 178–80.
30. Quoted in Mulhern 1991, p. 146.
31. Hill and Goodwin 1989, p. 39–44.
32. Ibid.
33. Ibid.
34. In Sakheim 1992, p. 6.
35. Ibid., p. 7.
36. Cohn 1975, p. 590.
37. Cohn 1975, p. 225.
38. Jerome D. Frank, *Persuasion and Healing*, The Johns Hopkins University Press, 1973.
39. As quoted on *Sonya Live*, CNN, May 3, 1993. Journal Graphics, Inc. Transcript no. 288.
40. As quoted on *The Fifth Estate*
41. Sakheim and Devine 1992, p. xvi.
42. From an interview with Lipstadt on *Fresh Air*, National Public Radio, December 17, 1993.
43. Lipstadt 1993, pp. 23–24.
44. Lipstadt 1993, pp. 25–26.

10. MULTIPLE PERSONALITY DISORDER: THE CREATION OF A SICKNESS

1. Bass and Davis 1988, p. 424.
2. Ross et al. 1989, pp. 62–65.
3. Personal interview with the authors, 1992.

4. Video aired on the Canadian television show *Fifth Estate*.
5. Smith 1989, p. 55.
6. Bliss 1986.
7. Putnam 1989, p. 72.
8. Ibid., p. 177.
9. Bliss 1986, p. 138.
10. Ibid., p. 125.
11. McHugh 1993, p. 5.
12. Herzog 1984, p. 210.
13. Putnam 1989, p. 82.
14. Ibid., p. 34.
15. Ibid., p. 79.
16. Ibid., pp. 190–91.
17. Ibid., p. 73.
18. Ibid., p. 71.
19. Ibid., p. 90.
20. In McHugh 1993, p. 5.
21. Ibid.
22. Bliss 1980, pp. 285–93.
23. Braun 1986, p. 11.
24. Wilbur 1986, p. 138.
25. Putnam, p. 91.
26. McHugh 1993, p. 5.
27. Spanos 1986, p. 41.
28. Goldstein and Farmer 1993.
29. Bliss 1986, p. 249.
30. McHugh 1993, p. 5.
31. Torem 1989, p. 92.
32. Ross et al. 1989, pp. 62–65.
33. Horevitz 1983.
34. Ibid., p. 144.
35. Brassfield 1983, pp. 146–52.
36. Ross et al. 1989, pp. 62–65.
37. Bliss 1984, no. 7, pp. 135–98.
38. Bliss 1983, pp. 114–23, and Braun 1980.
39. Bliss 1986, pp. 125–26.
40. Ibid., p. 13.
41. Ibid., pp. 13–14.
42. Caul, D. 1984.
43. Caul, D., et al. 1986, p. 149.
44. Mason, L. A., and T. S. Brownback. "The Emergence of Two Multiple Personalities in a Group" in *Dissociative Disorders 1985: Proceedings of the Second International Conference on Multiple Personality/Dissociated States.*
45. Putnam 1989, p. 36.
46. Orne and Bates. In press.
47. Ibid.
48. Ross 1989, p. 18.
49. Ibid., p. 19.
50. Disturbed by the recent rise in the diagnosis of the disorder, Dr. Herbert Speigel, who treated Sybil for a time, has broken a long self-imposed silence on the case. Based on his evaluation of this most famous patient, he has suggested that her behavior was in large part role playing learned in therapy.
51. Merskey 1992, pp. 327–40.

52. Ibid., p. 337.
53. Coon and Milistien 1990, p. 135.
54. Bliss 1986, p. 132.
55. From an interview with a former MPD patient on the *Fifth Estate* television show.
56. In the proposal, which has circulated widely within the therapy and literary community, he goes on to claim that "It appears that Sirhan Sirhan, who shot Robert Kennedy, was mind controlled, and this raises the question of whether Lee Harvey Oswald was also controlled."

11. THERAPY OF A HIGH PRIESTESS

1. Quoted in *Chicago* magazine, September 1992, p. 126.
2. Unless otherwise noted, all quotes and details of Anne Stone's story were taken from personal interviews with her and her husband.
3. Quoted in the *Los Angeles Times*, April 3, 1991, Part B, p. 1.
4. Ibid., April 23, 1991, Part A, column 1.
5. Quoted in *Chicago* magazine, September 1992, p. 127.
6. Braun, B. Taped presentation given at the Midwestern Conference on Child Sexual Abuse and Incest, University of Wisconsin, Madison, October 12, 1992. In the lecture Braun said that in normal use, a high dose of Inderal is 160 milligrams and that he sometimes prescribes doses as high as 1600 milligrams.
7. This and the following quotes are from the October 12, 1992, lecture.
8. Quoted in the *Los Angeles Times*, April 3, 1991, Part B, p. 1.
9. Ibid.

12. THE MURDER, THE WITNESS, AND THE PSYCHIATRIST

1. Terr 1994, pp. 2–3.
2. Ibid., pp. 3–4.
3. MacLean 1993, pp. 438–39.
4. All quotes from therapists Barrett and Reider were taken from transcripts of the trial of George Franklin.
5. MacLean 1993, p. 340.
6. Terr 1994, p. 85.
7. Ibid., p. 12.
8. Interview with the authors.
9. Terr 1994, p. 22.
10. Interview with the authors.
11. Terr 1994, p. xii.
12. Ibid., p. xiii.
13. Terr 1993.
14. Terr 1990.
15. Terr 1988.
16. Terr 1994, pp. 40–41.
17. Terr 1990, p. 79.
18. Terr 1994, pp. 40–41.
19. Ibid., p. 56.
20. Ibid., p. 36.
21. Interview with the authors.
22. Terr 1994, p. 40.

13. DEATHS IN THE FAMILY

1. Gil 1993.
2. Bass and Davis 1988, p. 22.
3. Ibid., p. 73.

CONCLUSION: THE ETIOLOGY OF RECOVERED MEMORY THERAPY

1. In Masson 1984, p. 271.
2. Ibid., p. 131.
3. Bass and Davis 1988, p. 347.
4. Herman 1992, p. 13.
5. Freud, Standard Edition 3:204.
6. Masson 1984, pp. 104–5.
7. Freud, Standard Edition 3:269.
8. Crews 1993, p. 60.
9. Ibid., p. 10.
10. This unpublished comment was written in response to an academic article criticizing recovered memory therapy.
11. Kuhn 1970, p. 10.
12. Crews 1993, p. 62.
13. Ibid., pp. 62–63.
14. Pazder 1980, p. 252.
15. Ross 1989, p. 123.
16. Guze 1992, p. 80
17. McHugh 1994, pp. 17–18.
18. Ibid., p. 29.
19. Valenstein 1986, pp. xi–xii.
20. Ibid., p. 147.

APPENDIX: THREE PAPERS

1. Williams 1993.
2. Ibid.
3. Briere and Conte 1993.
4. Herman and Schatzow 1987.
5. Herman and Schatzow 1984.

Bibliography

Ackerman, R. J. 1983. *Children of Alcoholics*, 2d. ed. New York: Simon & Schuster.

Adams, K. M. 1991. *Silently Seduced*. Deerfield Beach, Fla.: Health Communications, Inc.

Adessa, M., et al. 1989. "Turning Around Bulimia with Therapy." *Psychology Today* (September):14.

Allen, C. V. *Daddy's Girl*. New York: Wyndham Books.

Allison, R. B. 1984. "Difficulties Diagnosing the Multiple Personality Syndrome in a Death Penalty Case." *International Journal of Clinical and Experimental Hypnosis* 32(2):102–17.

Arkes, H. R. 1981. "Impediments to Accurate Clinical Judgment and Possible Ways to Minimize Their Impact." *Journal of Consulting and Clinical Psychology* 49(3):323–30.

Baker, R. A. 1990. *They Call It Hypnosis*. Buffalo: Prometheus Books.

———1992. *Hidden Memories*. Buffalo: Prometheus Books.

Baldwin, C., and C. Orange 1993. *New Life, New Friends*. New York: Bantam Books.

Barbasz, M. 1990. "Treatment of Bulimia with Hypnosis Involving Awareness and Control in Clients with High Dissociative Capacity." *International Journal of Psychosomatics* 37(1–4):53–56.

Bass, E., and L. Davis 1988. *The Courage to Heal*. New York: Harper & Row.

Beckman, K. A., and G. L. Burns 1990. "Relation of Sexual Abuse and Bulimia in College Women." *International Journal of Eating Disorders* 9(5):487–92.

Berger, G. 1990. *Violence and the Family*. New York: Franklin Watts.

Bernheimer, C., and C. Kahane, eds. 1985. *In Dora's Case*. New York: Columbia University Press.

Blake-White, J., and M. Kline 1985. "Treating the Dissociative Process in Adult Victims of Childhood Incest." *Social Casework*, 394–402.

Bliss, E. L. 1980. "Multiple Personalities: A Report of 14 Cases with Implications for Schizophrenia and Hysteria." *Archives of General Psychiatry* 47:285–93.

———1983. "Multiple Personalities and Related Spontaneous Self-Hypnotic Disorders." *American Journal of Clinical Hypnosis* 26:114–23.

———1984a. "A Symptom Profile of Patients with Multiple Personalities, including MMPI Results." *Journal of Nervous and Mental Disease* 172:107–202.

———1984b. "Spontaneous Self-Hypnosis in Multiple Personality Disorder." *Psychiatric Clinics of North America* 7:135–98.

———1986. *Multiple Personality, Allied Disorders, and Hypnosis*. New York: Oxford University Press.

Blume, S. E. 1990. *Secret Survivors*. New York: Ballantine.

Boskind-White, M., and W. C. White 1983. "Bingeing and Purging." *Glamour* (May):258–59, 310.

Bottoms, E. L., P. R. Schaver, and G. S. Goodman 1993. "Profile of Ritualistic and Religion-Related Abuse Allegations Reported to Clinical Psychologists in the United

States." Paper presented at the annual meeting of the American Psychological Association, San Francisco.

Bowers, K. S. 1991. "Dissociation in Hypnosis and Multiple Personality Disorder." *International Journal of Clinical and Experimental Hypnosis* 34(3):155–76.

Boyer, P., and S. Nissenbaum 1974. *Salem Possessed.* Cambridge: Harvard University Press.

Bradshaw, J. 1988. *Bradshaw on the Family.* Deerfield Beach, Fla.: Health Communications.

———1992. *Lear's* (September).

Brady, M. 1992. *Beyond Survival.* New York: HarperCollins.

Brassfield, P. P. 1983. "Unfolding Patterns of the Multiple Personality Through Hypnosis" *American Journal of Clinical Hypnosis* 26(2):146–52.

Braun B. G. 1980. "Hypnosis for Multiple Personality." In *Clinical Hypnosis and Medicine,* ed. H. Wain.

———, ed., 1986. *Treatment of Multiple Personality Disorder.* Washington, D.C.: American Psychiatric Press.

———1989. "Iatrophilia and Iatrophobia in the Diagnosis and Treatment of MPD." *Dissociation* 2(2):66–69.

———1990. "Unusual Medication Regimens in the Treatment of Dissociative Disorder Patients: Part 1: Noradrenergic Agents." *Dissociation* 3(3):144–50.

Brewer, C. 1991. *Escaping the Shadows, Seeking the Light.* San Francisco: HarperSanFrancisco.

Brickman, J. 1984. "Feminist, Nonsexist, and Traditional Models of Therapy: Implications for Working with Incest." *Women and Therapy* 3(1):49–67.

Briere, J. 1989. *Therapy for Adults Molested as Children.* New York: Springer Verlag.

———1992a. *Child Abuse Trauma.* Newbury Park, Calif.: SAGE Publications.

———1992b. "Studying Delayed Memories of Childhood Sexual Abuse." *APSAC Advisor* (Summer):17–18.

Briere, J., and J. Conte 1993. "Self-Reported Amnesia for Abuse in Adults Molested as Children." *Journal of Traumatic Stress* 6(1):21–31.

Briere, J., and D. M. Elliott 1993. "Sexual Abuse, Family Environment, and Psychological Symptoms: On the Validity of Statistical Control." *Journal of Consulting and Clinical Psychology* 61(2):284–88.

Briere, J., and M. Runtz 1988. "Post Sexual Abuse Trauma." *Journal of Interpersonal Violence* 2(4):367–77.

Britton, A. G. 1992. "The Terrible Truth." *Self* (October): 188–202.

Bronson, C. 1989. *Growing Through the Pain.* New York: Prentice-Hall/Parkside.

Browne, A., and D. Finkelhor 1968. "Impact of Child Sexual Abuse: A Review of the Research." *Psychological Bulletin* 99:66–77.

———1984. "Initial and Long-Term Effects: A Review of the Research." In *Child Sexual Abuse.* ed. D. H. Schetky and A. H. Green, 143–79. New York: Brunner/Mazel.

Bryer, J. B., B. A. Nelson, J. B. Miller, and P. A. Krol 1987. "Childhood Sexual and Physical Abuse as Factors in Adult Psychiatric Illness." *American Journal of Psychiatry* 144:1426–30.

Burpee, S. A. 1992. "Testimony to Senate and Assembly Codes Committee Regarding the Statute of Limitations for Sexual Offenses Committed Against Children." Unpublished.

Calof, D. L. 1993a. *Multiple Personality and Dissociation.* Park Ridge, Ill.: Parkside.

———1993b. "Facing the Truth About False Memories." *Networker* (September/October):39–45.

Campbell, T. W. 1992. "Therapeutic Relationships and Iatrogenic Outcomes: The Blame-and-Change Maneuver in Psychotherapy." *Psychotherapy* 29(3):474–80.

Caul, D. 1984. "Group and Video Techniques for Multiple Personality Disorder." *Psychiatric Annals* 14:43–50.

Caul, D., R. G. Sachs, and B. G. Braun 1986. "Group Therapy in Treatment of Multiple Personality Disorder." In *Treatment of Multiple Personality Disorder*, ed. B. G. Braun. Washington, D.C.: American Psychiatric Press.

Chase, T. 1987. *When Rabbit Howls*. New York: Jove.

Chu, J. A., 1992. "The Critical Issues Task Force Report: The Role of Hypnosis and Amytal Interviews in the Recovery of Traumatic Memories." *ISSMP&D News* (June):6–9.

Chu, J. A., and D. L. Dill 1990. "Dissociative Symptoms in Relation to Childhood Physical and Sexual Abuse." *American Journal of Psychiatry* 147(7):887–92.

Claridge, K. 1992. "Reconstructing Memories of Abuse: A Theory-Based Approach." *Psychotherapy* 29(2):243–52.

Clark, K. R. 1993. "Season of Light/Season of Darkness: The Effects of Burying and Remembering Traumatic Sexual Abuse on the Sense of Self." *Clinical Social Work Journal* 21(1):25–43.

Cohn, N. 1975. *Europe's Inner Demons*. New York: Basic Books.

Colao, F., and M. Hunt 1983. "Therapists Coping with Sexual Assault." *Women and Therapy* 2(2):205–14.

Coons, P. M. 1989. "Iatrogenic Factors in the Misdiagnosis of Multiple Personality Disorder." *Dissociation* 2(2):70–76.

Coons, P. M., and V. Milistien 1990. "Self-Mutilation Associated with Dissociative Disorders." *Dissociation* 3:135–43.

Council on Scientific Affairs 1985. "Scientific Status of Refreshing Recollection by the Use of Hypnosis." *Journal of the American Medical Association* 253(13): 1918–23.

Courtois, C. A. 1988. *Healing the Incest Wound*. New York: W. W. Norton.

Crabtree, A. 1992. "Dissociation and Memory: A Two-Hundred Year Perspective." *Dissociation* 5(3):150–54.

Crews, F. 1993. "The Unknown Freud." *New York Review of Books*. November 18.

Daly, L. W., and J. F. Pacifico 1991. "Opening the Doors to the Past: Decade Delayed Disclosure of Memories of Years Gone By." *The Champion* (December):43–47.

Davis, L. 1990. *The Courage to Heal Workbook*. New York: Harper & Row.

de Young, M. 1982. *The Sexual Victimization of Children*. Jefferson, N.C.: McFarland & Co.

Edward, J. 1987. "The Dream as a Vehicle for the Recovery of Childhood Trauma." *Clinical Social Work Journal* 15(4):356–60.

Ehrenreich, B., and D. English 1978. *For Her Own Good*. Garden City, N.Y.: Anchor Press/Doubleday.

Elkind, D. 1988. "Eating Disorders." *Parents* (April):190.

Ellenson, G. S. (1986)."Disturbances of Perception in Adult Female Incest Survivors." *Social Casework* (March):149.

Emslie, G. J., and A. Rosenfeld 1983. "Incest Reported by Children and Adolescents Hospitalized for Severe Psychiatric Problems." *American Journal of Psychiatry* 140(6):708–11.

Engel, B. 1989. *The Right to Innocence*. New York: Ivy Books.

Erdelyi, M. H. 1990. "Repression, Reconstruction, and Defense: History and Integration of the Psychoanalytic and Experimental Frameworks." In *Repression and Dissociation*, ed. J. L. Singer, 1–32. Chicago: University of Chicago Press.

Esterson, A. 1993. *Seductive Mirage*. Chicago and La Salle: Open Court.

Faria, G., and N. Behlohlavek 1984. "Treating Female Adult Survivors of Childhood Incest." *Social Casework* 65(8):465–71.

326   BIBLIOGRAPHY

Feinauer, L. L. 1990. "Comparison of Long-Term Effects of Child Abuse by Type of Abuse and by Relationship of the Offender to the Victim." *American Journal of Family Therapy* 17(1):48–56.

Feldman, G. C. 1993. *Lessons in Evil, Lessons from the Light*. New York: Crown.

Fennig, S., and E. Bromet 1992. "Issues of Memory in the Diagnostic Interview Schedule." *Journal of Nervous and Mental Disease* 180(4):223–24.

Fine, C. G. 1989. "Treatment Errors and Iatrogenesis Across Therapeutic Modalities in MPD and Allied Dissociative Disorders." *Dissociation* 2(2):77–82.

Finn, S. E., et al. 1986. "Eating Disorders and Sexual Abuse: Lack of Confirmation for a Clinical Hypothesis." *International Journal of Eating Disorders* 5(6):1051–60.

Finney, L. D. 1990. *Reach for the Rainbow*. New York: Putnam.

Forward, S., and C. Buck 1988. *Betrayal of Innocence*. New York: Penguin Books.

Frank, E., and W. Wright 1991. *Sins of the Father*. New York: Fawcett Crest.

Frank, J. D. 1972. "The Bewildering World of Psychotherapy." *Journal of Social Issues* 28(4):27–43.

————1973. *Persuasion and Healing*. Baltimore: Johns Hopkins University Press.

Frankel, F. H. 1993. "Adult Reconstruction of Childhood Events in the Multiple Personality Literature." *American Journal of Psychiatry* 150(6):954–58.

Franklin, E., and W. Wright 1991. *Sins of the Father*. New York: Crown.

Fredrickson, R. 1992. *Repressed Memories*. New York: Simon & Schuster.

Freud, S. 1953–74. *Standard Edition of the Complete Psychological Works of Sigmund Freud*. London: Hogarth Press.

Friedman, W. J. 1993. "Memory for the Time of Past Events." *Psychological Bulletin* 113(1):44–64.

Ganaway, G. 1991. "Alternative Hypotheses Regarding Satanic Ritual Abuse Memories." Paper presented at the ninety-ninth annual convention of the American Psychological Association, San Francisco.

————1989. "Historical Versus Narrative Truth: Clarifying the Role of Exogenous Trauma in the Etiology of MPD and Its Variants." *Dissociation* 2(4):205–20.

Gannon, J. P. 1989. *Soul Survivors*. New York: Prentice-Hall Press.

Gil, E. 1983. *Outgrowing the Pain*. New York: Dell.

Gilbertson, Alan, et al. 1992. "Susceptibility of Common Self-Report Measures of Dissociation to Malingering." *Dissociation* 5(4):216–20.

Goldstein, E. 1992. *Confabulations*. Boca Raton, Fla.: SIRS Books.

Goldstein, E., and K. Farmer 1993. *True Stories of False Memories*. Boca Raton, Fla.: SIRS Books.

Gould, C. 1992. "Diagnosis and Treatment of Ritually Abused Children." In *Out of Darkness: Exploring Satanism and Ritual Abuse*, ed. D. K. Sakheim and S. E. Devine, 207–48. New York: Lexington Books.

Gould, S. J. 1981. *The Mismeasure of Man*. New York: W. W. Norton.

Greaves, G. B. 1992. "Alternative Hypotheses Regarding Claims of Satanic Cult Activity: A Critical Analysis." In *Out of Darkness: Exploring Satanism and Ritual Abuse*, ed. D. K. Sakheim and S. E. Devine, 45–72. New York: Lexington Books.

Green, A. H. 1993. "Child Sexual Abuse: Immediate and Long-Term Effects and Intervention." *Journal of the American Academy of Child and Adolescent Psychiatry* 32(5):890–902.

Greenfeld, M. 1990. "Disclosing Incest: The Relationships That Make It Possible." *Journal of Psychosocial Nursing* 28(7):20–23.

Guze, S. B. 1992. *Why Psychiatry Is a Branch of Medicine*. New York: Oxford University Press.

Haaken, J., and A. Schlaps. 1991. "Incest Resolution Therapy and the Objectification of Sexual Abuse." *Psychotherapy* 28(1):39–47.

Herman, J. L. 1981. *Father-Daughter Incest*. Cambridge: Harvard University Press.

———1992. *Trauma and Recovery*. New York: Basic Books.

Herman, J. L., and E. Schatzow 1984. "Time-Limited Group Therapy for Women with a History of Incest." *International Journal of Group Psychotherapy* 34(4):605–16.

———1987. "Recovery and Verification of Memories of Childhood Sexual Trauma." *Psychoanalytic Psychology* 4(1):1–14.

Herzog, A. 1984. "On Multiple Personality: Comments on Diagnosis, Etiology, and Treatment." *International Journal of Clinical and Experimental Hypnosis* 32(2): 210–21.

Hicks, R. D. 1991. *In Pursuit of Satan*. Buffalo: Prometheus Books.

Hilgard, J. R. 1970. *Personality and Hypnosis*. Chicago: University of Chicago Press.

Hill, S., and J. Goodwin 1989. "Satanism: Similarities Between Patient Accounts and Pre-Inquisition Historical Sources." *Dissociation* 2(1):39–44.

Hoff, J. 1991. *Law, Gender, and Injustice: A Legal History of U.S. Women*. New York: New York University Press.

Holmes, D. S. 1990. "The Evidence for Repression: An Examination of Sixty Years of Research." In *Repression and Dissociation*, ed. J. L. Singer. Chicago: University of Chicago Press.

Horevitz, R. 1983. "Hypnosis for Multiple Personality Disorder: A Framework for Beginning." *American Journal of Clinical Hypnosis* 26(2):138–45.

Horn, M. 1993. "Memories Lost and Found." *U.S. News and World Report*. November 29, 52–63.

Israels, H., and M. Schatzman 1993. "The Seduction Theory." *History of Psychiatry* 4:23–59.

Jaroff, L. 1993. "Lies of the Mind." *Time* (November 29):52–59.

Johnson, J., and S. Padilla 1991. "Satanism: Skeptics Abound." *Los Angeles Times*, April 23, 1.

Johnson, M. K., et al. 1988. "Phenomenal Characteristics of Memories for Perceived and Imagined Autobiographical Events." *Journal of Experimental Psychology: General* 117(4):371–76.

Jones, E. 1961. *The Life and Work of Sigmund Freud*. New York: Basic Books.

Kaminer, W. 1992. *I'm Dysfunctional, You're Dysfunctional*. Reading, Mass.: Addison-Wesley.

Katz, S. J., and A. E. Liu 1991. *The Codependency Conspiracy*. New York: Warner Books.

Kinsler, P. J. 1992. "The Centrality of Relationship: What's Not Being Said." *Dissociation* 5(3):370–76.

Kinzie, J. D., et al. 1986. "The Psychiatric Effects of Massive Trauma on Cambodian Children." *Journal of the American Academy of Child Psychiatry* 25(3):370–76.

Klaits, J. 1985. *Servants of Satan*. Bloomington: Indiana University Press.

Kleinman, A. 1988. *Rethinking Psychiatry*. New York: Free Press.

Kline, M. V. 1984. "Multiple Personality: Facts and Artifacts in Relation to Hypnotherapy." *International Journal of Clinical and Experimental Hypnosis* 32(2):198–209.

Kluft, R. 1987. "The Simulation and Dissimulation of Multiple Personality Disorder." *American Journal of Clinical Hypnosis* 30(2):104–17.

———1988. "On Treating the Older Patient with Multiple Personality Disorder: 'Race Against Time' or 'Make Haste Slowly'?" *American Journal of Clinical Hypnosis* 30(4):257–66.

———1989a. "Iatrogenic Creation of New Alter Personalities." *Dissociation* 2(2): 83–91.

———1989b. "Reflections on Allegations of Ritual Abuse." *Dissociation* 2(4):191–93.

Krauthammer, C. 1993. "Defining Deviancy Up." *New Republic* (November 22): 20–25.

Kris, E. 1955. "The Recovery of Childhood Memories in Psychoanalysis. In *The Psy-

choanalytic Study of the Child, ed. R. S. Eisler et al., 54–88. New York: International Universities Press.

Kritsberg, W. 1993. *The Invisible Wound*. New York: Bantam.

Kuhn, T. S. 1970. *The Structure of Scientific Revolutions*, 2d ed. Chicago: University of Chicago Press.

Kunzman, K. A. 1990. *The Healing Way*. San Francisco: Harper & Row.

Lacey, J. H. 1990. "Incest, Incestuous Fantasy and Indecency." *British Journal of Psychiatry* 157:399–403.

Langs, R. 1973. *The Techniques of Psychoanalytic Psychotherapy*. New York: Jason Aronson.

———1982. *The Psychotherapeutic Conspiracy*. New York: Jason Aronson.

Lanning, K. V. 1989. "Satanic, Occult, Ritualistic Crime: A Law Enforcement Perspective." *The Police Chief* (October):62–83.

Laurence, J. R., and C. Perry 1983. "Hypnotically Created Memory Among Highly Hypnotizable Subjects." *Science* 222:523–24.

Lehrman, K. 1987. "Anorexia and Bulimia: Causes and Cures." *Consumer Research* (September):29–32.

Levine, H. B., ed. 1990. *Adult Analysis and Childhood Sexual Abuse*. Hillsdale, N.J.: Analytic Press.

Lew, M. 1988. *Victims No Longer*. New York: HarperCollins.

Lipstadt, D. 1993. *Denying the Holocaust*. New York: Free Press.

Lloyd, H. R., R. G. Valgady, and W. W. Tyron 1992. "Evaluation of Mental Health Issues of Memory in the Diagnostic Interview Schedule." *Journal of Nervous and Mental Disease* 180(4):215–22.

Loftus, E. F. 1979. *Eyewitness Testimony*. Cambridge: Harvard University Press.

———1993. "The Reality of Repressed Memories." *American Psychologist* 48(5):518–37.

Loftus, E. F., and S. A. Christianson 1989. "Malleability of Memory for Emotional Events." In *Aversion, Avoidance, and Anxiety: Perspectives on Aversively Motivated Behavior*, ed. T. Archer and L.-G. Nilsson, 311–22. Hillsdale, N.J.: Erlbaum Associaties.

Loftus, E. F., and G. R. Loftus 1980. "On the Permanence of Stored Information in the Human Brain." *American Psychologist* 35(5):409–20.

Lubrano, A. 1993. "Ritual Abuse, Deadly Memories: Are Macabre Tales Fictions or Felonies?" *Newsday*, May 10, 15.

Lueger, R. J., and T. P. Petzel 1979. "Illusory Correlation in Clinical Judgment: Effects of Amount of Information to Be Processed." *Journal of Consulting and Clinical Psychology* 47(6):1120–21.

Lynn, S. J. "Accuracy of Recall by Hypnotically Age-Regressed Subjects." *Journal of Abnormal Psychology* 95(3):298–300.

McClure, M. B. 1990. *Reclaiming the Heart*. New York: Warner Books.

McHugh, P. R. 1992. "Psychiatric Misadventures." *American Scholar* 61(Autumn):497–510.

———1993. "Multiple Personality Disorder." *Harvard Mental Health Newsletter* (Fall):4–6.

———1994. "Psychotherapy Awry." *American Scholar* 63(Winter):17–30.

MacLean, H. N. 1993. *Once Upon a Time*. New York: HarperCollins.

McShane, C. 1993. "Satanic Sexual Abuse: A Paradigm." *Journal of Women and Social Work* 8(2):200–12.

Malmquist, C. P. 1986. "Children Who Witness Parental Murder: Posttraumatic Aspects." *Journal of the American Academy of Child Psychiatry* 25(3):320–25.

Maltz, W. 1991. *The Sexual Healing Journey*. New York: HarperCollins.

Masson, J. M. 1984. *The Assault on Truth*. New York: HarperCollins.

Mayer, R. S. 1991. *Satan's Children*. New York: Avon.

Meehl, P. E. 1960. "The Cognitive Activity of the Clinician." *American Psychologist* 15(1):19–27.

Merskey, H. 1992. "The Manufacture of Personalities." *British Journal of Psychiatry* 160:327–40.

Mesic, P. 1992. "Presence of Minds." *Chicago* (September): 101–30.

Miller, A. 1986. *Thou Shalt Not Be Aware*. New York: Meridian.

————1990. *Banished Knowledge*. New York: Doubleday.

————1993. *Breaking Down the Wall of Silence*. New York: Meridian.

Mulhern, S. 1991. "Satanism and Psychotherapy." In *The Satanism Scare*. ed. J. T. Richardson, J. Best, and G. B. David. New York: Aldine de Gruyter.

Nash, M. R., et al. 1993. "Long-Term Sequelae of Childhood Sexual Abuse: Perceived Family Environment, Psychopathology, and Dissociation." *Journal of Consulting and Clinical Psychology* 61(2):276–83.

Neisser, U. 1993. "Memory with a Grain of Salt." Paper presented at the False Memory Syndrome Conference, Philadelphia.

Neisser, U., and N. Harsch. 1992. "Phantom Flashbulbs: False Recollections of Hearing the News about Challenger." In *Affect and Accuracy in Recall: Studies of "Flashbulb Memories."* ed. E. Winograd and U. Neisser. Cambridge, U.K.: Cambridge University Press.

Nurcombe, B., and J. Unutzer 1991. "The Ritual Abuse of Children: Clinical Features and Diagnostic Reasoning." *Journal of the American Academy of Child and Adolescent Psychiatry* 30(2):272–76.

Ofshe, R. 1992a. "Coercive Persuasion and Attitude Change." In *Encyclopedia of Sociology*, ed. E. F. Borgatta and M. L. Borgatta, 1:212–24. New York: Macmillan.

————1992b. "Inadvertant Hypnosis During Interrogation: False Confession Due to Dissociative State; Misidentified Multiple Personality and the Satanic Cult Hypothesis." *International Journal of Clinical and Experimental Hypnosis* 40(3):125–26.

————In press. "Making Grossly Damaging but Avoidable Errors: The Pitfalls of the Olio/Cornell Thesis." *Journal of Child Sexual Abuse*.

Ofshe, R., and M. Singer. In press. "Recovered Memory Therapy and Robust Repression: Influence and Pseudo-memories." *International Journal of Clinical and Experimental Hypnosis*.

Ofshe, R., and E. Watters 1993. "Making Monsters." *Society* (March/April): 4–6.

Orne, M. T. 1979. "The Use and Misuse of Hypnosis in Court." *International Journal of Clinical and Experimental Hypnosis* 27(4):311–41.

Orne, M. T., and B. L. Bates. In press. "Reflections on Multiple Personality Disorder: A View from the Looking-Glass of Hypnosis Past." In *The Mosaic of Contemporary Psychiatry in Perspective*. New York: Springer Verlag.

Palmer, R. L., et al. 1990. "Childhood Sexual Experiences with Adults Reported by Women with Eating Disorders: An Extended Series." *British Journal of Psychiatry* 156:699–703.

Pearson, R. W., M. Ross, and R. M. Dawes. In press. "Personal Recall and the Limits of Retrospective Questions in Surveys." In *Questions About Questions: Meaning, Memory, Expression and Social Interaction in Surveys*, ed. J. Tanur. Sage Press.

Peterson, B. 1991. *Dancing with Daddy*. New York: Bantam.

Pettinati, H. M., ed. 1988. *Hypnosis and Memory*. New York: Guilford Press.

Phillips, M. 1993. "The Use of Ego-State in the Treatment of Posttraumatic Stress Disorder." *American Journal of Clinical Hypnosis* 35(4):241–48.

Pope, H. G., and J. I. Hudson 1992. "Is Childhood Sexual Abuse a Risk Factor for Bulimia Nervosa?" *American Journal of Psychiatry* 149(4):455–63.

Poston, C., and K. Lison 1989. *Reclaiming Our Lives*. Boston: Little, Brown.

Price, D. A. 1990. "Corporate Headquarters of the Mind." In *Handbook of Hypnotic Suggestions and Metaphors*, ed. D. C. Hammond, 344. New York: Norton.

Prozan, C. K. 1992. *Feminist Psychoanalytic Psychotherapy*. Northvale, N.J.: Jason Aronson.

———1992. *The Technique of Feminist Psychoanalytic Psychotherapy*. Northvale, N.J.: Jason Aronson.

Putnam, F. W. 1989. *Diagnosis and Treatment of Multiple Personality Disorder*, New York: Guilford Press.

———1991. "The Satanic Ritual Abuse Controversy." *Child Abuse and Neglect* 15: 175–79.

Pynoos, R. S., and K. Nader 1989. "Children's Memory and Proximity to Violence." *Journal of the American Academy of Child and Adolescent Psychiatry* 28(2):236–41.

Richardson, J. T., J. Best, and D. G. Bromley 1991. *The Satanism Scare*. New York: Aldine de Gruyter.

Rieff, D. 1991. "Victims, All?" *Harper's Magazine* (October):49–56.

Rogler, L. H., R. G. Malgady, and W. W. Tryon 1992. "Evaluation of Mental Health." *Journal of Nervous and Mental Disease* 180(4):215–22.

Rose, E. S. 1993. "Surviving the Unbelievable." *Ms.* (January/February):40–45.

Rosenfeld, A. A., C. C. Nadelson, and M. Kriefer 1979. "Fantasy and Reality in Patients' Reports of Incest." *Journal of Clinical Psychology* 40:159–64.

Rosenham, D. L., and M. E. P. Seligman 1984. *Abnormal Psychology*. New York: W. W. Norton.

Ross, C. A. 1984. "Diagnosis of Multiple Personality During Hypnosis: A Case Report." *International Journal of Clinical and Experimental Hypnosis* 32(2):222–35.

———1989. *Multiple Personality Disorder: Diagnosis, Clinical Features and Treatment*. New York: John Wiley.

Ross, C. A., G. R. Norton, and G. A. Fraser 1989. "Evidence Against Iatrogenesis of Multiple Personality Disorder." *Dissociation* 2(2):61–65.

Rush, F. 1980. *The Best-Kept Secret: Sexual Abuse of Children*. Bradenton, Fla.: Human Services Institute.

Sakheim, D. K., and S. E. Devine, eds. 1992. *Out of Darkness*. New York: Lexington Books.

Salter, S., and C. Ness 1993. "Buried Memories, Broken Families." *San Francisco Examiner*. April 4–9, 1–10.

Saxe, G. N., et al. 1993. "Dissociative Disorders in Psychiatric Inpatients." *American Journal of Psychiatry* 150(7):1037–42.

Schetky, D. H., and A. H. Green 1988. *Child Sexual Abuse*. New York: Brunner/Mazel.

Schimek, J. G. 1987. "Fact and Fantasy in the Seduction Theory: A Historical Review." *American Psychoanalytic Association Journal* 35(4):937–64.

Schreiber, F. R. 1973. *Sybil*. New York: Warner Books.

Schultz, R., B. G. Braun, and P. K. Richar 1989. "Multiple Personality Disorder: Phenomenology of Selected Variables in Comparison to Major Depression." *Dissociation* 2(1):45–51.

Schwartz, H. J. 1990. "Association of Bulimia with Sexual Abuse." *American Journal of Psychiatry* 147(7).

Shapiro, L. 1993. "Rush to Judgment." *Newsweek* (April 19):54–60.

Shearer, S. L., and C. A. Herbert 1987. "Long-Term Effects of Unresolved Sexual Trauma." *American Family Physician* 36(4):169–79.

Sheehan, P. W., D. Statham, and G. A. Jamieson 1991. "Pseudomemory Effects and Their Relationship to Level of Susceptibility to Hypnosis and State Instruction." *Journal of Personality and Social Psychology* 60(1):130–37.

Shengold, L. 1989. *Soul Murder*. New York: Fawcett.

Siegel, D. R., and C. A. Romig 1990. "Memory Retrieval in Treating Adult Survivors of Sexual Abuse." *American Journal of Family Therapy* 18(3):246–56.

Singer, J. L., ed. 1990. *Repression and Dissociation.* Chicago: University of Chicago Press.

Singer, M. T., and R. Ofshe 1990. "Thought Reform Programs and the Production of Psychiatric Casualties." *Psychiatric Annals* 20(4):188–93.

Slothower, J. 1987. "Battle of the Binge." *Health* (October):19–20.

Smith, M. 1993. *Ritual Abuse.* San Francisco: HarperCollins.

Smith, M., and L. Pazder 1980. *Michelle Remembers.* New York: Congdon & Lattes.

Smith, M. C., and R. F. Mollica 1992. "Issues of Memory in the Diagnostic Interview Schedule." *Journal of Nervous and Mental Disease* 180(4):225–26.

Smith, S. G. 1989. "Multiple Personality Disorder with Human and Non-human Subpersonality Components." *Dissociation* 2(1):52–56.

Spanos, N. P. 1986a. "Hypnosis and Multiple Personality." *Progress in Experimental Personality Research* 14:3–62.

———1986b. "Hypnosis, Nonvolitional Responding and Multiple Personality: A Social Psychological Perspective." *Progress in Experimental Personality Research:* 1.

Spanos, N. P., et al. 1986. "Hypnotic Interview and Age Regression Procedures in the Elicitation of Multiple Personality Symptoms: A Simulation Study." *Psychiatry* 49:298–311.

———1991. "Secondary Identity Enactments During Hypnotic Past-Life Recognition." *Journal of Personality and Social Pathology* 61(2):308–20.

Spence, D. P. 1982. *Narrative Truth and Historical Truth.* New York: W. W. Norton.

Steiger, H., and M. Zanko 1990. "Sexual Traumata Among Eating-Disordered, Psychiatric and Normal Female Groups." *Journal of Interpersonal Violence* 5:74–86.

Steinem, G. 1992. *Revolution from Within.* Boston: Little, Brown.

Stuart, G. W., et al. 1990. "Early Family Experiences of Women with Bulimia and Depression." *Archives of Psychiatric Nursing* 4:43–52.

Summit, R. C. 1983. "The Child Sexual Abuse Accommodation Syndrome." *Child Abuse and Neglect* 7:177–93.

———1992. "Misplaced Attention to Delayed Memory." *ASPAC Advisor* (Summer): 21–25.

Swanson, L. and M. K. Biaggio 1985. "Therapeutic Perspectives on Father-Daughter Incest." *American Journal of Psychiatry* 142(6):667–74.

Swink, K. K., and A. E. Leveille 1986. "From Victim to Survivor: A New Look at the Issues and Recovery Process for Adult Incest Survivors." *Women and Therapy* 5(2/3):119–41.

Tavris, C. 1992. *The Mismeasure of Woman.* New York: Touchstone.

Terr, L. C. 1983. "Chowchilla Revisited: The Effects of Psychic Trauma Four Years After a School Bus Kidnapping." *American Journal of Psychiatry* 140:1543–50.

———1990. "Children's Responses to the Challenger Spacecraft Disaster." Paper presented at the annual meeting of the American Psychiatric Association, New York.

———1988. "What Happens to Early Memories of Trauma? A Study of Twenty Children Under Age Five at the Time of Documented Traumatic Events." *Journal of the American Academy of Child and Adolescent Psychiatry* 27(1):96–104.

———1990. *Too Scared to Cry.* New York: Basic Books.

———1991. "Childhood Traumas: An Outline and Overview." *American Journal of Psychiatry* 148(1):10–20.

———1994. *Unchained Memories: True Stories of Traumatic Memories Lost and Found.* New York: HarperCollins.

Thigpen, C. H., and H. M. Cleckley 1984. "On the Incidence of Multiple Personality Disorder: A Brief Communication." *International Journal of Clinical and Experimental Hypnosis* 32(2):63–66.

Tice, L., et al. 1989. "Sexual Abuse in Patients with Eating Disorders." *Psychiatric Medicine* 7(4):257–67.

Torem, M. S. 1989. "Iatrogenic Factors in the Perpetuation of Splitting and Multiplicity." *Dissociation* 2(2):92–98.

————1992. "The Use of Hypnosis with Eating Disorders." *Psychiatric Medicine* 10(4):1992.

Tower, C. C. 1988. *Secret Scars*. New York: Penguin Books.

Trevor-Roper, H. R. 1968. *The Crisis of the Seventeenth Century*. New York: Harper & Row.

Valenstein, E. 1986. *Great and Desperate Cures*. New York: Basic Books.

Van Benschoten, S. C. 1990. "Multiple Personality Disorder and Satanic Ritual Abuse: The Issue of Credibility." *Dissociation* 3(1):22–30.

van der Hart, O., and P. Brown 1992. "Abreaction Re-evaluated." *Dissociation* 5(3): 127–40.

Vanderbilt, H. 1992. "Incest: A Chilling Report." *Lear's* (February):49–77.

Victor, J. S. 1993. *Satanic Panic*. Chicago and La Salle: Open Court.

Viderman, S. 1979. "The Analytic Space: Meaning and Problems." *Psychoanalytic Quarterly* 48: 257–91.

Wagstaf, G. F. 1981. *Hypnosis, Compliance and Belief*. New York: St. Martin's.

Watters, E. 1991. "The Devil and Mr. Ingram." *Mother Jones* (January/February).

Weiss, B. L. 1992. *Through Time into Healing*. New York. Simon & Schuster.

Weiss, R. 1988. "Bulimia's Binges Linked to Hormones." *Science News:* 182

Westerlund, E. 1993. "Counseling Women with Histories of Incest." *Women and Therapy* 2(4):17–31.

Williams, L. M. 1992. "Adult Memories of Childhood Abuse: Preliminary Findings from a Longitudinal Study." *APSAC Advisor* (Summer):19–21.

————1993. "Recall of Childhood Trauma: A Prospective Study of Women's Memories of Child Sexual Abuse." Paper presented at the annual meeting of the American Society of Criminology, Phoenix.

Wilson, G. T., C. M. Franks, K. D. Brownell, and P. C. Kendall 1984. *Annual Review of Behavior Therapy and Practice*, vol. 9. New York: Guilford Press.

Winograd, E., and U. Neisser., eds. 1992. *Affect and Accuracy in Recall*. New York: Cambridge University Press.

Wood, G. 1978. "The Knew-It-All-Along Effect." *Journal of Experimental Psychology* 4(2):345–53.

Wright, L. 1993. "Remembering Satan." *New Yorker*, May 17 and 24.

————1994. *Remembering Satan*. New York: Knopf.

Young, W. 1992. "Recognition and Treatment of Survivors Reporting Ritual Abuse." In *Out of Darkness*, ed. D. K. Sakheim and S. Devine. New York: Lexington Books.

————et al. "Patients Reporting Ritual Abuse in Childhood: A Clinical Syndrome Report of 37 Cases." *Child Abuse and Neglect* 15:181–89.

Index